The Intercultural Challenge
of Raimon Panikkar

FAITH MEETS FAITH SERIES

The Intercultural Challenge of Raimon Panikkar

Edited by
Joseph Prabhu

ORBIS BOOKS

Maryknoll, New York 10545

The Catholic Foreign Mission Society of America (Maryknoll) recruits and trains people for overseas missionary service. Through Orbis Books, Maryknoll aims to foster the international dialogue that is essential to mission. The books published, however, reflect the opinions of their authors and are not meant to represent the official position of the society.

Library of Congress Cataloging-in-Publication Data

The intercultural challenge of Raimon Panikkar / edited by Joseph
  Prabhu.
     p.   cm.
  Includes bibliographical references.
  ISBN 1-57075-056-4 (alk. paper)
    1. Panikkar, Raimundo, 1918– . I. Prabhu, Joseph. II. Series:
Faith meets faith.
BL43.P36I58 1996
230′.2′092 — dc20

                            96–31970
                             CIP

Contents

Part III
PRAXIS

Part IV
RESPONSE

Preface

Raimon Panikkar's contributions, both theoretical and practical, to the worlds of religion and scholarship are legion. From the history and phenomenology of religions, philosophy and theology, through cosmology and the philosophy of science, comparative studies, indology, scriptural exegesis, mysticism and spirituality, to peace studies and ecology, cross-cultural hermeneutics and interreligious dialogue, he has over a fifty-two-year writing career poured out his learning, experience and wisdom into some fifty books and five hundred major articles in six languages. What is more, this was achieved not in ivory-tower isolation, but in the midst of teaching, lecturing and pastoral responsibilities and involvement in a number of organizations, movements and journals. In a reversal of the laws of thermodynamics and aging, his productivity only seems to increase as he grows older; in the last year alone, four new books have appeared and soon we shall see the publication of at least three more, including his Gifford Lectures, *The Rhythm of Being*.

The need for a volume that attempts a synoptic view of so protean a thinker has long been felt. It is perhaps understandable that readers of more limited interests and competencies are familiar with some aspects of his work, but unaware of others and of the comprehensive world view that underlies and unites them all. In an era of specialization, it at times confounds the imagination that there are people who not only have a holistic vision but have made themselves masters of the several fields enveloped within it.

This, however, has not been the only challenge in the reception of Panikkar's work. He is as much of a poet as a philosopher, a mystic as a theologian and the tensions among mythos, logos and spirit which he has written about so insistently are embodied in his consciousness and his prose. Panikkar simply does not think straight. His mind leaps in a mandalic pattern, constantly creating fresh projections of a central intuition and showing their interrelatedness, or to shift to a musical analogy, crafting new harmonies out of a basic melodic structure. Those of a more linear and piecemeal temper typically respond to his compositions with respectful puzzlement, if not dazed incomprehension.

It was partly in order to ease this condition that this volume was conceived, though the proximate occasion for putting it together was to honor him on his seventy-fifth birthday. From the start it was obvious that no one volume could encompass his myriad interests and contributions, so I felt it might be more manageable if the book concentrated on three central areas of his thought: its metaphysical foundations, his "catholic" theology, and their practical implications.

ix

That plan dictated the choice of topics and contributors. It was gratifying to see that, besides the present essayists, many others whom I contacted responded generously and I regret that considerations of space and of structure precluded inclusion of their essays. My sincere thanks, however, go to Harvey Cox, Louis Dupré, Denis Goulet, Klaus Klostermaier, Kana Mitra, Carl Raschke, Paul Ricoeur and Leonard Swidler.

It goes without saying that I am deeply grateful to the authors of the articles featured in the book, many of whom not only sent in their contributions in a timely manner but did so under great pressure. When one tries to coordinate the schedules of people spread over three continents, it is perhaps inevitable that there will be delays. But I should like the contributors to know how much I appreciate their generosity, patience and understanding.

It is a matter of grave regret that one participant in this venture is no longer able to receive my thanks in person. Frank Podgorski — priest, theologian, Indologist and Director of the South Asian Studies Program at Seton Hall University — passed away on 30 June 1995, some weeks short of his fifty-sixth birthday. Father Podgorski's connection with Panikkar goes back twenty years, during which time he regularly reviewed Panikkar's books and, of course, produced his own work. He will be much missed.

Four others deserve special thanks. Maria Carmen del Tapia, Panikkar's long-time secretary, has responded to my inquiries in her usual helpful and efficient manner. Paul Knitter, the editor of the Faith Meets Faith series in which this book is being published, has helped me with his editorial skills and wise counsel, as has William Burrows, my long-suffering friend, who has steadily nudged me and this book along. Tina Krueger, my former student, very graciously helped with some of the word-processing chores.

Without the generous award of a two-term sabbatical leave during the academic year 1993–94 by California State University, Los Angeles, this book might have taken even longer to complete. I was able to spend that year as a Senior Fellow at the Center for the Study of World Religions at Harvard, an experience as congenial as it was stimulating, for which I owe thanks to the Director, Larry Sullivan, and the wonderful staff, in particular to Kit Dodgson for her many kindnesses.

My debt to my mother is too great for adequate acknowledgment. Her support and encouragement of my intellectual pursuits have sustained me over the years, as has her personal example. My daughter, Tara, patiently bore the privations associated with a preoccupied father; her frequent queries about the state of the "Panikkar book" kept me on the straight and narrow.

My deepest thanks, however, go to Raimon Panikkar himself, friend and mentor for over thirty years. I first encountered him as a college freshman in 1964 in India, speaking characteristically on "Time and Eternity," and it perhaps says something about his impact that I still vividly remember most of the lecture. The friendship that subsequently developed has been one of the great blessings of my life. This volume, produced together with others, is a token of my gratitude, as indeed was my editing of the nine different drafts of his "Response" to give it just the right note of spontaneity (leaving aside his idiosyncratic system of capitalization). I wanted the book to appear as part of the celebration of his seventy-fifth birthday in 1993, but I am glad that it comes out in time for the fiftieth anniversary of his ordination to the priesthood on 29 September 1996. *Tu es sacerdos in aeternum.*

Joseph Prabhu

Introduction

Lost in Translation
Panikkar's Intercultural Odyssey
JOSEPH PRABHU

> *But nothing's lost. Or else: all is translation*
> *And every bit of us is lost in it.*
>
> — James Merrill

I

It significant, I think, that the very first published article in 1944 by Raimon Panikkar bears the title "Síntesis: Visión de síntesis del universo." It says something about both the cast of his mind and his intellectual ambition that at the age of twenty-six, pursuing as he was at the time studies in chemistry and philosophy, he would dare to write an essay of that scope. Our age of specialized and increasingly fragmented knowledge is not accustomed to such sweeping and synoptic projects. Yet, if such an integral vision of reality, reminiscent of an Augustine, a Nicholas of Cusa or a Hegel, is to be assayed in our time, there are few people better qualified than Panikkar to do so. For one thing, there is his expertise in the many different fields in which he has written and lectured: the natural sciences, philosophy, theology, religious studies, cultural history, indology, spirituality, and politics. For another, there is the cross-cultural scope of his learning, his knowledge of at least a dozen languages and of both Western and non-Western philosophical and cultural traditions. Panikkar claims to be at home in four "worlds": the Christian, in which he was brought up; the Hindu, the world of his father; the Buddhist; and the modern secular world. He

Joseph Prabhu is Professor of Philosophy at California State University, Los Angeles, Visiting Scholar at the Graduate Theological Union, Berkeley, and Visiting Professor of Religious Studies at University of California, Berkeley. He has been a Senior Fellow at the Center for the Study of World Religions at Harvard and is author of the forthcoming book *Hegel and the Dark Face of Modernity.*

1

has written about them both separately and in interaction. Finally, in addition to synchronic width there is a diachronic depth which makes him spontaneously see life in millennial terms from the perspective of the last six to eight thousand years of human history. In terms of the temporal imagination of Indic cultures, this breadth of perspective is nothing unusual and indeed might be considered conservative. It does, however, provide an intriguing contrast to a culture that thinks in terms of monthly surveys and the latest opinion polls.

There is something else, however, that is striking about that early essay besides its synthetic ambition — the proclamation of a vision in the very title. It says something about the origins and the inner consistency of Panikkar's work that over a fifty-year period spanning forty books and at least five hundred major articles he has broadened, deepened and clarified it in a number of different ways, ringing a few changes of accent and emphasis, perhaps, on a basic rhythmic structure of a "cosmotheandric *perichorēsis,*" but otherwise remaining remarkably true to that initial vision. Here again the contrast between the hard-edged and empirical temper of a predominantly scientific age and the mystical and holistic imagination of Panikkar, respectful of empirical detail and historical nuance and yet striving for an integrative unity, could not be more palpable. The irony is that Panikkar is both scientist and mystic, a combination that these days at least is not as discordant as in the heyday of positivism. Hence the title of one of his forthcoming books, *Sacred Secularity.*

Even as I mention these conventional academic categories, I am aware of how inadequate they are to capture the peculiar qualities of Panikkar's life and work. As if his encyclopedic learning and synthetic efforts were not enough, there is a further achievement to confound us. All his vast erudition is put at the service of an essentially practical goal: learning and living the wisdom of life. Like the philosophers of old, who took the etymology of the word seriously and made philosophy a mode of life, an art of living, Panikkar has said that for him philosophy is both the love of wisdom and the wisdom of love.[1] Once again the difference between his style of thinking and that common in the contemporary West is marked. Since at least Descartes, philosophical thinking has become *wissenschaftlich* and discursive, tending more to a theory of thinking properly than the actual practice of proper thinking. For Panikkar, by contrast, philosophy is a style of life that engages the whole of existence and whose goal is the fundamental transformation of the human personality as it both mirrors and molds reality. Such an aim would nowadays be seen as merely edifying or inspirational and categorically different from systematic or scientific endeavors, as even a brief glimpse at the conventional classifications in present-day academia would indicate. Such is the split between theory and practice in a technological age that we would regard it as a confusion and conflation of categories to countenance a thinking geared to point us in the direction of wholeness and holiness. This is not to say that he has not written in a wide variety of styles and gen-

---

1. Panikkar, "Philosophy as a Life-style" in *A Dwelling Place for Wisdom,* Westminster/John Knox Press, Kentucky, 1993.

res from the "scientific" to the "homiletic," the "systematic" to the "pastoral"; through all of them, however, a single cosmotheandric vision shines through, a grounding of all being in what he calls the trinitarian structure of reality.

Then again, within the field of religious studies itself, which has been Panikkar's affiliation for a good part of his professional career, he does not easily fit within the traditional boundaries: theology, phenomenology, history of religions or comparative religion. In typical fashion, Panikkar engages in all these endeavors simultaneously, not feeling it necessary to make any rigid distinctions among them even while being appreciative of their methodological structures and strictures. This, of course, is quite frustrating for more conventional scholars respectful of sharp methodological boundaries, which makes it hard to "place" or "situate" Panikkar within the contemporary maps of the field.

The foregoing may hint at some of the difficulties that a contemporary English-speaking audience may encounter in reading Panikkar. While he has been widely published in English, it represents only one of the six languages in which he ordinarily composes his works and some of what has appeared in English is a translation from French, German, Italian, Spanish or Catalan. Add to this his learning in Greek, Latin, Sanskrit, Pali, Hebrew and a few other languages, and his desire to cram it all densely into a relatively brief text (albeit supplemented by numerous footnotes), which continually refers to other writings of his, that purportedly explain things more fully, and you have some idea of both the richness and obscurity of his work. Long-time readers are familiar with some of his neologisms — *Christophany, ontonomy, tempiternity, katachronism,* etc., coinages which are tokens of the very "interculturation" he proposes. And indeed to his English-speaking readers Panikkar is probably best known as one of the pioneers and most creative thinkers in the field of interreligious and intercultural encounter. His contributions in these areas are, however, not adequately understood without some acquaintance with his positions as a metaphysician and philosopher of religion and the practical implications they carry.

What motivated this volume was the desire to honor Panikkar with a Festschrift, but one which would expound and critique his work and in the process make it better understood. Given his multifarious contributions in so many different areas, it was obvious that no one book would be sufficient to accommodate his diverse interests. Fortunately, there has been at least one other Festschrift and one entire journal issue felicitating Panikkar that I am aware of.[2] Hence, as editor of this particular work, I thought it might be better to concentrate on a few fundamental facets of his thought in order to illuminate the *Gesamtkunstwerk* a bit more clearly, an instance of Panikkar's *pars pro toto* principle put into effect. The contributors have done that admirably within the limits of their assigned topics and it would be inappropriate for me to comment on their essays, something which Panikkar himself does in his "Response." What I should like to add is a brief overview of Panikkar's life and work and a

---

2. See *Philosophia Pacis,* ed. Miguel Siguan, Símbolo Editorial, Madrid, 1989, and "Panikkar at Santa Barbara," *Cross Currents,* vol. 29, no. 2, Summer, 1979.

few comments on select aspects of his thought, which might help to situate the different essays comprising the volume.

II

Nowhere does the tale about the elephant and the six blind men apply more aptly than in the case of Panikkar. Not only will there be many different interpretations but it is doubtful that any one person, including Panikkar himself, can provide a view of the "whole elephant." This is entirely consistent with his position of life being led at a level deeper than the *logos* and with his distinction between a "synthesis" and a "system," the former an integration of different bodies of knowledge and experience that is essentially open-ended and fluid, the latter a conceptual mapping of concepts, categories and relations that aims at both consistency and completeness. In a post-Hegelian and Gödelian age, the difficulties of such systematic knowledge are familiar and do not need to be rehearsed. In any case, it goes without saying that this is a personal interpretation.

In my view, two thematic strands intertwine and weave through Panikkar's work, one synchronic and the other diachronic, reflecting the modalities of space and time, or of geography and history, that he has lived both existentially and professionally. The synchronic thread is represented by his cross-cultural and intercultural work: his account of the four traditions he claims to embody, the Christian, Hindu, Buddhist and secular-humanist, and their mutual fecundation and correction. Here, at the theoretical level is where we can locate his work on cross-cultural hermeneutics and at the practical level his guidelines for inter- and intra-religious dialogue. This, as I have said, is the work for which he is best known, at least in the North American context. His work in the philosophy of science and cosmology in the 1940s and 1950s and now again in the 1980s and 1990s points in the direction of what I am calling the diachronic moment — his philosophical-theological interpretation of world history culminating in a fulfillment of what he calls "cosmotheandric consciousness" — the realization that God, humankind and the world exist not as independent but as interpenetrating and mutually constituting realities. In this phase of his architectonic is to be placed his work on the history of human consciousness and the gradually emerging forms of religious awareness and the new cosmology he proffers in critique and supplementation of previous cosmologies (see *The Cosmotheandric Experience,* the forthcoming *The Conflict of Kosmologies* and his Gifford Lectures, *The Rhythm of Being*). These elements, the synchronic and the diachronic, are the two elliptical foci of an essentially mystical apprehension of reality articulated in "trinitarian" terms.

In what follows I should like to explore some of the experiential sources of his "theology," although the word is at best an approximation of his particular activity. The prospectus of the 1989 Gifford Lectures describes his attempt "to liberate the Divine from the burden of being God" and, indeed, the lectures themselves were delivered in Edinburgh under the title "Trinity and Atheism:

The Housing of the Divine in the Contemporary World." Panikkar, as Francis D'Sa points out in his essay, is no monotheist, that is, no believer in an isolated, sheerly transcendent God, but rather a radical trinitarian who prefers to speak of the Divine as one of three constitutive dimensions of reality. His theology, or a-theology, takes its point of departure not from scripture or philosophy but from spiritual experience, both his own and that of others. His affinities here are with the mystical and monastic theologies of the West and with the experientially based articulations of spiritual insight characteristic of the East. This abundance of spiritual experience is then reflected on and ordered by a metaphysical disposition which again draws upon the philosophical traditions of both East and West.

Panikkar's assertion that he "left" Europe as a Christian, "found" himself a Hindu and "returned" as a Buddhist, without ever having ceased to be a Christian, has been often cited and indeed accurately describes his life trajectory.[3] He was born in Barcelona in 1918 of a Spanish Roman Catholic mother and an Indian Hindu father and brought up in the strictest Roman Catholic orthodoxy. Great as the influence of his father might have been in other ways, it did not extend to his religious upbringing. Panikkar's exposure to the world of India as a youth was scholastic rather than ritualistic and consisted of the study of the Sanskrit classics under the supervision, among others, of the Spanish Sanskritist Juan Mascaro. His first relatively brief encounter with India in the flesh occurred in 1954 and it was only from 1955 onward that he had prolonged contact. His real "finding" of Hinduism started then, while he was working on his third doctorate at the Lateran University, Rome, which was granted in 1961 and subsequently was published as *The Unknown Christ of Hinduism*. His first doctorate was in philosophy in 1946, dealing with the concept of nature, and his second in 1958 was in chemistry with a thesis on the philosophy of science on the topic of the ontonomy of science and its relation to philosophy, both from the University of Madrid.

All three theses reveal that from his youth his interests, whether in science, philosophy or theology, gravitated toward problems concerning the Ultimate, the mystery, the depths of life. This is remarkable, or perhaps in hindsight not altogether surprising, when one considers the outer turmoil of Europe and the world at the time. Panikkar grew up in pre-Franco Spain between the end of the First World War, which did not much affect Spain, and the Spanish Civil War which brought great destruction. Panikkar left Spain for Germany to pursue his studies at the University of Bonn only to encounter, after three years there, the outbreak of the Second World War, which compelled his return to Barcelona. He was ordained a Roman Catholic priest in 1946 and is presently attached to the diocese of Varanasi in India.

No account of his life can neglect this aspect because it is central to his self-identity. On the one hand, he has long meditated on the role, lifestyle and

---

3. *The Intra-religious Dialogue,* Paulist Press, New York, 1978; 2d ed. ATC, Bangalore, 1984, p. 2.

self-understanding of the priesthood in the modern world in its continuities and discontinuities with traditional models. On the other hand, he has so explored the depth dimensions of human life in general as to reveal its universal "priestly" aspect, connected with our intrinsic relatedness to life. In *Blessed Simplicity: The Monk as Universal Archetype* Panikkar deals specifically with the conception of the monk in modern times, but his remarks carry over, I believe, with some qualifications, to the priesthood. Here is an autobiographical comment that sheds light on his understanding of his priestly vocation:

> Since my early youth I have seen myself as a monk, but one without a monastery, or at least without walls other than those of the entire planet. And even these, it seems to me, had to be transcended — probably by immanence — without a habit, or at least without vestments other than those worn by the human family. Yet even these vestments had to be discarded because all cultural clothes are only partial revelations of what they conceal; the pure nakedness of total transparency only visible to the simple eye of the pure in heart.... By monk, *monachos,* I understand that person who aspires to reach the ultimate goal of life with all his being by renouncing all that is not necessary to it.[4]

Panikkar's "Hinduism" was a relatively late development and one hermeneutically shaped by his prior European Christian background and training. Late as it may have been it was nonetheless profound, as any reader of *The Vedic Experience,* the ripe fruit of many years of living in and reflecting on the worlds of Hinduism, can quickly discern. In some sense, he was following in the footsteps of other Christian thinkers[5] who similarly wanted to build bridges and mediate between Christian and Hindu theologies, and in particular in the footsteps of Fr. Jules Monchanin and Henri Le Saux (Swami Abhishiktananda), two French Benedictine monks who had come to India in 1939 and 1948, respectively, to devote themselves to the contemplative life lived in a completely Indian form. I mention this to highlight at least two features of Panikkar's encounter with Hinduism and Buddhism: first, it was shaped more by contemplative and spiritual imperatives than by purely academic ones; second, he gravitated more toward the speculative and metaphysical than the ritualistic.

In spite of a long immersion in Hindu and Buddhist life, Panikkar claims that he never ceased being a Christian. There have been as many critics who have accused him of having a very Christian interpretation of Hinduism and Buddhism as the reverse. He remains undismayed by such criticisms. Hindu-Buddhist-Christian existence will obviously seem heterodox and even heretical to those who prefer to remain within traditional boundaries. He has responded to his Christian critics in many different ways, including his invocation of the distinction among "christendom, christianity and christianness." The first is a

---

4. *Blessed Simplicity: The Monk as Universal Archetype,* The Seabury Press, New York, 1982, pp. 6 and 10.

5. See Robin Boyd, *An Introduction to Indian Christian Theology,* I.S.P.C.K., Delhi, India, 1975.

historical-sociological reality, the second an immanent, sacramental one, while the third, christianness, refers to the Ultimate Mystery, called by many different names, all of them obviously inadequate. The Mystery undergirds the first two realities and yet transcends them. One cannot directly approach this Mystery, which Panikkar as a Christian calls by the symbol "Christ," and which members of other traditions call by other names. As Panikkar puts it:

> The faith that I still desire to call Christian, though others may prefer to call it simply human, leads to the *plenitude* and hence to the *conversion* of all religion, even though up-to-date it has only succeeded, from a judaic substructure, in converting to a greater or lesser extent helleno-latin-gothic-celtic "paganism." This same faith is at the present time engaged in the process of converting modern secularism.[6]

And, he might have added, of being converted by it.

Perhaps the most daring of Panikkar's attempts at charting a Hindu-Buddhist-Christian spirituality within a still Christian self-understanding came in his early and path-breaking little book first published in 1970 as *The Trinity and World Religions*. Here he imposes a trinitarian structure on Hinduism and an advaitic structure on Christianity, both "trinity" and "advaita" being alternative symbols for the cosmotheandric Mystery. Drawing on traditional and unacknowledged, submerged dimensions of the Christian trinity, Panikkar attempts to connect Buddhism with the silent, self-emptying dimension of the Father; Christianity, Judaism and Islam, as religions of the word, with the Son, the incarnate Word; and advaitic Hinduism with the immanent, radically inner dimension of the Spirit. In doing so it is not his purpose imperialistically to provide a Christian grid onto which other traditions can be forced. Rather, taking Christianity as his point of departure, he wants to show that Christianity has no monopoly on trinitarian understanding and that such understanding enriched by the contributions of different traditions can in fact deepen and transform all of them.

Above all, Panikkar brings into play here two archetypes which run through his advaitic trinitarianism: *śūnyatā* and *kénosis* on the one hand and *pleroma* and fullness on the other. Rowan Williams, in a perceptive essay on Panikkar entitled "Trinity and Pluralism," has captured the dialectic of emptiness and form well:

> For Panikkar, the trinitarian structure is that of a source, inexhaustibly generative and *always* generative, from which arises form and determination, "being" in the sense of what can be concretely perceived and engaged with; that form itself is never exhausted, never limited by this or that specific realization, but is constantly being realized in the flux of active life that equally springs out from the source of all. Between form, "logos," and life, "spirit," there is an unceasing interaction. The Source of all does not and cannot exhaust itself simply in producing shape and structure; it also produces that which dissolves and re-forms all structures in endless and

---

6. *The Trinity and World Religions,* 1970, p. 4.

undetermined movement, in such a way that form itself is not absolutized but always turned back towards the primal reality of the source.[7]

This is the philosophical *Grundstruktur* that Panikkar fleshes out imagistically:

> In spite of every *effort* of the Father to "empty himself" in the generation of the Son...there remains in this first procession, like an irreducible factor, the Spirit, the non-exhaustion of the source in the generation of the Logos. For the Father, the Spirit is, as it were, the return to the source that he is himself. In other, equally inappropriate, words: the Father can "go on" begetting the Son, because he "receives back" the very Divinity which he has given up to the Son. It is the immolation or the mystery of the Cross in the Trinity. It is what Christian theologians used to call the *perichorēsis* or *circumincessio,* the dynamic inner circularity of the Trinity.[8]

The trinity is the ontological foundation of Panikkar's multifaceted doctrine of pluralism, which is a quite different notion from what is usually understood by that term. In the debates between exclusivists, inclusivists and pluralists, *pluralism* has come to mean the liberal idea of many equally valid paths to salvation or the view that the various religions constitute phenomenal manifestations of one transcendent noumenon, a *Ding-an-sich.*[9] Panikkar's view is almost the opposite. He does not think that one can trump religious pluralism by metaphysical universalism, because there is as much diversity in metaphysics as there is in religion. Furthermore, the Mystery by definition cannot be objectified or made into some neutral transcendent essence of which the different faiths are manifestations. Most important, Panikkar questions the presuppositions behind the very attempt at a universal theory of religions.

Panikkar's pluralism starts by disputing the hallowed equation of Being and Thinking by a suggested overcoming of what he calls a threefold reductionism: "Reason is not the whole of Logos," "Logos is not the whole of Man" and "Man is not the whole of Being."[10] He might have added that Being is not the whole of the Real, given the apophasis that he builds into the trinity. Like Whitehead, Panikkar emphasizes the spontaneity and novelty of the Divine, so that even God is not transparent to him-or herself. Freedom is the supreme aspect of Being. Being speaks to us in many different ways and to listen to Being is far more than just thinking it. Far from difference getting explained away in the identity of the One, Williams is right when he says:

7. Rowan Williams, "Trinity and Pluralism," in *Christian Uniqueness Reconsidered: The Myth of a Pluralistic Theology of Religions,* ed. Gavin D'Costa, Maryknoll, N.Y., Orbis Books, 1990, p. 3.

8. *The Trinity and World Religions,* ibid., p. 60.

9. See John Hick, *An Interpretation of Religion,* Yale University Press, New Haven, 1989.

10. "The Myth of Pluralism: The Tower of Babel — A Meditation on Non-Violence," in *Cross Currents,* Summer, 1979, op.cit., pp. 214–16.

The heart of this ontology could be summarized by saying that *differences matter*. The variety of the world's forms as experienced by human minds does not conceal an absolute oneness to which perceptible difference is completely irrelevant. If there is a unifying structure, it does not exist and cannot be seen independently of the actual movement and development of differentiation, the story of life-forms growing and changing.[11]

Unity is possible, then, when one pierces the different "appearances," not to get at a static Reality beyond but rather to arrive at the realization that the Real expresses itself dynamically in and through its appearances. The Real is real only in its appearances. Ewert Cousins describes this aspect of Panikkar's thought well when he writes:

> He has extended Francis of Assisi's cosmic sense into the religious experience of mankind. He sings a Franciscan hymn to the fullness of creation, but he has transposed it to another key.... He rejoices in the varieties of religious experience with the same gusto with which Francis rejoiced in the varieties of flowers, animals and birds. And this joy extends to the varieties of cultures and languages and into natural sciences and the forms of secular culture.[12]

Each religion has unique features and presents insights that are mutually incommensurable. This is so because of their holistic character, which makes it both illegitimate and unproductive to compare them in a direct, straightforward manner. Comparison implies a neutral standard or yardstick applied to the items being compared, but there is no neutral *tertium quid,* no a priori common ground that can mediate between religious traditions. Each such claim or insight has to be understood and evaluated in its own proper context, and contexts tend to be radically different.

This emphasis on religious pluralism carries over to culture, given the close ties that exist between religion and culture. Each culture gives religion its language, while each religion gives culture its ultimate contents. The parallel here to global theologies or universalistic theories of religion is a kind of cultural colonialism that starts with the unquestioned belief in the validity and superiority of a particular culture and then tends to measure other cultures in terms of its own standards. Panikkar's targets are both general and specific. In general, he is against the homogenization of life brought about by cultural colonialism, but in particular he points to the worldwide hegemony of the modern Western world view and its very particular notions of science, technology and rationality. To talk of hegemony is to imply that all other cultures are at present under the sway of the modern West, but the West is now, according to Panikkar, in a state of deep internal crisis, about which I shall say more presently.

To return to the theme of pluralism, perhaps one of the most provocative assertions of Panikkar is that each statement of what he calls a basic experi-

---

11. Williams, op. cit., p. 4.
12. Ewert Cousins, *Cross Currents,* Summer 1979, op. cit., p. 152.

ence, a primordial apprehension of reality, has to be understood and judged in its own context. These contexts are not just factually but also in principle irreducible to one another, this irreducibility being an expression of Panikkar's metaphysical claim that the very nature of truth is pluralistic. His intent here is manifold: to safeguard the integrity of different cultures and prevent their absorption or assimilation by dominant others; to prevent the absolutization of one's own point of view by the realization that others can and do see things differently; to elicit from such self-relativization a desire to dialogue with others on the presumption that we might have something to learn from them; and, in instances where there is a fundamental incompatibility of views, to push in the direction of compromise or "agreeing to disagree" rather than giving in to destructive impulses.

Two different, though associated, questions arise here: first, what precisely are Panikkar's general conceptions of reason and truth; and second, whether these conceptions lead him either to a self-refuting relativism or to equivocation or contradiction. Gerald Larson, for example, believes that Panikkar equivocates in his use of truth between a multi-valued logic in which straightforward truth-claims are no longer warranted, and an ordinary two-valued logic in which he asserts that religions embody truth in pluralistic and incommensurable ways. Larson wonders whether Panikkar, in asserting that the nature of truth itself is pluralistic, does not fall into self-referential paradox like that, for instance, of Epimenides the Cretan in his statement, "All Cretans are liars." These are actually two distinct issues. As Bertrand Russell argued in his famous "Theory of Types," some self-referential paradoxes can be taken care of by carefully distinguishing between meta- and object languages. The more serious charge, however, has to do with the propriety of claiming that at least some of the language of religion goes beyond reason, while not only using reason to make that very point but also using it within supposedly "supra-rational" discourse. There is, in other words, an unclarity and slippage in the uses of *truth* and *reason*.

Regarding the first point, Panikkar wants to relativize rationality to what he calls a particular myth or paradigm, and there are as many myths as there are cultures or subcultures. Pluralism at this level denies that there is one overarching norm of rationality and affirms by contrast that there are many such norms, some of which are incompatible. This is, at a descriptive level, unexceptionable, except perhaps to some positivists or dogmatic rationalists. The interesting question, I think, is whether the matter should be left there. If I see a person washing his hands a hundred times in a normally clean environment in the space of thirty minutes and he gives me reasons for his behavior, those reasons may be internally coherent and no doubt convincing to the subject. That, however, is not sufficient to render that particular action in that particular context "rational," even though the person concerned may think it is. The problem with an internalist position like Panikkar's is that it may render itself immune from criticism from outside. Take, for example, the case of sanctioned female circumcision in certain cultures. Would it be enough to say that the women of those cultures are "content" and are convinced of the rationality of the procedure? Panikkar, in his notion of dialectical and dialogical dialogues, does not shy away from such questions and argues that such dialogues leave room for criticism. However, someone criticizing such a practice would not, I think, be content with saying that her criticism *simply* reflects her societal myth. She might quite properly insist that she is not just imposing the norms of her culture but in fact offering something more general. The context of discovery, in other words, is not co-extensive with the context of validity. Reason, as against mere belief or opinion, does lay claim to a context-transcending power.

Such context-transcendence applies even more strongly to the notion of truth. Granted that truth arises in a particular context, that does not, however, relativize it just to that context. As Francis D'Sa puts it in his essay:

> The discovery of a truth may originate in a christian, hindu or buddhist context, but if it is true, then it must be true for all. Hence, the original moment (and place) of discovery, however privileged it may be socio-logically, is hermeneutically speaking just a formulation of that truth; it can never claim to be *the* formulation of the truth, much less the truth itself. Thus it is not possible to formulate truth exhaustively for truth being identical with reality, can never be exhausted by the Logos.[13]

Panikkar's *pars pro toto* principle says much the same thing. Indeed, all his cross-cultural hermeneutics presupposes that truth which originates in one context can be articulated in such a way that it becomes meaningful in other contexts. Thus, for example, Christians have no monopoly on Christ and the trinity, and the truth represented by those symbols is sufficiently universal to have echoes in non-Christian traditions. Likewise, in writing about "Man" in his philosophical anthropology, Panikkar would seem to be as universalist as, say, Chomsky in linguistics or Freud in psychology.

What Panikkar is trying to negotiate, then, is the distance between particularity and universality and between difference and unity. Each culture or mythic context comes up with a unique formulation of truth, which, being unique, is irreducible to another. Nevertheless, to the extent that each is a formulation of truth and not just something purely subjective, that truth is universal, though not necessarily in that particular form. This is Panikkar's notion of homeomorphic equivalents. Thus, for example, in his treatment of human rights he wants to mediate between two extremes, both of which he considers illegitimate: on the one hand, the imposition of the notion of human rights in, for example, its Lockean form on cultures for whom Locke's ideas may be quite alien and alienating; and, on the other, a simple dismissal of the idea just because of its putative Western origin.

Panikkar, as I read him, is an ontological universalist and a linguistic/cultural pluralist. While he cannot deny that his metaphysics is obviously particular, he is committed to certain general beliefs about reality that hold universally (relative, of course, to his myth), but when it comes to linguistic/cultural formulations of

---

13. Francis D'Sa, "The Notion of God in Panikkar," in this volume.

that reality, he is a pluralist in that no linguistic interpretation can hold universally, for the simple reason that it represents a cultural particularization of the truth. As he says in his reply to Larson,

> Some saying and its contra-*dictory* cannot be said in truth. We grant the validity of this principle where it belongs — language. But from language to reality there is a jump. Relativity still holds. Here it is the relativity of language.[14]

At the ontological level Panikkar is close to Hegel in his doctrine of the "concrete universal": we cannot abstract the particular and the universal apart from each other; rather, the universal is the entire field of concrete reality organized around a dimensionless moving center that cannot itself be represented. Each concrete reality, therefore, in some sense expresses the whole in a unique, indispensable way, just as a single drop of water expresses the whole ocean. What gives it its individuality is that it holds the ocean in *this* particular form.

Given this ontological understanding, Panikkar's epistemological pluralism comes into play. Truth is the whole, but each cultural formulation at its idealized best represents the *totum in parte*. It does this insofar as it strives for self-understanding in relation to the whole, that is, as it tries to glimpse the ocean from the perspective of the single drop and to see "the movement of which our situation is a moment."[15] It is the ontological rhythm that prescribes the epistemological beat and the swing to and fro from "moment" to "movement," from part to whole. As Panikkar once expressed it, his slogan is not *"e pluribus unum* but rather *e pluribus totum."*[16] There is, thus, no question of demeaning our particular *Sitz im Leben* because of its particularity and inevitable partiality, but, conversely, there is equally no warrant for absolutizing it either.

One reason Panikkar invites the charges of relativism and of equivocation is that most of his discussion of reason and truth is expressed in ontological terms, but there is still a gap to be filled between ontological conditions and normative principles for belief and action. Ontological conditions do not by themselves settle epistemological issues, which, while they cannot be separated from ontological concerns, nevertheless need to be distinguished from them. It is true that all assertions are relative to a context or "myth," but some myths are more general than others. Thus, the affirmation of the intrinsic dignity of human beings and the rejection of apartheid are widely accepted, but the denunciation of war or capitalism is not. To say that a particular culture sees things from within its particular horizon or out of its specific "window" does not in itself settle the question of the quality or validity of either the window or the seeing. That is, one's window may be foggy or distorted as, for example, in the case of racist or sexist prejudice, or our judgments may, for other reasons — error, delusion, wishful thinking and so forth — be wrong. These questions are

14. See Panikkar, "Response," in this volume.
15. Williams, op. cit., p. 5.
16. See my report of a talk of Panikkar's at Harvard in *Harvard University Center for the Study of World Religions News,* Fall, 1994, p. 1.

not decided by the unexceptionable claim that we all see through our respective windows or myths. That insight does not by itself provide us with standards for assessing myths.

Consider the difference between two statements:

1) It is right in culture A to practice cannibalism.

2) It is right for culture A to practice cannibalism.

In conformity with the Panikkarian principle of trying to understand the other as it understands itself, that is, of "standing-under" its myth, Panikkar would presumably urge us to suspend judgment until we at least attempt to put ourselves in the other's shoes. *Tout comprendre n'est pas tout pardonner.* If "we" from culture B, say, criticize people in culture A, it is not just that we are imposing our standards on others, but rather we are claiming something more general: that this is what is right, given the best moral standards available, whether they originate with us or with others. Of course, that judgment itself is made in a particular context or out of a particular myth, but that fact does not diminish the truth of the judgment. It merely reminds us of our human finitude and historicity, and that as such no human judgment can claim a God's-eye view. It does not, however, provide us with standards by which either to make or assess claims.

So concerned is Panikkar with the dangers of cultural imperialism and epistemological hubris, that he firmly rejects all pretensions to universality. As he says in his "Response":

> What I have called the *pars pro toto* effect...is a non-universal way of approaching from our particular perspective the universality we all intend....If the knowing subjects are real, no single subject can claim to speak for all other subjects, and thus reasonably raise the claim to universality.[17]

Coming from a background like Panikkar's, where he has seen a technocratic Western modernity aggressively establish cultural hegemony over the non-western world — west and non-west being cultural rather than strictly geographical markers — one can understand his strong reaction to universalistic pretensions. It is not just a political development that he is bemoaning, but one which represents a distortion and a diminishment of Being, as the wisdom of eastern and southern cultures either gets crushed beneath the juggernaut of western cultural colonialism or, what amounts to much the same, gets trivialized as folklore or exotica. In Panikkar's view a genuinely cross-cultural perspective of the common challenges and problems we face is not just a matter of justice or irenics but one equally of truth.

Precisely for that reason, one may ask whether in theoretical terms Panikkar presents the strongest case for his position by his stark repudiation of the idea of universal validity. After all, in terms of his own argument, which criticizes modern nominalism and subjectivism and the priority afforded to epistemology

---

17. See Panikkar, "Response," in this volume.

artificially separated from its ontological ground, one would expect notions of "objective truth" (in the sense of an idealized, rational, inter-subjective consensus) and of "universal validity" (suitably qualified to indicate its open, fallible and revisable character) to play a larger role in his thinking than they do. The ontological foundation of Panikkar's cross-cultural hermeneutics would seem to be the insight expressed well by Gadamer, that we are ineluctably *immer mehr Sein als Bewusstsein,* that Being's apprehension of us is both more fundamental and more extensive than our apprehension of Being. If that is true, "universal validity" could be interpreted not as the colonialistic attempt to speak for others, but rather as an attempt to present a point of view that we believe to be true, because it is supported by what appears to us objectively as the best and most compelling reasons and evidence available — much as Panikkar himself does. The phrases "point of view," "we believe," "what appears to us," indicate the inevitable subjective element, but such subjectivity does not invalidate the possibility of objectivity. The old and time-honored distinctions between *doxa* and *episteme,* prejudice and reason, partiality and impartiality rest on the ability of thought to rise above its subjectivity and offer a more objective view. And it is precisely that offer that allows others to challenge our claim to universal validity by presenting other reasons and evidence, some of which may well establish that what we thought to be general turns out to be merely particular. The dialectic of truth epistemically considered operates in this realm of an idealized inter-subjective rational *agōn,* which we are driven to because of our ontological conditioning.

In general, it seems to me that Panikkar conflates two quite distinct senses of universality, descriptive and prescriptive. As he correctly points out, the belief in intrinsic human dignity is not as a matter of descriptive fact universally held. That does not mean, however, that it should not (prescriptively) be universally subscribed to. The same distinction operates in the case of the reasons that Panikkar adduces for his belief. His view about the divine ground of human beings is not a universal one (descriptively), but this from Panikkar's point of view is an error precisely because of the implicit objective claim, that whether some people recognize it or not, it is *true* that there is such a divine ground.

III

Queries about truth in the context of pluralism open out into the question of truth in the context of his work as a whole. Panikkar has always insisted that the trinity and the pluralism it grounds are not just narrow, provincial theological concerns but views about reality, which have resonance at a number of different levels, metaphysical, cultural and political. As such, his theology goes together with a cosmology and a normative way of life to comprise a comprehensive world view.

Panikkar's full-fledged treatment of cosmology is due to appear shortly as *The Conflict of Kosmologies,* but he has written about it often enough to provide us with a fairly clear picture of his views. Needless to say, I can here only sketch them in very broad strokes. In any case, my purpose in this section is not to get into a discussion of cosmological matters, but rather to pursue a different line of argument and to raise what I think are fundamental epistemological questions.

Perhaps one way of covering such vast territory is to present a few representative selections from Panikkar's writings which give at least a flavor of his thinking on this topic:

> There is rather one, though intrinsically threefold relation which expresses the ultimate constitution of reality. Everything that exists, any real being, presents this triune structure expressed in three dimensions. I am not only saying that everything is directly or indirectly related to everything else: the radical relativity or *pratītiya-samutpāda* of the buddhist tradition. I am also stressing that this relationship is not only constitutive of the whole, but that it flashes forth ever new and vital in every spark of the real.[18]

> There is no need of epistemological mediation because ontologically everything is ultimate mediation, or rather communion. Everything is, because it mediates. Everything is in relation because everything is relation or, if you take the person to be essentially relationship...everything is personal.[19]

> Cosmic confidence...is the confidence *of* the cosmos itself of which we are a part inasmuch as we simply are. It is a subjective genitive: the confidence itself is a cosmic fact which we presuppose all the time...what the principle of non-contradiction does in the logical field, the cosmic confidence performs in the ultimate order of reality.[20]

> In the dialogue between Bellarmino and Galilei regarding the ultimate question of science.... Bellarmino was right and Galilei wrong. There cannot be real science (knowledge, *scientia, gnōsis, jñāna*) disconnected from a (theo-) cosmological context and vice versa, there can be no theology without science. The perversion...concerns the very method of knowing and its substitution by calculating...we can calculate without love, but we cannot truly know without love.[21]

The provenance and ethos of this world view with its ideas of universal correlations, isomorphism, the human being's kinship with an eternal Reason and Love, the natural world's participation in a divine drama in which human consciousness constitutes an essential and defining moment — are more akin to Eckhart and Dante, the Vedas and early Buddhism than to anything that a modern scientific naturalist could identify with. And, indeed, Panikkar minces

---

18. *The Cosmotheandric Experience,* ed. Scott Eastham, Orbis Books, Maryknoll, N.Y., 1993, p. 60.
19. See Panikkar, "Response," in this volume.
20. Ibid.
21. Ibid.

no words in calling modern science perverse, because if there is one thing that the scientific revolutions of the sixteenth and seventeenth centuries did it was to free nature from subservience to human knowledge and purposes, establish it as self-contained and independent and in fact reverse the medieval, divinely sanctioned anthropocentrism with a gradually developing naturalism that sees humans more and more as natural products. Banished from this naturalistic world are notions of *entelechies,* ontological hierarchies and intrinsic meaning. And if Panikkar chooses to call such a world view perverse, the modern naturalist would, I suppose, quite genuinely find his to be nostalgic, sentimental and hyper-personal. The new notions of infinities in space, time and number shatter the closed, finite world of immediate communication and of value-determined hierarchies of being. As Nietzsche expressed it with characteristic pathos, ever since Copernicus, "Man has been falling from a center to an x," which he cannot determine, lost as he is in the universe with its infinite multiplicity of worlds.[22]

It is not just the naturalist, however, who would find Panikkar's world view atavistic. The same break from the medieval hierarchies of being that triggered modern natural science in the West also produced another science that characterized itself as new — Vico's anti-Cartesian *Scienza Nuova,* which provided the metaphysical basis of modern scientific history with its maxim *"verum et factum convertuntur."* Vico and Descartes, opposed as they may have been in other respects, were united in seeing nature and history as fundamentally different from each other. Both saw the rupture which modern subjectivism, with its accent on constructionism and the priority of problems of knowledge and method over content, created with respect to ancient and medieval cosmologies. Different as the subject matter of the modern natural sciences and the humanities may be, they are united in seeing nature as an object rather than in terms of "communion," "relationship," *"perichorēsis"* and the like. It is not surprising, therefore, that Panikkar has the same negative response to historical consciousness as a metaphysical frame of reference as he has to modern science. The relativization of human reason to both "myth" and "spirit" is meant to undermine the pretensions of a historical consciousness that limits its scope to the human world and to meaning within that narrow segment. From the standpoint of historical consciousness and the strong sense of contingency it brings along with it, the "cosmic confidence" that Panikkar articulates looks like a throw back to bygone eras of *physis* and cosmos, of *ṛta* and *sanātana dharma,* whose stable and timeless forms underpin the world of change.

The discussion about mediation that Panikkar refers to in his "Response" took place between us within this metaphysical context. Once the reflective turn is made — Panikkar's second kairological moment — mediation is inescapable, in that the immediacies of knowledge and faith are either empty or themselves mediated. Panikkar challenges this on the grounds that mediation

---

22. Karl Löwith, *Nature, History and Existentialism,* Northwestern University Press, Evanston, 1966.

for him presupposes the equation of Being and Intelligibility, which assumption he denies. That assumption, however, is not the only alternative; even critics of rationalism like Pascal or Kierkegaard see the inescapability of mediation, which is but an expression of our finitude and historicity. As Goethe says, "The true is godlike; it does not appear immediately, we must ascertain it from its manifestations."

For Panikkar these manifestations are in the nature of a direct communion, and immediate revelation, making mediation unnecessary, at least at the ultimate level. His notions of myth and symbol point to a pre-reflective awareness of the interrelatedness, and even more, innerrelatedness of all reality. Hence his invocation of the Mīmāṃsā concept of *apauruṣeyatva* and the Buddhist idea of *pratītiya-samutpāda* in sharp contrast to the Greek notion of *hen kai polla,* the latter inevitably creating the dualism of the knower and the known, the former avoiding it because everything is in relation.

> There is no need for epistemological mediation, because ontologically everything is ultimate mediation or rather communion. Everything is, because it mediates.... The epistemological question is not ultimate. There is no split between epistemology and ontology. The *logos* of the *on* is not mere *episteme,* it is a dimension of the *on* itself. Ontology becomes epistemology only when the *verbum entis* becomes the *verbum mentis,* that is, i.e., when our *logos* divorces the *on.*[23]

Some of this critique of the modern priority given to epistemology and mediation will be familiar to Western readers from similar critiques proffered by Heidegger and Wittgenstein. The cognitive enterprise cannot be seen as either autonomous or foundational, because it stands within a life-context and an on-going ontological "happening." Panikkar's view is, however, more radical than either Heidegger's or Wittgenstein's, because there is an explicit finitude and historicity in their thinking that Panikkar seemingly denies or, at least, qualifies. Here again I want to press a point made earlier. Granted that the separation of epistemology from ontology is unwarranted, the distinction between the two is not. Once we reach the stage of the intentionality and the self-consciousness of thought, is it still possible to talk of *svayamprakāśa,* or self-illuminating and non-intentional communication? Granted that the subjectivism of modern philosophy in either its nominalist or its realist variants may be legitimately criticized, does that permit us in a post-critical age to talk of a primordial revelation, of a direct, unmediated contact with reality? It seems to me that the ontological interrelatedness of all things, including ourselves, and hence our participation in reality, do not by themselves settle the epistemological questions occasioned by the fact of reflective consciousness.

What interests me as much is the larger question: Is Panikkar's cosmotheandric vision a viable historical possibility, or does it represent rather a vision of great beauty and compelling power, but one that is, in Hölderlin's famous

---

23. See Panikkar, "Response," in this volume.

lament, "too late"?[24] That is, granted the *aporias* of modernity and the limitations of both modern science and historical consciousness, is the way forward Panikkar's way or will it take other directions? His answer is articulated in terms of the "new innocence," the cosmotheandric moment which would incorporate the distinctions of the second ("enstatic") moment without losing the unity of the first ("ecstatic") moment. The very idea of a new innocence is problematic, as Panikkar himself recognizes.

> Innocence is innocent precisely because once spoiled it cannot be recovered. We cannot go back to the earthly paradise, much as we might long to do so....The third moment is a conquest, the difficult and painful conquest of a new innocence. The first innocence is lost forever.[25]

The question is whether innocence in any form is possible for us.

This brings us back to the question of truth, which I posed at the beginning of this section. What evidence or reasons are there for justifying his confidence? Such contemporary evidence as there is seems to be ambiguous. The movements in contemporary Western philosophy are in pragmatist, historicist or deconstructionist directions, all of which in different ways privilege the contingent and the changeable and the resolutely secular (as against sacred secularity). The movements in science, while going beyond objectivism or positivism, seem to point in a direction different from the privileging of human consciousness and personalism that is so marked a feature of the cosmotheandric vision. As against these historical trends Panikkar wants to raise the power of a mystical vision that is "tempiternal" and as such is meant to stand as a corrective to our own "*duerftige Zeit.*" How in this difficult area does one distinguish truth from wishful thinking, what is real, even if astringent, from what is consoling? There is as yet no clear answer from Panikkar beyond a scathing critique of the present that already presupposes the correctness of his position.

This raises the question whether Panikkar is right in his historical judgment about the time now being ripe for the third cosmotheandric moment that he calls the new innocence to indeed maintain the distinctions of the second "humanistic" moment without losing the unity of the first "primordial" one. My sceptical remarks in this section indicate that in my judgment Panikkar underestimates the rupture created by the modern scientific and epistemological revolutions. While the healing of the great divisions between cosmos and history caused by these developments may be immensely desirable, the question of truth that I

---

24. See Hölderlin's poem "Brot und Wein," with its haunting lines:

> Aber Freund! wir kommen zu spät. Zwar leben die Götter,
> Aber über dem Haupt in anderer Welt
> Endlos wirken sie da and scheinens wenig zu achten
> Ob wir leben, so sehr schonen die Himmlischen uns
> Denn nicht immer vermag ein schwaches Gefäss sie zu fassen
> Nur zu Zeiten erträgt göttliche Fülle der Mensch

25. *The Cosmotheandric Experience,* pp. 50–51.

have raised sharpens the issue of evidence and warrants for an emerging cosmotheandrism of the sort Panikkar envisages. It is not enough to say that the
modern world is bamboozled by the "myth of history" and that what is needed
is a new myth and a new vision. They may be needed but is need a sufficient
epistemological basis for assertions of fact or plausibility? To think so is not
to take sufficiently seriously the challenge posed by the modern sciences and to
beg the question in favor of the pre-modern period. It may further be argued that
there is an incommensurability between the pre-modern and the modern that by
definition renders any synthesis difficult. If views cannot even be made commen-
surate, how can they be sublated? To make good his claim that his is a genuinely
post-modern vision, Panikkar will have to do more than simply present his cosmotheandrism. *Die Anstrengung des Begriffs* that Panikkar, following Hegel,
valorizes points towards a more strenuous justificatory argument.

IV

The appropriateness of the title of this book should by now be obvious. The
intercultural challenge that Panikkar poses is one that radically questions modern and post-modern world views, not only for their ethnocentricity and cultural
imperialism, but even more for their severely restricted outlook. By the same
token, it is a diminishment of Panikkar's real challenge to see him only as a
cross-cultural philosopher of religion and theologian, as he tends very often to
be viewed, without at the same time understanding the comprehensive vision
that underlies and animates these roles. One reason for providing the metaphysical and cosmological background to his theology and scholarship in the field
of religion is to present him as a holistic thinker who has tried to incorporate
the experience of several millennia of a culturally diverse human history into a
vision that, at least in intent, is forward looking.

Since his early writings, Panikkar has been talking of our time as a time of
kairos and crisis, a time of special significance fraught with both danger and opportunity. In all his work with its talk of "the end of history" and the need for a
radical transformation and metamorphosis, and our preparation for it in terms of
a personal and collective *metanoia,* there is a palpable sense of a certain order
coming to an end and a new configuration struggling to be born. This, as we
approach the end of our century and millennium, no longer sounds as prophetic
and revolutionary as it once may have. With the collapse of colonial hegemony,
the recrudescence of ethnic and cultural conflict and the reversion to more primal identities and loyalties, and above all with the increasing scepticism about
scientism and the technological culture it spawns, the passing of the "modern"
world is now widely accepted. The very designation post-modern attests to this,
as indeed does the frequent use of the prefix post as a marker, though people
differ widely in their accounts of what exactly has come to an end and what is
replacing or displacing it.

Panikkar, with his background and interest in modern science and its connections with philosophy and religion, is in large part concerned with drawing

out the metaphysical implications of post-Copernican science and with showing both how discontinuous such science is with that practiced in other times and cultures and, its great achievements notwithstanding, its increasingly deleterious consequences for global civilization. Not only does such science with its mathematical formalism deal exclusively with the measurable and quantitative aspects of reality to the neglect of qualitative concerns like value, meaning or purpose, but also, with its rigid dichotomy of the knower and the known, and its stress on the objectifiable, wrenches the activity of knowing from its ontological context and thus brings about an alienation of the knower both from the world and from himself or herself as a part of and participant in that world. The ecological crisis we are experiencing is, from a metaphysical standpoint, the direct result of this science-induced alienation. The stress on love as an epistemological imperative is not in Panikkar's case a pious platitude but an urgent summons to a renewed awareness of our cosmotheandric solidarity. In pressing him, as I did in the preceding section, for a rigorous philosophical argument about how we might get there, given the ruptures of modern science and the worldwide hegemony of a technocratic civilization, I am at the same time articulating a political concern about how we might resist what Husserl, and following him Heidegger, have called the "europeanization of the earth."

On this point, Panikkar is under no illusions. All cultures now fall under the dominance of the modern west and its economico-technological ideology. The so-called East Asian "economic miracle" merely betokens the extension of this ideology to that part of the world as it exploits the conditions of a skilled labor force and new markets. It has very little to do with questioning, leave aside subverting, the predominant technological world picture. Panikkar's intercultural challenge is to be situated within this historical-political context for the many dimensions of his work to be properly appreciated. Until such time as we penetrate to the historical and metaphysical roots of our present crises, ecological, cultural and political, we will only be spinning our wheels in a swamp, engaging perhaps in a few cosmetic changes but otherwise leaving the status quo intact.

Panikkar's interculturality goes much deeper than preaching tolerance and setting guidelines for interreligious exchange. It is, I suppose, not inaccurate to describe him as "the apostle of interreligious dialogue,"[26] as long as one realizes that one is talking more of an apostle like Paul than some of the others, one who understands the full implications of bridging and mediating worlds and cultures.

By way of tying together the diverse threads of this essay and bringing it to a conclusion, I want to highlight a few further dimensions of Panikkar's intercultural challenge. At its most basic, interculturality stands at the opposite pole to a cultural colonialism, the belief in the unquestioned validity and superiority of a single culture. Such monoculturalism usually goes along with an ideology of evolutionism, in which other cultures and perspectives are placed on a single evolutionary scale and absorbed within the last, most "complete" and "fulfilled" item on that scale. As opposed to this, interculturality implies

---

26. See Leonard Swidler, *After the Absolute,* Fortress Press, Minneapolis, 1990, p. 44.

an openness to, and willingness to learn from, other cultures, grounded in the acknowledgment of the partiality and relativity of one's own cultural tradition. It is thus also opposed to a certain variety of so-called multiculturalism that stresses sheer difference and insists on being immured within one's particular language, religion, culture, racial or ethnic tradition. The central political task for our times, as Panikkar makes clear in another recent book, *Peace and Cultural Disarmament,* is the creation of a new paradigm of coexistence among the various cultures, races and religious traditions within a single interconnected civilization. Much of his cross-cultural hermeneutics from his notion of "dialogical dialogue" to his "diatopical hermeneutics" may be seen as directed toward this political goal, which has occupied him also in his work at the Directorate of Peace at UNESCO in Paris.

Cultural disarmament refers not just to the dangers of monoculturalism and difference-based tribalisms, but also to the hope that an economico-technological ideology stressing human domination and control over the rhythms of life will increasingly give way to a cosmotheandric harmony. This hope has resonance at many different levels. Metaphysically, it points to a view of life where the cosmic, the human and the divine dimensions of existence are seen in their innerrelatedness. Epistemologically, it gestures toward a balancing of the claims of reason, myth and symbol. Politically, it signals a new paradigm of solidarity with the cosmos and the divine and of peaceful coexistence and creative cooperation with one another. It is to Panikkar's credit that he has buttressed this hope both by going to the roots of our crises and by suggesting a way out. As we contemplate the increasing anomie of our world at the end of this century, this cosmotheandric vision is not without appeal.

PART I

Metaphysical Foundations

1

The Notion of God

FRANCIS X. D'SA, SJ

INTRODUCTION

Among the few modern thinkers to treat of the notion of God positively and somewhat at length is the Canadian philosopher-theologian Bernard J. F. Lonergan. Lonergan goes about this discussion by first investigating the notion of being. This examination leads him to the conclusion "that the idea of being would be the content of an unrestricted act of understanding that primarily understood itself and consequently grasped every other intelligibility."[1] He then proceeds to work out his concept of an unrestricted act of understanding. Here, "it becomes manifest that it is one and the same thing to understand what being is and to understand what God is."[2] The notion of God, as Lonergan conceives it, implies that God is the creator,[3] that he is "the first agent of every event, every development, every emergent,"[4] that he is "the ultimate final cause of any universe, the ground of its value, and the ultimate objective of all finalistic striving"[5] and that "God is personal."[6] "Moreover, as the idea of being is the notion of a personal God, so too it implies a personalistic view of the order of the universe."[7] In a second major step Lonergan sets out to *affirm* the existence of God. The outline of his argumentation is as follows: "If the real is completely intelligible, God exists. But the real is completely intelligible. Therefore God exists. To begin from the minor premise, one argues that being is completely intelligi-

Francis X. D'Sa, SJ, is Professor of Theology at DiNobili College, Pune, India, and visiting Professor of Indology at the University of Innsbrück, Austria.

1. Bernard J. F. Lonergan, *Insight: A Study of Human Understanding,* Philosophical Library, New York; Darton Longman and Todd, London, New Impression, 1973, p. 657.
2. Ibid., pp. 657–68.
3. Ibid., p. 663.
4. Ibid., p. 664.
5. Ibid.
6. Ibid., p. 668.
7. Ibid., p. 669.

ble, that the real is being, and that therefore the real is completely intelligible."[8]
"There remains the major premise, namely, if the real is completely intelligible, then complete intelligibility exists. If complete intelligibility exists, the idea of being exists. If the idea of being exists, then God exists. Therefore, if the real is completely intelligible, God exists."[9]

It has been asserted that Lonergan's method, built on "the pure desire to know"[10] "provides the heuristic intentional thrust which reaches *beyond all cultural and religious borders.*"[11] James Brown informs us that Vernon Gregson in his book *Lonergan, Spirituality, and the Meeting of Religions,* "clearly illustrates the value of Lonergan's method for understanding and relating spirituality to the meeting of religions and secular consciousness,"[12] topics with which Panikkar has concerned himself for the greater part of his life. Specifically, Lonergan's treatment of the notion of God is a modernized version of the scholastic version of the same. Indeed, years later, looking back at chapter 19 of *Insight,* Lonergan himself confessed that there he had approached the question of God "in the old manner of the Aristotelian-Thomist tradition."[13]

My reason for mentioning Lonergan is not so much to critique his position from the Panikkarian perspective as to highlight Panikkar's own contribution. Lonergan, a profound christian thinker from the West, "indubitably maintains that there is an epistemology and a metaphysics implicit in Christian revelation."[14] Panikkar, a profound christian, buddhist, hindu and secular thinker, would be far removed from such a stance. Against such a Lonerganian backdrop, then, the specificity of Panikkar's approach to the Divine should stand out strikingly.

INTRODUCTION TO PANIKKAR'S THOUGHT

To understand Panikkar's thought it is necessary to take note of the womb where his seminal ideas were conceived; this will point to the context of his concepts. From early years Panikkar has been at home both in India and in Europe, that is, in the christian and secular traditions of Europe as well as in the hindu and buddhist traditions of India; in the field of science as well as in the world of philosophy, theology and religion.[15] His voluminous writings with very erudite and often rare references as well as extensive bibliographies from diverse fields testify not only to his versatile temperament but to the universe

---

8. Ibid., p. 672.

9. Ibid., p. 673. For a detailed treatment see Bernard Tyrell, *Bernard Lonergan's Philosophy of God,* Gill & Macmillan, Dublin, 1974.

10. *Insight,* p. 348.

11. James Brown's review of Vernon Gregson, *Lonergan, Spirituality, and the Meeting of Religions,* Lanham, Md.: University Press of America, 1985, in *Cross Currents,* Spring, 1987, p. 106. My emphasis.

12. Ibid., p. 104.

13. Lonergan's Foreword to Bernard Tyrell's *Bernard Lonergan's Philosophy of God,* p. x.

14. Tyrell, op. cit., p. 17.

15. Panikkar, "Philosophy as Life-Style," pp. 199–201.

in which he lives, moves and has his being. If some have found his thought difficult to follow it is due not only to his neologisms and the originality of his ideas but also and more probably to the fact that these readers themselves may have been nurtured in the well of one culture, not in the ocean where the waters of different traditions meet. In his writings Panikkar repeatedly makes statements like the following: "I am attempting to speak a language that will make sense for the follower of more than one philosophical tradition — a risky task perhaps, but necessary if one is to do justice to a cross-cultural investigation."[16] Or again: "I 'left' [Europe] as a Christian. I 'found' myself a Hindu and I 'return' a Buddhist, without having ceased to be a Christian."[17] From a multireligious and multicultural biographical background such as this Panikkar has felt the urge to live reality to the fullest, "a concern for ultimate issues — not in a merely theoretical way, but by the total participation of the person."[18] Says Panikkar: "My personal circumstances (biological, historical and biographical) led me to accept the risk of conversion without alienation, assumption without repudiation, synthesis or symbiosis without syncretism or eclecticism."[19] Panikkar has experienced intercultural dialogue in his own person as an *intra* religious experience.[20]

UNDERSTANDING PANIKKAR'S PREUNDERSTANDING

The overriding concern of Panikkar in his writings is to communicate cross-culturally, and this not merely through "morphological" and "diachronical" hermeneutics.[21] "Diatopical hermeneutics stands for the thematic consideration of understanding the other without assuming that the other has the same basic self-understanding and understanding as I have. The ultimate human horizon, and not only differing contexts, is at stake here. The method in this third moment is a peculiar *dialogical dialogue, the dia-logos* piercing the *logos* in order to reach that dialogical, translogical realm of the heart (according to most traditions), allowing for the emergence of a myth in which we may commune, and which will ultimately allow understanding (standing under the same horizon of intelligibility)."[22] There is here a clash of horizons that is not merely temporal but also cultural. "If morphological hermeneutics spell [sic] out of the implicit treasures of one particular culture and if diachronical hermeneutics bridges the temporal gap in human cultural history, diatopical hermeneutics tries to bring together radically different human horizons."[23]

---

16. Panikkar, *Myth, Faith and Hermeneutics,* p. 381.
17. Panikkar, *Intrareligious Dialogue,* p. 2.
18. "Philosophy as Life-Style," p. 199.
19. Ibid., p. 201.
20. Ibid., p. 201.
21. *Myth, Faith and Hermeneutics,* pp. 8–9.
22. Ibid., p. 9.
23. "Philosophy as Life-Style," p. 205. In almost all his writings Panikkar is at pains to point out that the Logos is one mode of consciousness. There is another mode of human consciousness where the Spirit is fundamental. "There is a trend of 'crypto-subordinationism' in the western tra-

There are two assumptions here: first, no one formulation of a truth (wherever and by whomsoever it may have been discovered) can ever be identified with the truth itself; and second, it should be possible to interpret any truth cross-culturally. If the first points to the regionalization of truth, the second stresses its universalization.[24] It is these two aspects of reality which diatopical hermeneutics tries to reconcile. The universalization aspect derives from the fact that truth's grasp of us is primordial and hence more immediate and intimate than our grasp of truth. Our grasp, due to our finitude, is episodic, partial and particular.

What therefore Panikkar probably means with the "ultimate human horizon" that is at stake is this: There is no such thing as a private truth or even for that matter a christian, hindu or buddhist truth. The discovery of a truth may originate in a christian, hindu or buddhist context, but if it is true then it must be true for all. Hence the original moment (and place) of discovery, however privileged it may be sociologically, is hermeneutically speaking just *a* formulation of that truth; it can never claim to be *the* formulation of the truth, much less the truth itself. Thus it is not possible to formulate truth exhaustively, for truth being identical with reality, can never be exhausted by the Logos. That implies that every culture has its own experience and expression of the truth of real-

---

dition which cannot be overcome by any number of otherwise well-intentioned pneumato*logies,* let alone phenomenologies. The Spirit can neither be reduced nor subordinated to the Logos....The human organ for the Spirit is the *mythos.* Myth and Logos go together, but their link is not dialectical, nor is it mythical: rather it is the link which constitutes both of them....In other words, there is no *logos* without *mythos* — of which the *logos* is the language — and there is no *mythos* without the *logos* — of which the *mythos* is the ground" (ibid., p. 202).

The question that diatopical hermeneutics addresses is both temporal and cultural. It is a coming face-to-face of two worlds and entering into a dialogue, and not a mere discussion. Dialogue, for Panikkar, has to do with testimony and witness, not with argument as in discussion. Hence dialogical dialogue is a transcending, a going beyond the *logos* but a going beyond *through* the logos to the mythos, which the *logos* reveals and from which it has emerged. The function of the dialogue is to open to the hearer the *mythos* of the one who gives testimony. The dialogue is the bridge from and to the *mythos.* It is only when the hearer enters into the *mythos* of the speaker that intercultural and interreligious dialogue takes place. Hence for Panikkar *understanding* implies always a standing under the spell of the same *mythos.* The specific *mythoi* of the cultures have to give way to the emergence of a common *mythos* if understanding is to take place. The ultimate human horizon is, of course, Mythos which, because it is ultimate, we can never cross. Its function is to point in the direction of a commonality which we never fully attain; it is a constant call to enter ever more deeply into the unity of Reality.

24. For Panikkar the "relationship between truth and the expression of truth in concepts and symbols is one of the most central philosophical problems. Truth has the inbuilt claim to be universally valid, here and there, yesterday and tomorrow, for you and for me. Yet my grasping and formulating it cannot sustain the same claim without charging all the others who do not agree with me with stupidity or wickedness. Hence the necessary *via media* between agnostic relativism and dogmatic absolutism. This is what can be called relativity....Our particular case is a typical example of the *pars pro toto:* from the optic of the inside it looks like the whole; from the outside it looks like a part, a fragment....Here lies the crux. We cannot but aim at the *totum,* and yet we often forget that all we see is the *pars* which we then take *pro toto....*In brief, we need a new hermeneutic: the diatopical hermeneutic that can only be developed in a *dialogical* dialogue. This would show us that we must take neither the *pars pro toto,* nor believe that we see the *totum in parte.* We must accept what our partner tells us: simply that we take the *totum pro parte,* when we are aware of the *pars pro toto;* which is obviously what we will retort right back to him. This is the human condition and I would not consider it to be an imperfection" (Inter-Culture XVII. 1. 82 [Janvier-Mars 1984], pp. 37–38).

ity. But still the exigency of the unity of reality — which is manifested in the urgent need to communicate cross-culturally — urges us to make the effort to articulate the experience of truth in such a manner that it becomes meaningful in the different contexts of diverse cultures. It is here that diatopical hermeneutics becomes topical.

Now not only has Panikkar given us the theoretical underpinnings of his diatopical hermeneutics; he has offered us a number of concrete diatopical hermeneutic interpretations of Vedic sacrifice,[25] the myth of Prajāpati,[26] the myth of Śunaḥśepa,[27] Advaita and bhakti,[28] karma,[29] the trinity,[30] etc. The interpretations illustrate how "diatopical hermeneutics tries to bring together radically different human horizons."[31] Human horizons do not come together when American wheat fills Russian stomachs or African cocoa becomes Swiss chocolate — this is more the outcome of political and economic marriages of convenience than of human concern. But human horizons coalesce when, for example, "Asian" karma is interpreted as karma that affects all human beings, their history as well as their cosmos; or when the myth of Śunaḥśepa is read as the myth of the human condition; or when the trinity is shown to be an integral "part" of the religious experience of all traditions.

In order to communicate (better still, to commune) cross-culturally Panikkar has developed diatopical hermeneutics based on dialogical dialogue which takes the *topoi* and their respective horizons seriously. The reason for this is that the insights of these horizons have to be preserved in a broader horizon of intelligibility. This happens when the different horizons fuse and we begin to participate in the same Mythos.

Diatopical hermeneutics is not just a matter of intellectual interpretation. Its base is experiential in the first place. The more we participate in the same Mythos the deeper is the communion between "us" and "them" and the result is a "we." To explain this we need to introduce Panikkar's understanding of consciousness.

Mythos is an important ingredient of Panikkar's understanding of consciousness. His contention is that consciousness can be neither simply identified with nor exhausted by the Logos.[32] Mythos is as much and as important a characteristic of consciousness as Logos. Logos is the foreground, the expression, the thought, and Mythos is the background, the horizon, the unthought.[33]

Mythic awareness is a *sui generis* kind of consciousness. It cannot be objectified but it is that which permits objectification. It cannot be expressed but it is that which helps bring forth expression. It cannot be grasped but it is that

---

25. Panikkar, *The Vedic Experience: Mantramañjarī,* pp. 346–432.
26. *Myth, Faith and Hermeneutics,* pp. 66–95.
27. Ibid., pp. 98–184.
28. Ibid., pp. 278–79.
29. Ibid., p. 238.
30. Panikkar, *The Trinity and the Religious Experience of Man.*
31. "Philosophy as Life-Style," p. 205.
32. "Witness and Dialogue," pp. 238–39.
33. "The Philosophical Tradition," p. 345.

which allows us to grasp something. It cannot ever be reduced to the foreground because it is that which constitutes the foreground.

There is a general tendency to reduce consciousness to the Logos, to equate consciousness with the Logos. The underlying presupposition is that whatever we know can be thematized, explained and analyzed. This rests on the belief that there is nothing in consciousness which cannot be put in words. What is overlooked in the process is that the consciousness which puts the contents into words itself cannot be put in words! The Logos dimension of consciousness is not everything. But it is the dimension which puts into words what is experienced and thought. Its peculiarity is that its consistency is based on reason, because of which reasoning and argumentation (=dialectics) play a major role in this realm. But reasoning and argumentation presuppose a consciousness which itself is beyond such reasoning and argumentation since it is the base on which they function. This base is the mythic dimension of consciousness.[34]

Furthermore, the Logos alone would not be able to convey meaning, much less meaningfulness. One could say that if speaking is done through the Logos, its meaning derives from the Mythos. But if the Mythos can speak only through the Logos, it is equally true that the Logos can mean only through the Mythos. Background and foreground always go together; one without the other is not possible.

Now if we examine this a little more closely we shall notice that no meaning in itself can attract, inspire, move or motivate. Only a meaning that is meaningful, full of meaning, is capable of that. But a meaning that is in no way meaningful is empty and dead; it does not mean anything. It does not have the Spirit. It is the Spirit alone that gives life, makes meaning meaningful, by lending "meaning" to meaning.

Now if Logos is the thought and Mythos the unthought, the Pneuma is the unthinkable. "The way leads from myth to *logos* to the *pneuma.*"[35] The Pneuma has a dual function: inspiring and fulfilling. She draws meaning from Mythos, inspires it to become word and attracts it to herself so that by filling it with meaning she can make it and keep it meaningful. Meaningfulness is "unthinkable." "The unthinkable does not exist in itself as a fixed dimension; at any given moment it is the provisional, the historical that accomplishes itself in the future, in hope.... Receiving the *pneuma* is a permanent passage, a *pascha,* a

---

34. Ibid., pp. 344–45: "Man knows through the *logos* that he unearths from myth and that he still remains in myth. *Mythos* is the second dimension of speech itself, the silence between the words, the matrix that bears the words....If I try to explain myth with the *logos,* I can only represent it *in illo tempore* which is interpreted as past. No living myth — and we all live in myths — can be interpreted through the strainer of mythology. The light of the *logos* dispels the darkness of myth and myth measured by the standard of the *logos* cannot withstand it. *Logos* finds *mythos* ridiculous, just as myth is not disconcerted by mythology.... For *logos* has also a mythical connection, otherwise it could not exist. *Mythos* is also an organ of philosophy, but neither as reflexive consciousness, nor as a second-class organ somehow subordinate to the *logos. Mythos* is not ancillary to *logos.* The mythical dimension does not mean that I think the unthought — for then it would obviously cease to be unthought. It is an important task of philosophy to admit *mythos* as an organ *sui stante,* a contact with reality."

35. Ibid., p. 346.

pilgrimage; the procession from *mythos* through *logos* to *pneuma* is endless. Precisely this pneumatic dimension guarantees the constant openness into which we may take a step forward."[36] Reception of the pneuma is important because without her there is no openness. This implies that without her our myths turn into mythology:[37] With her however our horizon of understanding can grow and function.

It is the Pneuma then that draws all meaningfulness from the Mythos. However, we do not find or experience meaningfulness in itself. It is the Logos dimension that is made meaningful but this happens only on the background of the Mythos. This, in turn, is so because of the constant and continual pull that Pneuma exercises in our lives — an attraction which on the one hand can never be satiated in space-and-time but on the other, if missing, drains all meaning from our lives.

The openness, which is a gift of the Pneuma, is made intelligible in the Mythos and is experienced in the Logos. The usual fallacy consists in attributing all this to the Logos alone, in concluding that consciousness can be exhaustively expressed by the Logos alone and in forgetting that the mythic and pneumatic dimensions are as real and important as the Logos dimension.[38]

To illustrate all this let us return to the earlier part of our discussion on dialogue. The essence of dialogue is grounded not in the Logos but in the Mythos. "Myth reveals itself in dialogue just as the *logos* liberates itself in dialectics."[39] There is authentic dialogue only when there is a common Mythos in which the dialogue partners participate. The function of real dialogue is not so much to focus on the Logos (where the formulations and the doctrines hold sway) as to point to the Mythos and to reveal the common horizon. The latter is the outcome of the fusion of horizons which itself is the result of the reception of the Pneuma. Dialogue is like sailing together on the sea of a common Mythos and being driven in an unknown direction by the winds of the self-same Pneuma. In such an enterprise even the Logos can take on an unusual function, namely that of witness and testimony, and not merely of reasoning and argumentation.

Now the fact that we are being driven by the winds of the Pneuma implies that our sails are open to these winds. This "existential openness" is what Panikkar calls faith.[40] The Pneuma can inspire us only when we are open to her.

---

36. Ibid., p. 347.

37. Mythology, for Panikkar, consists in reifying the myth and in interpreting it literally. Unlike myth, mythology for Panikkar has negative connotations.

38. Ibid., pp. 342ff.

39. "Witness and Dialogue," p. 239.

40. "Faith as a Constitutive Human Dimension," p. 207. "One is open to what one is not or, rather, to what one has not yet become. Real openness means the possibility of being: openness to Being. It implies a capacity to be ever more and more filled, an 'in-finite' receptivity, because Man is not 'finished,' finite. Man is open because he is not closed, he is not complete because he is itinerant, not definite, not 'finished,' in-complete. The existential openness of faith represents Man's capacity for his non-finitude, that is, his in-finity. No person considers himself as finished, as having exhausted the possibilities of becoming. The opening of which we speak is constitutive of the human being, the other side of what we call contingency. This latter appears when we look backwards, to our foundation, thus discovering that we do not have in and of ourselves the ground

Furthermore, Panikkar understands faith on two levels: faith as a constitutive human dimension, that is, faith as a human structure that opens up the person; and the act of believing, the act, namely, in which the structure of openness is actuated. Both of these are to be distinguished from belief, which is the expression of the act of faith. Though we cannot separate the three it is important to distinguish them.[41]

It is Panikkar's merit that he has liberated the notion of faith from the clutches of rationalism on the one hand and subjectivism on the other, and brought it into the realm of the cosmotheandric. He can therefore appropriately speak of "the universe of faith and the pluriverse of beliefs," because it is only in the universe of faith that "the experience of faith which is a primal anthropological act"[42] makes the human enter into the realm of the Divine. Though the Divine realm is one, the entrances, namely beliefs, are many. Belief for Panikkar is intimately connected with the act of believing (=faith). Making use of Panikkar's theory of symbol, one could assert that belief is the symbol of faith and faith is the symbolized experience. If beliefs em*body* faith, faith *anima*tes beliefs.[43]

Belief, according to Panikkar, is a *sui generis* phenomenon. Its meaning is not its content. "The peculiar difficulty in the phenomenology of religion is that the religious *pistema* is different from and not reducible to the Husserlian *noēma*. The *pistema* is that core of religion which is open or intelligible only to a *religious* phenomenology. In other words, the belief of the believer belongs essentially to the religious phenomenon. There is no 'naked' or 'pure' belief separate from the person who believes. This being the case, the *noēma* of a religiously skeptical phenomenologist does not correspond to the *pistema* of the believer. The religious phenomenon appears only as *pistema* and not as mere *noēma*."[44]

Believing, expressed in a belief, is a special human act which cannot be paraphrased into words. The expression, however indispensable to the "believing," is not the content of this act. In the act of believing the Logos is only a pointer

---

of our own existence. The former, i.e., the existential opening, appears when we look forward, towards the goal, the end, the transcendent, etc. and discover that we are not complete" (p. 208).

41. "Faith and Belief," pp. 56–57: "Faith cannot be equated with belief, but faith always needs a belief to be faith. Belief is not faith, but it must convey faith. A disembodied faith is not faith. A belief that does not always point to a beyond that outsoars and in a sense annihilates it is not belief but fanaticism. Faith finds expression in belief, and through it men normally arrive at faith. Where Men live in a homogeneous cultural world, most never notice that tension between faith and belief. They look on dogmas, which are simply authoritative formulations of belief, almost as if they were faith itself, half-forgetting that they are dogmas *of* faith. When cultural change or an encounter between religions robs the notions hitherto bound up with faith of their solidity and unmistakable correspondence to faith, naturally a crisis erupts. But this is a crisis of belief, not of faith. Undoubtedly the bond between the two is intimate; it is in fact constitutive, since thought itself requires language, and belief is the language of faith. Hence what begins as a crisis of belief turns into a crisis of faith, as a rule due to the intransigence of those who will tolerate no change because they do not distinguish between faith and belief."

42. Ibid., p. 59.

43. Ibid., pp. 40–61.

44. "EPOCHÉ in the Religious Encounter," p. 89.

to the Mythos; and so the focus of belief, genuinely understood, is the Mythos. That is why Panikkar can say: "Belief is taken to be the vehicle by which human consciousness passes from *mythos* to *logos*."[45] On the other hand, belief reveals the myth from which it derives and in which it remains rooted.[46]

The way we look at reality, the way we consider what is real and what is false, all this is determined by our Mythos. Our understanding of truth and reality is dependent on our Mythos. Cultures are differentiated according to the *mythoi* they believe in. These *mythoi* are further differentiated "regionally" and "individually." A living Mythos is assimilated diversely according to differences in space and time. In the *myth of history* what is true and what is false is determined by what "really" happened.[47] But in the *myth of cosmos* what is true and what is false is not determined by what happened but by what is seen as forming a harmonious whole with the cosmos.[48] Our ideas of reality and consequently our notion of "God" too will differ according to the Mythos in which we live.

Hence, once we are aware of the function of Myth and its role in human consciousness our questions too will be of a different kind. For then we shall be aware of the nature and limits of the Logos. All our questions and answers belong to the realm of the Logos. In the realm of faith the Logos has a different role compared to its role in the cognitive realm. Whereas in the cognitive realm reasoning built on consistency is important, that is not so in the realm of faith. Beliefs are often mistakenly understood as cognitive statements, but they have a function of their own. To identify the linguistic expression of belief with the act of believing, to understand the verbal expression of belief with its content is to reify the belief. It is like mistaking the pipeline for the water. Understanding the nature of belief will guard us against reducing a *pistema* to a *noēma*. "Belief articulates the myth in which we believe without 'believing' that we believe in it. To believe is not to hold a belief as one holds an object of knowledge."

The notion of God, then, differs according to the Mythos of the times and cultures. Panikkar sees three major moments of consciousness in the last ten thousand years of human memory thus: the first was dominated by the *myth of cosmos,* the second by the *myth of history* and the third is the *global myth* that is emerging.[49] Panikkar's treatment of Mythos is of immense help in placing in correct perspective the different religious traditions of the human race and even notions like the "atheism" of Buddhism.[50] Panikkar's theo-logy (that is, his

45. *Myth, Faith and Hermeneutics,* p. 5.

46. It is understandable then that for Panikkar dialogue has to take place at the level of belief and not at the level of doctrine or discussion.

47. "Śunahśepah: A Myth of the Human Condition," p. 99: "One of the myths of the modern West is history. History is the landmark to which we refer the incontestability of facts, and in terms of which we criticize other myths. For Western Man, historical facts are the hard and inescapable reality.... Except for those who live in the myth of history, historical facts are merely events that have not reached their full reality."

48. Francis X. D'Sa, "Myth, History and Cosmos," in *Jeevadhara* 14:79 (1984), pp. 9–26.

49. Panikkar, "Colligite Fragmenta," pp. 19–91.

50. Panikkar, *The Silence of God,* and "The God of Being and the 'Being' of God: Religion and Atheism," in *Myth, Faith and Hermeneutics,* pp. 350–60.

notion of God) has been aptly characterized as the theology of the future since the *global myth* which he is drawing our attention to is only an emerging myth.[51] A brief account of it should be germane to our discussion.[52]

PANIKKAR'S COSMOTHEANDRISM

If the first moment of consciousness consisted of a "pre-reflexive attitude in which Nature, Man and the Divine are still amorphously mixed and only vaguely differentiated"[53] and the second of the "historical attitude in which the discriminating process of individualization proceeds from the macro- to the microsphere,"[54] the third (catholic and cosmotheandric) moment tries to "maintain the distinctions of the second moment without forfeiting the unity of the first."[55]

The cosmotheandric vision takes up every insight without extrapolating it, preserves specificity without sacrificing unity, and promotes communion in an atmosphere of distinction and differentiation. As we shall see, cosmotheandrism re-collects not only the insights of the various religious traditions but also of dreaded "isms" such as atheism and secularism.

Panikkar contends that "the cosmotheandric vision might well be considered the original and primordial form of consciousness. In fact, it has glimmered since the beginnings of human consciousness as the undivided vision of the totality."[56] Human beings are inclined to concentrate on parts and aspects of reality, with the result that the vision of the totality has suffered. The *kairos* of our times will be the discovery of a "second innocence."[57]

Panikkar has different formulations for cosmotheandrism. I quote just three of them. One, "There is a kind of perichorēsis, 'dwelling within one another,' of these three dimensions of Reality, the Divine, the Human and the Cosmic — the I, the you and the it."[58] Two, "The cosmotheandric principle could be stated by saying that the divine, the human and the earthly — however we may prefer to call them — are the three irreducible dimensions which constitute the real,

51. Ewert H. Cousins, "Raimundo Panikkar and the Christian Systematic Theology of the Future," *Cross Currents* 29 (Summer, 1979), pp. 141–55.

52. Up till here we have briefly acquainted ourselves with such foundational categories of Panikkar's thinking as *mythos, logos, pneuma,* faith and belief. Of these for Panikkar, myth, faith and hermeneutics "represent the threefold — cosmotheandric — unity of the universe, that unity which neither destroys diversity nor forgets that the world is inhabited, that God is not alone and that knowledge is based on love" (*Myth, Faith and Hermeneutics,* p. 10). Panikkar's "overcoming a threefold reductionism" could be adduced as a sort of "negative" summary: "i) Reason is not the whole of Logos....ii) Logos is not the whole of Man....iii) Man is not the whole of Being" (Panikkar, "The Myth of Pluralism: The Tower of Babel — A Meditation on Non-Violence," *Cross Currents* 29: 2 (1979), pp. 214–15.

53. "Colligite Fragmenta," p. 68.

54. Ibid.

55. Ibid.

56. Ibid., p. 69.

57. Ibid., p. 72.

58. Panikkar, "The Myth of Pluralism: The Tower of Babel — A Meditation on Non-Violence," p. 217.

i.e., any reality inasmuch as it is real."[59] And three, "The times begin to be ripe now to gather again the broken pieces of these partial insights into a new wholistic vision: there is no matter without spirit and no spirit without matter, no world without Man, no God without the Universe, etc. *God, Man and World are three artificially substantivized forms of the three primordial adjectives which describe Reality.*"[60]

Of the three, the last formulation is the most radical. We have one non-dual Reality which is trinitarian. There is no such thing (or being) as God, or World or human being. We always have a Reality which is divine, cosmic and human. These dimensions are not identical; indeed according to Panikkar they are irreducible. The stress may now be on the divine, now on the cosmic or human but whatever the focus the other two dimensions are always present.[61]

When elucidating these three dimensions Panikkar makes it clear that no dimension is absent in any being whatsoever. First of all, "every being has an abyssal dimension, both transcendent and immanent. Every being transcends everything — including, and perhaps most pointedly, 'itself,' which, in truth, has no limits. It is, further, infinitely immanent, i.e., inexhaustible and fathomless."[62] The reason for this is obvious. Every being "belongs to every being as such. To place limits on being — *qua* being — is to destroy it."[63] "To isolate a being — where this is possible — would amount to stifling it, killing it, cutting the umbilical cord which unites it to being. In harmony with the greater part of human tradition, I call this dimension divine, but this does not imply that another name would not or could not do. The basic view here is the infinite inexhaustibility of any human being, its ever open character, its mystery — if we allow the word in this connection — its freedom, another language might prefer."[64] In order to understand this we have to distance ourselves from the "substantialist" mode of thinking and have recourse to the "cosmotheandric" vision.

Similarly, every being participates in the human dimension. What Panikkar means by this is that "every real being...is within the range of consciousness; it is thinkable and, by this very fact, connected with man's awareness.... We cannot speak, or think, or affirm anything whatsoever — positively or negatively — about anything which is not connected with our consciousness. The very act of affirming or negating anything establishes a connection.... All this does not

---

59. Ibid., p. 74.

60. "Philosophy as Life-Style," p. 206. My emphasis.

61. Ibid. See too "Colligite Fragmenta," pp. 73–74: "Without ignoring a certain hierarchical order, this vision does not locate the center in God — an impossible task in any case, once Man is aware that it is he who does this — but it allows the three dimensions to find their center each time in the free interplay between them. Let me try to explain this further.... The cosmotheadric principle could be stated by saying that the divine, the human and the earthly — however we may prefer to call them — are the three irreducible dimensions which constitute the real, i.e., any reality inasmuch as it is real.... Everything that exists, any real being, presents this triune constitution expressed in three dimensions.... The Cosmotheandric intuition is not a tripartite division among being, but an insight into the threefold core of all that is, insofar as it is."

62. "Colligite Fragmenta," p. 75.

63. Ibid.

64. Ibid.

mean, obviously that Pluto — or any other being, for that matter — has to be known or thinkable by any or every conscious human being. It simply means that thinkability and knowability as such are features of all that is."[65] It is important to grasp Panikkar's explanation. The human dimension of every being consists in its thinkability and knowability — by a human being. Anything real in this world must be related to human beings. "In so many words, the waters of human consciousness wash all the shores of the real — even if Man cannot penetrate the *terra incognita* of the interior — and by this very fact, Man's being enters into relation with the whole of reality."[66]

In an analogous manner every being "stands in the World and shares its secularity."[67] Whatever is related to human consciousness has its roots in this universe. Panikkar goes to the extent of asserting that "God without the World is not a real God, nor does he exist."[68] He then goes on to explain that "this does not mean that God has a body like ours.... By analogy, God's body differs from ours. On the other hand, it does not mean that God is without matter, space, time, body and that every material thing that is, is God's, or more precisely, God's thing, God's own World."[69] Panikkar concludes from this: "Were it not for matter and energy, or time and space, not only would human discourse and thinking be impossible, but God and Consciousness would also recede into sheer nothingness and meaninglessness. The final foundation for the belief that something exists is that the World exists; the ultimate basis for Man's hope is the existence of the World."[70]

According to Panikkar cosmotheandric reality is *ontonomous;* each "being" — it now becomes difficult to articulate since there are no "beings" as such left in this vision — has its own appropriate law — *nomos tou ontos* — which dovetails into the law of all other beings so that we have a harmonious whole. Panikkar contrasts the ontomic order with heteronomy (where the lower orders of being are dependent on the higher) and autonomy (where one order of beings is independent of the others).[71] In an ontonomic order there is neither higher nor lower, only interdependence and interconnectedness according to the law of each being.

Understandably then cosmotheandrism does away with the distinction between the secular and the sacred. For here the secular is sacred and the sacred is secular.[72] Similarly it rejects the separation of time and eternity. In the new vision time is the symbol of eternity; where there is neither time nor eternity but tempiternity, i.e., "that form of existence which does not so much encompass as pierce the three dimensions of time, and yet it does not abandon them entirely

---

65. Ibid., pp. 76–77.
66. Ibid., p. 76.
67. Ibid., p. 78.
68. Ibid., p. 79.
69. Ibid., pp. 79–80.
70. Ibid., p. 80.
71. Panikkar, *Kultmysterium in Hinduismus und Christentum,* pp. 78–86.
72. Panikkar, *Worship and Secular Man,* pp. 9ff.

in order to uncover the transtemporal core of time itself."[73] Cosmotheandrism implies that Reality is a network of relationships, the totality of which Panikkar calls "radical relativity."[74]

PANIKKAR'S CHRIST

One of the names, and more precisely one of the major symbols that Panikkar has employed extensively for the cosmotheandric reality is the symbol of Christ.[75] When he first employed it in The *Unknown Christ of Hinduism*, it gave rise to a spate of misunderstandings on almost all sides. The word *Christ*, coming as it does from the Christian world, has not found favor with protagonists of the other religious traditions. And Christians themselves have not all been happy about this usage. However most of the critics, it seems to me, have not understood Panikkar's Christ; much less have they grasped what it is that Panikkar is proposing.[76]

Hence a few clarifications about Panikkar's usage of the name of Christ are called for.

Panikkar starts from the fact that "Christ is an ambiguous term. It can be the greek translation of the hebrew Messiah, or it can be the name given to Jesus of Nazareth. One may identify it with the Logos, and with the Son or equate it with Jesus. The nomenclature that I personally would like to suggest in this connection is as follows: I would propose using the word Lord for that Principle, Being, Logos or Christ that other religious traditions call by a variety of names and to which they attach a wide range of ideas. I am not making any claim here to solve the problem, and shall thus continue to use the name of Christ, for I believe it is important that the figure of Christ should regain its complete fullness of meaning, but I shall do so in a way that is devoid either of polemic or apologetic. Each time that I speak of Christ I am referring (unless it is explicitly stated otherwise) to the Lord of whom christians can lay claim to no monopoly."[77] The name Christ "carries with it the heavy reality of history, good and bad."[78] But God, Matter, Consciousness or names such as Future, Justice, Love are also living symbols that he could use.[79] In his Introduction to the second and revised edition of *The Unknown Christ of Hinduism* Panikkar states that "Christ stands for that center of reality, that crystallization-point around which the human, the divine and the material can grow. Rama may be another such name, or Krishna, or (as I maintain) Īśvara, or Purusha, or even

73. Panikkar, "Time and Sacrifice," p. 697.

74. "Philosophy as Life-Style," p. 202.

75. Peter Slater, "Hindu and Christian Symbols in the Work of R. Panikkar," *Cross Currents* 29: 2 (1979), p. 182.

76. Panikkar, "The Category of Growth in Comparative Religion: A Critical Self-Examination," pp. 92–113.

77. *The Trinity and the Religious Experience of Man*, p. 53.

78. Panikkar, *The Unknown Christ of Hinduism*, p. 27.

79. Ibid.

Humanity."[80] More important, Christ is a symbol of the cosmotheandric Reality. "Christ is still a living symbol for the totality of reality; human, divine and cosmic. Most of the apparently more neutral symbols such as God, Spirit, Truth and the like truncate reality and limit the center of life to a disincarnate principle, a non-historical epiphany, and often an abstraction."[81]

In reply to a criticism that in his treatment of Christ and Christianity he is guilty of reductionism, Panikkar makes a triple distinction which, he asserts, is valid for all religions. The sociological dimension, the sacramental dimension and the transcendental mystery make up any religion. Panikkar calls the transcendental aspect of any and every religion the Christ. In this context the following comment of his should be of interest. "I should stress immediately that I consider this threefold division valid in any religion, so that if a Christian could call these levels: *Christendom, Church, Christ,* a Buddhist may call them *Sangha, Dharma, Nirvāṇa,* a Hindu *Sampradāya, Karma, Brahman,* a Muslim, *Umma, Qurán, Allah.* I am not saying that even for those traditions including the Christian, these names are the only possible ones (*religion, grace, God,* for instance). Even more, none of these three levels is exhaustively described by any of the mentioned words. This is not because they are false, but because they are incomplete."[82] To this statement we have to add another that for Panikkar the symbol of Christ " 'recapitulates' in itself the Real in its totality, created and uncreated."[83]

In order to grasp Panikkar's understanding of Christ three points have to be kept in mind: the concept of symbol, Christ as the symbol of the cosmotheandric Reality and Christ in the trinitarian context.

Symbol, for Panikkar, is the thing itself in as much as it manifests itself. The manifestation of the thing is not identical with the thing, but it is not separate either. Thing and manifestation are one. The symbol symbolizes the symbolized reality. To reduce the symbolized reality to the symbol and vice versa is to overlook the symbolic difference. The symbol is the face of the symbolized. The symbolized reality cannot be known except through the symbol. A smile, for instance, is the symbol of symbolized joy in the heart. The latter is visible only through the former, never in itself. On the other hand, the smiling face without the joy in the heart is really a mask that is put on, not really a symbol. A real symbol "contains," that is, makes present, "re-presents" the symbolized reality without being identical with it.[84]

---

80. Ibid.
81. Ibid.
82. Panikkar, "Response to Harold Coward," in *Cross Currents,* 29: 2 (1979), p. 191.
83. *The Unknown Christ of Hinduism,* p. 28.
84. *Myth, Faith and Hermeneutics,* pp. 6–8. cf. "The Supreme Experience: The Ways of East and West," pp. 301–02: "A symbol is precisely the thing; not the 'thing in itself,' which is a mental abstraction, but the thing as it appears, as it expresses and manifests itself. The symbol of a thing is neither another thing nor the thing in itself but the very thing as it manifests itself, as it is in the world of being, in the epiphany of the 'is'.... The symbol is not another reality, it is not another thing, nor the thing as we may imagine it in some nonexistent ideal realm. It is the thing as it really appears, as it really 'is,' in the realm of beings. The symbol is nothing but the

Christ, as the symbol of the cosmotheandric Reality, "contains" the two poles: the divine on the one hand and the cosmic on the other. Panikkar finds this symbol the most appropriate in the circumstances. "I find in the general pattern of the christian mediator all the functions which all those other names are supposed to perform: being immanent and transcendent, temporal and sempiternal, of the past and of the future, in history and transhistorical, spiritual and material, etc. In spite of the resistance that this interpretation may find (disregarding the imperfections of my personal effort), the christian mediator seems to represent the most universal archetype or, phenomenologically speaking, that which can be more readily universalized without losing concrete identity. A whole Christology is obviously implied here."[85]

The discerning reader will not have failed to note that Panikkar's Christ is in effect a *trinitarian* Christ. And Panikkar does not hide this fact; on the contrary he highlights it. "Within the Christian tradition this Christ is incomprehensible without the Trinity. A non-Trinitarian Christ cannot be totally human and totally divine."[86]

In order to allay the fears of the overzealous christian, who may feel that Panikkar has not done enough justice to the Jesus of history, Panikkar has repeatedly stated that Jesus is the Christ but that the Christ is not Jesus.[87] The reality of the Christ is much larger than that manifested in Jesus. We are familiar with the Christ revealed in Jesus but ignorant about his other aspects revealed elsewhere; one of the prime aims of Panikkar's controversial book *The Unknown Christ of Hinduism* was to draw attention to unknown aspects of the Christ which (Panikkar claims) are revealed in Hinduism.[88] Some aspects were revealed in Jesus; others in Hinduism and some more in the other religious traditions of humankind. When Panikkar speaks of the unknown Christ of Hinduism he is not implying that these aspects were unknown to Hinduism but known to Christianity. Rather he is referring to the Christ-aspects revealed in Hinduism but as such have remained unknown to both the hindus and the christians.[89]

PANIKKAR'S TRINITY

The focus of Panikkar's trinitarian insight is "the universality of the experience and the reality" of the triangular consciousness of *I, Thou* and *We*. These

---

symbol *of* the thing, that is (subjective genitive), the peculiar mode of being of that very thing which outside its symbolic form *is* not and cannot *be,* because ultimately being is nothing but symbol. To be able to discover the symbolic difference, i.e., to discover me as symbol of myself or in other words, to realize that my own being is one of the real symbols of the I (certainly not my little ego), could perhaps be called one of the ways to reach the supreme experience."

85. "The Category of Growth in Comparative Religions: A Critical Self-Examination," in *Harvard Theological Review* 66 (1973), pp. 113–140. The quotation is from pages 124–25 and is not be to found in the article with the same name in *The Intrareligious Dialogue.*

86. *The Unknown Christ of Hinduism,* p. 28.

87. *The Trinity and the Religious Experience of Man,* p. 53: "Jesus of Nazareth is the Christ but the Christ is not Jesus."

88. Ibid., pp. 14–15.

89. Ibid., p. 26.

are mutually constitutive. No *I* is possible without the *We*, which in its turn cannot be without the *I* and the *Thou*. The *I* can address the *Thou* only in the spirit of the *We*. There can be no *I in itself*, no *Thou in itself* and no *We* independent of *I* and *Thou*. *I*, *Thou* and *We* presuppose each other. Ultimate Reality consists of the network of relationships among the *I*, the *Thou* and the *We*.[90]

From the reservoir of our conscious life we seem to be aware of what *I*, *Thou* and *We* mean. At least we think so. But as a matter of fact, it is only in a profound relationship that we experience the *We;* our experience of the *I* in our everyday life is really not an *I;* it is the Ego masquerading as the *I*. Fundamentally, we are a *Thou*. Our finitude, which is responsible for our total dependence for our being "outside" of ourselves, is what makes clear to us that our *I*-consciousness is not perfect, not full. Our dependence is an expression of our *Thou*. Our dependence is for our being, for our consciousness and for our self-consciousness. This dependence for our self-consciousness is in fact the expression of our *Thou* nature. Our experience of *Thou* is an experience of dependence, dependence on the *I*. Similarly with our *We* experience; it is an experience of a community of *Thou*-s. Thus our analogy of the network of *I*, *Thou* and *We* relationships certainly limps. Its strong point, however, is that we are still able to appropriate the mutuality of this triangular consciousness. Even though our *I, Thou* and *We* consciousness is finite, imperfect and "accidental," still it is an experience basic to our personhood.

If now we can take an experience like this and "apply" it to our understanding of the Trinity, the point of entry, as Panikkar rightly remarks, is the "Son."[91] The Son is the *Thou,* the absolute *Thou*. It is only from the Son that we can know about the Father. About the Father himself — in himself — we can say *nothing;* he is, as Panikkar puts it, *an-onymous*[92] he has no name. From our point of view the *I* is *nothing, no-thing, is not,* has no *existence:* "In the Father the aphophatism (the *kenosis* or emptying) of Being is real and total."[93] In no way do we have any idea, much less any experience of the absolute *I*. That is why we cannot speak about him. God is Silence total and absolute, the silence of Being — and not only the being of silence. His word, who completely expresses and consumes him, is the Son. The *Father has* no being, the Son is *his* being. The source of being is not being.[94] The Father is the *I*, thoroughly transcendent and therefore utterly ineffable. Transcendence can neither reveal itself nor incarnate itself — if it is to remain transcendent.[95]

Similarly the Spirit, the Spirit of communion between *I* and *Thou,* is the *We* of the Trinity,[96] i.e., divine immanence which can neither reveal itself nor incar-

---

90. Ibid., pp. xiv–xvi.
91. *The Trinity and the Religious Experience of Man,* p. 52.
92. Ibid., p. 44.
93. Ibid., p. 46.
94. Ibid., pp. 47–48.
95. Ibid., p. 59.
96. Ibid., p. 61: "The Trinity is, indeed the real mystery of Unity, for true unity is trinitarian. For that reason, properly speaking, there is no *Self* in the reflexive sense. The *Self* of the Father is the Son, his *in-himself* is the Spirit. But the Son has no *Self;* he is the Thou of the Father;

nate itself — again, if it is to remain divine immanence.[97] Neither *I* nor *We* are Being; *I* is the source of Being and *We* the ground of Being. If the transcendent *I* is the silence of Being, it is the silence of the Buddha, the silence of *nirvāṇa* and *śūnyatā*. Buddhism focusing on this apophatic aspect has developed its own approach to the Ultimate Mystery.[98] If the immanent *We* is the ground of Being we cannot relate to it; at the most we can realize it through insight and enlightenment in the manner of the Upaniṣadic approach. This *We* is "not this," "not that;" it is indescribable.

Ewert Cousins has neatly summed up Panikkar's insightful reflections on the Trinity thus:

> In his discussion of the Trinity, Panikkar describes three aspects of the divinity and three corresponding forms of spirituality: (1) the silent, apophatic dimension, which he relates to the Father, since the Father expresses himself only through the Son and of himself has no word or expression; (2) the personalistic dimension, which Panikkar relates to the Son, since the Son is the personal mediator between God and man, through whom creation, redemption, and glorification flow; and (3) the immanent dimension, which Panikkar relates to the Spirit, since the Spirit is the union of the Father and the Son. According to Panikkar the apophatic spirituality of the Father is similar to the buddhist experience of nirvāṇa. The personalist spirituality of the Son has its roots in Yahweh's revelation to the Jews; from the Christian perspective, its completion is the person of Christ. The immanent spirituality of the Spirit has its resonance in the advaitan Hindu doctrine of the non-duality of the self and the Absolute.[99]

It is understandable now why Panikkar insists that, "correctly speaking, then, it is only with the Son that man can have a personal relationship. The God of theism, thus, is the Son; the God with whom one can speak, establish a dialogue, enter into communication, is the divine Person who is in-relation-with, or rather, is the relationship with man and one of the poles of total existence."[100] With this we have returned to the trinitarian Christ. Because "every word about the Father can only refer to the one of whom the father is Father, that is, to the Word, to the Son."[101] The Son is not only the visibility of the invisible, he is also the

---

his *Self* in relation to his Father is a Thou. Similarly with the Spirit; the Spirit 'in himself' is a contradiction. There is only the Spirit *of* God, of the Father and Son. He is the One sent. He is neither an I who speaks to another, nor a Thou to whom someone else speaks, but rather the *we* between the Father and the Son — that we which encompasses also the whole universe in a peculiar way. Strictly speaking one cannot even say that the Father is an I, if one takes it to be a sort of 'absolute subject.' The son is assuredly the Thou of the Father. Furthermore, the Son is the World. The speaker is known only in the World. He is nothing outside this speaking which is his son. This is why in relation to us the divine I appears only in the *thou* of the Logos through the *we* of the Spirit. There is no room for egoism in the Trinity."

97. Ibid.
98. Ibid., p. 47.
99. Cousins, op. cit., p. 147.
100. *The Trinity and the Religious Experience of Man,* p. 52.
101. Ibid., p. 47.

expressibility of the inexpressible. Indeed he is the full and total expression of the inexpressible *I*. The expression is the *Thou*. The Christ is the fullness of the *Thou; with him, in him and through him everyone and everything exists.* There is no one and nothing that is not theandric. We can therefore appreciate Panikkar's rhetoric that "the Trinity is one of the deepest problems Man can ask about himself, his God, about Creation and Creator, and one of the most universal."[102]

Similarly it should also be obvious now why Panikkar says the following about the Christ:

> He is at the center of the divine processions, being "originated" and "origi-nating" (in the consecrated language, being begotten and co-inspiring): at the center of time gathering in himself the three times and being present throughout in each case in the corresponding way, namely at the begin-ning, at the end and in between — the angelic, the human, the corporeal, the material. There is not a single "type" of reality which is not repre-sented in Christ.... Christ is not only the sacrament of the Church, but also the sacrament of the World and of God.[103]

This conception of the mediating Christ as the symbol of the cosmothean-dric Reality, on the one hand, and as the visibility of the Trinity, on the other, has tremendous consequences. On this background one can grasp, for instance, Panikkar's preoccupation with the emergence of the secular spirit. In his writ-ings, like *Worship and Secular Man,* "Time and Sacrifice: The Sacrifice of Time and the Ritual of Modernity," "The End of History: The Threefold Structure of Human-Consciousness," "Man as a Ritual Being" — Panikkar draws the conse-quences of such a vision. On the cosmotheandric backdrop his *sacred secularity* substantiates itself as the *kairos* of our times.

PANIKKAR'S NOTION OF GOD

It might sound paradoxical that an essay dealing with Panikkar's notion of God comes to speak of it only in the conclusion. However, I think, this is as it should be, as the essay must have made amply clear. For Panikkar there is no such thing as God; God as such simply does not exist. Repeatedly he expresses his criticism of the "notion" of God. "One could perhaps sum up the experience of modern Man with an overstatement by saying that God did not save Man and so Man has abandoned him. An abandoned God, obviously, amounts to a dead God, a God denied. And the *deus ex machina* invoked by the pale deism of the 'intellectuals' is no longer needed to keep the cosmic machine going."[104] "God is meaningless without creatures."[105] "Modern man has killed an isolated and insular God; contemporary Earth is killing a merciless and rapacious Man,

---

102. Ibid., p. xii.
103. *The Unknown Christ of Hinduism,* p. 28.
104. "Colligite Fragmenta," p. 55.
105. Ibid., p. 74.

and the gods seem to have deserted both Man and Cosmos."[106] "God is not only the God of Man, but also the God of the World. A God with no cosmological and, therefore, no cosmogonical functions would not be God at all, but a mere phantom."[107]

And when Panikkar does speak of God, his manner is refreshingly meaningful. "God is that dimension of more and better for the World as much as for Man. Not only Man, but also the Cosmos is unachieved, not finished, infinite. The Cosmos does not expand mechanically or unfold automatically; it also evolves, grows, moves toward an ever new universe."[108]

In a certain sense Panikkar is an iconoclast, his protestations notwithstanding. Take this example: "God is not the absolute Other (regardless of the philosophical difficulty inherent in this formulation: absolute transcendence is contradicted by the very thought of it). Nor is God the same as we."[109] But he does not stop there; he continues:

> I would say that God is the ultimate and unique I, that we are his "thous," and that our relation is personal, trinitarian and nondualistic. But the cosmotheandric vision does not need to be couched in such terms. It is enough to say that Man experiences the depth of his own being, the inexhaustible possibilities of and for relationship, his non-finite (i.e. in-finite) character — for he is not a closed being and cannot put limits on his own growth and evolution. Man discovers and senses an inbuilt *more* in his own being which at once transcends his own private being. He discovers another dimension which he cannot manipulate. There is always more than meets the eye, finds the mind or touches the heart. This *ever more* — even more than perceiving, understanding and feeling — stands for the divine dimension.[110]

These lines are perhaps the best summary of Panikkar's "notion of God." They put forward accurately how he conceives of the Divine in a way that could be meaningful to any person of good will. In the synopsis of his Gifford Lectures Panikkar informs us that his lectures "give vent to the suspicion that most of the traditional ideas about 'God' are inadequate for carrying the burden imposed upon the word by our present day consciousness."[111] In place of the answers of the different "theisms" (= theism, monotheism, a-theism, deism, polytheism and pantheism) which he finds unsatisfactory he introduces the notion of *Radical Trinity,* which stands for the human invariants of the divine, the human and the cosmic. This is the cosmotheandric invariant.

"The modern civilization is not an exception *even if the word for the Divine is understood as Future, Justice, Liberty and the like.* This seems to be more than

---

106. Ibid., p. 91.
107. Ibid., p. 88.
108. Ibid., p. 88.
109. Ibid.
110. Ibid., p. 88.
111. Synopsis of Panikkar's Gifford Lectures, p. 1.

just an historical fact. It seems to be also linked with the structure of the human mind. It might as well be a true character of the Real."[112] Panikkar's experience of the Divine points to the fact that the Divine is the monopoly neither of the "religions"[113] nor of the believers. Indeed, these lectures contest the division between believers and unbelievers:

> They attempt to demolish the wall of religious apartheid without building an artificial commune. There are, of course, several and incompatible world-views, but the humanness we all have in common is more than a sharing in an elusive human nature and in some somatic commonalities. It is also a sharing in a divine destiny through a faith which is previous to its articulations in beliefs and belief-systems. It is a sharing in a destiny which is more than the survival of the human family or the planet Earth. Human History is a sharing in the very Destiny of Being. The temporal eschatology of an Omega point in a linear future ultimately only postpones the final end. The Trinity as the very symbol for the Rhythm of Reality does not offer a cheap consoling picture but certainly a more realistic and fascinating hope.[114]

Finally Panikkar's notion of the Divine, while taking account of all the positive and negative insights of the past, critiques them in a way that purifies them of their dogmatism and lopsidedness, and then gathers them up, not in a larger theoretical framework but in a higher and more holistic unity which obviously we never attain definitively but toward which we can move with faith in the Divine, hope in the cosmic and love for the human. Faith will see to it that we are always open to goodness and growth, to service and selflessness, and to the Unknown and the Unexpected. Hope will make us feel at home in the cosmos, which is not merely our past but our future as well. And love will reveal that humans are not mere humans. They are the ones who discover "the housing of the Divine in the contemporary world."

---

112. Ibid., p. 5. My emphasis.

113. Ibid., p. 6: "Is it possible to live a truly 'religious' life, a full human existence while transcending all theisms? The answer is yes. Worship persists, but free from idolatry. Prayer remains, but free from superstitions and being a project of human frustrations. Love is not split into service of God and concern for our fellow-beings. The 'Presence of God' is not an act of the memory or the will. The Sacred and/or the Holy are then purified of all taboos. Each being recovers its dignity and human freedom is not reduced to making choices. Ethics finds its basis in the very nature of Being. Human knowledge does not need to be divorced from sacred knowledge and the vexing conflict between reason and faith, Science and Religions is dissolved. True piety does not disappear, and humanism is no longer anthropocentric. The rift between philosophy and theology is healed and all sciences rediscover their proper ontonomy. Furthermore the experience of the divine dimension is compatible with different ideas about the Deity according to the diverse religious traditions of humankind which are then seen as concrete expressions of the deeper cosmotheandric intuition. We are Divine as much as the Divine is Human — without confusion and division.... The Divine is an abstraction. But so is Man, and equally so the Cosmos. Divine Destiny, Human History, and cosmic Existence are inseparable. The being of God is not the god of Being."

114. Ibid., p. 7.

SELECTED BIBLIOGRAPHY OF RAIMON PANIKKAR

Kultmysterium in Hinduismus und Christentum: Ein Beitrag zur vergleichenden Religionstheologie. Freiburg & München: Karl Alber, 1964.

The Trinity and the Religious Experience of Man. Maryknoll, N.Y.: Orbis Books; London: Darton, Longman & Todd, 1973.

Worship and Secular Man. Maryknoll, N.Y.: Orbis Books; London: Darton, Longman & Todd, 1973.

"Colligite Fragmenta: For an Integration of Reality," in *From Alienation to At-Oneness.* Proceedings of the Theology Institute of Villanova University. Edited by F. A. Eigo. Villanova, Pa.: Villanova University Press, 1977, pp. 19–91.

The Vedic Experience: Mantramañjarī: An Anthology of the Vedas for Modern Man and Contemporary Celebration. Los Angeles and Berkeley: University of California Press; London: Darton, Longman & Todd, 1977.

The Intrareligious Dialogue. New York: Paulist Press, 1978.

"Faith and Belief," in *The Intrareligious Dialogue,* pp. 39–61.

"EPOCHÉ in the Religious Encounter," in *The Intrareligious Dialogue,* pp. 78–90.

"The Category of Growth in Comparative Religions: A Critical Self-Examination," in *The Intrareligious Dialogue,* pp. 92–113.

"Philosophy as Life-Style," in *Philosophers on Their Own Work.* Bern, Frankfurt, Los Angeles: Peter Lang, 1978, pp. 199–201.

"The Texture of a Text: In Response to Paul Ricoeur," in *Point of Contact* 2: 1 (April–May 1978), pp. 51–64.

"Time and Sacrifice: The Sacrifice of Time and the Ritual of Modernity," in *The Study of Time III.* Edited by J. T. Fraser. New York: Springer, 1979, pp. 683–727.

Myth, Faith and Hermeneutics. New York: Paulist Press, 1979.

"Śunaḥśepa: A Myth of the Human Condition," in *Myth, Faith and Hermeneutics,* pp. 98–184.

"Faith as a Constitutive Human Dimension," in *Myth, Faith and Hermeneutics,* pp. 188–229.

"Witness and Dialogue," in *Myth, Faith and Hermeneutics,* pp. 232–56.

"The Philosophical Tradition," in *Myth, Faith and Hermeneutics,* pp. 336–48.

"The God of Being and the 'Being' of God: Religion and Atheism," in *Myth, Faith and Hermeneutics,* pp. 350–60.

"The Law of Karma and the Historical Dimension of Man," in *Myth, Faith and Hermeneutics,* pp. 362–88.

The Unknown Christ of Hinduism. Revised and enlarged edition. London: Darton, Longman & Todd; Maryknoll, N.Y.: Orbis Books, 1981.

"The Jordan, the Tiber and the Ganges: Three Kairological Moments of Christic Self-Consciousness," in *The Myth of Christian Uniqueness: Toward a Pluralistic Theology of Religions.* Edited by John Hick and Paul F. Knitter. Maryknoll, N.Y.: Orbis Books, 1987, pp. 89–116.

"Anima Mundi-Vita Hominis-Spiritus Dei: Some Aspects of a Cosmotheandric Spirituality," in *Actualitas Omnium Actuum.* Festschrift für Heinrich Bech zum 60 Geburtstag. Edited by Erwin Schadel. Frankfurt: Peter Lang, 1989, pp. 341–56.

The Silence of God: The Answer of the Buddha. Maryknoll, N.Y.: Orbis Books, 1989.

"Trinity and Atheism: The Housing of the Divine in the Contemporary World." A series of ten lectures (synopsis of Panikkar's Gifford Lectures 1988/89).

2

Metaphysical Pluralism

JOHN B. COBB, JR.

No one has wrestled more courageously with the issue of pluralism than Raimon Panikkar. It is for him not only a theoretical issue but a practical one as well, and he struggles with its meaning for the Roman Catholic Church of which he is a faithful member. It is also a deeply existential issue. He is himself profoundly Indian and profoundly Christian, and he knows that none of the usually recommended ways of understanding and connecting these facets of his being suffices.

No one in our day, or perhaps in any day, has been better qualified to guide the church's reflection on pluralism. This is first and foremost because of the radically pluralistic character of his own existence. But it is also because of his wide-ranging scholarship. He understands the religious traditions of both East and West not only as they have shaped him personally but also through years of research and informed reflection. He understands profoundly the close relation of language and religious meaning, and he has accumulated a wide knowledge of the languages in which the diversities of meaning are embodied.

Panikkar understands that pluralism is an issue in ethics, politics, and culture as well as in religion. He sees that it arises at the point at which the mutual toleration of differences breaks down, where "live and let live" does not suffice. It arises when practical proposals and alternative assertions of truth appear irreconcilable.

A common response to this pluralism, at least in religion, is to posit that behind and beyond all the conflictual diversity there is something common. The religions offer alternative paths up the same mountain or alternative ways of approaching and conceiving the same inconceivable Absolutes. Panikkar sees immediately that this will not do. This solution is offered from a perspective that

John B. Cobb, Jr. was Professor at the School of Theology, Claremont, from 1958 to 1990. Since then he has retained a part-time position in the Department of Religion of the Claremont Graduate School. Among his writings are *Christ in a Pluralistic Age* and *Beyond Dialogue: The Mutual Transformation of Christianity and Buddhism.*

supposes that religious pluralism can be overcome by metaphysical universalism. Beyond the diverse accounts of the mountains ascended, the metaphysician claims to provide a neutral or universal account of the one mountain all the religions inadequately describe. Or beyond the diverse accounts of God, Brahman, and Nirvāna, the metaphysician claims to point to the mountain of which all these are phenomenal manifestations. Against this, Panikkar rightly points to the diversity of metaphysics. The philosophical situation is as pluralistic as the religious one. One cannot solve the pluralism of religions by claiming universality for one's own metaphysics.

I greatly appreciate Panikkar's contribution here. His analysis seems to me quite accurate. Further, I appreciate and share his sense of the appropriate practical response: to continue dialogue with one another in mutual respect and cosmic trust without knowing where this will lead. I admire the consistency with which he holds to this position even when others seem evil in his eyes.

I ground my agreement with Panikkar both theologically and philosophically. At a conference at Temple University in October 1984, at which Panikkar also spoke, I explained how "a Christocentric catholic theology" leads me to a position quite similar to his.[1] My assignment now is to discuss pluralism in metaphysical terms; so I will not rehearse my theological commitments.

The rejection of the universalistic claims of particular metaphysics is also, inescapably, a metaphysical statement. Panikkar and I are both caught in this trap. Panikkar argues that "reason is not the whole of Logos," that "Logos is not the whole of Man," and that "Man is not the whole of Being."[2] He also disagrees with Husserl's view that consciousness is always consciousness-of, affirming instead, with Indian thought generally, that there is "pure consciousness." These metaphysical assertions are important to his argument for pluralism, his critique of other metaphysics, and his own stance of openness. Indeed, a much fuller metaphysics could be gleaned from his writings.

My point here is not to criticize. His position is consistent and appropriate. But since I am going to describe my own metaphysical stand toward pluralism, I want to note that doing so is not at odds with Panikkar's approach. The reasons for this approach appear as we consider the alternative ways of critiquing universalistic claims of particular metaphysics.

First, one can assert that all metaphysical statements are meaningless. Second, one can show that all metaphysics is relative to praxis, culture, language, social location, and so forth. Third, one can show that a particular position is metaphysically inadequate. Panikkar emphatically distances himself from the first of these options and adopts the second. Nevertheless, in the process of adopting the second and justifying it, he discloses metaphysical beliefs of his own that show why the kinds of universal claims so often made by philosophers are inappropriate. In my opinion this cannot be avoided. One

---

1. Leonard Swidler, ed., *Toward a Universal Theology of Religion* (Maryknoll, N.Y.: Orbis Books, 1987).

2. Raimundo Panikkar, "The Myth of Pluralism," *Cross Currents* (Summer 1979), pp. 214–15.

cannot overcome the universalization of inadequate metaphysics without making assertions about the nature of human beings, human thought, and the world that are themselves metaphysical — at least implicitly. Hence Panikkar can argue in favor of metaphysical pluralism only from a metaphysical point of view.

Does this mean that we universalize our own metaphysics in the process of denying that any metaphysics can be universalized? Yes and no. Yes, we do treat a particular metaphysics as accurate in the process of displaying the inappropriateness of the kinds of universalizing that we find unacceptable. No, we need not assume that ours is the one adequate or appropriate basis for accomplishing this task. And, indeed, we can recognize that the need to accomplish this task is itself the product of a particular perception of the situation — not a universal one. In principle, I think, these qualifications are present in Panikkar's formulations, although inevitably many of his metaphysical statements are presented in far less qualified fashion.

My approach to these issues is from the "process" tradition. I note this because at one point Panikkar dismisses process theology as wanting "to be universal from a perspective which is seen as universal only from within the system."[3] My point is only that process thought is innocent of this desire. My point is only that, as far as I can see, Panikkar is in the same situation. His metaphysical claims appear to him universally valid, but of course they appear that way only to some — not to all. The question is not, I think, whether one is in this situation; for to assert that all metaphysical claims are relative is to involve oneself in a universalistic account of the situation. The question is rather whether one reflects on what it means to be in this situation and thus relativizes one's own work. Since not all process thinkers have been equally self-conscious about the need to do this, there is little doubt that Panikkar can make a case against us. But in principle, the awareness that all thinking is a process immersed in a larger process points to this self-relativization. In the case of the greatest process philosopher, Alfred North Whitehead, this was fully explicit and suffuses the tenor of his work. Whatever the sins of individual process theologians in stating particular convictions with too little qualification, I judge that as a group we are less guilty than most — perhaps no more guilty than Panikkar himself. I, for example, began my career with a book on *Varieties of Protestantism.* I followed that with *Living Options in Protestant Theology.* When I turned to contributing to the constructive task, I entitled my first attempt, "A Christian Natural Theology." That was a fully self-conscious choice explained in the book itself. That book appeared in 1963, before the theme of pluralism had become so prominent in theology. I hope, therefore, that Panikkar will not too quickly dismiss his would-be allies.

---

3. Ibid., p. 205.

A PROCESS APPROACH TO PLURALISM

Process metaphysics speculates that the world is composed of a vast plenum of events of all sorts. Each event is an inexhaustible creative synthesis of antecedent events. No two are identical. The patterns of relationship among the events are also inexhaustible. Human events are enmeshed inextricably in this total matrix.

Confronting this infinite complexity, the human mind has primarily the task of discerning and establishing structures that are important to practical life. It also functions to find answers to questions that express curiosity. We all know that in the end many answers found in this primarily theoretical quest have also turned out to have practical importance in both religion and science.

Although in all cultures reason has had both these functions, their respective importance has varied. Further, diverse cultural practices and languages have selected differing features of the inexhaustible matrix for attention and emphasis. Each in this sense constructs its own world. Yet *constructs* is misleading when used alone. The construction is always based on discernment.

Discernment is necessarily of some features of the inexhaustible complexity in which we are all immersed. It is necessarily highly selective. The ideal of discerning everything at once is utterly remote from any human possibility. The question is not whether discernment abstracts from the whole — it does — but whether the abstractions are useful, relevant, and illuminating.

Construction introduces interpretation and relates what is discerned in ways that may resemble or differ widely from the relations of the events in which the elements are discerned. Interpretation and patterning may also be more or less useful, relevant, and illuminating. In any case, they build up a world of human meaning and direct human activities. The events embodying these meanings become an important part of the total matrix of events in which we are enmeshed.

Discernment and construction are not in fact separated from one another. What is discerned of the given reality depends on prior construction, just as what is constructed is affected by what is discerned. In addition there is a secondary discernment into features of what has been constructed. The effort to distinguish the elements of primary discernment from the constructions in which they are enmeshed is a difficult one, of whose success one can never be sure.

Given this metaphysical speculation, how shall we understand the plurality of religious traditions, especially when their claims about truth and goodness clash? First, we will see that these claims arise from their respective constructions. Since these have developed from different discernments, and since there is no assurance that the interpretations and the patterns established among them are accurate, we will not be surprised that there is conflict. We will encourage adherents of all traditions to recognize that they have constructed worlds of meaning that are of great value to themselves but should not be treated as universal truths.

Second, however, we will also expect that adherents of each tradition decline to be fully relativized. Some may be prepared to agree that much of the theory and practice they prize is relative to the specifics of their histories and cultures, but most will insist that in and through the culturally specific there is also an apprehension of what is universal and universally important. We will expect that they are right, because we believe that there are elements of primary discernment as well as of construction in all tradition, and we will accordingly support the conviction that sheer relativity is not the last word.

Third, the fact that there are elements of discernment in all religious traditions will not lead us to assume that what is discerned in all is the same. That the same or at least similar aspects of the inexhaustible matrix of events have been discerned independently in several cultures is certainly possible, but it should be asserted only when it can be shown by careful examination. The fact that all cultures have religious aspects does not in itself entail that all have discerned the same or even similar things. There is no assurance, for example, that what is experienced as sacred in one culture will also be what is experienced as sacred in another. On the contrary, we will be equally open to discovering that what have been discerned are quite different features of the total matrix. Especially since what is discerned is so deeply influenced by construction, we will expect that differences are important at this level as well.

This is a highly abstract statement. Let me offer some more concrete judgments about diverse foci of attention and resultant discernment derived from the foregoing understanding of the relation of thought to reality. Consider first what happens in cultures whose constructions lead them to discern that they are indeed constructions. Buddhism is the example par excellence. Some very influential people, beginning with Gautama, concluded that the constructed world of meaning led to suffering and that this suffering could be escaped as persons became free from the influence of all construction. Such freedom would lead to a life of pure discernment in the terms I have proposed.

Sometimes Buddhists claim that this discernment is wholly non-selective and exhaustive. In terms of the metaphysics here proposed, this is impossible. The constructs in which we find meaning are a major factor of selectivity in discernment, so that when their influence is removed, more can be discerned. But the human organism is already a system of selection and amplification. The inexhaustible complexity of reality is far beyond the human capacity to appropriate, even the capacity of the enlightened Buddhist.

Others who recognize that there is a large constructive element in their cultural world of meaning draw differing conclusions. They, too, recognize that the received construction distorts and falsifies in at least some respects, but this does not lead them to try to overcome the process of construction altogether. Instead, it leads to the goal of improving the construction to make it more functional, or more correspondent to reality, or some combination of the two. The Greek religio-philosophical movements were of this sort. In modern times religious energies were poured into the scientific enterprise. At times the social and psychological sciences have been looked to for salvation. The features of reality discerned and conformed to have been quite diverse in these various movements.

In other instances this distinction of construction and discernment has not been thematically considered. What has seemed important has been righteousness. What is discerned in human experience is the distinction between what occurs and what might have occurred, a purpose partly realized, partly missed. This leads further to discernment of the causes of missing the mark as well as of a source of the mark. It leads also to attention to ways of assuaging the guilt that is intensified through this emphasis. Needless to say, I have in mind the Abrahamic traditions.

In recent times in the West there have been those who have held that there is no discernment at all — only construction. They advocate deconstruction, and some suggest that seeing through the constructional character of our worlds will be our ultimate liberation. The seeing through is itself discernment of the character of our worlds of meaning, hence it is an exaggeration to say that they deny all discernment. What they deny is primary discernment into features of a world that is not humanly constructed.

Still other traditions have grown out of and encouraged discernment of patterns in the natural and social worlds. In China Taoism represents the former, Confucianism, the latter. Taoists discerned the patterns of reciprocity, balance, and harmony in natural events. Confucianists discerned patterns of human behavior and social order that led to stable and harmonious political life.

At a highly abstract level generalizations can be made about all of these movements. All see something wrong and propose ways of righting it. But to go beyond that in identifying commonalities is quite dubious. It would have to be shown that what the Buddhist experiences in pure discernment is what the Abrahamic religions have discerned as the source and call for righteousness in human life. It would have to be shown that the patterns of order discerned in nature by the Taoist are the same patterns as those discerned by Greek philosophers and modern natural scientists.

If these commonalities cannot be shown, that does not indicate that one is right and the others wrong. It indicates only that in the inconceivably complex totality of events, different features have been discerned and diversely interpreted and ordered. On the other hand, that does not entail a stance of neutrality. All religious traditions tend to exaggerate the importance of their own achievements. All neglect the degree of abstraction involved in their discernments and the simplifications and distortions involved in their constructions. All thereby damage their own adherents as well as benefit them, and none opens itself as willingly to the potential contributions of others as one could wish. Judgments about the extent of these failures are warranted by the perspective here offered.

Today, as religious traditions are forced to deal with one another, many adherents revert defensively to absolutes that carry little conviction. The result is fanaticism. But others find increasingly in the heart of their own discernments reason to believe that others may have discerned something, too. This leads to a willingness to give and take, to teach and receive.

WHITEHEADIAN SPECULATIONS FOR THE ORDERING
OF THE PLURALITY

Although the vision of myriads of complexly interrelated events is the foundational feature of process metaphysics, there are additional levels of speculation by individual process thinkers that provide further ways of ordering religious diversity. These further speculations may prove wrong without invalidating the most fundamental aspects of the metaphysics, but I share an example taken from Whitehead because, thus far, it has seemed illuminating to me in my efforts to correlate some of the major religious traditions. I share it also to show that process thought can develop a plurality of typologies of religious systems. Pluralism is important at this level as well.

Whitehead discerns in every event a conjunction of the disjunctive many, that is, of other events. He speculates that the ultimate truth about the world is that "the many become one and are increased by one."[4] The new "one" is itself one of many new events that participate in the disjunctive that become conjunctively the next new events. So the process continues, on and on. This ultimate reality that characterizes every matter of fact Whitehead calls "creativity." Creativity is not a thing or a process or an event or an activity. But one could identify it as "process itself" or "activity itself," quite analogous to "being itself" in those philosophies that think of the world as made up of beings rather than events. Creativity in itself, like being in itself, has no form or character of its own. Although it is not an actual entity, it is not abstract either; for it is that by virtue of which actual entities are actual.

The form of each event, each instantiation of creativity, is largely derived from the forms of the events that make up the many out of which it constitutes itself. But this is not, by itself, an adequate account. If it were, the present would be the wholly determined outcome of the past. Of course, many philosophies accept this conclusion; but Whitehead discerns — especially, but not only, in human experience — an element of decision, a cutting off of some possibilities in favor of others. For him, what is genuinely possible for each event is more varied than what becomes actual in it. This means that in the constitution of the one out of the many, there is not the causal efficacy of the past but also the effective relevance of possible ways of interpreting, ordering, and supplementing what is received from the past and, thereby, of responding to the past creatively instead of only conformally. Thus the realm of possibility, of what Whitehead calls "eternal objects" is a second ultimate factor in the metaphysical situation alongside formless creativity.

There is a third factor as well, one that I have already mentioned. It is the world itself in all its everchanging particularity and actuality. At any given moment this is the entire past relative to whatever locus in the space-time continuum is taken as the present.

---

4. Alfred North Whitehead, *Process and Reality,* corrected ed., David Ray Griffin and Donald W. Sherburne, eds. (New York: The Free Press, 1978), p. 21.

These three factors found in the analysis of any event are all, in an important sense, *ultimate*. That is, they are not hierarchically arranged, and none is merely derivative from the others. Indeed, the relation of any pair is better thought of as non-dual, for they mutually require one another. There can be no creativity apart from the eternal objects, and there can be no creativity or eternal objects apart from the actual world. Equally, there can be no actual world apart from creativity and the eternal objects, and no eternal objects apart from creativity and the actual world.

This metaphysical triad turns out to be useful in the interpretation of the diversity of religious traditions. One of Panikkar's illustrations of differences between India and the West can illustrate part of this. He points out that, especially in India, one image of final destiny is the falling of a drop of water into the ocean. To Western ears this often appears profoundly unacceptable, since Westerners identify themselves with the *drop* of water in its distinction from other drops of water. The particularity of the drop (hence, personal identity as understood in the West) is lost as the drop merges with the ocean. To Indians, on the other hand, the true self is not lost, for the true self is the water of which the drop is but a passing form.

The water here represents Ātman, or Brahman, or Being, which resembles what in Whitehead's language is "creativity." To realize that one is nothing but an instance of this external, indestructible, ultimate, releases one from all anxieties attendant on identifying oneself in one's difference from others.

The image of the drop of water leads more to the Hindu vision than to the Buddhist. It suggests a common substance underlying all things or of which all things are composed. Buddhism resembles process thought in denying that there are things composed of substances and affirming instead that there are events which are instantiations of dependent origination. This corresponds closely with Whitehead's doctrine of creativity.

But whether the term is Ātman or *dependent origination,* the aspect of reality which is discerned and toward which attention is directed is much the same. The question is: Of what am I, and of what are all others, ultimately composed? What am I when all transient forms are stripped away? The Vedantist Hindu answers Ātman, or Nirguna Brahman, Brahman without attributes. The Buddhist says dependent origination or emptiness. There is nothing left when all particularity is stripped away, for the event is nothing but an instance of dependent origination.

This line of questioning has not preoccupied the West, although it has appeared from time to time. On the contrary, the West has attended to form. This is particularly apparent in the Platonic tradition. But the Hebrews also understood creation and redemption as forming and reforming and transforming. They concentrated attention on the contrast between what is and what might be and upon the choices made by human beings among real options. The goal is a new heaven and a new earth — not the realization of what has always been and what always will be.

In those traditions that seek the realization of what is beneath the particularizing forms or in and through all particularization by forms, the sacred connects itself with this realization, or with that which is realized in and through it. In the Abrahamic traditions, the sacred connects itself with the Creator, the One who forms all things and who then promises new forms, provides alternatives, and calls for the realization of some of these and the rejection of others. In a quite different way, the Platonic tradition also associates the sacred with the highest forms or with the One who is pure form or who knows all forms.

There have been others for whom the natural world itself is sacred. To live rightly is to live according to nature, to accord with its rhythms, to embody its harmonies. For them, it is a mistake to concentrate either upon underlying reality or upon the forms that particularize, whether in their function as particularizing or in their character as atemporal universals. It is unity of form and matter in concrete actuality that elicits wonder and provides value. Taoism represents this style of religious life, but in this it is continuous with much of primal and contemporary religiousness as well.

Viewed thus, these three ways of being religious are all valid and conformal to what-is. What each discerns is real, and as its constructions encourage further penetration into the facet of reality, each has gained a deeper wisdom. However different the discernments may be in the three ways, they cannot contradict one another. They are, like all discernments, complementary.

The situation with respect to the constructions associated with these discernments is quite different. Almost inevitably each is so formulated as to belittle the others if not so as to contradict them. The goal of dialogue is to work through these constructions to the discernments they express and defend, so that their complementary character can become visible and the possibility arises for appropriation by each of insights gained by the other. Whitehead's speculations can facilitate some aspects of this process.

THE PERMANENCE OF PLURALISM

Process metaphysics does not lead to the expectation that eventually a single religion or a single metaphysic will emerge synthesizing the discernments of all and correcting all their exaggerations and distortions. There are several reasons for discouraging any such expectation.

First, it would not be a happy outcome. The elements of zest and adventure so important to the process vision would be dulled where variety was thus greatly reduced.

Second, the ongoing process repeatedly brings the plurality together into new unities, but each of these unities remains quite particular. It is the unity of just that plurality, and as a creative unity it adds its own distinctive contribution. Elsewhere other pluralities are forming other unities. These unities jointly constitute new pluralities. Consensus in some area is likely to be accomplished by new disagreements in others.

Third, there is no reason to think that jointly the religious traditions have already discerned all that is worth discerning in the matrix of events. Quite the contrary. Precisely as we interact and learn from one another, we will raise new questions, direct attention to new features of reality, and, we may hope, gain new discernments through which all that we have heretofore thought and felt will be transformed. Today, for example, feminists are discerning much about our constructions to which we had previously been oblivious, and they are adding to our primary discernments as well. Religious traditions that are open to change can never be the same again.

The basic pattern I am proposing among religious traditions is one of mutual openness leading to mutual transformation. As long as we are thinking of the great traditions that have endured for millennia and won the allegiance of millions of civilized people, I strongly affirm that we should approach them in this spirit. But there are other cases that require closer attention. I choose three interesting examples: Naziism, primitive religions, and Mormonism.

Panikkar rightly stresses that as an individual Christian facing an individual Nazi a case can be made for openness. We should never close ourselves to a fellow human being. But does that mean that we would approach Naziism as a system expecting to find there discernments that would enrich us?

One can never be sure, but my answer is provisionally negative. Certainly there are some discernments into human character, into how power can be effectively exercised, and into means of manipulating the attitudes of intelligent people through propaganda. But at the primary level crucial to religious traditions it is doubtful that Naziism can contribute. It seems to show more how valid, familiar initial discernments can be distorted and the results absolutized in ways that are humanly immensely destructive.

Primitive religion presents a quite different situation. Native American religion can serve as an example. When first encountered by Christians it appeared superstitious and naive. The label *primitive* encourages that perception among many even today. The term *primal* is better. It may be still better to speak of the religion of hunting and gathering peoples.

One trouble with the term *primitive* is that as religion grew more sophisticated, it appropriated whatever discernments were present among primitive people and refined and supplemented them. That would mean that whatever true insights the older religions had were already appropriated by us and included in a higher synthesis. In that case there would be no point in dialogue, for there would be no reason to expect to learn. Differences could be located on a scale of progress rather than in parallel developments with divergent discernments.

But on closer contact we find that the situation is quite different. Native Americans have insights into the natural world and human relations herewith, for example, that have been lost in the course of civilization. "Civilization" can no longer appear to us as an unambiguous gain. The wisdom and life of the hunter-gatherer are in many ways superior to ours. To listen and learn are eminently appropriate.

I choose Mormonism as a third example. A religious movement with quite distinctive teachings Mormonism broke off from the mainstream of Protestantism in the United States. It clearly has some features of community life that are admirable and attractive. The question is whether it possesses discernments lacking in the mainstream of Christianity so that dialogue can be a source of important learning.

I am skeptical that this is the case. There is no doubt that the Mormons have constructed a world of meanings divergent from the Christian mainstream. Some discernments preserved in the mainstream seem muted in this movement. But it is not clear that there are fresh supplementary discernments here of the sort that would justify fundamental dialogue. Of course, this need not exclude dialogue at many other levels.

THE SELF-RELATIVIZATION OF METAPHYSICS

I have now sketched a view of religious pluralism based on a particular metaphysics. But that metaphysics is only one among many possible and actual accounts of the world. Perhaps the world is in fact exhaustively graspable in thought. Or perhaps it is totally opaque to thought. Perhaps there are no primary discernments, only constructions. Or perhaps exhaustive discernment is possible once all construction is obliterated. Perhaps the world is composed of matter in motion so that events are merely the byproduct of movements of material particles. Or perhaps the only events are human ones. Perhaps all events are illusory and only the one underlying substance is real.

I have personally considered and rejected those options. But others have considered and rejected mine and adopted some version of one or another of these. I have no platform beyond our two points of view from which I can pronounce my metaphysics superior. I can show that our two systems have different consequences and argue that the consequences of mine are better. But the other can derive different judgments of value from different metaphysics and reverse the conclusion. There is a circularity of argument between metaphysics and values.

What effect should my awareness of this plurality of metaphysics have on me? From the point of view of my own metaphysics it calls me to constant dialogue. If my own formulations are based on limited discernment of the whole, I have something to learn from others whose discernments have led to different formulations. This does not lead to equal interest in dialogue with all. Some metaphysics appear to me to offer no discernments not already appropriated in my own and to lack some present in mine. Some seem to be derived from constructions that once seemed plausible but now do not. But others are clearly offering discernments that are new and enriching from the point of view of process thought. For example, Heidegger's analysis of *Dasein* and of *Sein,* Buber's treatment of the I-thou relation, structuralism's illumination of synchronic patterns of thought, deconstructionism's clarification of the nature of construction and its results — all open new horizons of thought and reflection for the process thinker. Of course, there are features of the teaching of all these people I can accept only with qualifications. There are also features I can only reject, especially features of their denials of positions other than their own. On the whole, a process thinker judges that people are more reliable when they are affirming and articulating their positive discernment than when they are denying those of others.

It is of the nature of process thought to understand itself as in process. There is no certain or irreformable core, however strongly one may be convinced of some formulations. Everything is always open for reconsideration. The expectation is that all of its ideas will some day be superseded, although it expects also that this supersession of ideas will still include the pre-linguistic discernments expressed in particular and imperfect ways in current formulations.

But to show that a measure of openness to the plurality of metaphysics is built into process thought still fails to go to the heart of the matter. What about those philosophies that seem wrong or outdated? For example, what about philosophies that reject pluralism altogether, claiming to offer the final and inclusive truth?

The fact that sincere, intelligent, and well-informed people hold that position is a reminder to me of the relativity of my own. It does not prevent me from judging that their position too is relative, whatever claim they make to the contrary. And since just that relativity is what they deny, I am unable to escape the situation of believing that they are simply wrong. At this point my ability to be a metaphysical pluralist reaches its limits. The issue then shifts to the practical plane, and there, of course, the existence of plurality must be recognized and affirmed by pluralists whatever position absolutists may adopt.

There is no place from which to think other than the utterly particular place at which one finds oneself from moment to moment. What we think on every topic is relative to that particularity. But thought also involves *some* transcending of sheer particularity. Otherwise it is not thought at all. The question is how far that transcending goes, and this difference from instance to instance.

For my part, thought has convinced me that I am but one among many thinkers, that I think as I do because of my own history and the multifarious influences upon me, but that my thinking has been tested and checked in ways that seem appropriate to me and also from some perspectives other than my own. I believe the same is true of others — in some cases more, and in some cases less. This is, as I experienced it, a fundamentally pluralistic situation. That others disagree, I acknowledge, and I recognize their right to do so, but my own convictions are not thereby weakened, and on the basis of my convictions I will oppose any effort on their part to enforce conformity to their ideas while supporting their right to maintain absolutistic views themselves. I believe that in all this I am close to Panikkar's position. I rejoice in the degree of agreement to which widely differing life histories have brought us.

3

Panikkar's Philosophy of Language

HAROLD COWARD

We live, move and have our being in language. Even to criticize its faults and limitation to the extent of negating it, we have to use language. Language is not an aspect of thought, but its very essence. As Bhartṛhari, the great Indian philosopher of language, put it:

> There is no cognition without the operation of words; all cognition is shot through and through by the word. All knowledge is illumined through the word.[1]

Raimon Panikkar shares this high evaluation of language but adds to it a strong sense of joy in divine words. He quotes from the Ṛg Veda, "May you delight in these my words."[2] Anyone who has heard Panikkar speak or read his writing knows that for him language is joy and inspiration but yet not lacking in careful criticism and analysis. In this Panikkar follows both Western and Eastern traditions in the philosophy of language and yet adds an additional quality that is uniquely his own.

Aristotle established the classical Western conception of humans as the beings who have language (*logos*). Although animals can use signs and sounds to signal one another, humans alone seem to possess the ability to think and speak, and at the same time to be aware of what they are thinking and speaking.

Harold Coward is Professor of History and Director of the Centre for Studies in Religion and Society, University of Victoria. His many publications include *Pluralism: Challenge to World Religions* and (as co-author with K. Kunjunni Raja) *The Philosophy of the Grammarians*. He is founding editor of *The Hindu-Christian Studies Bulletin* and one of the founders of the Society for Hindu-Christian Studies. He is a member of the Royal Society of Canada.

1. Bhartṛhari, *Vākyapadīya* I: 123, translated by T. R. V. Murti in Foreword to Harold Coward, *The Sphoṭa Theory of Language.* New Delhi: Motilal Banarsidass, 1986, p. vii.
2. Ṛg Veda 1, 25, 18 as translated by R. Panikkar in *The Vedic Experience: "Mantramañjarī."* Berkeley: University of California Press, 1977, p. 29.

Language not only distinguishes humans from animals, it also mediates human knowledge. All knowledge of ourselves and all knowledge of the world comes to us through language.[3] This points up the extreme difficulty of studying language. All thinking about language must, by virtue of human limitations, be done within language itself. One cannot get outside of language so as to examine it objectively. Language must be used to study language from within. In recognition of this difficulty some scholars have coined a special name for the task — *metalanguage*.[4]

J. G. Herder and Wilhem von Humboldt may be taken as the founders of Western linguistic science.[5] Emphasizing the naturalness of language Herder and Humboldt developed an idealistic philosophy of language. Critical contributions to the study of language were also made by Kant and Hegel. Hegel called language the medium through which the subjective spirit is mediated with the being of objects.[6] In this century Ernst Cassirer has expanded the philosophy of language to include the natural sciences, the humanities and all human cultural activity. This is very much like the breadth that we find in Panikkar's philosophy of language. Both Cassirer and Panikkar recognize that an essential characteristic of language is that it finds within itself its own criteria for truth and meaning. On one point, however, Panikkar parts company with Cassirer. Cassirer begins from the presupposition that language, art and religion are parallel "forms" of representation.[7] The difficulty here arises because of the fact that as far as human knowledge is concerned, all of it is encompassed within language. Religion, especially, is not a form separate from language but occurs within language. Panikkar's view of language, as we shall see, is inclusive enough to avoid this problem.

Similar problems of narrowness arise when one turns to contemporary linguistic philosophy, where language seems restricted to the printed word and then analyzed for a one-to-one correspondence with objective reality. Panikkar is quick to identify such labeling activity as the making of signs or terms and as being quite distinct from living words which function as symbols.[8] Contemporary linguistic philosophy reduces language to the formal word empirically referenced, something far removed from the idealistic notion of natural language from which Herder and von Humboldt, taking their cue from Aristotle, had started. When words are seen only as carriers of information much of the fullness of language is lost. Throughout his writing Panikkar remains sensitive

3. Hans-Georg Gadamer, "Man and Language," in *Philosophical Hermeneutics,* trans. D. E. Linge, pp. 59–68.

4. See, for example, Frits Staal, "The Concept of Metalanguage and Its Indian Background," in *Journal of Indian Philosophy* 3, 1975, pp. 315–34.

5. Gadamer, "Man and Language," p. 61.

6. Gadamer, "The Nature and Things," in *Philosophical Hermeneutics,* p. 76.

7. Ernst Cassirer, *Language and Myth,* translated by Susanne K. Langer. New York: Dover, 1946, pp. 8–9.

8. Raimundo Panikkar, "Words and Terms," *Instituto di Studi Filosofici,* Roma, 1980. See also "Hermeneutics of Comparative Religion: Paradigms and Models," *Journal of Dharma,* 5, 1980, p. 50.

to the fullness of the word and the reality it evokes — even to the fullness of the silence of the Buddha.[9]

As well as Western philosophy of language, Panikkar is also strongly influenced by Indian speculations on language. These were present in the Vedas before the advent of recorded history and have continued in an unbroken tradition up to the present.[10] The Indian approach to language was never narrow or restrictive. Language was understood in relation to consciousness — consciousness not restricted even to human consciousness. All aspects of human experience and the world were thought of as illumined by language. It is remarkable that in the ancient hymns of the R̥g Veda a semi-technical vocabulary was already developed to deal with such linguistic matters as composition, poetic creation, inspiration, illumination, vision and so on.[11] There was careful concern for both the phenomenal and metaphysical dimensions of language. With early scientific training and his later immersion in the Vedas,[12] Panikkar stands squarely in this Indian linguistic tradition. This helps Panikkar avoid the two reductionistic mistakes of much modern thought, namely, of reducing language, to being a merely human convention having only empirical referents or of a metaphysical reduction that so devalues the meanings of words that language ends up as obscure mysticism. Like the great Grammarians of the Indian tradition, men like Panini, Patañjali and Bhartr̥hari, Panikkar is concerned with the function of language in the everyday empirical world and with its function as scripture and myth.

Grounding himself in the Indian philosophy of language, Panikkar emphasizes the necessity of human relationship for the experience of the word. As Western scholars are just now realizing,[13] it is the human context that gives language its heart, that keeps words from degenerating into mere signs, or as Panikkar would say, "terms." The Indian tradition has always stressed the oral words, the experience of its vibrations by speaker and hearer. It is the enacted word, says Panikkar, which is powerful, creative and transforming. Words become real to us not just by objective theoretical analysis, but by the classical idea of "study," which includes commitment to them, speaking them aloud and so representing them in ourselves. Only then, maintains Panikkar, is the translation of the original experience of a text possible — and this is the goal of his *Mantramañjarī,* not translation but a bringing of the reader/hearer into an exis-

---

9. Raimundo Panikkar, "The Silence of the Word" *Word out of Silence: A Symposium on World Spiritualities, Cross Currents,* 24, 1974, pp. 154–71.

10. P. K. Chakravarti, *The Linguistic Speculations of the Hindus.* Calcutta: University of Calcutta, 1933.

11. Frits Staal, "The Concept of Metalanguage and Its Indian Background," *Journal of Indian Philosophy,* 3, 1975, p. 319.

12. See *The Vedic Experience: "Mantramañjarī."*

13. See, for example, the current emphasis among biblical scholars on the reader-response interaction. Bernard C. Lategan, "Reference: Reception, Redescription and Reality," in *Text and Reality: Aspects of Reference in Biblical Texts* by Bernard C. Lategan and Willem S. Vorster. Atlanta: Scholars Press, 1985, p. 67.

tential reenactment of the Vedas.[14] Thus the title, *The Vedic Experience* rather than *A Translation of the Vedas*. This goal of the existential study or experience of the word is defined by Patañjali at *Yoga Sūtra* 2:44 as *svadhyaya* — chanting of the *mantra* ending in communion with the divine.[15] Modern scholars such as Walter Ong,[16] Werner Kelber,[17] Jacques Ellul[18] and others[19] are agreeing with this stress on the need for the oral experience of the word if it is to have transforming power. Panikkar also makes the point that the existential involvement in the word ends in a requirement for action. While Panikkar grounds himself in the linguistic imperative found in Indian texts like the Bhagavad Gītā[20] and those of the Pūrva Mīmāmsā,[21] this aspect of his philosophy of language connects in surprising ways with the contemporary Grammatology of Jacques Derrida.[22]

Having situated Panikkar's philosophy of language in its traditional and contemporary contexts, let us now enter a detailed study of his thought. In presenting Panikkar's position we will employ the following headings: (1) Language out of Silence; (2) The Distinction between Terms and Words; (3) Word as Dynamic Interaction; and (4) Translation as Reenacted Language.

LANGUAGE OUT OF SILENCE

Drawing on Vedic texts, Panikkar suggests that silence is the source of every real word. Panikkar situates silence at the source of our being, at Brahman, which is at the same time the source of language. "That's why Word is Brahman, and why there are authentic and inauthentic words. And that's why the lie, untruthfulness, is perhaps the capital sin (Sathapatha Brahmana II: 2, 2 20)."[23] Panikkar is careful not to make silence the ultimate beyond language, as the Buddhist would. He presents silence not as a language itself, but as contiguous with Śabdabrahman, the silence that is in all words. Language "words" or "fills out" but does not exhaust the silence. Language comes out of silence and takes us back into silence — the place where we all meet. We cannot define silence but we can speak silence by letting the pregnant force of Śabdabrahman burst forth into words. *Vāc* (speech), says the Brahmana, is truly "the womb of the

14. *The Vedic Experience: "Mantramañjarī,"* p. 27.

15. *Patañjali's Yoga Sūtras,* translated by Rama Prasad. New Delhi, Oriental Books, 1978, p. 168.

16. Walter Ong, *The Presence of the Word.* New Haven: Yale University Press, 1967. See also his more recent *Orality and Literacy: The Technologizing of the Word.* London: Methuen, 1982.

17. Werner H. Kelber, *The Oral and Written Gospel,*. Philadelphia: Fortress, 1983.

18. Jacques Ellul, *The Humiliation of the Word.* Grand Rapids, Michigan: Eerdmans, 1985.

19. Books continue to appear treating the importance of the oral word. See, for example, Brian Stock, *The Implications of Literacy.* Princeton: Princeton University Press, 1983; William A. Graham, *Beyond the Written Word: Oral Aspects of Scripture in the History of Religion.* Cambridge University Press, 1987; and Harold Coward, *Sacred Word and Sacred Text: Scripture in World Religions.* Maryknoll, N.Y.: Orbis Books, 1988.

20. *The Bhagavad Gītā,* translated by R. C. Zaehner. Oxford: Oxford University Press, 1969.

21. See Ganganatha Jha, *Pūrva-Mīmāmsā in its Sources.* Varanasi: Banaras Hindu University, 1964.

22. Jacques Derrida, *Of Grammatology.* Baltimore: Johns Hopkins University Press, 1974.

23. Panikkar, "The Silence of the Word," p. 165.

universe."[24] Language is the firstborn of silence, the sacrifice of silence. "Any real word is word because it comes out of silence; but it is more; it is precisely authentic word because it *is* (spoken) silence."[25] According to Panikkar there is an intrinsic and constitutive polarity between silence and word. One does not exist without the other, and it is the one which makes possible the other. "The relationship between silence and the word is a non-dualistic one, and neither monism nor dualism will do justice to their intrapenetration."[26]

In his discussion of the origin of language Panikkar is consistent with the Hindu and Christian tradition. In the Vedas language is directly identified with the Divine (Brahman). The Ṛg Veda states that there are as many words as there are manifestations of Brahman.[27] Even in the later Hindu scriptures, the Āraṇyakas and Upaniṣads, there is a continued equating of speech and Brahman. As the Bṛhadāraṇyaka Upaniṣad states: *Vāg vai brahmeti,* "Speech, truly is Brahman."[28] And at the level of Brahman speech is the silence ready to burst forth into illumination, the *paśyanti vāk,* as Bhartṛhari would call it.[29] A parallel viewpoint is expressed in Christian scripture at the beginning of the Gospel according to Saint John: "In the beginning was the Word, and the Word was with God, and the Word was God."[30] In both traditions the sensitive soul (the Hindu *ṛsi,* the Hebrew prophet) has silenced his or her own thoughts and opened himself or herself to experience the speaking silence of the Divine Word. The *ṛsi* or the prophet is not a composer of the Vedic hymn or Hebrew prophecy but the seer of an eternal truth. From the Hindu perspective the language of the Veda is a "rhythm not composed by the intellect but heard, a divine Word that came vibrating out of the Infinite to the inner audience of the man who had previously made himself fit for the impersonal knowledge."[31] The *ṛsi's* initial silent vision is said to be of the Veda as one, as a whole, the entirety of Brahman. As the unity of the Veda unfolds it reveals the language of scripture and the forms for all ordinary world use. The Hindu Grammarians set forth rules (the Prātiśakhyas) for prosody, phonetics, accentuation and *sandhi* to ensure that the oral form of the Veda and everyday language use would be preserved and passed on with little loss or distortion. The great Indian philosophers of language, Patañjali and Bhartṛhari, conveyed the essence of this philosophy of language in their writings. At the center was a battle to keep language use pure so that the word out of silence could be clearly heard, understood and enacted. Panikkar continues

24. Atharva Brahmana II: 38.
25. Panikkar, "The Silence of the Word," p. 156.
26. Ibid., p. 163. Panikkar notes that "there are escapist silences and repressed silences, as well as empty words and nonsensical chattering; it is only such non-authentic words or silences that are at variance. Any authentic silence is pregnant with words which will be born at the right time" (p. 163).
27. Ṛg Veda 5. 10. 2 and 10. 114. 8.
28. Bṛhadāraṇyaka Upaniṣad 4. 1. 2.
29. *Vākyapadīya* I: 142.
30. John 1:1.
31. Aurobindo Ghose, *On the Veda.* Pondicherry: Sri Aurobindo Ashram Press, 1956, p. 6.

this tradition in his distinction between "words" and "terms," which is the core of his philosophy of language.

THE DISTINCTION BETWEEN "WORDS" AND "TERMS"

Whereas the Hindu Grammarians are worried that sloppy and egocentric word use would rob language of its revelatory power, Panikkar sees the modern threat to language originating in the scientific use of words. Having been trained as a scientist, Panikkar is sensitive to the requirement for a scientific language which allows for exactitude and measurement, for the need to speak objectively of the world of empirical objects. For each such object there is an epistemic sign: "tree," atom," "wine," and so on. Panikkar calls these signs "terms" because they are empirically verifiable within certain conditions. Such terms are exactly translatable into any language. Should a particular language have no name for an object, a term can quite easily be invented.[32] Such terms are the result of human convention. "Words," however, are the real substance of language and are quite different from "terms." Panikkar explains:

> The uniqueness of language lies in "words" which, unlike terms, reflect a total human experience. They are not objectifiable because (of being) not totally separable from the particular instance in which they are used, and the meaning they are given. Each word is uniquely used and every usage of a single word is equally unique, in that each of us gives different shades of meaning to the same word and one person uses a single word in a variety of ways. Consequently, words like "justice," "god," "Brahman" which have no empirical referent, cannot be understood outside the human experiences crystallized around them, which vary with history, geography, psychology, and so on. They cannot be transplanted outside these contexts but have rather to be transplanted along with the soil in which they are rooted, the world-view which gives them meaning.[33]

This use of "words" has been the foundation and essential characteristic of human civilizations and religions.

The difficulty in the modern, especially Western world, is that the use of scientific language has become dominant. Often the so-called educated person communicates through "terms" and no longer speaks "words." Education, says Panikkar, often amounts to supplanting words with terms. While this has the positive result of allowing humans to gain scientific and technological control over the world of empirical objects, there is also a negative effect. The negative aspect arises when the objective world is judged to be the only important and ultimately real world. The world of words, which includes much that is valued in human civilizations and religions, is reduced to a medieval anachronism.

---

32. Raimundo Panikkar, "Hermeneutics of Comparative Religion: Paradigms and Models," *Journal of Dharma*, 5, 1980, p. 50.
33. Ibid.

The metaphoric richness of words is ruled out because it does not meet the requirement of having a one-to-one referent. Terms remain as the only language acceptable to the scientific outlook.[34] Nominalism, in which each term represents one concept, is the basis of scientific language. It is also the foundation of technological society, which "uses names as signs, as references scientifically defined, as more or less univocal ciphers pointing toward states of affairs scientifically organized and ordered."[35] But real things are not sufficiently represented by scientific terms. Scientific language captures only objectified forms — the "it" of things.

But the scientific is not the most important aspect of language. It leaves out the *are* and the *am,* the you (thou) and the I (am). The sphere of the person and the realm of human life is ignored.[36] Words, for Panikkar, are living symbols. As a symbol, a word is not an isolated entity but embodies a circle of communication from speaker to hearer.

> A word is only a word if it is spoken by somebody (the speaker); if it has a sound, a sensuous countenance (the spoken with); a meaning, a sense (the spoken of); and a receiver, a hearer (the spoken to) to whom and for whom we speak and who in a way draws our own words out with his/her/its presence, influence, expectations, range of perceptivity, interests and the like.[37]

The whole world is constituted by all of these four aspects: the speaker uttering the word, its physical sound, its meaning contents and its hearer. Taken together these four aspects form the indestructible unity of the word. None can be isolated from the other aspects. The word is not a constructed unity of these independently existing component parts, as our scientific mentality would lead us to believe. Language itself is the a priori ground upon which these aspects of the word depend for their existence.

Unlike scientific terms, which are universal in meaning and thus translatable into any language, words are problematic when we experience the encounter of world views and religions. While terms function to orient us in the universal world of objects, words are symbols which give meaning to our lives in the contexts of people and Gods.[38] Thus words cannot be translated but only transplanted in another human context (but more of that below). A term may stand for something else, but a word does not. A word does not point to something totally separate from itself. Panikkar means this quite literally. "If we did not have the word 'justice' we would have not justice. . . . This appears to be a tautology, and in a certain sense it is a *qualified tautology* as are all ultimate utterances, as they have no ground beyond them; and language is ultimate."[39]

---

34. R. Panikkar, "Words and Terms," pp. 120–21.
35. Ibid., p. 120.
36. Ibid., p. 123.
37. Ibid., p. 124.
38. Raimundo Panikkar, *The Intrareligious Dialogue.* New York: Paulist Press, 1978, p. xxv
39. Panikkar, "Words and Terms," p. 125.

In taking this strong stand on the ontological priority of language, Panikkar aligns himself with both the Hindu tradition and with important currents in contemporary Western thought. Within Hinduism Bhartṛhari maintained that *vāk,* speech, is the ground of all consciousness. It is through the a priori existence of the word that all knowledge and communication is possible.[40] Due to the a priori existence of the unitary word in consciousness (the *sphoṭa*), its manifestation as inner meaning (*artha*) and uttered sound (*dhvani*) is possible. The logic of language for both Bhartṛhari and Panikkar is that the unity of the whole word is prior to the existence of its parts. In contemporary Western thought the French philosopher Jacques Derrida takes a parallel line in his contention that "there is nothing outside the text."[41] For Derrida, as for Panikkar and Bhartṛhari, there is no metaphysical "other" outside the text or speech which starts or constitutes language. Although terms may have external referents words do not. As Derrida contends, there is no referent outside of the spoken or written text. This is not a Buddhist move, as some have mistakenly assumed.[42] Language is not being treated as *vikalpaḥ* or mere imaginary construction possessing no way to get a grip on reality — the Buddhist analysis. For Bhartṛhari, Panikkar and Derrida language is itself the very stuff of our experience. All three would find common cause against those who maintain that language has no purchase on reality. This is made clear when all three thinkers see words, not as eternal forms esoterically separated from real life, but as embodied in the dynamic becoming of space and time.

WORD AS DYNAMIC INTERACTION

For Panikkar a word, unlike a term, is not objectifiable — it is not "over there."[43] Whether we use language in our everyday relationships or in our encounter with the divine, our words are experienced as a dynamic interaction with reality. For Panikkar language is strongly existential.

> Time and space belong to the word *qua* word.... Each word is unique. Each time I say "yes," "daddy," "I love you," "I disagree," "God," "Peter," "justice," it is not a mere labeling for the sake of clarification and classification. It is a calling or an answering (i.e., a swearing, an oath) for the sake of saying something which is inseparable from the saying itself and which cannot be reduced to the mere "contents" of the saying. The content depends on the container, and vice-versa.... Every authentic word is a sacrament.[44]

40. For a full exposition of this position see Coward, *The Sphoṭa Theory of Language.*

41. Christopher Norris, *Deconstruction: Theory and Practice.* London: Methuen, 1982, p. 41.

42. Bhartṛhari, in his day, was mistakenly called a Buddhist. Derrida's position has been misrepresented as a Buddhist analysis of language (see Robert Magliola, *Derrida on the Mend.* West Lafayette, Indiana: Purdue University Press, 1984). Panikkar's emphasis on silence might lead some to attempt a Buddhist interpretation, but he carefully guards against such a result (see his discussion with Alan Watts of his "The Silence of the Word," *Cross Currents,* 24, 1974, p. 165).

43. Panikkar, "Words and Terms," p. 127.

44. Ibid., p. 126.

Like Buber[45] Panikkar maintains that words manifest and embody I-Thou relationships. "Not only is there no I without a Thou and vice-versa, for the I is only such if there is a Thou, and conversely; but there is neither I nor Thou without the word."[46] The word uttered reveals me to you. It is a vow and a commitment. "It implies fidelity and the risk that you may not admit my cry, my affirmation, my prayer, my opinion, or understand my saying."[47] Words reveal and commit us to one another in ways that cannot be reduced to objectifiable statements — no matter how hard the lawyers may try. Words are constitutive expressions of our human relationships. Each time a word is said it is a new word. Lovers never tire of saying "I love you." Nor do such words become empty, manipulative or boring repetitions. Each saying anew is heard afresh, as in the chanting of a powerful *mantra*. The same dynamics obtain in religious language, in the saying of the Jesus Prayer, the preaching of a parable or the chanting of the Lord's name. Such words constitute, maintain and develop our experience of the divine. To understand a particular word one must experience its testimony and participate in its myth.[48]

Language, for Panikkar, is a mode of being human. It is not a set of terms having objective referents. In speaking words one experiences the double sense: of calling and of being called. Words are dynamic rather than passive. In human interaction words impose upon us imperatives for action. Words are not neutral or objective. They are living symbols which embody within themselves our corporate wisdom[49] and relate that wisdom in a fresh way to the new situation in which we find ourselves. This also means that there is no word without connection to an entire language and group of people. There is no such thing as an isolated, neutral or *tabula rasa* word. Panikkar cites the Heideggerian metaphor *Haus des Seins.*

> The word is the habitat of Being: That which *has* being. To put it differently: the "*itself*" of the word is an "I-Thou-It-Self," it is the "in-between" or the respectiveness, and not a mere *it*. A word "in-itself" means the integral word, the linguisticality in which all speakable things share: it means a word in its-Self.[50]

The word is the sphere of Being in which the speaker and the hearer commune. Preachers, teachers and parents can detect the empty repetition of words. Although such words may have a meaning in themselves, they convey no real meaning when devoid of personal conviction in the life of the speaker and/or

45. Martin Buber, *I and Thou*. New York: Charles Scribners, 1958.

46. Panikkar "Words and Terms," p. 125.

47. Ibid., p. 127.

48. Raimundo Panikkar, *Myth, Faith and Hermeneutics*. New York: Paulist Press, 1979, pp. 237–39.

49. Here one must acknowledge the quite different ways in which this "corporate wisdom" is conceived: from Bhartṛhari's *sphoṭa* concept of revealed truth in the East to Carl Jung's Western notion of historically layered archetypes in the collective unconscious. Panikkar partakes of both but locates himself more strongly with Bhartṛhari and the Vedas.

50. Panikkar "Words and Terms," p. 128.

the hearer. Attempts to remove the word from the context of human interaction and isolate its essential meaning only succeed in killing the word. The word's meaning is in the dynamic and creative commitment of the speaker-hearer relationship.

An important characteristic of the speaker-hearer relationship is that the words must be spoken. The Indian Sanskrit tradition has always maintained that language is speech — the spoken word. Speech requires the context of a relationship. Even the yogi in lonely meditation chanting a *mantra* is understood as speaking the mantric word in relationship — if not to a personal Lord, then to the impersonal *ṛta* or divine order of the universe (still very much a relationship requiring the sincere commitment of the yogi). The modern idea that words can be abstracted from spoken interaction and written down as impersonal knowledge is seen by the Hindu philosophy as a fundamental misunderstanding of the way in which language operates. Attempts to teach using words removed from relationship would be judged as doomed to failure, for the power, creativity and inspiration of the word is contained in the speaking relationship. Although scientific terms may be mastered outside of the speaker-hearer context,[51] human wisdom demands that it be spoken in a context which takes account of its past history, present practice and future possibilities. Only then is the word fully alive. A recent review of the function of scripture in the world religions shows that it is the spoken word (the "lively word" as the Puritans called it) that has power to transform lives.[52]

Panikkar, too, emphasizes that a word to be a word has to be spoken. The life of a word, he says, is similar to the life of a person. We are free and yet at the same time constrained by the context in which we live. "We share in life and we live in life; we live it and are it, without having been its creators."[53] So also with words. We share in the "life" of a word as we learn it and use it. We may even modify the meaning of a word as we live with it and within its linguistic relationship. As the Hindu tradition taught, a living word has no author. It is *apauresheya* or uncreated. No one decides "this is what this particular word will mean." Such human-created conventions are signs or terms rather than living words. Words as living symbols claim and culture us. We live within them and therein find the meaning of our human existence. Cultures fall, says Panikkar, because they confuse terms with words. Modernity, for example, takes scientific and technological terms to be the real words. This use of terms so objectifies our relationships with persons and things that the significance which words would convey is lost. Modern language devalues culture and seems to many to be empty of meaning. Like Derrida, who deconstructs the objective referencing

---

51. Teachers involved in creating computer-assisted instruction programs have quickly come to the conclusion that the more user-friendly the computer program, the more effective will be the learning. "User-friendly" means that the interaction between the student and the computer should approximate the interaction which would take place with a living teacher.

52. See Harold Coward, *Sacred Word and Sacred Text: Scripture in World Religions.* Maryknoll, N.Y.: Orbis Books, 1988.

53. Panikkar, "Terms and Words," p. 129.

of language so as to reveal its inherent inner meaning, Panikkar distinguishes between "terms" and "words" so as to sensitize us to the essential requirement for language to contain and be contained in committed human interaction.

Panikkar offers a very simple criterion for differentiating terms from words. "We can use terms in which we do not believe without lying. We cannot do the same with words."[54] Only the lover can authentically say "I love you" to the beloved. Only a Jew can really say the *Shema,* or a Muslim the *distich* or a Christian "Christ is Lord." When said by nonbelievers the same statements are terms rather than words. The required criterion of the speaking taking place within a relationship of commitment is absent.While the nonbeliever is merely repeating terms, the believer is reenacting his or her profession of faith with each saying. Each profession of faith by the believer is a newly nuanced set of words possessing sacramental power. Words are much more than just containers of cognitive contents; they embody human relations. "Word is relation, is love as much as meaning, embraces the listener as much as the speaker, it entails your voice as much as the ears and hearts of those with whom you communicate: they elicit from you the adequate words."[55]

For Panikkar, the model of language as dynamic human interaction comes to be employed as a paradigm for intrareligious dialogue,[56] for the comparative study of religion[57] and for the translation of religious texts.[58] Since space limitations preclude an examination of all three, let us conclude with Panikkar's application of his philosophy of language as a paradigm for the translation of the Vedas.

TRANSLATION AS REENACTED LANGUAGE

Since words involve existential participation in the speaker-hearer circle of communication, the act of translation is much more complex than a mere transposition of terms from one language to another. For Panikkar, translation of the Vedas requires that "the reader is brought close to reenacting culturally the Vedic experience for himself."[59] The task of the translator is to allow the Vedic words "to become living symbols once again and thus to be grafted onto the living growth of modern Man's cultures."[60] To assimilate a living symbol from another language and culture is not to interpret it or to paraphrase it or to understand it on the merely mental level. This would be to translate in terms rather than words. Consistent with his philosophy of language, translation, for Panikkar, enables the reader to assimilate the words from another culture into his or her own life. In translating the Vedas Panikkar's goal is to enable the Vedas to

---

54. Ibid., p. 130.
55. Ibid., p. 131.
56. Panikkar, *The Intrareligious Dialogue,* pp. xxivff.
57. Panikkar, "Hermeneutics of Comparative Religion: Paradigms and Models," pp. 49–51.
58. *The Vedic Experience: Mantramañjarī,* pp. 20ff.
59. Ibid., p. 20.
60. Ibid., p. 19.

be reenacted in modern human experience. The aim is not correct term-for-term translations. Rather, "philological accuracy consists in human fidelity, and the 'correct' version is the outcome of a correct shift of symbols, of such a sort that the reader is brought close to reenacting culturally the Vedic experience for himself."[61]

For Panikkar, language is a revelation of the Spirit within the context of human relationship. Each language has new words which represent a new disclosure of reality. Each set of words is the physical and metaphysical crystallization of centuries of human experience. The challenge to the translator is to find those authentic words through which we can enter into communion with another culture, another time, another revelation of reality.[62] The task in translating the Vedas is to present the total experience of Vedic people "against the present-day human horizon, in order to make the former intelligible and to enrich, challenge, and perhaps eventually transform the latter."[63] Neither a term-for-term or a paragraph-for-paragraph translation will serve this need. What is required, says Panikkar, is that the whole *śruti,* the whole Vedic experience, be transposed into our own personal experience.

> We have to learn another language or another world view, no longer as we used to learn a foreign idiom, but as we learn our own language. Children learning to speak do not refer to an objectified world, nor do they relate the particular word of one language to a corresponding word in another language; they assimilate, they understand, they use a word to express a state of consciousness and eventually a reality which is not disconnected from the word they are using.[64]

This is also the aim of translation — to find a modern word which will symbolize the experience of the speaking, hearing and living relationship embodied in the ancient Veda.

Just as there are no fixed and unchanging words, so there are no immutable translations. Words are living, changing symbols. The task is not to find the best word to translate the Vedic *ātman,* but to confront the same problem in our words that the Vedic thinker confronted in *ātman.* To do this requires that the modern Westerner using English, with its inbuilt Jewish-Helleno-Christian presuppositions, be prepared to enlarge these presuppositions so as to make room for the different Vedic experience of human consciousness. Doing this will also enable our words to evolve and enrich themselves. Language will become more universal in the sense of being capable of expressing the experiences of another culture, yet without losing its own concrete particularity.[65] While using terms as one-for-one translations may not challenge, change or enrich one, the experience of the living words of another culture will. This is the experience that

---

61. Ibid., p. 20.
62. Ibid., pp. 19–20.
63. Ibid., p. 21.
64. Ibid.
65. Ibid., p. 25.

words necessarily bring to us in acts of translation, in the comparative study of religion or in interreligious dialogue.

For Panikkar, language is the manifestation of the Spirit. While the scientific use of terms plays an important role in modern civilization, such terms cannot express the essential core of human relationship, culture and religion. Only words, as living symbols of the Spirit, can do that. Only words can engage us with the divine silence which is their source, make meaningful our human relationships and enable us to translate each other's religious experience so that it becomes an enrichment of our own.

4

Contra Pluralism

GERALD JAMES LARSON

INTRODUCTION

Raimon Panikkar's work in recent years has been important by way of focusing attention on one of the crucial problems in contemporary religious and philosophical thought, namely, the problem of *theoretical* pluralism.[1] The adjective *theoretical* is important here in order to distinguish Panikkar's program from other discussions of what might be called ordinary uses of the term *pluralism*. Martin Marty, for example, distinguishes three types of ordinary or conventional pluralism: "mere pluralism," "utter pluralism," and "civil pluralism."[2] "Mere pluralism" is the simple recognition in a given context that there are all sorts of things to be taken into account. "Utter pluralism" is an exasperated recognition in a given context that there are so many impulses, opinions or ideas floating about that it is seemingly impossible to find any basis for consensus. "Civil pluralism" is a sophisticated and tutored recognition in a given social and political environment, allowing, on one level, the greatest possible

---

Gerald James Larson is Rabindranath Tagore Professor of Indian Cultures and Civilizations and Director of the Indian Studies Program at Indiana University, Bloomington. He is author of many articles and books on Indian philosophy and religion and contemporary philosophy, of which the most recent is *India's Agony over Religion*.

1. For purposes of this paper, I am focusing on five of Panikkar's recent essays: (a) "Aporias in the Comparative Philosophy of Religion," *Man and World* 13, 3–4 (1980), pp. 357–83; (b) "Religious Pluralism: The Metaphysical Challenge," in L. S. Rouner, ed., *Religious Pluralism* (Notre Dame: University of Notre Dame Press, 1984), pp. 97–115; (c) "The Invisible Harmony: A Universal Theory of Religion or a Cosmic Confidence in Reality?," in L. Swidler, ed., *Toward a Universal Theory of Religion* (Maryknoll, N.Y.: Orbis Books, 1987), pp. 118–53; (d) "The Jordan, the Tiber and the Ganges: Three Kairological Moments of Christic Self-Consciousness," in J. Hick and P. F. Knitter, eds., *The Myth of Christian Uniqueness* (Maryknoll, N.Y.: Orbis Books, 1987), pp. 89–116; and (e) "What Is Comparative Philosophy Comparing?," in G. J. Larson and E. Deutsch, eds., *Interpreting Across Boundaries* (Princeton: Princeton University of Press, 1988), pp. 116–36.

2. Martin Marty, "My Virtue Is Better Than Your Virtue," public lecture, University of California, Santa Barbara, January 12, 1989.

diversity of views and lifestyles, yet seeking, on another level, to identify those minimal conditions for order and communication that permit a mixed polity to survive. The United States with its separation of church and state together with its so-called civil religion would presumably be an exemplum of Marty's "civil pluralism." India as a modern, secular nation-state would presumably be another.

Panikkar's concern is not primarily with any one of Marty's ordinary or conventional types, but rather with the underlying intellectual assumptions or presuppositions in any formulation of the notion of pluralism. Panikkar's concern, in other words, is with the philosophical basis or lack thereof of pluralism, or as he puts it, "the metaphysical challenge" of pluralism.[3] Panikkar frequently casts his discussions in terms of specifically "religious pluralism," partly, I suppose, because he is most comfortable with the discourses of the history of religions, theology and religious studies, but partly also because the discourses of religious traditions are in many ways the most diagnostically significant examples of what is at stake in seriously maintaining a posture of pluralism. Panikkar, however, could just as easily have addressed other sorts of discourses as well, for example, contemporary literary theory, the so-called new historicism, deconstruction, post-modernism and a host of other humanistic and social scientific perspectives in which notions of pluralism are currently being discussed. In this regard one thinks of the recent exchange between Clifford Geertz and Richard Rorty about the possibility of an "anti-anti-ethnocentrism," with Geertz worrying about the "uses of diversity" and Rorty glorying in his "Postmodernist Bourgeois Liberalism" without intellectual foundations.[4] In this latter exchange, though the discourses are those of cultural anthropology and philosophy, the underlying theoretical issue of pluralism closely parallels Panikkar's discussion.

In any case, in the present chapter I propose to argue

(1) that Panikkar's formulation of the problem of *theoretical* pluralism is basically correct;

(2) but that, unfortunately, when so formulated, the notion of pluralism becomes unintelligible in a two-valued (truth-falsehood) logic, inasmuch as the principle of the excluded middle is violated;

(3) and that, therefore, the notion of pluralism so formulated is as self-defeating as any formulation of relativism and as tripped up by the problem of self-referentiality as any formulation of universalism or absolutism.

Or putting the matter into the idiom of the Geertz-Rorty exchange, I wish to contend that a position of "anti-anti-ethnocentrism" is not a *tertium quid.*

---

3. Panikkar, "Religious Pluralism," op. cit., pp. 97–115.

4. Clifford Geertz, "The Uses of Diversity," The Tanner Lecture on Human Values, *Michigan Quarterly Review* (Winter 1986), pp. 105–23; Richard Rorty, "On Ethnocentrism: A Reply to Clifford Geertz," *Michigan Quarterly Review* (Summer 1986), pp. 525–534. See also Richard Rorty, *Contingency, Irony and Solidarity* (Cambridge: Cambridge University Press, 1989), especially the final chapter entitled "Solidarity," pp. 189–98.

It is simply a restatement of ethnocentrism, however sugar-coated to improve the taste or assist the digestion. It is, as Rorty rightly recognizes, the ideological ethnocentrism of "Postmodernist Bourgeois Liberalism" or some cultural variant thereof.[5]

Let me express the thrust of what I wish to argue in a somewhat different, and admittedly polemical, manner. Jean-Paul Sartre in *Search for a Method* comments that there have been only three "moments" of creative intellectual work in modern Western thought between the seventeenth-century and the twentieth, namely, the "moment" of Descartes and Locke (in the developing social reality of mercantile capitalism), the "moment" of Kant and Hegel with Kierkegaard as counterpoint (in the developing social reality of industrial capitalism), and the "moment" of Marx (in the developing social reality of finance capitalism and bureaucratic statism).[6] The point of Sartre's periodization, of course, is not that intellectuals or "ideologists" in a given period were all Lockeans, Kantians, Marxians, and so forth, but rather that the creative "moments" provided the idiom or intellectual framework of a period, concerning which one could be either for or against, but *in* which the problems of the emerging social reality were largely discussed. Each "moment" articulated in its context "the humus of every particular thought and the horizon of all culture."[7] Sartre argues further that the next creative theoretical "moment" after Marx cannot yet even be conceived. Says Sartre: "But we have no means, no intellectual instrument, no concrete experience which allows us to conceive of this freedom or of this philosophy."[8] In my view, Sartre's periodization is diagnostically interesting, and I am inclined to agree that we have not yet reached the threshold in which we can adequately conceive of a new creative "moment." To be sure, we have reached the point at which it is increasingly obvious that theoretical and practical Marxism is bankrupt, that the Western-style nation-state system with its bipolar foci of power is breaking up, that the global inequity of the current world economic system is rapidly becoming delegitimized, that the resurgence of religious world views is largely parochial and/or without transnational or even national significance in most instances, and that *glasnost* and *perestroika* are everywhere being hailed (except, of course, in Beijing, Beirut, Jerusalem, Belfast, Ludhiana, Teheran, Rangoon, Buenos Aires, Managua and a host of other places).[9] We have reached, in other words, the last, gasping instant of the "moment" of Marx, namely, *pluralism,* positively as the new "pluralism of the left" (or what can be characterized as the ideology of *glasnost* of the "neo-visible hand,"

5. Rorty, Contingency, *Irony and Solidarity,* op. cit., pp. 192, 197.

6. Jean-Paul Sartre, *Search for a Method,* trans., H. E. Barnes (New York: Vintage Books, Random House, 1968), p. 7.

7. Ibid.

8. Ibid., p. 34.

9. Three recent books provide an intriguing analysis of the present state of world civilization, particularly powerful by reason of their basically pro-American orientation, namely, Paul Kennedy, *The Rise and Fall of the Great Powers* (New York: Random House, 1987); Peter F. Drucker, *The New Realities* (New York: Harper & Row, 1989); and Zbigniew Brzezinski, *The Grand Failure* (New York: Charles Scribner's Sons, 1989).

namely, "democratic" socialism and its varieties), and, of course, negatively as the "pluralism of the right" (or what can be characterized as the ideology of the "neo-invisible hand," namely, global "free" trade, word-processed finance capitalism with computer chips, or even more negatively, as the "neo-gloved hand," namely, the totalitarian tendencies of the national security state). *Pluralism,* in other words, is a non-theoretical recognition of the status quo of global social reality in the latter decades of the twentieth century. Posing as a "live and let live" diplomatic cordiality, it is, in fact, little more than a literally mindless ideology that fosters the politicization of the religious (via the "pluralism of the left" — for example, secular humanism, liberation theology, feminist ideology, and so forth) and the religionization of the political (via the "pluralism of the right" — for example, the Islamic Revolution in Iran, Sikh extremism in the Punjab, Zionism, American Falwellism, and so forth).[10] Most important of all, pluralism (perhaps unwittingly if taken in its "pure" Panikkarian form as will be shown in the sequel) is a classic case of making a virtue out of necessity. That is to say, by undercutting a common rational framework for serious intellectual reflection, it marginalizes the intellectual life in all of its forms and thereby eliminates any intellectual persuasive basis for changing or transforming the status quo beyond that of the contingencies of the will to power and the privileges of status and wealth in modern social reality. To quote Sartre once again: "One of the most striking characteristics of our time is the fact that history is made without self-awareness."[11] To paraphrase Marx, what I wish to argue is the following: the criticism of pluralism is the beginning of all criticism for our time.

THE TERMS *RELIGION* AND *TRUTH*

Before turning to Panikkar's formulation of the problem of theoretical pluralism, it is important to understand how the two terms *religion* and *truth* will be used in the discussion. In this regard I shall simply follow Panikkar's lead, not in the sense that I completely agree with Panikkar's formulation (although overall I think that his characterizations are quite useful), but rather in the sense of maintaining consistency with Panikkar's account of theoretical pluralism, which I think is correct. Put into good Indian philosophical idiom, I want to be fair and consistent in my statement of the *pūrva-pakṣa* so that my *siddhānta* has the most telling effect.

First, then, the term *religion.* According to Panikkar, *religion* is

the set of symbols, myths and practices people believe gives ultimate meaning to their lives. I stress the believing factor, for religion is never

---

10. For interesting discussions of the processes of "politicization" and "religionization," see Roland Robertson, "Church-State Relations and the World System," in T. Robbins and R. Robertson, eds., *Church-State Relations: Tensions and Transitions* (New Brunswick: Transaction Books, 1987), pp. 39–51.

11. Sartre, op. cit., p. 29.

just an objective set of values. Religion is always personal and necessarily includes the belief of the person.[12]

Panikkar makes clear, furthermore, that he is not interested in all aspects of religion but rather with "the intellectual side of religions":

> In a word, there is a constitutive link between a certain conception of reality, which can be expressed intelligibly, and the religion which espouses it. It should be clear from the very outset that we are dealing with the intellectual side of religions, which is where the problem of pluralism arises. And it is in this respect that we speak of truth in religions. Religious conflict, therefore, is rooted in each religion's primordial apprehensions.[13]

Panikkar also specifies what he means by "primordial apprehension" as follows:

> A basic experience (*Grunderfahrung*) or primordial apprehension of reality refers to that mostly spontaneous and often uncritical human attitude which subsequently expresses itself in a set of more or less organically linked symbols, myths and practices. This basic experience, which does not need to be self-conscious, is at the origin of a particular religion and conditions the ultimate convictions regarding the nature of reality and the meaning of life.[14]

Regarding the notion of *truth,* Panikkar comments as follows:

> Let us understand by *truth* that quality or property of reality which allows things to enter into a *sui generis* relation with the human mind and which finds its main expression in human language. Truth may entail a correspondence between things and our thinking, or it may be a construction of our mind or of a supreme mind. At any rate, truth implies a certain correlation between our faculties of apprehension and what they apprehend. The question of truth is a question of the intellect and for the intellect. The truth of religion is not its symbols, myths and practices but the intellectual content of them, its interpretation. We are concerned here with the interpretations given to basic experiences underlying religions. A *true religion* is an ambiguous phrase. Religions can only be true or false inasmuch as they speak to our mind and our mind reflects upon them. In this sense a true religion has to fulfill these two conditions:
>
> 1. It has to deliver the promised goods to its members; in other words, it needs to be truthful to its own tenets...; it must achieve existential truth, honest consistency.
>
> 2. It has to present a view of reality in which the basic experience is expressed in an intelligible corpus that can sustain intelligent criticism

---

12. Panikkar, "Religious Pluralism," op. cit., pp. 98–99.
13. Ibid., p. 98.
14. Ibid., p. 99.

from the outside without falling into substantial contradictions.... A true
religion must achieve essential truth, authentic coherence.[15]

To summarize, "Religions," according to Panikkar, are "sets of symbols,
myths and practices people believe." "Religions" grow out of "primordial apprehensions" (*Grunderfahrung*), which may or may not be self-conscious. These
apprehensions "condition" "the ultimate convictions" that are generated among
people and come to be expressed "in a set of more or less organically linked
symbols, myths and practices." The question of "truth" is not in the symbols,
myths and practices themselves, however, but rather in the intellectual content
or the intellectual interpretation of the symbols, myths and practices as they are
set forth in an "intelligible corpus," which finds its "main expression in human
language," and can be assessed *internally* in terms of "existential truth, honest
consistency" and *externally* in terms of "essential truth, authentic coherence."

THE PROBLEM OF THEORETICAL PLURALISM

Here again I shall simply follow Panikkar's lead, since, as I have already
suggested, his formulation of the problem of theoretical pluralism is, in my view,
basically correct. First Panikkar makes clear that "religious pluralism" is not the
same as "the plurality of religions."[16]

Pluralism, according to Panikkar, whether linguistic, cultural, philosophical
or religious, is much more than Marty's "mere pluralism," "utter pluralism," or
"civil pluralism," all of which are little more than recognitions of plurality rather
than pluralism.[17] In other contexts, Panikkar puts his point in an even stronger
fashion.[18] He also says that pluralism is not a meta-world view that permits a
plurality of world views.[19]

Panikkar sets forth what does count as pluralism when he says:

We have a situation of pluralism *only when we are confronted with mutually exclusive and respectively contradictory ultimate systems. We cannot,
by definition, logically overcome a pluralistic situation without breaking
the very principle of noncontradiction* and denying our own set of codes:
intellectual, moral, esthetic and so forth. [emphasis added][20]

Panikkar's formulation of the notion of pluralism thus denies any universal
theory of whatever kind. As he himself puts it:

My thesis is clear: a universal theory of whatever kind denies pluralism. Any alleged universal theory is one particular theory, besides many
others, that claims universal validity, thus trespassing the limit of its own

---

15. Ibid., pp. 99–100.
16. Ibid., p. 16.
17. Panikkar, "The Invisible Harmony," op. cit., pp. 124–25.
18. Panikkar, "What Is Comparative Philosophy Comparing?," op. cit., p. 118.
19. Panikkar, "The Invisible Harmony," op. cit., p. 125.
20. Ibid.

legitimacy. Further, no theory can be absolutely universal, because theory, the contemplation of truth, is neither a universal contemplation, nor is (theoretical) "truth" all that there is to Reality.[21]

Panikkar's argument against universal theory of whatever kind is reminiscent of Richard Rorty's formulation. Says Rorty, regarding all those "who have not yet gone postmodern":

These liberals hold on to the Enlightenment notion that there is something called a common human nature, a metaphysical substrate in which things called "rights" are embedded, and that this substrate takes moral precedence over all merely "cultural" super-structures. Preserving this idea produces self-referential paradox as soon as liberals begin to ask themselves whether their belief in such a substrate is itself a cultural bias. Liberals who are both connoisseurs of diversity and Enlightenment rationalists cannot get out of this bind. Their rationalism commits them to making sense of the distinction between rational judgment and cultural bias. Their liberalism forces them to call any *doubts* about human equality a result of such irrational bias. Yet their connoisseurship forces them to realize that most of the globe's inhabitants simply do not believe in human equality, that such a belief is a Western eccentricity. Since they think it would be shockingly ethnocentric to say "So what? We Western liberals do believe in it, and so much the better for us," they are stuck.[22]

This also entails, of course, that Panikkar's own notion of pluralism cannot be a universal theory and that, therefore, truth itself is pluralistic.[23] Moreover, Panikkar argues further, if pluralism entails the denial of universal theory of whatever kind and the denial that truth is one, pluralism likewise must be distinguished from relativism, or put another way, pluralism need not entail relativism, although it does imply perspectivism and relativity.

The pluralism of truth is a much more serious and disturbing hypothesis than the obvious recognition of *perspectivism* and *relativity*. To admit that truth is perspectival should not offer any difficulty, although on that ultimate level the problem emerges as the question of what is the most adequate perspective in order to have the most accurate vision of things. And this obviously cannot be again another perspective without a *regressus ad infinitum.*

The relativity of truth, once it is distinguished from *relativism,* should also not be difficult to accept. Relativism destroys itself when affirming that all is relative and thus also the very affirmation of relativism. Relativity, on the other hand, asserts that any human affirmation, and thus any truth, is relative to its very own parameters and that there can be no absolute truth, for truth is essentially relational. The latter case is the reverse

---

21. Ibid., p. 132.
22. Rorty, "On Ethnocentrism," op. cit., pp. 531–32.
23. Panikkar, "The Invisible Harmony," op. cit., pp. 126, 128.

of the former. Relativism destroys itself if we affirm it. Relativity on the other hand is presupposed in the act of denying it.[24]

Panikkar has succeeded, I think, in constructing a formulation of the notion of pluralism that is conceptually tight, reasonably consistent, properly differentiated from other positions, straightforward in following its own implications and exceedingly provocative. It is the *only* sustained, careful and serious presentation of the notion of pluralism in the contemporary literature of religious studies and philosophy, so far as I am aware, and in this sense we have all learned a great deal as a result of Panikkar's efforts. That I take issue in the sequel with Panikkar's formulation is a measure of my respect for the man and his contributions, or putting the matter somewhat differently, a serious, critical argument deserves an equally serious, critical response.

TOWARD A CRITIQUE OF PLURALISM

It may be helpful, first of all, to locate the pluralist position within the range of possible positions regarding the set of things we call religions. Simply acknowledging that there is such a set of things is not necessarily to be a pluralist. A pluralist, rather, is someone who takes a particular cognitive attitude toward the set along the lines of "more than one but less than all." That is to say, the pluralist position argues that a unified cognitive attitude toward all the members of the set of things we call religions is not warranted or does not do justice to the nature of the truths (more than one) of religions. This entails, of course, that no universal affirmative claims are possible regarding the set as a whole. If I could devise an affirmative claim that pertains to all members of the set of things we call religions that does not exclude or contradict at least one fundamental claim of a member of the set, I could not be a pluralist. Hence, "more than one but less than all." Truth with respect to religions is neither singular (pertaining to one only) nor universal (pertaining to all together or some sort of unanimity). Truth with respect to religions is, rather, plural. The set of things we call religions is to be construed serially, with each member of the set articulating in its context a particular cognitive interpretation of its primordial apprehension that may well be perfectly true in its environment both in terms of internal consistency and external coherence, but may also well be mutually exclusive and contradictory with respect to some (at least one) other member of the set. Moreover, there can be no privileged position, or perhaps better meta-position, outside or above the set that would enable one to assess the mutually exclusive and contradictory claims within the set. If such a meta-position would be claimed, the pluralist would argue that the claimed meta-position, by reason of self-referentiality, is simply one more serial position within the set.

The pluralist position, of course, is only one position among several positions that could be or have been taken toward the set of things we call religions. Three

---

24. Ibid., p. 127.

other obvious positions immediately come to mind; namely, (a) the inclusivist position, (b) the exclusivist position, and (c) the reductionist position.[25]

The inclusivist argues that truth is universal and general, that all members of the set of things we call religions have within them certain aspects of this universal and general truth such that the particularities within any given member of the set that exclude or contradict which is universal and general may be more or less ignored or reinterpreted from the perspective-determining truth. The exclusivist argues that truth is singular and general, that one and only one member of the set of things we call religions represents a correct interpretation and that all other members of the set are, at best, approximations, or at worst, false accounts, of the one singular truth that is nevertheless generally true. The reductionist argues that truth is not really an important issue in dealing with the set of things we call religions, that it is possible and profitable to look at the set of things we call religions as manifestations of social organization, cultural expression or personal identity, leaving aside whether such organizations, expressions or identities are true in some general sense — truth, in other words, has only methodological and/or propositional significance and the so-called truth-claims of the set of things we call religions need to be reduced to their proper frame of reference, which is outside the set.

There are, then, at least four positions that could be and have been taken regarding the truth of the set of things we call religions:

I. The inclusivist position — truth universal and general

II. The exclusivist position — truth singular and general

III. The pluralist position — truth plural and particular

IV. The reductionist position — truth irrelevant

By way of brief exemplification, one would identify, I suppose, Hegel, Whitehead, Śankara, and the great mystics, with the inclusivist position. Orthodox theologians within Christianity, Islam, Judaism, and so forth, would represent for the most part the exclusivist position. Panikkar and probably Richard Rorty would be well-known spokesmen for the pluralist position. Durkheim, Freud, Weber, Berger, Wittgenstein, among others, would be examples of the reductionist position.

Interestingly, given the present analysis of the various positions, many who claim to be pluralists are not really so. What sometimes is construed to be the "privileged pluralism" of a John Macquarrie or a Paul Tillich or many of those involved in "dialogue" between religious traditions is not really pluralism in Panikkar's (or Rorty's sense). These positions for the most part are simply themes and variations on the exclusivist position. Similarly, what might be called the "personalist pluralism" of Wilfred Cantwell Smith as set forth, for example,

---

25. For an interesting discussion of the varying positions regarding questions of religious truth, see Patrick John Mahaffey, "Religious Pluralism and the Question of Truth," unpublished doctoral dissertation in religious studies, University of California, Santa Barbara, 1988.

in his intriguing book *Towards a World Theology,* is not a Panikkarian pluralism.[26] It is simply a reworking of the inclusivist position. Likewise, most phenomenologists of religion, including Eliade, Kristensen, and van der Leeuw, whom one might be tempted to call "descriptive pluralists," are in reality exponents for the most part of the reductionist position with respect to their strict phenomenological work that explicitly brackets the issue of truth.

Having identified and located the pluralist position within the range of possible positions regarding the set of things we call religions, let me now turn to appraising the pluralist position in terms of its propositional truth-claims. I propose to do this using two distinct sets of propositional relations; namely, the set of relations derived from the traditional western framework known as the square of opposition, and second, the set of relations derived from Nāgārjuna's well-known *catuṣkoṭi,* the so-called tetralemma.[27] I am fully aware, of course, that the pluralist position finally rejects both frameworks of relations. I am also fully aware that modern traditions of propositional logic and mathematical logic range far beyond the western square of opposition or Nāgārjuna's *catuṣkoṭi.* The point of the exercise is not to defend the traditional square of opposition or Nāgārjuna's *catuṣkoṭi,* but rather to show how the pluralist position differs from these two frameworks of relations, and why. In what follows I shall also be referring to the so-called three laws of thought; namely, (1) the principle of identity ("If anything is A it is A" or "If any proposition is true it is true"), (2) the principle of contradiction ("Nothing can be both A and not A" or "No proposition can be both true and false"), and (3) the principle of the excluded middle ("Anything must be either A or not A" or "Any proposition must be either true or false").[28] Another perhaps somewhat simpler formulation is as follows:

(1) the principle of identity: "A=A";

(2) the principle of contradiction: "not both A and not-A";

(3) the principle of the excluded middle: "either A or not-A" or "not-not-A implies A."[29]

Yet another variant is the following:

(1) the principle of identity: "A must remain A throughout";

26. Wilfred C. Smith, *Towards a World Theology* (Philadelphia: The Westminster Press, 1981).

27. For useful elementary discussions of the traditional western square of opposition, see M. R. Cohen and E. Nagel, *An Introduction to Logic and Scientific Method* (London: Routledge and Kegan Paul Ltd., 1934), pp. 67ff.; and Irving M. Copi, *Introduction to Logic,* 3rd ed. (New York: The Macmillan Co., 1968), pp. 130–51. With respect to Nāgārjuna's *catuṣkoṭi,* I shall be following three distinct interpretations as follows: R. C. Pandeya, "The Logic of *Catuṣkoṭi* and Indescribability," in J. L. Mehta, ed., *Vedānta and Buddhism* (Varanasi: Centre of Advanced Study in Philosophy, Banaras Hindu University, 1968), pp. 25–36; R. H. Robinson, "Some Logical Aspects of Nāgārjuna's System," *Philosophy East and West,* vol. 6 (1957), pp. 291–308; and Frits Staal, *Exploring Mysticism* (Berkeley: University of California Press, 1975), pp. 33–46.

28. This is Cohen and Nagel's formulation, op. cit., pp. 181–82.

29. This is Staal's formulation, op. cit., p. 38.

(2) the principle of contradiction: "A cannot be both B and not-B at the same time and in the same sense";

(3) the principle of the excluded middle: "A must be either B or not-B."[30]

Prima facie one is tempted to suggest that Panikkar's formulation of the pluralist position is off the propositional map either in terms of the square of opposition or in terms of the *catuṣkoṭi,* and furthermore, that it violates or abuses all three laws of thought. Such, however, is not the case. The Panikkarian pluralist position does make certain propositional claims, and at no point does it violate, in my view, either the principle of identity or the principle of contradiction. Indeed, if it did *not* make propositional claims and if it *did* violate the principle of identity and the principle of contradiction, it would not be a position at all. It would be little more than irrational gibberish. Put another way, the Panikkarian pluralist position presupposes or requires a propositional network and presupposes the principle of identity and the principle of contradiction. The fault of the Panikkarian pluralist position, if "fault" is the correct term, is that it wants to have its cake and eat it too! That is to say, the pluralist position calls into question the principle of the excluded middle. This in itself is not necessarily a fatal flaw in a position. It is quite rational to question the principle of the excluded middle in certain contexts or for certain purposes — hence, my caveat above: "if 'fault' is the correct term." The problem, however, is that if one calls into question the principle of the excluded middle, one then goes beyond a two-valued logic. The meaning of the word *true* then changes. In a three-valued logic, in which the principle of the excluded middle is not accepted, the meaning of the word *true* no longer pertains to assertions. What is true or what is the case in a three-valued logic means "neither true nor false within a two-valued logical frame." This is not the same, it should be noted, as indeterminacy. Truth or falsity may well be, and indeed often are, indeterminate in a two-valued logic. "Neither true nor false" in a three-valued logic means, rather, that truth or falsity in the two-valued logical sense is *in principle* impossible to determine and, hence, meaningless.

But before proceeding further with the problems of a two-valued or three-valued logic, let me first clarify the Panikkarian pluralist position in terms of the square of opposition and the *catuṣkoṭi.* First, the so-called square of opposition (see diagram on page 82).[31]

Now, regarding the set or class of things we call religions, the inclusivist position presumably argues some form of the A claim, *All S is P;* the exclusivist position presumably argues some form of the I claim, *Some (at least and in fact, one) S is P;* the reductionist position presumably argues some form of the E claim, *No S is P.* One might think at first glance that the pluralist would perforce have to argue the O claim, *Some S is not P.* Interestingly, however, this is not Panikkar's claim. The O claim (*Some S is not P),* for example, could

---

30. This is Pandeya's formulation, op. cit., p. 30.
31. I have reproduced the square as found in Copi, op. cit., p. 133.

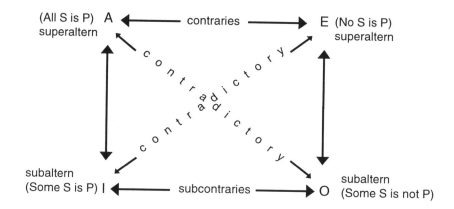

take the form that some of the set of things we call religions, namely, Judaism, Christianity and Islam, to the extent that they accept one or another form of the biblical God, are warranted religious interpretations, whereas some of the set of things we call religions, namely, Hinduism, Buddhism, Jainism, and others, to the extent that they do not accept one or another form of the biblical God are unwarranted religious interpretations. The latter, namely, *Some S is not P,* at least leaves open the possibility that *Some S is P* by reason of the principle that subcontraries cannot both be false, though they might both be true. By the same token, however, *Some S is not P,* also leaves open the possibility that No S is P, namely, the reductionist position. The pluralist will not take this position because, in fact, it is not what the pluralist wants to argue, or put another way, it is not really the pluralist position. The purpose of the pluralist position is not to show simply that *All S is P* is contradictory and that *No S is P* and *Some S is P* are possible but undetermined. The pluralist position is more radical than that. The pluralist position wants to argue that truth itself is plural, that truth means more than one thing. The pluralist position, in other words, must be a form of *Some S is P* (and in that sense parallel with the exclusivist position) but with the remarkable proviso that the singular and yet generally true exclusivist claim is, in fact, plural, that there is more than one exclusivist claim and that these claims may be equally true. Such a position does not violate the principle of identity (any such serial interpretation is what it is); neither does it violate the principle of contradiction (for the claim is *not* that each serial interpretation is what it is "at the same time and in the same sense"). But it does violate the principle of the excluded middle. The pluralist position wants to persuade us that it is *not* the case that "A must be either B or not-B" or that it is *not* the case that "not-not-A implies A." Truth itself is plural. Put another way, there is a kind of truth over and above the conventional two-valued kind, and, of course, it is at that point that it goes beyond the square of opposition and begins to become what Panikkar calls "the dethronement of reason and the abandonment of the monotheistic paradigm" or the abandonment of "the monomorphism of a monolithic reality." Put less dramatically, it simply means the abandonment of a two-valued logic.

Turning now to Nāgārjuna's *catuṣkoṭi,* it must be said at the outset that there is a good deal of controversy regarding the manner in which the so-called tetralemma should be interpreted. For present purposes I shall present briefly the interpretations of Richard H. Robinson, Frits Staal and R. C. Pandeya.[32] It is useful to mention these three by way of showing why there is some controversy surrounding the matter and by way of comparison with the traditional square of opposition already mentioned.

Richard H. Robinson's interpretation has the merit of framing the *catuṣkoṭi* in a manner that quantifies the constituent terms, thereby bringing the *catuṣkoṭi* into line with the traditional western square of opposition. Regarding any matter of interpretation to the extent that one wishes to make a general or universal claim (beyond that of everyday or conventional discourse), there are four and only four possible positions to take, namely

I. All x is A;

II. No x is A;

III. Some x is A *and* some x is not-A;

IV. No x is A *and* no x is not-A.

Nāgārjuna, according to Robinson, rejects each possible position, thereby showing that no proposition is valid in a general, universal or absolute sense. Says Robinson: "No proposition is valid except within a set of validating conditions."[33] By way of comparison with the square of opposition (see the A, E, I and O forms of the traditional square above) Robinson comments as follows:

> Since "No x is not A" equals "All x is A," the fourth lemma is a conjunction of the E and A forms. The third lemma is a conjunction of the I and O forms. The fourth lemma is a conjunction of the contradictories of the conjuncts of the third lemma; "No x is A" is the contradictory of "Some x is A," and "No x is not A" is the contradictory of "Some x is not A." Thus there is a reciprocity between the third and fourth lemmas. Negation of the conjuncts of one always produces the other.
>
> In these formulas, "x" stands for the attributes of the entity in question. According to the commentaries, which lemma is affirmed or denied depends on what set of attributes constitutes one's universe of discourse. In one frame of reference, a given lemma will be affirmed, and in another it will be denied. This is tantamount to saying that no proposition is valid except within a set of validating conditions. Consequently, no proposition is valid in an absolute sense.[34]

---

32. See note 27 above for full citation.
33. Richard H. Robinson, *Early Mādhyamika in India and China* (Madison: University of Wisconsin Press, 1967), p. 57.
34. Ibid.

Frits Staal points out that the problem with Robinson's interpretation is that there is no textual evidence for the quantification of terms in the tetralemma (in terms of "all," "no," and "some") and that, therefore, Robinson's interpretation is unsatisfactory.[35] Staal suggests a simpler rendering, namely,

I. A;

II. not-A;

III. A and not-A;

IV. either A or not-A (or, not-not-A implies A).

In this rendering, lemma I represents identity; lemma II represents difference; lemma III represents the principle of contradiction; and lemma IV represents the principle of the excluded middle. Nāgārjuna, Staal continues, rejects each of the lemmas, and there is nothing irrational in so doing. Says Staal:

> There is nothing irrational in the Mādhyamika rejection of these clauses. In rejecting the third clause, the denial of the principle of noncontradiction is rejected, not the principle of noncontradiction itself. As regards the fourth clause, it is possible and rational to either accept it or to reject it.[36]

Staal also points out an interesting twist regarding the principle of the excluded middle in the fourth clause.

> If we were to accept the fourth clause of the *catuṣkoṭi,* it would be tantamount to denying the validity of the principle of the excluded middle. As we have just seen, that is not irrational. If we reject the fourth clause, as the Mādhyamika philosophers did, we are free to accept the principle of the excluded middle. But we don't have to, since denying the denial of the excluded middle only implies the excluded middle if we accept the principle of double negation, which is itself equivalent to the excluded middle.[37]

Alas, it is possible to have one's cake and eat it too, at least under certain conditions, but more on that in the sequel.

R. C. Pandeya offers yet a third interpretation of the *catuṣkoṭi.*[38] According to Pandeya, the four lemmas are as follows:

I. A;

II. not-A;

III. A and not-A;

---

35. Staal, op. cit., p. 37.
36. Ibid., p. 39.
37. Ibid.
38. Pandeya, op. cit., pp. 25–34.

IV. *either:* not (A and not-A);
   or: not (A or not-A).[39]

In other words, the fourth lemma is *either* a conjunctive denial, thereby affirming the principle of contradiction, *or* a disjunctive negation, thereby denying the principle of the excluded middle. Pandeya argues that since Nāgārjuna has already dealt with the principle of contradiction in his treatment of the third lemma, it is unlikely that he would deal with it again in the fourth lemma. The fourth lemma, in other words, is probably a different proposition from the third. Hence, he prefers to take the fourth lemma as a disjunctive negation, or, in other words, as involving the principle of the excluded middle. But, again, interestingly, we can observe the twist that Staal pointed out above, namely, that in denying the denial of the excluded middle, the excluded middle is itself invoked. Regarding the excluded middle, to quote Staal again, "it is possible and rational to either accept it or to reject it."[40] In any case, Pandeya argues that the Mādhyamikas reject the principle of the excluded middle for the most part, since in their system assertion has no place. The principle of identity and the principle of contradiction, Pandeya suggests, operate in any system of logic. The principle of the excluded middle operates only when assertion is brought into a system. Concludes Pandeya:

> Mādhyamikas do not accept a truth-value logic and consequently there is no place for assertion in their logic. Therefore in their system, if A is not found to be B, then *not necessarily* "A is not-B."[41]

Thus far my critique of the Panikkarian pluralist position has been basically positive. I have been trying simply to exhibit and/or tease out what appears to be the case in maintaining the pluralist position. The only negative implication of the critique up to this point is the somewhat surprising realization that the pluralist position is not really as radical as it claims to be. Far from "dethroning" reason, the pluralist position fully accepts the principle of identity and the principle of contradiction. It calls into question the principle of the excluded middle, to be sure, but that in itself is hardly grounds for claiming that reason is being dethroned. It simply means that in some situations it may be necessary to go beyond a two-valued logic. Moreover, I have tried to show that it is quite possible to "map" the pluralist position either in terms of the western square of opposition or Nāgārjuna's *catuṣkoṭi*. To be sure, the pluralist position is off the map in some sense in both frameworks, but it is quite possible to see what the pluralist position is claiming in either framework.

What, then, is the problem? The problem, I submit, is one of equivocation, and at this point, alas, my critique becomes negative. As mentioned earlier, the Panikkarian pluralist position is a classic case of wanting to have its cake and eat it too, not, unfortunately, it must now be recognized, in the reasonable sense

39. Ibid., p. 33.
40. Staal, op. cit., p. 39.
41. Pandeya, op. cit., p. 30.

of recognizing that there may well be occasions when assertion is no longer warranted, but rather in the seriously flawed sense that one can then proceed to make assertions of pluralistic "truth" regarding the set of things we call religions. On one level, it calls into question a two-valued logic. It is *not* the case given the set of things we call religions that "one" is true and the others false, or that "all" are true in some sense, or that "no" religions are true in some sense, or that "some" are true and "some" are not true in a univocal sense of truth. On another level, however, it *is* the case that truth itself is plural and that we are able to have something like a plurality of exclusive "truths," construed serially. In moving from the former level to the latter level, however, the meaning of the word *true* has radically shifted. On the latter level, the word *true* really means "neither true nor false in the sense of a two-valued logic."

But what is the warrant for continuing to use the word *true* on this latter level, or the word *false* for that matter, since what is being asserted is that in the kind of world in which we live there are some things which cannot adequately be dealt with in terms of a true-false two-valued logic. It is precisely at this point, I submit, that the Panikkarian pluralist position involves an equivocation. It wishes to continue to make assertions, namely, that there is a plurality of exclusive "truths," from the vantage point of three-valued (or a multi-valued) logic in which assertion is no longer warranted. And at this point the equivocation does not simply involve the denial of the principle of the excluded middle, although its methodology up to this point has been indeed based on the denial of the principle of the excluded middle. At this point it falls into contradiction and becomes self-defeating. Why? Since it continues to make assertions. If my position reaches a point at which I can no longer make assertions, I cannot then assert that my position is true. I can only assert that my position is neither true nor false in terms of a two-valued logic. Put another way, I cannot say that "true" equals "neither true nor false" without falling into contradiction, because, in fact, I am then committed to saying that it is true that the set of things we call religions are neither true nor false but that each one severally (or taken serially) is perfectly true in terms of internal consistency and external coherence! They might be "beautiful," "noble," "worth preserving," "entities to be taken seriously," and a host of other things, but they cannot be perfectly "true" if they are neither true nor false!

When once this equivocation is recognized, the Panikkarian pluralist position collapses, and one might well ask if there is another way of framing the pluralist position that does not finally equivocate and fall into contradiction. Two possibilities come to mind, namely, that of Richard Rorty and that of Mādhyamika philosopher Nāgārjuna. Rorty's position, if one can call it a position, is that there is no way of rationally establishing any position. We live in a radically pluralist post-modern world, and the better part of wisdom is to get on with it the best we can, utilizing whatever possible from our historically derived experience and acting compassionately whenever possible. This is, indeed, a pluralist position, but it is hardly a *theoretical* pluralist position, since it argues, to the contrary, that there is no such thing as a theoretical pluralist position. It simply asserts plurality, and thus, is a position, finally, of sheer immediacy. If not completely untutored, it is at best a plea for tutored common sense.

Nāgārjuna's position, I think, offers considerably more, but though superficially close to Panikkar's pluralism, in fact, finally, is a dramatically different animal. It is, I would argue, what I have characterized throughout this paper as a reductionist position. That is to say, given the set of things we call religions, or given sets of whatever things, a true-false two-valued logic has only limited application within contexts of empirically validating conditions. The ultimate *truth-* claims of the set of things we call religions go beyond the empirical validating conditions that would enable us to say that they are either true or false. Hence, the claims put forth by the set of things we call religions are simply *śūnyatā*, not at all in the sense that they are false but, rather, in the sense that they are neither true nor false. They point to a realm or a level which takes us beyond a true-false two-valued logic, a realm or level that one might characterize as a nonrational as opposed to irrational or rational. To drag this realm or level into the true-false, two-valued logic of ordinary life is to fanaticize the rational life and to trivialize the spiritual life. The great merit of this sort of reductionist position is that it is rationally compatible with a post-modern scientific world, while at the same time making clear that the spiritual life has its place as well. Moreover, it provides a useful criterion for determining when religious claims are being improperly employed in our ordinary life-world of conventional social reality.

But let me bring this essay to a conclusion. My title is "Contra Pluralism," not in the sense of denying that we all live in a pluralistic world. Of course, we live in a pluralistic world. Rather, I am denying that truth is pluralistic. I am not a *theoretical* pluralist, nor can any of us be theoretical pluralists, *because there is no such thing as a theoretical pluralist position.* When one clearly sees the equivocation in the Panikkarian pluralist position, the theoretical position itself collapses. *Either* it falls into the sheer immediacy of plurality, thereby irrationally leaving everything as it is, *or* it falls back onto the throne of reason from which it had hoped to escape, thereby rationally having to justify itself. Three-valued or multi-valued logics are indeed possible rationally so long as we remember that we cannot reintroduce them into the two-valued framework in any meaningful sense. There is no *tertium quid* that would allow us to believe anything or everything. The rational life is still worth living, *pace* the pluralists among us.

PART II

Christian Implications

5

The Mystical Basis of Panikkar's Thought

BEVERLY J. LANZETTA

Whether mysticism is seen to refer to union with a transcendent deity or to the underlying ordinariness that is the "thusness" of life, it provides a heritage, consistent across cultures, of oneness. The oneness of reality is the quintessential mystical insight, eloquently expressed through the centuries in diverse cultural and religious settings, and which forms the heart of the interreligious quest. Because there is something in the human person that continues to have faith in an underlying commonality to life, the contemporary scholar is challenged to undertake a new and radical interpretation of the salvific journey in light of the pluralism of seemingly disparate world views. Raimundo Panikkar is one such scholar who has devoted the last thirty years to a systematic and rigorous mystical approach to interreligious dialogue, and who has taken seriously the challenge of investigating the philosophical foundations of the task.

One of Panikkar's most creative contributions to cross-cultural research is his focus on the mutual fecundation or *perichorēsis* that constitutes the inner life of reality. In the world's mystical literatures, a dynamic interrelationship exists between oneness (alternately called "nothingness," openness, desert) and the multiplicity of the world: *samsara* is *nirvāṇa,* theism is desert and desert is theism, *yesh* is *ayin* and *ayin* is *yesh,* form is emptiness and emptiness is form. Unity is the ground of plurality; plurality the existential playground of unity. For Panikkar, this radical dynamism, where Reality is neither "this nor that," permits the very plurality and incommensurability of the world:

> Every being is what it is precisely because it is itself an ensemble of re-
> lationships and enters into intimate, constitutive relationship with other

Beverly J. Lanzetta, Assistant Professor of Religious Studies at Grinnell College, is author of *The Path of the Heart* and the forthcoming book *The Other Side of Nothingness: Towards a Theology of Radical Openness,* as well as articles on mysticism, interreligious thought, and contemporary spirituality.

beings. And this relationship is such that it forms a radical unity that does not render things uniform, but, on the contrary, permits them to be diverse. Unity, then, and not the contrary, is the fundamental fact. This radical unity of relativity is intimate to each thing, and yet at the same time it is transcendent, inasmuch as no thing really exhausts it, nor indeed all things together.[1]

It is this dynamic, mystical perspective on the mutual reciprocity of unity and diversity, that Panikkar sees as constitutive of the building up of reality, and that distinguishes his work in the philosophy of religion. No other scholar, to my knowledge, has so systematically and creatively set about articulating the hermeneutical challenges that a mystical, and global, view of reality demands.

THE PERENNIAL PHILOSOPHY AND COSMOTHEANDRISM

In some respects Panikkar's thought has antecedents in the perennial philosophy which embraces the multiplicity of mystical expressions as evidence for a cross-cultural "common core" or "oneness." Thus, while each tradition is accorded its own unique manifestation, the perennialist philosophers hold that underlying all religious forms is a primordial tradition which is universal and immemorial. Aldous Huxley, in his book, *The Perennial Philosophy,* wrote:

A version of this Highest Common Factor in all preceding and subsequent theologies was first committed to writing more than twenty-five centuries ago, and since that time the inexhaustible theme has been treated again and again, from the standpoint of every religious tradition and in all the principal languages of Asia and Europe.[2]

Panikkar's perspective, however, differs from that of the perennialists in one significant respect: he views the multiple manifestation of religious expressions as *constitutive* of Reality and hence *internal* to the interreligious task, and *not* as relative stages along the way to an overarching Tradition or Oneness. Because this distinction is vital to understanding the center around which Panikkar's scholarship revolves, the following section will explore in more depth some of the main philosophical principles of the perennial philosophy.

The two intertwining themes of the perennial philosophy are "tradition" and *"scientia sacra."* With respect to tradition, perennialists like Seyyed Hossein Nasr envisage the term to be a comprehensive one which encompasses the entire range of divine-human relations formalized by a particular religion.[3] The traditionalist school proposes that religion can be studied only from the depths of the esoteric dimension which informs it. Further, the traditionalist school contends

---

1. Raimundo Panikkar, *The Silence of God: The Answer of the Buddha,* trans. Robert R. Barr (Maryknoll, N.Y.: Orbis Books, 1989), p. 140.

2. Aldous Huxley, *The Perennial Philosophy* (New York: Harper and Brothers, 1945), p. vii.

3. See Frithjof Schuon's development of the perennial philosophy in *The Transcendent Unity of Religions* (New York: Harper & Row, 1975); and Seyyed Hossein Nasr, ed., *The Essential Writings of Frithjof Schuon* (Amity, N.Y.: Amity House, 1986), especially pp. 1–136.

that any form, concept, archetype, revelation, or manifestation, even a divine manifestation, is the "relative Absolute." The Absolute, by definition, is that which exists prior to any distinction; it is the unknown, primal source:

> Tradition . . . places absoluteness at the level of the Absolute, asserting categorically that only the Absolute is absolute . . . every determination of the Absolute is already in the realm of relativity. The unity of religions is to be found first and foremost in this Absolute which is at once Truth and Reality and the origin of all revelations and all truth.[4]

Behind the diversity of traditions exists a Primordial Tradition "which constituted original or archetypal man's primal spiritual and intellectual heritage received through direct revelation when Heaven and earth were still 'united.' "[5] Each subsequent tradition embodies a new vertical revelation from the Primordial Origin, and therefore contains within itself a comprehensive spiritual originality.

The basic premise of the perennial philosophy is that reality is essentially divided into two horizontal realms — essence and existence or esoteric and exoteric. At the level of essence, or what Frithjof Schuon calls "transcendent unity," all religions are included in an existential Unity that is absolute and undifferentiated.[6] At the level of existence, religions are diverse and multiform. The esoteric/exoteric distinction rests on the belief that humans live in a world of symbolic forms which are representative of, but never fully identified with, the transcendent to which they attest. Thus all religious figures, Buddha, Mohammed, or Jesus Christ, represent the "relatively absolute." It is only in the supreme Essence, in the domain of the esoteric, that the transcendent unity of religions is said to take place.

While tradition forms the backbone, *scientia sacra* is the heart of the perennial philosophy. In light of all the great mystical writings Nasr, for one, writes of *scientia sacra* as a pure metaphysics accessible to the mind through an illumination of an immediate nature. As an illuminating, sanctifying knowledge, *scientia sacra* is knowledge at the level of its archetype or principle which is essential to "penetrate into foreign universes of form and bring out their inner meaning."[7] Nasr asserts that the perennial philosophy reveals that Religion is of divine origin, and exists in its archetypal splendor separate from the vicissitudes of human existence. Further, as Ultimate Reality, it is beyond all determination and gives rise to a hierarchical universe composed of multiple levels of existence and states of consciousness, similar to the Neoplatonic world of descending order. Thus metaphysics is concerned not only with the relatively absolute, but also distinguishes between "grades of existence."[8] It is precisely in discerning this

4. Seyyed Hossein Nasr, *Knowledge and the Sacred* (New York: Crossroad, 1981), pp. 292–93.

5. Seyyed Hossein Nasr, "The *Philosophia Perennis* and the Study of Religion," in *The World's Religious Traditions,* ed. Frank Whaling (New York: Crossroad, 1986), p. 186.

6. See Frithjof Schuon, *The Transcendent Unity of Religions.*

7. Nasr, *Knowledge and the Sacred,* p. 291.

8. Ibid., p. 138.

hierarchical universe that the diversity of religious forms can be understood. The intrinsic, esoteric unity of religions is mystically apparent as knowledge ascends to its archetype. Thus, according to this view, the convergence of religions rests on an epistemological principle: the capacity for sacred knowing.

Panikkar's philosophical position, which at first glance appears related to that of the perennial philosophy, is built on a wholly different theological foundation. The trinitarian basis of Panikkar's thought prescinds from distinguishing between the relative and absolute Absolute. There exists a mutually fecundating relationship between the manifest and unmanifest dimensions of reality. This relationship is neither one nor two, but the complementarity of mutually affirming coincidences. Thus, the various religious manifestations, whether personal, archetypal, or revelatory, are not relative to an Absolute Oneness, but integral to its unfolding. Further, in the perennial philosophy, although the diversity of religions is celebrated within its own context, each religion is capable of retaining its own isolationist strand, in which the other, *as* other, is not truly needed, for it is only in the Absolute that reality can be said to occur.[9]

It is at this juncture that the clearest distinction can be made between Panikkar's work and that of the perennialists. While both speak of a spiritual oneness that occurs beyond distinctions, the perennial philosophy holds that unity is an esoteric pre-existent realm from which all religions have descended and to which they will return. Thus, the richness of diverse spiritual universes and revelatory expressions is important within their respective lineage, but spiritual illumination rather than mutual interpenetration is the necessary medium for the esoteric "return." Panikkar, on the other hand, understands the meeting of religions to take place through the *transformation* into spirit. This transformation is dynamic, communal, and historical. Dialogue, mutual understanding, and cross-fertilization among the mystical universes of each tradition are essential for transformation, since in his cosmotheandric project they are constitutive of the building up of reality. The process of dialogue, of understanding, of crossing over into the sacred realms of another tradition is the medium of transformation which draws the divine-cosmic-human encounter toward the cosmotheandric goal. It is from this perspective that Panikkar undertakes to carve out a new epistemology and an advaitic methodology in the context of intrareligious dialogue (a dialogue that occurs ontically within one's own being, but which needs access to the interreligious issue to do so).

THEANDRISM, PLURALISM, AND DIALOGUE

The remainder of this chapter will focus on three distinctive features of Panikkar's proposal for dialogue and understanding among religions. These can be summarized as theandrism, pluralism, and dialogical dialogue.

---

9. See Charles Wei-Hsun Fu, "A Taoist/Zen Response," in *Toward a Universal Theology of Religion,* ed. Leonard Swidler (Maryknoll, N.Y.: Orbis Books, 1987), pp. 157–58; Thomas Dean, "Universal Theology and Dialogical Dialogue," in *Toward a Universal Theology of Religion,* p. 172.

Theandrism

The mystery of the Trinity in classical Christian thought revolves around the three Persons in one God. The subject of lengthy debate and painstaking clarification, the early Fathers labored to articulate an understanding of the inner trinitarian life that neither suffered the error of tritheism, in which the three Persons were seen as three Beings, and hence three gods; nor marginalized the activities of the Persons to mere manifestations of the one God, in the case of modalism. In both instances, the profound subtlety of the intra-trinitarian *perichorēsis* (Latin, *circumincessio*) was in danger of being lost through substantialist thinking.[10] Thus, early trinitarian thought can be understood as a brilliant and successful attempt to preserve the mystery of the Three in One, or unity in diversity, that alone captures the absolute relativity and self-emptying of the divine. Further, the co-inherence of the three Persons, physically manifest in Jesus Christ as both fully human and fully divine, was expanded during the Patristic Period to embrace the whole of the divine-human encounter.

Drawing on the Greek, Bonaventurian notion of the Trinity, Panikkar places the world's religious traditions *interior* to the Godhead and depicts them as pluralistic self-revelations of divinity. His approach is mystical and is rooted in the intra-divine dynamism, the inner life of the Trinity. The trinitarian life is one of pluralism in oneness, or distinction in unity, that is constantly replenishing itself. The intra-divine self-emptying of the three Persons of the Trinity has an *ad extra* expression in the *perichorēsis* of the world. It is because of this absolute self-communication that the mystery of the Trinity is revealed as both simultaneously one and distinct. The activities of the three Persons are inseparable from the abyss of the Father from which they emerge and to which they return. Thus, according to Panikkar:

> God's radical relativity *ad extra* is a mirror image of the same radicality *ad intra:* that is to say, the whole universe, as image or "vestige" of the Trinity, is endowed with the character of radical relativity. Things "are" in the measure that they cease to be in order to give themselves to other things. Things are but reciprocal constitutive relationships.[11]

Because for Panikkar Christ and the Trinity are intimately interrelated, the mystery of cosmotheandrism is itself inseparable from the incarnation. He writes, "Within the Christian tradition this Christ is incomprehensible without the Trinity. A non-Trinitarian Christ cannot be totally human and totally divine."[12] It is only in Christ, as the *persona media* of the trinitarian processions, that we find the metaphysical principle which draws together the One and the

---

10. "Coinherence (Latin: *circumincessio:* Greek: *perichorēsis*) is the doctrine denoting the mutual indwelling or interpenetration of the three Persons of the Trinity whereby one is as invariably in the other two" and in such a way that the absolutes do not relativize one another (Alan Richardson and John Bowden, eds., *The Westminster Dictionary of Christian Theology* [Philadelphia: The Westminster Press, 1983], p. 112).

11. Panikkar, *The Silence of God*, p. 142.

12. Raimundo Panikkar, *The Unknown Christ of Hinduism* (Maryknoll, N.Y.: Orbis Books, 1981), p. 28.

Many in a fully theandric act. Panikkar holds that all religions are in movement toward the Mystery, whether that mystery is termed *nirvāṇa* or Christ. Humans yearn toward that which they are not yet, toward the ground of their being. Therefore men and women, as *anthropos,* are directed toward the same goal. This goal may have many names, and these names may appear divergent, even antithetical. But in fact all names are mutually fecundating realities leading toward the supername and theandric "thing," Christ. In Panikkar's view, Christ is the cosmotheandric principle and mediator in which all aspects of reality — human, divine, cosmic — coincide. As such, Christ is the theandric center of a dynamic procession and reciprocity at the heart of reality, both in its transcendent and immanent dimensions. Further, precisely because Christ is the second Person of the Trinity, he *is,* both in a divine and human capacity, fullness *and* emptiness. At the heart of reality, therefore, rests a sacred interrelatedness revealed in Christianity through the Trinity, and seen by Panikkar to be the fundamental cosmological, ontological, and epistemological principle.

It is from this twin trinitarian and christological focus that Raimon Panikkar begins to fashion his unique contribution to interreligious dialogue: the cosmotheandric principle. To Panikkar, the cosmos reflects the interrelatedness at the heart of the Trinity and thus draws all of creation into a oneness of distinctions which, like the relationship of the three Persons in the one God, cannot be said to be either "one" or "two." This intimate and inseparable relationship between God and Man is, for Panikkar, the *theandric* aspect of reality.

Taken from the early writings of Maximus the Confessor, the term " 'Theandric' designates the entirely unique and new relationship that is established in Jesus Christ as being both fully human and fully divine: God and man as cooperating for the benefit of the whole of creation, not separated and yet not mixed, not confused and yet in full harmony."[13] *Theandric,* for Panikkar, thus captures the essential dignity necessary to be human and embody the profound mystery of God in a way which neither maintains their distinction nor posits their eternal oneness, but which is neither one nor two. It is a term which avoids the extremes of both the personalist and transcendent views of God and which allows one to enter into the dimension of mutually affirming relation that is the heart of the mystery and the mysticism of the trinitarian life.

Ontological *perichorēsis* underlies Panikkar's belief in the inherent pluralism of reality which is, at the same time, one. The very nature of reality is plural, theandric, incommensurate, and in movement toward the self-emptying that alone is the measure of being. Because of Panikkar's seminal insight into a theandric ontology, knowledge must also be conceived as nondualistic and dialogic. In other words, the very epistemological foundation upon which religions have legitimated their own exclusiveness is no longer viable in a cross-cultural context. Knowledge itself must be dialogic and open to the "other" as a *necessary* means of ascertaining "truth." Truth itself is dialogic and plural.

---

13. Lars Thunberg, *Man and Cosmos* (Crestwood, N.Y.: St. Vladimir's Press, 1985), p. 71.

Pluralism

This cosmotheandric relationship takes new shape in Panikkar's theology as *pluralism*. It is pluralism which begins to fulfill Panikkar's belief that "for a truly cross-cultural religious understanding we need a new revelatory experience."[14] Pluralism becomes the expression best suited to convey the profound mutual interdependence and mutual distinction inherent to the mystery of the Trinity. Pluralism is not just a goal to reach or the mere searching for common ground, but the fundamental nature of things.[15] Panikkar clarifies that in using the term *pluralism* he is not referring to plurality, which implies difference; or pluriformity, in the sense of variety; or to diversity, which connotes an unattainable harmony. Instead, he sees *pluralism* as "an awareness leading to a *positive* acceptance of *diversity* — an acceptance which neither forces the different attitudes into an artificial unity, nor alienates them by reductionistic manipulations."[16]

Panikkar's sense that pluralism is at the root of reality precludes any attempt at a universalism of religions, if by that is meant an attempt to reach a global intellectual understanding based on the development of a common language.[17] In fact, for Panikkar, "the truth of religion can be gauged only within the unifying myth that makes self-understanding possible. If we want to cross boundaries, we will have to share in some common truths brought forth in the common endeavor."[18] Panikkar sees the attempt toward universalization to be the particular malaise, and at times the particular genius, of the Western intellectual heritage. The "project" of universalization, according to Panikkar, is rooted in the *logos* — *logos* as reason, as rationalism, even as understanding. Yet the quest for understanding, for discovering the "law" of each thing, for figuring out, in the end is a disguised form of power in which the intellect must reign supreme. Life shows us, Panikkar believes, its pluralistic nature; some problems are never answerable, others are incommensurate with the evidence, and further, we are confronted with "mutually exclusive and respectively contradictory ultimate systems."[19] In the midst of the tangible fact, attempts toward a universal theory, language, or system are not only reductionist but potentially dangerous. Dangerous because such systems invite a logic which defies the possibility for compassion, acceptance, sympathy, and suffering *without* understanding: we do not need to *know*, to *love*. Further, Panikkar questions the validity of a *logos* without its spirit, and without the silence and abyss of the Father:

---

14. Raimundo Panikkar, "Some Words instead of a Response," *Cross Currents* 29 (1979), p. 195.

15. Raimundo Panikkar, "The Myth of Pluralism: The Tower of Babel — A Meditation on Non-Violence," *Cross Currents* 29 (Summer 1979), p. 201.

16. Ibid., p. 208. For Panikkar's more recent discussion of pluralism, see "The Invisible Harmony: A Universal Theory of Religion or a Cosmic Confidence in Reality?" in Swidler, *Toward a Universal Theology of Religion,* pp. 124–32.

17. Panikkar, "The Invisible Harmony: A Universal Theory of Religion or a Cosmic Confidence in Reality?," p. 119.

18. Ibid., p. 129.

19. Ibid., p. 125.

Truth itself is pluralistic, and thus not one — nor many, for that matter. Pluralism is not plurality. To affirm that truth itself is pluralistic amounts to averring that there is no one all-encompassing or absolute truth.[20]

For Panikkar, what is required is a "new innocence," in which the silence, the joy, the unspoken, and the unthought can push their shoots up, breaking apart the hardened soil of human constructs. Remedy for this ultimate foundationlessness is found in a fundamental religious attitude, what Panikkar feels can best be described as a "basic trust in reality":

> Having discovered the precariousness of the individual . . . having discovered in the entire explanation of ourselves and of the universe at least one weak spot that makes the whole thing foundationless, we may as well make a jump, a *metanoia,* a conversion, and discover that, in spite of our efforts, we were all the time assuming an unconscious trust in reality, a confidence perhaps in life, certainly in "that" which makes the entire human enterprise an adventure, either with sense or meaningless.[21]

It is apparent from his notions of pluralism that Panikkar has shifted his position somewhat since his first confession of interreligious faith. If there is no absolute truth, how does Panikkar reconcile his earlier positions concerning Christ and the convergence of religions in light of the pluralistic nature of Reality? In a recent work, Panikkar refines his understanding of Christ and contends:

> that the christic principle is neither a particular event nor a universal religion. What is it then? It is the center of reality as seen by the Christian tradition. But this vision is only the Christian vision, not an absolutely universal one. It is the *christic* universal vision.[22]

In relation to dialogue, Panikkar believes that neither the claim that universality is inherent in Christianity, nor the negation of this claim are viable options in a pluralistic world. Rather, he proposes that religions will meet only in their transformation into Spirit; they do not meet in their forms or in their concern for salvation. "But 'they' do meet: they meet in the skies — that is, in heaven."[23] Imaging the various religions as separate rivers, Panikkar says we can attempt to solve the dilemma:

> The rivers do not meet, not even as water. "They" meet in the form of clouds, once they have suffered a transformation into vapor, which eventually will pour down again into the valleys of mortals to feed the rivers

20. Ibid., p. 128.

21. Ibid., p. 138. For another treatment of Panikkar's thought on the "new innocence" see "The New Innocence," *Cross Currents* (Spring 1977), pp. 7–15.

22. Raimundo Panikkar, "The Jordan, The Tiber, and the Ganges: Three Kairological Moments of Christic Self-Consciousness," in *The Myth of Christian Uniqueness,* ed. John Hick and Paul Knitter (Maryknoll, N.Y.: Orbis Books, 1987), p. 92.

23. Ibid.

of the earth. Religions do not coalesce, certainly not as organized religions. They meet once transformed into vapor, once metamorphosized into Spirit, which then is poured down in innumerable tongues. The rivers are fed by descending clouds, and also by terrestrial and subterranean sources, after another transformation, that of snow and ice into water. The true reservoir of religions lies not only in the doctrinal waters of theology; it lies also in the transcendent vapor (revelation) of the divine clouds, and in the immanent ice and snow (inspiration) from the glaciers and snow-laden mountains of the saints.[24]

Dialogical Dialogue

Panikkar's pluralistic universe requires a new methodology based on a vision of reality that is "incommensurable with either unity or plurality."[25] Panikkar has been the most consistent and prolific contributor toward the development of new methods and epistemologies for cross-cultural study. Throughout his lengthy career, Panikkar has been concerned with the One-and-Many problem which has plagued humankind since the inception of critical thought. This question has become telescoped in his recent works into a serious confrontation with the whole tenor of monotheism and the subject-object directive which underlies Western notions of reality. As a corollary, he takes issue with the philosophical response which has resulted in either monistic or dualistic answers to the same fundamental question.

Panikkar grounds his critique of humanity's religious thought in an advaitic or nondualistic approach. Applying a radical nondualism to every human endeavor, Panikkar seeks to redefine theology, epistemology, sociology, anthropology, and philosophy. His thought radiates out from a central focus on God as One and a corresponding cosmotheandrism.[26] Panikkar believes that the monotheistic view of reality arises from an untenable, and even potentially destructive, I-consciousness which then divides the world into I-It encounters or subject-object dichotomies. The objective world of *it* and the subjective world of *I* are merely two poles of a deeper *thou.*[27]

The non-dualistic understanding of reality shatters the whole Western metaphysical and ontological structure *insofar as* it is premised on God as transcendent Other, discerned through a structure of consciousness (I-It consciousness) which, by its very presuppositions, is too restrictive to perceive that Ultimate Reality to which it is drawn. Because of this fundamentally distorted view of reality, Panikkar understands the need for a new method capable of incorporating the "consciousness of other people about themselves and the world as well."[28] He calls this new method the *dialogical dialogue.* The dialogical dia-

---

24. Ibid.
25. Ibid., p. 109.
26. Raimundo Panikkar, "The Dialogical Dialogue," in Whaling, *The World's Religious Traditions,* p. 202.
27. Ibid., p. 204.
28. Ibid.

logue abandons the notion that reality is ultimately dialectical and therefore must be subordinated to the mind.

Dialogue is intensely communal, relying as it does on the witness and testimony of the dialogic partner. It is the shared participation in the discernment of deeper truths, and a shared breakthrough into the structures of reality to discern that which transcends them. The dialogic dialogue involves a mutual relationship of understanding between partners, and a willingness both to appreciate the values of the other and to alter any prior misconceptions. To pierce the layer of reason which surrounds encounters between traditions and individuals, partners in dialogue must be willing to enter into the sacred dimensions of other traditions and return with new insight and understanding.

Panikkar asserts that the dialogical dialogue is essential in personal, cross-cultural, or pluralistic situations which are not reducible to the *logos* and where one must go "through the logos...beyond the logos-structure of reality."[29] While the dialectical dialogue has a proper and important place in human life, and is necessary for the discernment and critical judgment which takes place in all human exchange, it is not sufficient when aimed at a dialogue of subjects. Further, Panikkar grounds the dialogical dialogue in the very roots of reality, insisting on a "radical dynamism" as the only proper basis for a new understanding as "reality is not given once and for all, but is real precisely in the fact that it is continually creating itself — not just unfolding from already existing premises or starting points."[30]

The issue which Panikkar is pursuing hinges on another critical assumption, not spelled out with the same forthrightness as his notion of advaita. It is what Gandhi called *ahimsa,* nonviolence. Nonviolence speaks to the heart of the interreligious encounter and to the dialogical dialogue which gives it structure and focus. Traditional dialectics, as developed in Western culture and thought, rewards power and serves as an instrument of power, even as a "will to power."[31]

Three practical applications of the dialogical dialogue as a method have emerged in Panikkar's works. These are his hermeneutics of dialogue, the notion of homology, and "Understanding as Convincement." Panikkar believes "there is no hermeneutics without tradition," but that there is tradition without hermeneutics, what he calls "authentic tradition."[32] The spirit behind this sentiment arises from an understanding that religion is both orthodoxy and orthopraxis, that God is not interpreted but *received.*[33]

According to Panikkar, the task of hermeneutics is to penetrate beyond the rational forms, beyond pure interpretation to a "total assimilation of the message of salvation" within a tradition.[34] Such an assimilation requires the totality

---

29. Panikkar, "The Dialogical Dialogue," pp. 207, 218.
30. Ibid., p. 211.
31. Ibid., p. 210.
32. Panikkar, "The Hermeneutics of Hermeneutics," *Philosophy Today* (Fall 1967), pp. 166, 168.
33. Ibid., p. 178.
34. Ibid., pp. 168–70.

of tradition, the *logos* as well as kerygma, the depths of a tradition's spiritual universes, and a sensitivity to the unspoken, untransmittable essence of faith. While Panikkar is cautious about making any definitive statements about the role of mysticism, the contention of this essay is that the thrust of his work points toward the need for an interreligious mystical hermeneutic.[35]

Panikkar elaborates on a hermeneutics of dialogue and proposes two principles which he feels are necessary for a proper hermeneutical method. To be truly interreligious, hermeneutics has to retain a complementary relationship between the "principle of homogeneity" and the "dialogic principle."[36] Traditional theological study invokes the former principle, which is based on the assumption that a religious truth can be understood only from within its own context. The dimensions of this context — cultural, historical, philosophical — all contribute to the proper understanding from within.

Although Panikkar himself believes that an understanding of homology precludes the development of a universal theology of religion, there is actually a complementarity between the two ideas. If homology is understood to involve the discernment of a common role in traditions which is represented by diverse concepts, categories, terms, and images, then it can become the basis for the building of a common spiritual language. While Panikkar asserts that this commonality cannot be imposed from without, he also affirms that it has the potential to be born from within. Panikkar even seems to confirm this when he says:

> If Christians are able to extricate from their own religion the christic principle, this principle can be experienced as a dimension at least potentially present in any human being, as long as no absolute interpretation is given. This could equally be said of a similar principle in other traditions (Buddhahood for instance).[37]

The dialogical dialogue, therefore, is primarily concerned with the underlying viewpoints from which diverse opinions arise. It is concerned with the multiple angles on reality, the pluralistic paradigms, if you will, from which a person embedded in a whole spiritual-cultural matrix approaches life. To deal with perspectives rather than details requires a new epistemology and a new understanding of the "knowing subject." Because the dialogical dialogue deals with the whole subject, any knowledge of the subject necessitates a "connaturality and identification" with the subject, since "we cannot understand a person's ultimate convictions unless we *somehow* share them." This attempt toward a

---

35. Panikkar writes, "It is with hesitation that I use the phrase 'mystical experiences,'" ("The Jordan, the Tiber, and the Ganges," p. 113).

36. Panikkar, *The Intrareligious Dialogue* (New York: Paulist Press, 1978), pp. 31–32.

37. Panikkar, "The Jordan, the Tiber, and the Ganges," p. 112. Thomas Dean also holds that Panikkar's notion of dialogue does not rule out, and is even complementary to, the idea of a universal theology (see "Universal Theology *and* Dialogical Dialogue," in Swidler, *Toward a Universal Theology of Religion,* pp. 162–74).

penetration into the sacred universes of another Panikkar calls the "principle of Understanding as Convincement."[38]

A REAPPRAISAL OF THE COSMOTHEANDRIC PROJECT

Despite the volume of Panikkar's contribution to the interreligious situation, responses, critiques, and dialogue with his position have been minimal until recently.[39] At this point I would like to point out certain underlying tensions in Panikkar's thought which may contribute to a lack of clarity in his position. Panikkar, for various reasons, does not feel fully at home in the Western mentality because he believes it reduces the ultimate ontological self-opaqueness of Being to metaphysical certainty and a search for absolute truths. As a corrective to what he perceives to be the oppressive effects of Western rationalism Panikkar proposes an anthropological and theological pluralism based on the advaitic (or nondualistic) tradition in Hinduism. In doing so, however, Panikkar runs two risks: (a) interpreting Christian experiences from within a nondualistic perspective without fully taking into account the historical, metaphysical, and ontological claims of Christianity; and (b) proposing a ground for dialogue on the basis of a cosmic Christian perspective which, among other things, is a difficult position from which to build an interreligious theology.

Another tension in Panikkar's thought revolves around the universalist-pluralist pole. On the one hand, Panikkar insists on pluralism as the ultimate truth about reality; yet he tries to create a universal paradigm for human religious life in the cosmic Christ. On the side of pluralism, Panikkar has proposed multiple ways of conceptualizing religious diversity and has consistently worked toward developing a cross-cultural hermeneutics.[40] The question now is how do religions concretely go about understanding pluralism, and what guidelines can be followed to move to the next step? In regard to a universal theology, Panikkar's position here seems contradictory. First, on what grounds does he distinguish his notion of cosmotheandrism from attempts by other scholars at constructing a universal theology? Second, his critique of Western rationalism and onto-theology seems to ignore his own dialogic ground rules. That is, dialogue works and is operable at all levels. If this is the case, and given his deep grounding in the Greek and Bonaventurian understanding of the Trinity, cosmotheandrism should be sensitive to the dialogic nature of *logos* and its ability also to be open to the other, as it participates in the "profound dialectic of con-

---

38. Panikkar, "Dialogical Dialogue," p. 215.

39. But see Kana Mitra, *Catholicism-Hinduism: Vedāntic Investigation of Raimundo Panikkar's Attempt at Bridge Building* (New York: University of America Press, 1987); Wei-Hsun Fu, "A Universal Theory or a Cosmic Confidence in Reality? A Taoist/Zen Response," pp. 154–61; Dean, "Universal Theology and Dialogical Dialogue," pp. 162–74; Bibhuti S. Yadav, "Anthropomorphism and Cosmic Confidence," in Swidler, *Toward a Universal Theology of Religion,* pp. 175–91. *Cross Currents* (Summer 1979) devoted a whole issue to a symposium on Panikkar's writings, with responses and critiques; also consult Ewert H. Cousins, "The Trinity and World Religions," *Journal of Ecumenical Studies* (1970), pp. 476–98.

40. See Panikkar, *The Intrareligious Dialogue.*

cealment and disclosure."[41] However, if he is saying something still more radical about *logos,* that is, even the most dialogic *logos* — *ultimate* dialogic *logos* — cannot exhaust all the opaqueness of Being (and I believe he is), then the next step is to develop some sort of mystical hermeneutic to clarify his position. This he has not yet done.

While Panikkar's work has been so highly creative and forward looking, it is a bit of a shock to encounter certain exclusive Christian elements. Panikkar in recent years has responded to criticisms of Christian imperialism by clarifying his position in terms of a *christic principle,* which he sees as no longer the exclusive property of Christianity. In any event, it is precisely on the issue of Christ or any other configuration of a cosmic christocentrism as the goal of all genuine religious quests that I must take issue with his position. It is in the silences, which he so eloquently expresses in his writings, that Panikkar's work comes to fruition and flourishes. And yet it is precisely on the move toward theistic Silence that Panikkar's cosmotheandric projects seems, in my eyes, to reveal the most tension.

The question I want to raise is the following. If Panikkar adheres to a radical relativity, and hence pluralism, how then does he retain Christ as the cosmotheandric goal and supername? To counter with the proposal that he is not speaking of Christ in solely Christian terms, but rather as that "principle" toward which all spiritualities yearn, does not speak to the *name* itself. Why, in the plurality and incommensurability of plural truth-claims, is the principle and "name above every name" Christ? Further, is not Panikkar's view of the human spiritual journey in trinitarian terms itself an attempt to onto-theologize diverse religious universes? Since Panikkar sees the radical relativity of the Trinity as related to codependent origination and finally to the silence of the Buddha,[42] it is difficult to understand how he reconciles radical relativity and ontic apophatism with Christ. This is a question that he has yet to answer. If, in trinitarian terms, the radical relativity, which *is* the unity (and here we are squarely in the realm of Christian orthodoxy), occurs only through the self-emptying of name (or death on the cross), how can Christ still be used as *the name?*

For Panikkar, Christ is the metaphysical principle where all spiritualities meet because he satisfies in classical Christian mysticism the role of *persona media.* Christ is the principle of unity and diversity; he embodies the transcendent-immanent dynamic precisely because he is trinitarian. In Panikkar's cosmotheandric understanding Christ *is* the goal of the transcendent-immanent mystery, for he is the only principle which satisfies the radical

---

41. Dean, "Universal Theology *and* Dialogic Dialogue," p. 171. Dean writes on this same page, "By admitting opacity into Being and Truth but not into Reason or *Logos,* Panikkar is perhaps unwittingly *perpetuating,* rather than truly *rethinking,* the very same concept of *logos* or reason that he accuses the partisans of universal theology of employing. A more radical critique, and one more consistent with his own epistemological and ontological premises, would be one that sees the *logos* or reason as also fully participating in the dialectics of openness and opacity that characterize Being and Truth."

42. See Panikkar, *The Silence of God.*

relativity intrinsic to unity in diversity. Yet what is overlooked in this analysis is the mystical articulation of a more prior relationship: one that occurs not between the immanent and economic Trinity, but between the indeterminate and determinate divinity. That is, not only is there a principle (Christ) that occurs between the revealed Trinity and the manifestation (Jesus) of that revealed Trinity in the world, but another principle (nothingness, abyss, silence) is operative between the Trinity and its hidden abyss — the never to be named. Here the Trinity itself sheds identity to return to its prior ground of indistinction and oneness, from which it has never been separate, and which is the *source* of its unity-in-diversity. As Meister Eckhart says, "Distinction comes from Absolute Unity, that is, the distinction in the Trinity. Absolute Unity is the distinction and distinction is the Unity."[43] The determinate divinity, or Trinity, reveals the radical relativity *ad-intra* and its relationship to radical relativity *ad-extra*. However, in both cases identity is still preserved, even if it is a "unity-in-diversity" identity. The Trinity-Unity dynamic, however, refers to a qualitative difference that is neither of the two — it is where *God* sheds identity to return to the indistinct abyss or nothingness.

> God Himself will never look into it [the indistinct ground] and never has looked into it, insofar as He exists in the mode and "property" of His Persons. . . . If God should ever look into it, it would cost Him all His divine names and His personal property. He must leave these out altogether if He wishes to look in.[44]

By focusing on the mysticism of the inner trinitarian life, without reference to the abyssal silence, Panikkar proposes solutions that in the end lead to the same anthropocentric orientation: some notion of reality in relation to "us." Yet, the very pluralism of the interreligious quest shatters the notion that there exists a self-understood, globally coherent self to which all humans share allegiance. What is this self, projected as an "us," against whom all religious claims are measured? If "distinction is indistinction," then where is the God that can be singled out as fulfilling the necessity of a self-emptying so complete as to lack a name? In the context of this perspective, I am inclined to say that no identity is sufficient, and therefore, that all names must be shed to enter the most indistinct of indistinctions, to be both plural and one, and neither plural nor one.

Despite these and other perceived tensions in his thought, Panikkar's efforts toward solving the interreligious dilemma have been striking, consistent, and intense. His proposals suffer the inconsistencies and contradictions which beset any speculative, pioneering study. At the same time, his willingness to enter into the sacred realms of Christianity and discover what he calls the "unknown Christ" of Hinduism, or the triadic dimensions of reality, or a "christic

---

43. Meister Eckhart, *Deutsche Werke* 1:173.2–5. Translation taken from Bernard McGinn, "The God beyond God: Theology and Mysticism in the Thought of Meister Eckhart," *The Journal of Religion* 61 (1981), p. 14.

44. *Meister Eckhart: Selected Sermons and Treatises,* trans. J. M. Clark and J. V. Skinner (London: Faber & Faber, 1958), p. 138.

principle" are steps toward legitimizing the viability and necessity of sharing sacred speech. Further, his equally stunning proposal that Ultimate Reality is not only not accessible to *logos* but not even fully accessible to *Itself* brings to mind a view of reality continually open to its mystical "otherness," dynamic, and perpetually unfolding. It is this attempt at articulating the radical openness of Christianity to itself and to others that is behind much of Panikkar's writings. While one may feel overwhelmed by the comprehensive brilliance of his thought, the boldness of his speculative project serves to propel interreligious dialogue into profoundly beautiful rivers of thought.

6

The Cosmotheandric Intuition
The Contemplative Catalyst of Raimon Panikkar
FRANK PODGORSKI

A single but deep insight anchors the contemplative catalyst of Raimon Pa-nikkar. More than knowledge acquired through scientific analysis, deeper than wisdom culled by philosophical probing, beyond awe arising from theologi-cal appreciation, surpassing and yet enriched by vast multicultural reflection from *all* of these disciplines, this intuition creates a unique frame to enhance Panikkar's reflections. Years ago, Panikkar named his perspective the "*cosmoth-eandric intuition.*" Trying to understand or "stand under" this same *mythos,* this reflection will: (1) recall this insight, (2) consider how Panikkar himself has translated this intuition to the contemporary contemplative tradition, and (3) then ask Panikkar to clarify further precisely how this extraordinary intuition may be shared and communicated more widely.

THE COSMOTHEANDRIC INTUITION

"We never seek things for themselves but for the *search,*" Blaise Pascal once observed. Reflecting on the experience of Thomas Merton, Rembert Weak-land noted that contemplation is *search* rather than satisfaction. Detectable beneath all of Raimon Panikkar's work is an insight he long ago termed the "cosmotheandric intuition."

Frank Podgorski (b. 11 September 1939, d. 30 June 1995) was Professor in and Director of the Asian Studies Department at Seton Hall University. An Indologist and priest of the Archdiocese of Newark, New Jersey, Father Podgorski was author of many works on yoga and interpretations of Eastern spiritualities for Westerners. A splendid colleague and a friend who gave generously of himself to all who met him, Frank is remembered warmly by Raimon Panikkar and the contributors of this volume. *Requiescat in pace.*

Asked in 1975 in Montreal to share this understanding, he replied:

The *cosmotheandric intuition* would be that vision which brings together every scientific thread as well as all the other manifestations of the human spirit and discovers, to put it simply, that: There is no God without man and the World. There is no Man without God and the World. There is no World without God and Man.[1]

Elaborating further, Panikkar spoke of (1) God as *"plus ultra,"* that infinite, mysterious dimension of *whatever is real.* (2) Man he termed *anthropos* as distinct from God. (3) World is the cosmos, the entire and total physical reality. Yet these three realities, although distinct and distinguishable, are *what they are* precisely because of being "interrelated" to each other. *Interrelatedness* is thus the hermeneutical key to understand and "stand under" the *mythos* which both reveals and yet conceals reality. Elsewhere Panikkar explained the *cosmotheandric principle* as an "intuition of the threefold structure of all reality, the triadic oneness existing on all levels of consciousness and reality."[2] On another occasion, he wrote:

The *cosmotheandric principle* could be stated that the divine, the human, and the earthly — however we may call them — are *three irreducible dimensions* which constitute the real, i.e., *any reality inasmuch as it is real.*[3]

For Panikkar then, meditation on Trinity is not merely speculative reflection on the inner life of the God but "equally an analysis of the heights of man."[4]

If Christian Trinity bid Panikkar ponder "triadic oneness" and "three irreducible dimensions of reality," then Vedānta, especially Advaita Vedānta, challenged to a unique vision of "Oneness." Meditating on the classic *"ekam eva ādvitīyam"* font of the Chāndogya Upaniṣad, Panikkar observes: "This One, this *ekam,* is qualified in a special way. It is, in fact, the qualifying word, *ādvitīya* (non-twoness), which renders the affirmation of Oneness so fruitful."[5] Consciousness reveals a profound and ineffable Oneness. "Pure consciousness cannot be dualistic, but advaitic knowledge is really ineffable. Consciousness is not *Vāc,* the word, but that which permits the word to be."[6]

Thus, two widely separated foundational fonts, *Trinity* and *ekam eva ādvitīyam,* generate a *cosmotheandric intuition* to inspire Panikkar. Perhaps this insight may also serve as a contemplative catalyst for others as well. Let us first glimpse how Raimon Panikkar arrived at this extraordinary insight, this

---

1. Raimundo Panikkar, "Ecology," *Monchanin* 7.3–5 (175):27.

2. Raimundo Panikkar, *The Trinity and the Religious Experience of Man* (Maryknoll, N.Y.: Orbis Books, 1973), p. xi.

3. Raimundo Panikkar, *"Colligite Fragmenta:* For an Integration of Reality," in F. A. Eigo, ed., *From Alienation to At-Oneness* (Villanova, Pa.: Villanova University Press, 1977), p. 74.

4. Panikkar, *Trinity,* p. xii.

5. Raimundo Panikkar, *The Vedic Experience: Mantramañjarī* (Berkeley: University of California Press, 1977), p. 656.

6. Panikkar, *Vedic Experience,* p. 688.

special reading of the Book of Life. In the mode of a contemplative seeker, let us "just look" at Panikkar coming to this understanding.

Contemplation resembles art. Like a poet, painter, or musician, a contemplative first *sees* and becomes inspired. Only then *may* this insight or *vision* of Beauty, Meaning, or Oneness be translated into a medium which is quite *incapable* of conveying that *vision*. Paradoxically, to the extent that this *vision* is communicated well, so may an artist or contemplative be said to speak effectively to a particular milieu.

Buried within the word *contemplation* is the root *tem,* which means "to cut." Of what severance, separation or *cutting off* do contemplatives speak? Recall, for a moment, the wonder and awe experienced at an especially meaningful moment of life, while at the same time *cutting off* your natural instinct to name, label or categorize such a moment. Recall the initial moment of "just looking" at a Pacific sunset, the astonishment of "seeing" more than a mere panorama from a mountain peak, the incredible moment of recognizing "infinity" in the eyes of another. Although everyday language might call these actions "just looking," contemplative "eyes" sometimes recognize a far more profound *vision*. At times they even describe this as a moment of "profound Oneness." Is it any wonder then that Teresa of Avila gave priority to training her novices in this art of "just looking"?

As the visionary "just looks," intuition may enable the contemplative to "see through" and beyond these very same vistas to a root cause. In language borrowed from the Scholastic Age of Christendom, a contemplative may discover the formal, material, efficient, and final cause of *whatever is.* In translating this understanding of *intellectus* which surpasses *ratio,* Raimon Panikkar coined the term *contuition.* Thus, for a contemplative, creation or genesis is not something buried in a remote, distant past; rather, creation continues to unfold, challenge, and touch each of us daily.

Similarly, a "profound simplicity" characterizes the contemplative; beneath the common experience of radical plurality, an emphatic "contuition" of "ineffable Oneness" is lived. "When contemplation is well-advanced, reasoning ceases, having reached its goal; feelings are transcended; and only the recollection of the origin and end of everything persists."[7] Ultimately then contemplation speaks of liberation as breaking free from the limitations of an imprisoning milieu. Yet paradoxically, the moment a contemplative or artist begins to tell of what has been seen, frustration and failure overwhelm. "He who knows, does not speak; he who speaks, does not know" was *spoken* by the *Tao Te Ching* many years ago. Yet like Chuang-tzu and similar to the Buddha following Enlightenment, the contemplative feels compelled to carve words, create images, and fashion pictures precisely in an impossible attempt to report, ineptly though it be, the *vision* that has been seen.

---

7. Elemire Zolla, "Traditional Methods of Contemplation and Action" in Yusuf Ibish and Ilena Marculescu, eds., *Contemplation and Action in World Religions* (Seattle: distributed by University of Washington Press, 1978), p. 116.

As startling and radical as his conclusions may sometimes seem, Panikkar's intuition is very much within the mainstream of Christian reflection. Although *cosmotheandric insight* follows more in the tradition of Bonaventure, Nicholas of Cusa, and the Spanish mystics, it also flows from the Greeks. Panikkar's approach to philosophy exhibits this well.

With awareness then that Panikkar speaks principally but not exclusively from a mystical orientation, let us now turn to the overarching frame of his *vision*. How can we "just look" at this *cosmotheandric insight?*

The Intuition

The Chinese tradition points to Chuang-tzu as a sage with a unique ability to dwell within Wholeness, a Oneness, which he pictured as a dynamic living Organism. "Just looking" at all the apparently opposite and contradictory forces of nature, a "sage simply leans on the sun and the moon, tucks the universe under his arm, merges himself with all things, and allows the confusion and muddle to be as it is" (*Chuang-tzu II, 8*). Underneath the chaos of common experience, the sage discovers and rejoices in a rhythm of harmonious Oneness.

Proclaiming a Oneness every bit as organic and alive as that of Chuang-tzu, Raimon Panikkar meditates on the cells of the Organism; there, he observes and discovers a network of dynamic "interrelatedness" which binds and weaves together the inner vitality of Life. Like a poet who sees the ocean in a single drop of water or like the artist who recognizes the tree in the acorn, Panikkar's emphatic "contuition" is mammoth, indeed, truly overwhelming. Coining the word *cosmotheandric,* Panikkar meditates on three irreducible dimensions of reality, (1) divine, (2) human, and (3) earthly, all interwoven and bonded within one Organism. No one of these dimensions can subsist without the other two. This foundational *cosmotheandric insight* invites, in Panikkar's words, to a "re-covery" and "dis-covery" or "new innocence." Hopefully, such *new innocence* will begin to "re-veal" a *mythos* capable of responding to the "critical transhistorical consciousness" arising in our day.

The context of our age is critical for Panikkar. Many, following Jaspers and Toynbee, have understood the ninth to the sixth centuries BCE as the Axial Age of Spirituality, a moment during which the "seeds" or foundational insights of several great spiritualities were sown throughout the world. Our "moment" then seems to be the beginning of a Second Axial Age, a mutational age when the maturing fruits of various spiritual traditions are on the verge of beginning to dialogue (*dia-logos*), to really speak with each other, to share (*communio*), and hopefully to "cross-fertilize" and enrich one another. Perhaps figures such as the Dalai Lama or Thomas Merton or Mahatma Gandhi or Abhishiktananda or Aurobindo are among the early models of those who have begun to be nourished by multicultural spiritual fonts.

Many others also point to this bold new age. Teilhard de Chardin observes a "planetization and a radical change in consciousness," Robley Whitson writes of the "coming convergence," Jean Leclercq simply assumes a "global mutation," while Jean Houston goes so far as to predict an "ontological"[8] break-through in our very understanding of the meaning of *human.*

What seems most needed for this coming Second Axial Age would be a more universal version of the classical Renaissance person, a "cross-cultural multi-dimensional personality who appropriates the complex forms of consciousness not only of his own civilization but of the world and who already lives comfortably with a mutational context that has not yet fully taken shape."[9] The work of Raimon Panikkar has to be situated *here,* at the very frontiers and crossroads of a new age. Drawing on mysticism as well as science, myth as well as logic, *intellectus* as well as *ratio,* heart as well as mind, he both calls for and contributes to this bold new spiritual search, a quest mature enough to be nourished and enriched by the heritage of the entire human community. From this mammoth perspective, Panikkar wishes to challenge all contemplatives to collect and gather the harvest of centuries of spiritual growth and cultivation. The harvest is overripe, yet the harvesters seem surprisingly few!

Yet Panikkar is too aware of provincialism and the many other limitations of history, of various histories, and of historicity, to attempt naively to construct but another myth of history, even a myth of global history. Too much is at stake! Parochialisms must *not* be allowed to project simply another global fantasy. Mammoth crises confront and overwhelm the entire human race; only a transhistorical solution may help.[10]

Precisely because of our all-encompassing crisis, Panikkar wishes to break open traditional categories and ways of thinking about *time* and *space.* Instead of neatly divided chronological estimates of past, present, and future, he prefers to reflect on (1) pre-historical, (2) historical, and (3) transhistorical epochs of consciousness. Beneath this arch, the *cosmotheandric intuition* reports on wisdom culled from various moments when the *kairos* or "spirit" discovered appropriate myths for a particular milieu. Each kairological moment reveals the mythos capable of stimulating and inspiring the people of that particular age.

At our critical juncture of historical crisis, all that can be done is to collect the data. Ours is a moment for harvesting the experience of the human spirit. We must listen with reverence to that which has been seen and is still being intuited, what *intellectus* and *nous* as well as *ratio* have revealed of a future and a past as well as of the present. Attempting to "stand under" the *totality* of our heritage may perhaps reveal a myth appropriate for our age. Certainly many of our most cherished myths badly need a new hermeneutic. Our antiquated myth of space with its neat threefold division of "gods beyond," "humans in between," and an "underworld below" cries out for fuller understanding. Similarly, our myth of time with its precise distinctions of "past, present and future" has already begun to ask both religion and science for insights into the mystery of "timelessness."

---

8. Jean Houston, "Importance of Meditation," *Journal of Dharma* 11.2 (1977):230–39.

9. Ewert Cousins, "Raimundo Panikkar and the Christian Systematic Theology of the Future," *Cross Currents* 29 (1979): 143–44.

10. Raimundo Panikkar, "Is History the Measure of Man? Three Kairological Moments of Human Consciousness," *The Teilhard Review* 16:1–2 (1981):43.

The *cosmotheandric* meditation wishes to draw on and learn from all fonts. If "Oneness" is discovered beneath a cloak of chaos, if the entire Organism is "re-membered," if the body of primordial Prajāpati once "dis-membered" in cosmic sacrifice is again recalled, perhaps then we may become inspired.

And so removing the chains of mere historicism while yet meditating on the story of the human heritage, Panikkar's meditation simply endeavors to harvest and collect the fruits of human consciousness. Even though some of these moments may at first appear blanketed by overly simplistic views, Panikkar still wishes to "re-call" and ask if these now obscured insights may still speak and find resonance in the human heart. As a tool to assist in this "re-search," Panikkar suggests three intertwined *kairological moments:* (1) a pre-historical ecumenic moment, (2) an economic moment of historical consciousness, and (3) the universal transhistorical moment.

A Pre-Historical Ecumenic Moment

> For Primordial Man, Nature is the *oikos,* the house, the habitat. Here the divine is subsumed in nature, or rather is not merely *natural* but sacred and ultimately one. The entire world is man's habitat.... He has no sense of nature, for he is part of it.... He is thus sacred, for the entire universe is sacred, and he is part of the Whole. Communion with reality is here coextensive with the absence of a separating or reflecting self-consciousness.[11]

Yet the epoch of history recognizes and responds to many of these same "unspoken harmonies" as well. The Vedic sages, the Pre-Socratics, Plato, and the Stoics all spoke of a world "filled with gods." Bonaventure, Francis of Assisi, Christendom, the Hindu priests, the *bodhisattvas,* Chinese sages, shamanic priestesses and priests from so many different lands and cultures all rejoiced in the goodness of their "sacred milieu." To this very day, in a land as technologically advanced as modern Japan, the calendar of village and urban festivals still offers opportunities for "the people and the gods simply to enjoy each other." Even the contemporary West's theology of the Mystical Body reflects this common intuition of the human heritage. "Simply to be alive is to be sacred" resonates within the human heart!

How impossible then to abandon a conviction so central to the *humanum,* whether Ancient, Tribal, Medieval, Renaissance, or even Contemporary! Do not the clouds of impending ecological disaster attempt to awaken a forgotten "sacred awe," a "cosmocentric consciousness" which long ago filled the human heart with rightful wonder before the mystery of simply being alive, of experiencing oneself as a cell within a vital dynamic Organism? How profound the wisdom when *humanum* lived life with genuine gratitude to and for both the cosmos and the gods who dwell within! Is it too late for frightened twentieth-century *humanum,* who now confesses so many god-like forces, to

---

11. Panikkar, *"Colligite,"* p. 40.

be completely beyond individual control, to simply *re-call* and learn from the mythos of the originating moment?

Historical Consciousness: An Economic Moment

The economic moment is our moment of human history. Science and humanism, its operative myths, already point to the need for a reformulation of contemporary mythos. "Man as the measure of all things," that antique maxim of Protagoras, best describes this anthropocentric spirit.

> After wondering at Nature, Man wonders at his own mind and is awe-struck to see that the physical universe seems to follow the laws his mind discovers and can formulate.... Truth is only what the human mind can see with clarity and distinction.... Reason becomes the Spirit and the Spirit the supreme reality, God.[12]

Yet this very deification of human self-consciousness, this glorification of individualism, carries with it a huge price. Certainly, the center of gravity has shifted from cosmos to *anthropos* during the historical age. Yet, as *humanum* separated from the patterns of the cosmos, as humankind tried to rise above nature, its disincarnate Spirit became isolated and alone and forgot its material, animal, and cosmic ganglia. When *logos* and *vāc* became reducible to "reasoning with clarity," even the primordial awareness of divinity seemed to flee. Thus *anthropos* arose and stood tall in the center of the stage only to discover that both cosmic and divine supports had vanished. Tellingly, human knowledge has become increasingly disturbed by its inability to discover real meaning within life and existence. And so, what is the real difference between primordial and historical *anthropos*?

The probing question of both the Buddha and Yoga remains critical. Is not *self-consciousness* (*ahaṃkāra, asmitā*) a dilemma and a mistake, a pride of conceit (*abhimāna*) when it asserts "self" so as to build an *anthropocentric* world? Has *anthropos* risen to great heights only to find itself unable to survive in the rarefied atmosphere of isolation?

This dilemma of *anthropos* is observable within the three major problems of our day: the ecological, humanistic, and theological crises. All are interrelated and intertwined. The ecological crisis may be summarized by observing that following almost an epoch of exploitation and neglect, the groans of the earth telling of the imminent exhaustion of vital resources finally seems to have awakened *anthropos* to the need for a radically new attitude toward nature. Will this challenge, perhaps, become a moment for *re-calling* a long forgotten communion with the cosmos? The humanistic crisis is rooted in the frustrating realization that, in spite of perhaps having the technological means to actually do so and despite even fleeting moments of "good will" and the "best of intentions," *anthropos* has utterly failed to create a truly human civilization. Indeed, statistics show that the gap between the well-fed and the starving increases rather than

---

12. Panikkar, *"Colligite,"* pp. 48–50.

decreases *daily*. For many, as Panikkar graphically depicted, the bomb has already fallen. Again, *anthropos* is forced to confess candidly the limitations of independence. This is

> an inner discovery of the limits of Man, limits whose cause is not some lack of factual know-how, but *something deeper,* something ultimately unfathomable.... Modern Man is aware that there are forces at work which he cannot master and with which he has not yet reckoned. The total solidarity, so long shunned by the elites, now devolves on the entire human race.[13]

All of these problems intensify the theological crisis of our day. As *anthropos* took center stage by abstracting *self* from the cosmos, so did communion with and consciousness of the gods change. The result is that today the divine, if mentioned at all, plays but a minor cosmetic role in the story of the *humanum*. Thus our age speaks of the "death of God" to describe the incompatibility between former understandings of God and a contemporary knowledge of *cosmos* and *anthropos*. "The God of history remains idle; the God of the philosophers is indifferent; and the God of religion does not seem very concerned about the human condition."[14] But is *God really dead?*

At this point, Panikkar begins to search for deeper understanding. Despite our immediate overwhelming crisis, "what has been experienced" does point to unfathomable depths. At various moments, this (*idam*) has been glimpsed in cosmos, *anthropos* or Somewhere Beyond. Even our current crises instruct in this matter. Humanism now confesses the impossibility of manipulating nature or the human, while science acknowledges the impossibility of a completely neutral, detached, objective stance. All of this suggests that our modern myths need to be broken so as to create new myths capable of inspiring and regenerating our age.

The Transhistorical Universal Moment

If awe is virtue for the ecumenic moment and if analysis is strength for the economic moment, then quest for a more visionary *logos* capable of synthesizing the best of all past wisdom is the challenge of the forthcoming transhistorical moment. Panikkar calls this the *catholic* moment. It is a moment for collecting and gathering together *all* legacies of the past, *all* the wisdom of the former ages, while still articulating a *mythos* able to draw *anthropos* forth from the ego-constructed prison of individualism. Panikkar adapts the word *catholic* to stress the universal virtues essential for this bold new age.

Now is a moment for universal understanding! Because "man increasingly senses that the center is neither a merely transcendent godhead, nor the cosmos nor himself,"[15] there is now need for a much more profound understanding of

---

13. Panikkar, "*Colligite,*" p. 54.
14. Ibid.
15. Panikkar, "*Colligite,*" p. 61.

mythos. Consequently, a radical *metanoia,* a complete change of heart, spirit, and mind is demanded to even glimpse this deeper *logos.* Yet Panikkar suggests that a new *ontonomic* order may be emerging.

> By ontonomy we mean that degree of awareness, which having overcome the individualistic attitude as well as the monolithic view of reality, regards the whole universe as unity so that the regulation of a particular being is neither self-imposed nor dictated from above, but a part of the whole discovering or following its destiny. Ontonomy is the realization of *nomos,* the law of *on,* being, at that profound level where unity does not impinge upon diversity, but where the latter is rather the unique and proper manifestation of the former. It rests on the *specular* character of reality, in which each *part* mirrors the whole in a way proper to it.[16]

Probing the insight that wisdom is especially "communion among *subjects,*"[17] a *cosmotheandric intuition* for the *transhistorical* moment of *universal* consciousness is suggested. This moment is specially an hour for gathering fragments, *colligite fragmenta,* for integration, for recalling that all constitutive parts of *whatever is* participate and share in profound communion. Such Oneness invites to genuine community of *all* within the Organism. Gradually, the realization dawns that "there is but *one,* though *intrinsically* threefold, *relation* which expresses the ultimate constitution of reality."[18] Within this *Oneness,* all reality, *whatever is,* is *relational.* Thus God, without creatures, is a meaningless hypothesis, just as *anthropos* without *cosmos* is also an abstract anomaly.

The *cosmotheandric intuition* attempts to recover this foundational trinitarian *relationship* underlying all reality. Interestingly, several anthropological studies suggest one invariant of human culture might very well be a penchant for formulating threefold divisions, be these spatial, temporal, cosmological, or metaphysical. "God revealed Himself threefold" (*Br. Up. I, 2–3*) then is by no means a Hindu monopoly. Pointedly, the "cosmotheandric vision discovers the trinitarian structure of everything — and that third dimension, the *divine* is not just a *third,* but precisely the *mysterium conjunctionis.*"[19] As this dawning trinitarian consciousness replaces customary dualism, the frustrating "dead-end" of God as *Totally Other* opens to a more familiar understanding of God as also *an-Other.* Absolute transcendence is recognized as a meaningless abstraction, whereas the cosmotheandric call of communion invites immanence to articulate deeper understanding.

Pleading for authentic integration and genuine *inter-communion* then, the *cosmotheandric intuition* identifies the *intrinsic interrelatedness* of *whatever is.* Panikkar summarizes this insight by the following aphorisms:

---

16. Raimundo Panikkar, *Worship and Secular Man* (Maryknoll, N.Y.: Orbis Books, 1973), pp. 28–29.

17. Panikkar, "*Colligite,*" p. 72.

18. Ibid., p. 74.

19. Ibid.

1. The links which connect everything else *constitute* these very things.

2. There are three real, although different dimensions of *one* and the same reality: divine, human and cosmic.

3. Man and, indeed, *all* of reality are more than *individual.*[20]

"Historical consciousness is coming to an end. Man is embarking upon a new venture . . . about which we know only that we shall act the more freely the more we allow the *internal dynamism of our deepest being* to express itself, without projecting beforehand what we are about to do and to be. *We are consciously participating in the very existence of the cosmotheandric reality.*"[21]

THE CONTEMPLATIVE CATALYST

It is one gift to unearth wisdom; it is quite another to share that inspiration. Much of Raimon Panikkar's life may be seen as an attempt to translate "what he sees" to the inner awareness of others. Benares, Harvard, and Santa Barbara make most sense when the contemplative catalyst of Panikkar seeks to draw forth (*e-ducere* — educate) more profound awakenings. If Panikkar's *kōans* seem more jolting in recent days, it is precisely because he senses so deeply the urgency to awaken contemplative awareness.

A unique opportunity presented itself in 1980. *Aides Inter-Monastères* (*A.I.M.*) invited Panikkar to Massachusetts to reflect with contemplatives in a monastic setting on the subject of "The Monk as Universal Archetype." Although most of those attending this symposium were Christian monks of the Western tradition, participants included some monks from the East as well as several Westerners, who, although not members of any monastic order, described themselves as "committed to the development of the monastic dimensions of their lives." In 1982 the records of this dialogue appeared under the title of *Blessed Simplicity.*[22] Here is Panikkar's clearest attempt to articulate the *cosmotheandric intuition* as a contemporary contemplative catalyst.

As Panikkar addressed this group, his special understanding of *monkhood* immediately became evident. It both enhanced and stimulated dialogue. For Westerners, contemplation has often been associated with monasteries and the monastic tradition, usually meaning a somewhat isolated abbey or spiritual center especially noted for fostering a quest for internal holiness. One unfortunate corollary of this attitude is a popular tendency to link contemplation with romantic "non-worldliness." Was this not one of the reasons why Christians objected so strongly to Thomas Merton's social critique? When Panikkar speaks of monasticism, almost spontaneously his reflections become multicultural and

---

20. Ibid., pp. 82–88.
21. Panikkar, "Is History the Measure," p. 45.
22. Raimundo Panikkar, *Blessed Simplicity: The Monk as Universal Archetype* (New York: The Seabury Press, 1982).

world-focused. Thus Jaina ascetics, Yogis, Hindu *saṁnyāsins,* Buddhist *bodhisattvas* and Zen monks in addition to Christian models add enriching color, dimension, and flavor to his vision.

Another special vantage point of these conversations concerned their adaptation of the very word *monk.* Sometimes (1) *monk* was understood as a vowed, formally committed follower of a particular tradition, such as, for example, The Rule of Benedict. At other times, (2) *monk* described a human ideal, an "archetype, that central dimension which exists in the human being."[23] Yet at still other times, (3) *monk* was also used to describe spiritual seekers, those not belonging to any particular monastic order but committed "to the monastic development of their lives." Each of these emphases was interspersed and intertwined within the dialogue and conversations.

New Innocence

To all of these "monks," Panikkar proposed a quest for "new innocence." Recalling a past in which some monks chose to "sail against the wind" and "swim upstream against the current,"[24] the prophetic monk challenges with special urgency in our day. Panikkar's principal thesis is that the impending crisis of the *collapse of history*[25] demands a radical shift in the focus of contemplation. If, in the past, monastic flight from the world (*fuga mundi*) gave eloquent testimony to transcendence, an impressive witness to a God or Absolute beyond the turmoil of the world, then the impending crisis of the collapse of human history demands a new paradigm to assist as we near this moment of transhistorical human consciousness.[26]

Within this bold new context, Panikkar begins to paint the broad outline of "new innocence." At "the end of the Platonic period of civilization, . . . we cannot *rely completely* on the *logos.* . . . We need a deeper ground which does *not* depend on our ideas, conceptions, or ideologies."[27] We now recognize only too deeply the limitations of mere thinking. In a word, "thinking *freezes* being."[28] Therefore, as the *Upaniṣads* taught us so long ago, it is imperative to simply let "being be . . . letting being escape."[29]

> It is a . . . total spontaneity. Being explodes itself into being, into word, into the expression of that being, into something which goes its own way, like an expanding universe which nothing and nobody — and certainly no being, no thinking, no lack of contradiction, no logic or logistics, no anything — can control or guide. Blissful spontaneity, yes, because what is most important is the *process,* the dance, the whole thing expanding. . . .

---

23. Ibid., p. 111.
24. Ibid., p. 30.
25. Ibid., pp. 106–8.
26. Ibid., pp. 34–35.
27. Ibid., p. 110.
28. Ibid., p. 122.
29. Ibid., p. 123.

Who would know the knower? You cannot know the knower, as the *Upaniṣad* says. There is no way to control the flow of reality. Thinking is not the ultimate parameter. Being is just...explosion! This would explain the monastic concentration on purifying the heart, the source of our being, and allowing the Spirit, which is Freedom, to direct, inspire us.[30]

The wisdom of dance, the joy of laughter, the spontaneity of song, the wonder of a sunrise, the bliss of love! Who dares explain or give rules for the personal transformation brought about by these experiences? Simply, *let being be!* "You think too much," Zorba the Greek complained. Just be, let being be, and become and create what it will. Let Tao follow its natural course!

Blessed Simplicity

Could a monk possibly show the way? Perhaps quaint monastic stereotypes may yet open to the truth and wisdom for which monks give their lives. If the "system" is truly off-center, contemplation may yet discover a path to the *center.*

In the past, monastic flight from the world (*fuga mundi*) most often accented simplification. Traditional monastic spirituality spoke of total abandonment as the path to God. An ideal was that all *others* and all *other* things be left behind in an explicit quest for the Wholly Other, the entirely transcendent God. Accordingly, contemplation became the most important human activity; it stimulated ever greater efforts at detachment from the world. "The *renunciation monastic* judges work to be his or her primary relation to the world; the effort demanded by work both sanctifies the world and prepares for the higher order of contemplation. This spirituality continually moves toward transcendence."[31] Thus the contemplative's entire life becomes a sign pointing to a God *hidden* behind human experience. Individual ascetical effort is characteristic of this path. Personal reformation of one's own life becomes the means of responding to God's muted voice. God is to be encountered in transcendence, which climaxes in the experience of death and resurrection.

Yet *bodhisattvas* and Chinese sages and Francis of Assisi also tell of the importance of other *ways.* Do not Chu Hsi and Wang Yang Ming know of a "quiet sitting" which leads to the discovery of an inner dynamism within our very being? Is not such *"contemplation"* viewed as useless unless tested in the crucible of the marketplace? Did not their Chinese ancestors speak of *chün-tzu* whose lives became so transfigured that they spontaneously and automatically transformed their social milieu?

Therefore *Blessed Simplicity* proposes a search for a *center* which is world probing rather than world fleeing. Simplicity, not simplification, becomes its prime ascetical norm. Such simplicity demands a "singlemindedness that has reduced everything to its quintessence and reached the ultimate transparency

---

30. Ibid.

31. Matthias Neuman, "New Approaches for Benedictine Studies: A Review Essay of Raimundo Panikkar's *Blessed Simplicity,*" *American Benedictine Review* 35.2 (1984): 134.

of truth."[32] The Christian gospels call this "purity of heart," the *Bhagavad-Gītā* speaks of "acting without seeking the fruits of one's actions," while *bodhisattvas* and sages simply model this behavior. "Simplicity through integration" searches for a *center* not only in transcendence but equally within the rhythms of the human and the cosmos. This quest invites a reading of the Book of Life within the mode of such "unspoken harmonies" as that of the *cosmotheandric insight.*

---

32. Panikkar, *Blessed Simplicity,* p. 30.

7

Panikkar's Advaitic Trinitarianism

EWERT H. COUSINS

The Trinity is central in the thought of Raimon Panikkar. From one perspective it is the pivotal point around which his thought turns; from another it is the alpha and the omega of the development of his thought throughout his academic career. From his doctoral dissertation at the Lateran University in 1961 to his Gifford Lectures in 1989, the Trinity has been foundational. Published in 1964 under the title *The Unknown Christ of Hinduism,* his doctoral dissertation dealt with the relation of the son to the Father in the Trinity in dialogue with Hindu thought.[1] It is significant that his Gifford Lectures, delivered in Edinburgh in April and May 1989, were entitled "Trinity and Atheism: The Housing of the Divine in the Contemporary World."[2] They contained a comprehensive treatment of the cosmos, the human, and the divine from the standpoint of a trinitarian structure of reality. Because the Trinity is foundational for Panikkar, it permeates all the other dimensions of his thought: his understanding of Christianity itself, of other religions, interreligious dialogue, pluralism in culture, the secular, politics, philosophy, science, and history.

In the prominence he gives to the Trinity, Panikkar is a classical theologian. From the Greek Fathers to the twentieth-century systematic theologies of Karl Barth, Paul Tillich, and Karl Rahner, most — although not all — Christian theologians have seen the Trinity as foundational to their visions: hence they

Ewert H. Cousins is Professor of Theology and Director of Program in Cross-Cultural Spirituality at Fordham University. He is an editor of the much-acclaimed Crossroad Books Series, "Classics in World Spirituality." Professor Cousins is author of the classic *Bonaventure and the Coincidence of Opposites* and, more recently, of *Christ of the Twenty-First Century.*

1. Panikkar's doctoral dissertation in theology was entitled and was defended at the Lateran University, Rome, in 1961. With the addition of an introductory chapter, it was published under the title *The Unknown Christ of Hinduism* (London:Darton, Longman & Todd, 1964), reprint ed. 1968 and 1977. In a revised and enlarged edition it was published with the subtitle *Towards an Ecumenical Christophany* (London: Darton, Longman & Todd, 1981; Maryknoll, N.Y.: Orbis Books, 1981) and issued in an Indian edition (Bangalore: Asian Trading Corporation, 1982).

2. Panikkar's ten Gifford Lectures were delivered at the University of Edinburgh over the period from April 25 through May 12, 1989, and will be published by Orbis Books.

developed other aspects of their theology in the light of the Trinity. Although Panikkar is classical in this, he is radically innovative in three other respects. First, he sees the Trinity in relation to religions which most earlier Christian theologians had no contact with or knowledge of. Second, he has brought to light an aspect of the Christian doctrine of the Trinity which has remained submerged in Christian history. I call this aspect Panikkar's *advaitic Trinitarianism,* for it developed out of his own inner dialogue with the advaitic tradition of Hinduism, and yet remains, I believe, authentically trinitarian in the full orthodox Christian sense of that term. Third, he sees that the Christian doctrine of the Trinity reveals a structure of reality that is more comprehensively universal than was perceived in the classical vestige and image tradition.

What do I mean by Panikkar's advaitic Trinitarianism? The term *advaita* is composed of the Sanskrit root *dv,* which means "two," and the alpha privative, meaning "not." Etymologically, then, the term means "not two." Metaphysically the term has been applied to a major strand of Vedānta philosophy which claims that reality is ultimately *advaita,* that is, not two. Taking their point of departure from texts in the Upaniṣads, advaitic philosophers have claimed that Brahman (the divine) and the world are not two. Stated another way, the advaitic position holds that only Brahman is and that the phenomenal world is an illusion — not that it does not exist, but its existence, in fact, is illusory in relation to the overwhelming reality of Brahman. From another point of view, if one begins with the differentiated multiplicity of the phenomenal world, with an advaitic intuition, one can grasp Brahman as the substratum of the phenomenal world — the undifferentiated ground beyond all multiplicity and differentiation. One can say of any portion and of all of the phenomenal world that it is Brahman, for no difference divides them. In either case the advaitic position can be called a monism, because, in effect, it reduces plurality to an undifferentiated unity.

It is absolutely crucial to state that Panikkar does not hold this monistic reading of *advaita,* either in his own use of the term or as a valid interpretation of the classical advaitic texts of the Upaniṣads. Rather, he takes the etymological meaning as his key: *advaita* simply means "not two." For him, this indicates that reality is not dualistic; it is not divided into separate segments. Rather, it is radically relational, organic, holistic. What may appear to be two, such as God and the world, can in a depth intuition, which Panikkar calls advaitic, be seen as not ontologically separated but related through complementarity. This is true not only of God and the world, but of the mutual relations of the persons in the Trinity.

Isn't Panikkar's merely a classical Christian trinitarian position? Why call it "advaitic"? Why import a term from Hinduism, especially when Panikkar does not use this term precisely in its traditional Hindu sense? The term, I believe, is appropriate for two reasons: Although Panikkar holds the traditional Christian position that there are differentiations within the divinity and between the divinity and the world, in each case he emphasizes their organic interrelationship. His thought gravitates to that advaitic point where the realities are "not-two" but intimately related. Second, and I think most importantly, he draws

into Christianity modes of perception that are culturally and religiously Eastern — perception through the experience of silence and the experience of the
ground beyond differentiation. In each case one grasps the "advaitic" or "not-
two" aspect of reality. In this sense, then, Panikkar's trinitarian theology merits
a distinctly Oriental, and most appropriately, Hindu adjective. From this advaitic
perspective, Panikkar views the inner life of God and the panorama of the finite
world, highlighting aspects that have remained veiled from classical Western
theology and philosophy, thus bringing to light newly available links between
Eastern and Western thought. It is precisely this advaitic dimension that expands Panikkar's thought to reflect the more comprehensive universal structure
of reality which he believes is emerging into human consciousness in our time.

   In the course of this essay I will explore Panikkar's advaitic Trinitarianism
as he has presented it in the major writings of his early and middle periods: *The
Unknown Christ of Hinduism* and *The Trinity and the Religious Experience of
Man.*[3] Unfortunately I cannot draw from his Gifford Lectures, since his text was
not available at the time of this writing. From my textual study I will attempt to
bring to light the advaitic element in his thought. In view of this I will highlight
his contribution to the history of Christian trinitarian theology, to the dialogue
of world religions, and to the emerging consciousness of the future.[4]

WRITINGS ON THE TRINITY

   The first major treatment of the Trinity in Panikkar's writings is found in his
dissertation, which he defended in 1961. The dissertation was published in 1964
as Part II and Part III of *The Unknown Christ of Hinduism.* As the title indicates, the work deals with Christ and not the Trinity as such. However, Panikkar
focuses not on the incarnate Christ but on the Logos in the Trinity, precisely in
relation to the Father. His approach parallels the historical development of the
doctrine of the Trinity, which reached a climax in the Council of Nicea in 325.
There, too, the focus was on the Logos in relation to the Father. It was only after
this relation was clarified that the doctrine of the Holy Spirit was defined at the
Council of Constantinople in 381.

   Panikkar's treatment takes the form of a commentary on the *Brahma-Sūtra,*
a central text in the Hindu spiritual and intellectual tradition. At the outset Panikkar states clearly that he is not attempting a traditional commentary but is
exploring a philosophical problem in and through the text: the problem of God

---

   3. See *The Unknown Christ of Hinduism; The Trinity and the Religious Experience of Man*
(London: Darton, Longman & Todd, 1973; Maryknoll, N.Y.: Orbis Books, 1973); revised edition
of *The Trinity and World Religions* (Madras: The Christian Literature Society, 1970); and "Toward
an Ecumenical Theandric Spirituality," *Journal of Ecumenical Studies* 5 (1968), pp. 507–34.
   4. This is not the first time I have addressed Panikkar's trinitarian theology (see Ewert
Cousins, "The Trinity and World Religions," *Journal of Ecumenical Studies* 7 (1970), pp. 476,
pp. 476–98; idem, "Raimundo Panikkar and the Christian Systematic Theology of the Future,"
Cross Currents 29 (1979), pp. 141–55. It is a pleasure for me now, after another decade, to return
to this topic with the enrichment provided by the further unfolding of Panikkar's thought and with
the broader perspectives that the intervening years have provided.

and the world. He claims that this is not merely a comparative study: "We do not intend to compare one philosophy with another, or to check the answer given by one tradition with a parallel answer of another, far less do we intend, for example, to compare God the Father with Brahman, or Īśvara with Christ."[5] Rather, he wishes to "make a philosophical study on a subject that as such belongs neither to the East nor to the West, leaning on the Indian philosophical tradition and explained in a manner intelligible to western thought."[6]

He proceeds by analyzing the meaning of the second aphorism of the text: "Whence the origin etcetera of this." He concludes that the full literal meaning of the sūtra consists in this: "Brahman is that whence the origination, sustentation and transformation of this world comes." Although there is general agreement on this point, he writes, divergences arise when thinkers explore the meaning of Brahman and *ātman,* or the self. He then proceeds to examine the problem through the commentary of Śaṅkara, whom he calls the Prince of Advaitans. He summarizes Śaṅkara's commentary as follows: Brahman is the cause of origination, sustentation, and destruction of this world. This cause, however, is not the object of sense-knowledge but "is discovered by a special experience: the advaitic intuition."[7]

Panikkar returns to the text of the *Brahma-Sūtra* and does an extended analysis of the philosophical issues that arise there. He draws these into focus around what he calls "the problem of the identity and diversity of God and the First Cause." He specifies this by stating that "the problem is that of the relation between, on the one hand, Brahman, the Absolute, the Transcendent, the Unknown and, on the other hand, Īśvara, the Lord, the Creator, the God."[8]

Panikkar points out the tension between Brahman and Īśvara in Hindu thought. Brahman is utterly transcendent, pure silence, pure nothingness in the sense that it is prior to being. In contrast, Īśvara is "properly speaking the revelation of Brahman, the first out-coming as it were of the unfathomable womb of Brahman. He is properly God."[9] Īśvara is also the personal aspect of Brahman and the creator of the world. Brahman is immovable, in-concrete, beyond all possibility of acting. "It is Īśvara that manifests, appears, descends in the form of *avatar* of the most different kinds."[10]

At this juncture Panikkar turns to Christ as Logos in the Trinity. "The Īśvara of our commentary points to what we like to call the Mystery of Christ, as a being unique in his existence and essence and as such equal to God. He is *really* God, not simply 'God' but 'equal to God,' 'son of God,' 'God from God.' "[11] As Īśvara manifests the absoluteness of Brahman, so Christ manifests the absoluteness of the Father.

---

5. Panikkar, *The Unknown Christ,* p. 99.
6. Ibid.
7. Ibid., pp. 107, 113.
8. Ibid., p. 148.
9. Ibid., p. 152.
10. Ibid., p. 153.
11. Ibid., p. 160.

Panikkar closes his book by pointing out the similar function of Christ and Īśvara. "In the realm of philosophy: the place made in Vedānta for Īśvara, his postulation for a role which the philosophical mind finds necessary in order to explain and connect God and the world without compromising the absoluteness of the former and the relativity of the latter, this place is filled by Christ in Christian thought."[12] This allows Panikkar to grasp the link between Christ and Īśvara and so to speak of the reality behind the name Īśvara as the Unknown Christ of Hinduism.

In 1981 *The Unknown Christ of Hinduism* appeared in a revised and enlarged edition.[13] Although he has extended his text and nuanced its statements, he has not substantially changed his position. His statement of his trinitarian position and its relation to interreligious dialogue remains basically the same in the two editions of this book.

BOOK ON THE TRINITY

Panikkar followed *The Unknown Christ of Hinduism* with a book on the Trinity as such. It has appeared in three forms: as a lengthy article in the *Journal of Ecumenical Studies* under the title "Toward an Ecumenical Theandric Spirituality"; as a book published in Madras, *The Trinity and World Religions;* and as a book in the United States in a slightly revised version under the title *The Trinity and the Religious Experience of Man.*[14] This last version contains an important preface, in which he clarifies what he considers the central insight of the book: his cosmotheandric and hence non-dualistic vision of reality. Although there is no substantial difference in these three versions, I will be using the last in treating this work. *The Trinity and the Religious Experience of Man* is different from *The Unknown Christ of Hinduism* in two basic respects: First, it deals with the entire Trinity — Father, Son, and Holy Spirit; second, it views the mystery of the Trinity not from the standpoint of a philosophical problem, as *The Unknown Christ of Hinduism* does, but from the standpoint of spirituality. Taking his categories from the three classical spiritual paths of the *Bhagavadgita,* Panikkar treats the way of *karma,* the way of *bhakti,* and the way of *jñāna.*

Since *karma* means "action," and in the Hindu context primarily the action of worship, Panikkar treats under this heading the spirituality of the worship of God, whether it be through a divine name like Yahweh or Allah, an icon, or an idol. In a provocative turn of phrase, he speaks of this kind of spirituality as "iconolatry."[15] He next describes the way of *bhakti,* or devotion, as that of personalism: "The way of devotion and love, *bhaktimārga,* is the normal blossoming of the personalist dimension of spirituality. The gift of oneself to the Lord, love of God, necessarily demands a meeting of persons."[16] The third way,

12. Ibid., p. 164.
13. See n. 1, above.
14. See n. 3, above.
15. Panikkar, *The Trinity and the Religious Experience of Man,* p. 11.
16. Ibid., p. 23.

the path of *jñāna,* or knowledge, he links to *advaita,* or non-differentiation. It is here that *The Trinity and the Religious Experience of Man* connects with his previous work in *The Unknown Christ of Hinduism.* For Panikkar, the spirituality of *advaita* is the spirituality of the Absolute. It does not worship God in iconolatry or respond to God personally out of love and devotion. Rooted in the Absolute, "the essential attitudes of *advaita* will consist rather in silence, abandonment, total conformity, absolute non-attachment."[17]

Panikkar develops this idea further. "*Jñāna-marga,* the way of knowledge, of pure contemplation, of ontological *theoria,* is the way *par excellence* of *advaita.* For the *advaitin* it is not a matter of transforming the world or even himself, as it is with the *karma-yogin.*" This spiritual path does not draw him to love God to the utmost, as *bhakti* does. "It is sheerly a matter of forgetting himself, of yielding totally to God, thus even of renouncing loving him — a renunciation of love which does not proceed from a lack of love but is, on the contrary, more profoundly the sign of a love that is purer and 'carried further,' a love which, having disappeared into the Beloved, has no longer any memory of itself."[18] In dealing with these three spiritual paths, Panikkar has implicitly identified the advaitic dimension of the Christian Trinity. He will highlight this dimension explicitly in the remainder of the book.

THE SILENCE OF THE FATHER

Panikkar begins his explicit treatment of the Trinity by stating: "My intention here is not to expound the doctrine of the Trinity; my desire is simply to show how in the light of the Trinity the three forms of spirituality described above can be reconciled."[19] He underlines the significance of this approach for the encounter of religions: "The Trinity, then, may be considered as a junction where the authentic spiritual dimensions of all religions meet."[20] He then proceeds to treat in separate sections the Father, the Son, and the Holy Spirit.

With the full force of his previous treatment of the Absolute in *The Unknown Christ of Hinduism,* Panikkar links the Father in the Trinity with the Absolute: "The Father is the Absolute, the only God, *o theos.*"[21] In a way reminiscent of Augustine, he views the Father from the perspective of the Son. Augustine saw the Father and the Son in terms of mutual relation in order to distinguish both from the divine substance.[22] Panikkar makes note of Augustine but transposes the latter's abstract treatment into the more dynamic and concrete approach of the Greek Fathers in the East and Bonaventure in the West. As Augustine says, the Father is the Father precisely because he begets the Son, and the Son is the Son because he is begotten by the Father. This mutual relationship of origin is

---

17. Ibid., p. 38.
18. Ibid., p. 39.
19. Ibid., p. 41.
20. Ibid., p. 42.
21. Ibid., p. 44.
22. Augustine, *De Trinitate,* V.

what distinguishes each from the other and both from the divine substance or the substratum of the divinity. Remaining abstract, Augustine does not take his approach farther into the concrete personal properties of the Father and the Son.

Panikkar, on the other hand, taking his lead from the Greek Fathers, links the substratum of the divinity with the Father: "The Nicene Creed," he says, "as also the greek Fathers and even Tertullian, affirms that the 'substratum' of the divinity resides in the Father."[23] Then he applies to the Father and the Son Augustine's approach through mutual relation. Although there is no subordinationism in the Trinity, the Father is the source of the divinity — the *fons et origo totius divinitatis,* as the Council of Toledo declared — and the Son is the outpouring of this fountain, the expression of this originating source; one can say that the Son is the divinity as expressed by the Father.

This allows Panikkar to formulate a number of statements that resonate with Hinduism and Buddhism. As he says, "Perhaps the deep intuitions of hinduism and buddhism, which come from a different universe of discourse than the greek, may help us to penetrate further the trinitarian mystery."[24] From this dialogic perspective, Panikkar develops a radical apophatism, or negative theology, of the Father:

> We may say: the Absolute, the Father, *is not.* He has no *ex-istence,* not even that of being. In the generation of the Son he has, so to speak, given everything. In the Father the apophatism (the *kenosis* or emptying) of Being is real and total. Nothing can be said of the Father "in himself," of the "self" of the Father.

At this point Panikkar makes a striking correlation with Buddhism:

> Is it not here, truly speaking, in this essential apophatism of the "person" of the Father, in the *kenosis* of Being at its very source, that the buddhist experience of *nirvāṇa* and *śūnyatā* (emptiness) should be situated? One is led onwards towards the "absolute goal" and at the end one finds nothing, because there is nothing, not even Being. "God created out of nothing" (*ex nihilo*), certainly, i.e. out of himself (*a Deo*) — a buddhist would say.[25]

This kenosis of Being can be called the silence of the Father. "Any attempt," he says, "to *speak* about the Father involves a contradiction in terms, for every word about the Father can only refer to the one of whom the Father is Father, that is, to the Word, to the son. It is necessary to be silent." Panikkar observes that "the most diverse religious traditions teach us that God is Silence." Since the Father is wrapped in silence, he may seem totally inaccessible to us. But, according to Panikkar, this is not the case, for "there exists in us a dimension — the deepest of all — that corresponds to this total apophatism."[26] Again Panikkar echoes Augustine here, for he too sees the human person as an image of the

---

23. Panikkar, *The Trinity and the Religious Experience of Man,* p. 45.
24. Ibid., p. 46.
25. Ibid., pp. 46–47.
26. Ibid., p. 48.

Trinity. One could correlate Panikkar's apophatic dimension with Augustine's notion of the reflection of the Father in the faculty of memory, but memory would have to be deepened beyond Augustine's understanding that it reflects the divine eternity to encompass the level of radical silence to which Panikkar is pointing.[27] In the light of this exploration of the Father as silence Panikkar concludes, "Properly speaking the spirituality of the Father is not even a spirituality. It is like the invisible bedrock, the gentle inspirer, the unnoticed force which sustains, draws and pushes us."[28]

The Son and the Holy Spirit

Panikkar turns next to the Son, treating him primarily as person, in a manner which correlates with the spirituality of personalism in the path of devotion or love. In another provocative statement Panikkar says: "Only the Son is Person, if we use the word in its eminent sense and analogically to human persons: neither the Father nor the spirit is a Person." Relating this to the spirituality of personalism, he says: "Correctly speaking, then, it is only with the Son that man can have a personal relationship. The God of theism, thus, is the Son, the God with whom one can speak, establish a dialogue, enter into communication, is the divine Person who is in-relation-with, or rather, is the relationship with man and one of the poles of total existence."[29]

In treating the Son, Panikkar does not follow the same strategy he used in dealing with the Father. There he used the mutual relation approach of Augustine, making it concrete and dynamic in the fashion of the Greek Fathers. This allowed him to bring to light the personal property of the silence of the Father in polar complementary with the Son as speech. I would suggest that this approach to the Son calls for a more basic treatment than Panikkar has explicitly made. What I mean is this: In polar contrast with the Father, the Son must be studied as the determinate aspect of the divinity — the divine Logos whom the theological tradition East and West saw as the receptacle of the determinate divine ideas as exemplars of the created world. The Son is light in contrast with the hidden darkness of the Father; he is determinate divine Logos in contrast with the undifferentiated abyss of the Father. It is precisely this determinate character of the Son that is the ontological ground for his unique personhood, as described by Panikkar.

Next Panikkar approaches the mystery of the Spirit through the notion of immanence. If the revelation of the Father is the revelation of God transcendent, then "the revelation of the Spirit, on the other hand, is the revelation of God immanent." But divine immanence is not merely negative transcendence. "It is quite a different thing from the divine welling in the depths of the soul. Essentially it signifies the ultimate inner-ness of every being, the final foundation, the *Ground* of Being as well as of beings."[30] He continues:

---

27. Augustine, *De Trinitate*, VIII-XV.
28. Panikkar, *The Trinity and the Religious Experience of Man*, p. 50.
29. Ibid., p. 52.
30. Ibid., pp. 58–59.

Could not one say that in spite of every *effort* of the Father to "empty himself" in the generation of the Son, to pass entirely into his Son, to give him everything that he *has,* everything that he *is,* even then there remains in this first procession, like an irreducible factor, the Spirit, the non-exhaustion of the source in the generation of the Logos? For the Father the Spirit is as it were, the return to the source that he is himself. In other, equally inappropriate words: the Father can "go on" begetting the Son, because he "receives back" the very Divinity which he has given up to the Son. It is the immolation or the mystery of the Cross in the Trinity. It is what christian theologians used to call the *perichōrēsis* or *circumincessio,* the dynamic inner circularity of the Trinity.[31]

In the spirituality of the Spirit, Panikkar sees a correlation with *advaita.* This position, which in Hindu thought addresses the problem of the relation of God and the world, can throw light on the intra-trinitarian problem in Christianity. "If the Father and the Son are not *two,* they are not one either: the Spirit both unites and distinguishes them. He is the bond of unity: the *we* in between, or rather within."[32] Panikkar accords to Hinduism a special role in illuminating the mystery of the Spirit: "There is no doubt that hindu thought is especially well prepared to contribute to the elaboration of a deeper theology of the Spirit." He points out that we cannot have personal relations with the Spirit, that one cannot pray *to* the Spirit, but only *in* the Spirit. "It is to this Spirit that most of the Upaniṣadic assertions about the Absolute point, when seen in their deepest light. One could cite almost every page of the Upaniṣads for examples. Indeed what is the Spirit but the *ātman* of the Upaniṣads, which is said to be identical with *brahman,* although this identity can only be existentially recognized and affirmed once 'realization' has been attained."[33]

The spirituality of the Spirit differs from that of the Son. "Faith in the Spirit cannot be clothed in personalist structure. It does not consist in the discovery of Someone, and even less in dialogue with him. It consists rather in the 'consciousness' that one is not found outside reality." One lives in the awareness that he or she is included in reality, enveloped and submerged in knowledge and love. "It is a kind of passivity: There is no longer any *me* to save, for one has grasped that there is an I who calls one by a new and completely hidden name."[34]

The Trinity and the Religious Experience of Man closes with an all-too-brief treatment of "theandrism," Panikkar's term for an integral spirituality which includes the realms of the divine, the human, and the cosmic. It is this dimension of the work that was highlighted in its original title when it appeared in the form of an article in the *Journal of Ecumenical Studies:* "Toward an Ecumenical Theandric Spirituality." Although theandrism is the culmination of Panikkar's thought, I cannot explore it adequately here since my task is to focus on his

---

31. Ibid., p. 60.
32. Ibid., p. 62.
33. Ibid., pp. 63–64.
34. Ibid., p. 64.

doctrine of the Trinity. Yet it is imperative that the reader realize that Panikkar's thought on the Trinity begins and ends with an integral incarnational-cosmic vision.

THE TRINITY AND WORLD RELIGIONS

Returning now to the Trinity, I would like to highlight how Panikkar sees the Trinity in relation to world religions. I have presented above most of his direct references to the Trinity and world religions as these appear in *The Trinity and the Religious Experience of Man*. However, I believe that these scattered observations do not do justice to the sharpness and comprehensiveness of his thought. I would like to give here my own summary of his position, inspired by his oral exposition of it to me when we first met in New York in 1967.

From a trinitarian point of view, the major religions of the world can be seen in the following way: Buddhism is the religion of the silence of the Father; Judaism, Christianity, and Islam (as well as Zoroastrianism) are the religions of the revelation of the Son; and Hinduism is the religion of the unity of the Spirit. In my first discussion with him, the most catalytic idea — the one that opened up the distinctiveness of his approach — was that the religions of the West (Judaism and Christianity, along with Islam) are religions of God's Word or Logos, of God's revelation given to prophets and written in words in books. This is the revelation of a personal God who calls for a personal response. At the same time, western secular culture is a culture of the word or *logos;* guided by the intellectual *logos* of the Greeks and the pragmatic *logos* of the Romans, Westerners approach reality in and through the conceptualized and the spoken word. Even the interreligious question is explored in dialogue (*dia-logon*) through thought, word, or speech.

Not so the Orient! Neither in its religious nor secular concerns. The Orient has other modes of perception, for example, silence and the sense of immersion in unity. These are not merely subjective states but modes of the perception of reality. It is precisely these modes of perception that Panikkar is drawing from, in view of his own cultural immersion in the Orient, and that he is attempting in his theology to evoke in his readers. To read him any other way would be to distort his purpose and his thought. This has been the major problem between Panikkar and his Western critics. Wrapped in their own all-embracing religious and cultural envelope of *logos,* they have either been baffled by his thought or have attempted unsuccessfully to translate it exclusively into *logos* structures. In my case, I was already alerted to what he was doing by the fact that I had wrestled with the issues of cultural pluralism and the diversities of group consciousness during four years of work with Native Americans.

With this methodological issue in mind, we can return to Panikkar's observation on Buddhism and the silence of the Father and to the non-differentiation of the spirituality of the Spirit in Hinduism. In each case Panikkar is attempting to evoke in his *logos*-bound Western readers these primordial modes of perception which have not been directly mediated by their culture. Once they are evoked, he relates them to the Christian experience of the Trinity, not in an exclusive, parochial fashion, but in an ecumenical horizon in which he liberates the perception of spiritual realities from the limits of a mere particularist interpretation. When one enters into this larger horizon, with these new modes of perception, one can see that Panikkar is not attempting to reduce all religions to Christianity; nor is he a disguised missionary trying to lure the Buddhists and Hindus of the world to Christian baptism.

THE TRINITY IN CHRISTIAN HISTORY

This raises a further question: How does Panikkar's advaitic Trinitarianism stand in relation to traditional Christian trinitarian theology? In keeping with his own methodology, we must first situate Christian trinitarian theology in its historical-cultural setting. That means within the context of Logos/*logos,* as described above. The doctrine of the Trinity emerged within Christian consciousness in a historical-cultural setting in which Logos/*logos* was predominant. Note that I am not attempting to separate the mystery of the Trinity from culture in such a way as to reduce the doctrine to its cultural forms or to make the cultural forms so extrinsic to the doctrine that they are superfluous. Rather, I am assuming that aspects of the mystery of the Trinity can be authentically revealed in different cultural forms and contexts.

With this assumption let us proceed. It is not surprising, then, that the emergence of the doctrine from its Jewish roots and its subsequent development through the centuries focused on Logos/*logos.* The Arian heresy and the declaration of the Council of Nicea in 325 were concerned with Christ as Logos. In fact, Nicea treated the Father in terms of his generating the Logos. Because Christianity is centered on Christ, and because Christ, as Logos, is the center of the Trinity, the Father and the Spirit are seen in relation to the Logos. It is the Logos that is the focus of differentiation and relations in the Trinity. For example, the Father is defined as the generating source of the Logos, and the Spirit is perceived as the unity of the Father and the Son. Because Eastern Christianity has rejected the Western doctrine of *Filioque,* the relation of the Spirit to the Logos would have to be nuanced accordingly. Taking this into account, we can say that Logos-centered Trinitarianism is as characteristic of the third-century theology of Athanasius as it is of the twentieth-century theologies of Barth, Tillich, and Rahner.

While not rejecting this Logos-centered Trinitarianism, Panikkar also perceives the Trinity from outside the Logos/*logos* historical-cultural context of the West: from the silence of Buddhism and the unity of Hinduism. When one plunges into the mystery of this silence and this unity, the differentiations constituted by Logos do not appear. Yet they are not absorbed into an all-encompassing monistic One; they remain in the advaitic sense described above: as not-two.

Throughout the centuries these non-Logos dimensions of silence and unity remained for the most part implicit in Christian theology. However, they did emerge explicitly in the Christian mystical tradition. For example, Meister Eckhart and his followers in the Rhineland experienced the "desert of the Godhead" beyond the trinitarian differentiations. This desert has great affinity with the silence of Buddhism and the non-differentiated unity of Hinduism. Depending on one's interpretation of Eckhart, this desert can be situated within the larger trinitarian structure of his theology and mysticism.[35]

Panikkar stands on the edge of a new era that is dawning for the human community. As he says in the program of his Gifford Lectures: "There is a certain consensus today in believing that we are facing a turning point in the History of Humankind. Plato and the Bible may be insufficient, or Śaṅkara and K'ung Fu Tzu for that matter. There is a felt need for a fresh experience of Reality." Perhaps more than any other thinker of our time, Panikkar has acted as an explorer, a guide, a herald, a midwife of this "fresh" experience of Reality.

By exploring Reality in depth from the vantage point of the Christian Trinity, by penetrating further through the Buddhist and Hindu modes of experience of silence and non-differentiation, Panikkar has reached an advaitic trinitarian structure he calls "Radical Trinity." He proposes this as the universal structure of Reality emerging in consciousness in the new era. "The Trinitarian intuition," he says, "is neither an exclusive christian doctrine, nor a monopoly of 'God.' It reveals the most fundamental character of Reality. Being is trinitarian."[36]

---

35. See Ewert Cousins, *Global Spirituality: Toward the Meeting of Mystical Paths* (Madras: University of Madras, 1985).

36. Raimundo Panikkar, Program for the Gifford Lectures, 1988/89, pp. 1, 5.

8

Christophany
The Christic Principle and Pluralism
GERALD T. CARNEY

Raimon Panikkar has developed a fundamental reaffirmation of the meaning of Christ in the context of religious and cultural pluralism. The encounter with pluralism often seems to present a fateful choice for or against the exclusive character of Jesus as Christ and the historical particularism of Christianity: there is no other name, only one way. Alternative Christian theological formulations affirm a plurality of holy names and saving paths or an inclusivism which somehow incorporates the other as a companion on one's own path. Panikkar's career-long pilgrimage into Christology expands the dimensions of Christ: a christic event which is not the exclusive property of Christianity. Understanding this christic fact in the context of pluralism leads to an awareness of Christ, not only as savior and revealer but as the Mystery, the constitutive principle, the creative source of the Reality in which all participate. The unfolding of the Mystery of Christ as christic principle, in each person and in the world, as in the theological imagination, is a Christophany.

In *The Unknown Christ of Hinduism,* Panikkar illustrates how the commentator on a sūtra text can fully explore and develop the significance of such a brief passage.[1] Taking the second aphorism of Bādārayava's Vedānta Sūtras[2] "Brahman is that from which the origin etc. (i.e., the origin, preservation, destruction) of the world proceeds" — Panikkar enters into the dynamism of this text, into the process of following that desire to know which is itself a participation in Brah-

---

Gerald T. Carney is Professor of South Asian Religions at Hamden-Sydney College. A past-president of the Virginia Consortium for Asian Studies, he has published articles on Hindu devotional traditions in *Journal of Dharma* and *Journal of Vaishnava Studies.* He is working on a biography of Baba Bharati (1857–1914), a Bengali Vaishnava who came to the United States in 1902 to convert the "Far West" to the love of Krishna.

1. Raimundo Panikkar, *The Unknown Christ of Hinduism,* rev. ed. (Maryknoll, N.Y.: Orbis Books, 1981), 97–162. Hereafter UCH.

2. "*Jamnādyasya yata.* "

man as the origin of the universe. The unfolding commentary reveals not only the knowing process of the commentator, not only the dynamic structure of the universe disclosed through that knowing, but also an experience of Īśvara, the Lord, the name of the principle of the world, that from which all things proceed, and to which all things return and by which all things are sustained.[3] In this experience of Īśvara in the Hindu text, Panikkar perceives a point of encounter with the presence of the Christ, not only the mediator turned both toward God and toward the world, but the reality of the world itself in God. In this essay, I want to explore Panikkar's treatment of this encounter.

I wish there were a single powerful text with which to participate in the dynamism of the Christological thought in Panikkar's work, but he presents us not with a series of aphorisms but with a complex body of published material, spanning more than thirty years, into which his understanding of the Christ is woven. A unity and direction can be expressed in bibliographical terms, in a propositional dialectic, or in a series of theological convictions. Realizing that there is no such sūtra or unifying quotation (*mahavākhya*), but hoping to reflect the positive character of christic affirmation in Panikkar's work, I would point to the relation between two terms: the *christic principle* and *pluralism*. In choosing such a dyad, along with crucial quality of the "and," I would be following Panikkar's study of "Hinduism and Christianity" and "God and the World" in *The Unknown Christ*. In this essay, however, I will be looking primarily at a development of the christic principle but always in the context of religious and cultural pluralism.

THE CHRISTIC PRINCIPLE

The process of commenting on this sūtra, following the path of inquiry into the relation between God and the world, emphasizes the desire to know, which underlies the dynamism of consciousness. This search leads to understanding the contingency of the world as one's own participation in the principle of Reality itself, that toward which and from which and by which we live. The Absolute is Brahman, beyond name and form. The principle that must be named is the Lord, Īśvara, God in relation to us as "thou." This Lord, turned both toward Brahman and the world, coexisting as identity and diversity, is the principle and sustainer of all finite existence, the "thou" which is addressed when consciousness inquires. In this unfolding of the Lord, Īśvara, Panikkar affirms the presence of the Mystery of Christ, of the one who is more than mediator, indeed the Reality in which one participates and into which one is incorporated, the transforming truth which is known and by which one is known.

Īśvara manifests the nondual nature of Reality: one without a second, *neither* monism *nor* multiplicity, identity *and* difference. There is nothing but God, "a God that as the absolute 'I' has an eternal 'Thou,' which is equal to him and which is nevertheless not a second, but always a Thou. This Thou, which is the

---

3. UCH, 155.

Son, is the whole Christ.... All beings participate in this Christ, find their place in him and are fully what they are when they become one with him, the Son. All that exists, i.e., the whole of reality, is nothing but God: Father, Christ and Holy Spirit."[4] The creation and full development of the multitude of beings in time is nothing but the fuller realization of their being in the Lord, Īśvara: "that from which the World comes forth and to which it returns and by which it is sustained, that is Īśvara, the Christ."[5]

This process of a Christian interpretation of a Vedāntic text shows the Christian a fuller sense, the role of Īśvara which "corresponds functionally to the role of Christ in Christian thought." Thus the activity of the Christ is not limited to an historical event; "Christ has always been at work everywhere...he was present not only when God created all things, fixing the heavens and commanding the waters, but also when the Indian rishis composed and handed down the śruti."[6]

Faithfulness to Christ involves attention to this discovery, the unfolding of the mystery of God's presence at work in Hinduism, indeed in all religions. And, if God is present and active in all religions, then Christ is present there also, this Christ in whom all things subsist, the Christ whose continuing activity awaits our discovery, the Christ who remains unknown to Christians who have neither discerned nor acknowledged this dimension of the Christian mystery. The fuller sense of the Hindu text leads to a deeper realization of Christ for Christians.

In two important essays,[7] Panikkar examines the question of Christian identity in relation to other religions not by reflection on the religious process of a Hindu text but from the theological structure of Christian history and from the dynamics of the affirmation of Christ as universal savior. Does the affirmation of authentic Christian identity involve a rejection or negation of the other in the name of Christ?

The historical development of Christianity shows how the Christian movement became a religion related to empire and culture. Amid the disintegration of empires and the post-modern recognition of the plurality of cultures, neither religio-political conquest nor cultural imperialism can characterize contemporary Christian relations with other religions. Instead, dialogic relationship with other religions and cultures becomes the way of becoming faithful to one's own tradition while affirming one's "constitutive relatedness"[8] to other people and traditions. In dialogue, conversion becomes a shared process, not of others' turning toward Christianity but of each turning "towards that reality round which Christianity itself is also turning,"[9] and to which the Christian also seeks con-

---

4. UCH, 161.
5. UCH, 162.
6. UCH, 165.
7. See Raimon Panikkar, "Christianity and World Religions," *Christianity* (Patiala: Punjabi University, 1969), 78–127 [hereafter CWR] and "The Meaning of Christ's Name in the Universal Economy of Salvation," in M. Dhavamony, ed., *Evangelization, Dialogue and Development* (Rome: Gregorian University Press, 1972), 195–218 [hereafter MCN].
8. CWR, 96.
9. CWR, 98.

version. Within this shared process of religious growth, the Christian affirms that "Jesus is the Lord" but also recognizes that "Christ, the Lord, stands for the *universal principle,* the ultimate pivot of everything, the beginning and end of reality."[10] While "Christianity would simply disappear if it did not bear witness to the Lord in Jesus,"[11] "the Lord, who is in Jesus, is also present, effective, hidden and unknown"[12] in other religions. The Lord is present everywhere, already engaged in activity, but this divine activity is not immediately recognizable as such and thus requires a process of unveiling the hidden presence of God, who always remains not fully known, a Reality with inexhaustible possibilities, a Mystery not fully disclosed. "The Lord being unchanged and unconfused in Jesus is equally inseparable and indivisible from any manifestation."[13] The christic principle, the Lord, is both concrete in Jesus and universal as Mystery.

Faithfulness to Christian tradition, continuity with its affirmation that there is only one name in which there is salvation, leads to an inquiry about who or what this name is,[14] and about the process of naming and the effect of invoking a name. The name is not a sign, and it is not just a symbol. A revelation takes place, an epiphany; the name becomes luminously transparent, evoking the presence of the Reality itself. The name has a twofold power: first, that of the *pars pro toto,* the ability of the part (the limited and particular name) to reveal and effect participation in the totality, the Reality which the name intends; and, second, the *ontonomic* power of constituting shared meaning, of transforming the autonomy of subject and object into a special kind of unity, of establishing a non-dualism that respects diversity in interdependence and relationship.

The name of Christ is not a particular or common name, identifying by differentiation or exclusion; naming the Christ involves invoking the power which creates and sustains the universe. If so, the name of the Christ is not limited to a particular individual identity, or to a particular space and time, or to a particular culture; the name of Christ is uttered as the identity of the living one in whom one participates with others, the life of the world with whom one enters into the communion which constitutes being-in-relationship. The name of Christ, the identity of this principle of self and community, cannot be invoked as an external, quantifiable object (just name and form, nāma/rūpa), as separable from self, *that* name. Rather, the name itself invokes a *thou,* the one in whom and by whom all persons exist, which can only be affirmed and understood by participation. Jesus Christ is the mediator, but "his mediatorship is not primar-

---

10. CWR, 102.

11. CWR, 114. Panikkar emphasizes that "it would amount to sheer contradiction in terms or mere jugglery of words to speak of a Christianity without Christ, or of Christ as Lord, without Jesus. This concreteness has in the past been a stumbling block for Christian dialogue with other religions but nobody for the sake of dialogue has a right to blur the issue by minimizing Jesus or overlooking the central Christian affirmation of the Lordship of Jesus."

12. CWR, 115.

13. CWR, 117. Here Panikkar uses epithets which self-consciously echo "the four famous adjectives of the Council of Chalcedon concerning the two natures of Christ, the divine and the human: inseparable, indivisible, unchanged and unconfused."

14. MCN, 197.

ily epistemological but ontological and thus it is ultimately not necessary to see him, provided we see through him; and one may dare say that the more transparent he is, the clearer is the vision through him."[15] The name of Christ, as no other name, describes not a wall but a window, not a bounded plot but a boundless panorama extending far beyond what the eye can see.

> Christ . . . is not the revelation, not the revealed name, but the revealer of the name. The name Christ reveals is a Supername, a name which was prepared before the sun, a new name so new that just to repeat it without putting one's mind and heart would be no longer the saving name, so secret that we cannot have it in front of us as an object, so saving that he who knows it — and the sounds and voices may be infinite — knows it for sure that in that name all the treasures of the godhead dwell in the most corporeal manner and also knows that that Name has splashed on the earth in innumerable tongues.[16]

In the various prefaces to *The Unknown Christ of Hinduism,* Panikkar seeks to expand the dimensions of the Mystery of Christ by "showing that there is in Hinduism a living presence of that Mystery that Christians call Christ."[17] Thus affirmation of faith in Christ includes humble acknowledgment of the inability of this affirmation to avoid all ambivalence: the presence of the Mystery Christians call Christ in other religious contexts and called by other names. This ambiguity points to the depth of the Mystery and to the human inability to comprehend it or to identify it by exclusion or by differentiation. The name of Christ is not just another defined object but a name above every other name. Panikkar argues that "that unknown reality, which Christians call Christ, [is] discovered in the heart of Hinduism, not as a stranger to it, but as its very principle of life."[18] Thus,

> a Christ who could not be present in Hinduism, who was not with every least sufferer, a Christ who did not have his tabernacle in the sun, a Christ who did not represent the cosmotheandric reality with one Spirit seeing and recreating all hearts and renewing the face of the earth, surely would not be my Christ, nor, I suspect, would he be the Christ of the Christians.[19]

This Christ is "that selfsame Mystery that attracts all other human beings who are seeking to overcome their own present condition."[20] Although Christ is the Mystery, the Mystery cannot be totally identified with Christ.

> Christ is but one aspect of the Mystery as a whole, even though he is the way when we are on that way. Only when we are not walking on them, i.e. when they are mere lines on a map, are there "many paths."

---

15. MCN, 217.
16. MCN, 218.
17. UCH, 5.
18. UCH, 20.
19. UCH, 20.
20. UCH, 22.

For the actual wayfarer, there is only one way. Not only is it unique, it is only a "way" if it gives access to the summit.... At the summit, the Christian realizes that he and his experience of the Mystery are inseparable, indistinguishable; thus you discover Christ in all those who have reached the Mystery, even if their ways have not been the Christian one. Likewise, you will have to concede that the Hindu who has reached realization, become enlightened, discovered *ātman-Brahman* or whatever, has realized the ultimate Mystery. Only for the Christian is the Mystery indissolubly connected with Christ; only for the Vaishnava is the mystery unfailingly connected with Vishnu or whatever has been the particular form for "attaining *mokṣa.*"[21]

Thus Hinduism and Christianity share a mystical non-dualism: each tradition is constituted by the mystery that is one but not the same. Christ is manifest not only as the historical Jesus but also as a divine epiphany which embraces humanity and the world as well, a cosmotheandric principle. So Christ "stands for that center of reality, that crystallization point toward which the human, the divine and the material can grow."[22] This understanding of Christ as the cosmotheandric reality appropriates some trinitarian imagery (as center of divine processions and of all realms of being) and the core of sacramental theology. In summing up his thesis, Panikkar states that

> there is something in every human being that does not alienate Man but rather allows Man to reach fullness of being. Whether the way is transformation or some other process, whether the principle is a divine principle or a "human" effort, or whether we call it by one name or another is not the question here. Our only point is that this cosmotheandric or Trinitarian, *purushic* or *īśvaric* principle exists.
>
> Christians have called it Christ, and rightly so. My suggestion is that they should not give it up too lightly and be satisfied simply with Jesus — however divinized. It is in and through Jesus that Christians have come to believe in the reality that they call Christ, but this Christ is the decisive reality.
>
> I repeat: It is not that this reality *has* many names as if there were a reality outside the name. The reality is many names and each name is a new aspect, a new manifestation and revelation of it. Yet each name teaches or expresses, as it were, the undivided Mystery.[23]

So there are not many Christs, but one Christ; other names for this undivided Mystery lead Christians to recognize the unknown dimensions of this Christ.

---

21. UCH, 24–25.
22. UCH, 26.
23. UCH, 29.

PLURALISM

Three later essays[24] situate the discussion of the christic principle within the context of religious pluralism[25] rather than within that of Hinduism. "Is there something specifically universal in the christic fact: Is Christ a universal symbol?"[26] This formulation of the question is not that of Christendom (considered as colonial empire or Western culture) nor that of Christianity as a particular religion; it does not claim a unique exclusivism nor does it admit a reductionism that would dilute the Christian affirmation. Rather, the question opens to the possibility of a wider understanding of Christian identity:

> If, on the one hand, Christianity is one religion among others, we should keep distinctions, jurisdictions, and boundaries as clear as possible. If, on the other hand, Christians believe in their commitment to a universal mystery — revealed to them in Christ — they will also share in the manifestation of the Sacred of other religions without imagining that they are betraying their own beliefs or despising those of others.[27]

Put slightly differently: "If Christians are able to extricate from their own religion the Christic principle, this principle can be experienced as a dimension at least potentially present in any human being, as long as no absolute interpretation is given."[28] "The identity of Christ is not our identification of Christ."[29] Thus, "the christic principle is neither a particular event nor a universal religion," but the center of reality as seen by the Christian tradition.[30] Christian identity or Christianness involves "living a personal religiousness, that is, a sort of religious attitude that constitutes a dimension of Man, one factor of the *humanum,* one aspect of the divine."[31] This image of Christian identity and self-consciousness, this Christianness, implies a different dynamism than a mechanistic model or the linear movement of history. The mystic appreciation of reality is "theoanthropocosmic," a relationship in depth which neither objectifies nor excludes, but constitutes the real. This dynamism eliminates the need

---

24. "The Jordan, the Tiber and the Ganges: Three Kairological Moments of Christic Self-Consciousness," in John Hick and Paul Knitter, eds., *The Myth of Christian Uniqueness: Toward a Pluralistic Theology of Religions* (Maryknoll, N.Y.: Orbis Books, 1987), 89–116 [hereafter MCU]; "The Crux of Christian Ecumenism: Can Universality and Chosenness Be Held Simultaneously?" *Journal of Ecumenical Studies* 26 (Winter 1989), 82–99 [hereafter Crux]; "Can Theology Be Transcultural? [Plenary Address at 1988 College Theology Society Meeting]," in *Pluralism and Oppression: Theology in World Perspective* (Lanham, Md.: University Press of America, 1991), 3–22 [hereafter CTS].

25. See MCU, 109–10; Raimundo Panikkar, "The Myth of Pluralism: The Tower of Babel — A Meditation on Non-Violence," *Cross Currents* 29 (Summer 1979), 197–230; "The Invisible Harmony: A Universal Theory of Religion or a Cosmic Confidence in Reality?," in Leonard Swidler, ed., *Toward a Universal Theology of Religion* (Maryknoll, N.Y.: Orbis Books, 1987), 118–153.

26. MCU, 90.

27. Crux, 97.

28. MCU, 112.

29. Crux, 91.

30. MCU, 90.

31. MCU, 102.

to search for a center. In such a relationship, there can be no absolute center; instead, as in trinitarian theology, the participants are constituted by relationship and mutual participation.

In the same pluralistic model, truth is neither one nor many. There are not many truths, but an acknowledgment of the limitations of any knowing before the Mystery. One's particular understanding of Christ is less than the reality of Christ. Panikkar uses this disparity to explain the priority of the principle of identity over the dialectical principle of non-contradiction. Rather than explaining self as *not being* something else, the principle of identity affirms the self to be all that it *is*. This Indic style of thought "tries to discover that which is most common, most present everywhere, most immanent, most identical to itself and to everything else to which identity can be applied and affirmed — *brahman*."[32] The Holy is not the absolutely Other but the most intimate, the basic; the ultimate reality is not the most transcendent but the most self-identical, the most deeply immanent. A familiar constellation of terms arises: *dynamism,* the *incarnate* and *concrete, non-dualism, participation,* and *mystery.* To these must be added the cognitional confidence in one's identity as the revealed truth and ontological confidence in the reality so revealed as the principle of one's being. When one's relation to religious truth is understood as confident participation in Mystery, the cognitional grounds for interreligious struggle and rejection of the other are undermined.

The affirmation of the Christian faith takes place within this pluralistic context. However, pluralism does not lead to affirming that there are many saviors or many Christs. Pluralism means "denying the meaningfulness of any quantitative individualization in the Mystery of Christ. The saving power which Christians call Christ — is neither one nor many."[33] One does not objectify and cannot stand numerically apart from the reality in which one exists; this most concrete reality cannot be grasped as an abstract universal. The Christ is Mystery, cognitively and ontologically, radically open to new understanding. Knowing and loving participation in this principle of being constitutes the religious path. "Christians may find in this christic principle the point of union, understanding, and love with all humankind and with the whole of the cosmos, so that in this concreteness they find the most radical human, cosmic and divine communion with reality — notwithstanding other possible homeomorphic equivalents."[34] The christic principle points to the ground of Christian life but remains humbly open to the activity of the spirit, transparent to the Mystery itself, faithful to the self-emptying character of Christ: "The Christian point of insertion is the kenotic experience of Christ, which entails acceptance of and openness to the Spirit."[35]

This essential openness is not a qualification, diffusion or limitation of the christic principle. That principle has a constitutive dynamism and freedom:

---

32. Crux, 90.
33. MCU, 111.
34. MCU, 112.
35. MCU, 112.

"The christic event has an inherent dynamism to take flesh wherever it can."[36] The activity of this incarnational dynamism includes ambiguity of direction, ambivalence of results, and lack of any absolute a priori justification. But this dynamism of freedom, this paradoxical principle of identity, is also the transformative principle at work in human experience:

> We become aware of this [incarnational] impulse insofar as we experience the Christic event to be connected with the destiny of the human race and with the very dynamism of Being. We are both actors in and spectators of the selfsame display of Reality. Not only the fate of the earth, but also the very life of the universe, is something about which we share the glory, the burden, and the responsibility.[37]

The concrete universality of the christic event, connected with the destiny of the human race and with the fate of the earth, but also with the dynamism of Being and the very life of the universe, calls forth a fundamental care for incarnate form, a kenotic and non-dual identification with this creative principle.

Identification with this principle, participation in its activity, and kenotic openness to its freedom constitute the mystic core of Christian life, a fundamental choice about the spiritual path:

> The future of Christian history will show whether this effort at incarnation follows the pattern of the Grand Inquisitor or the Spirit of Bethlehem, under the witness of the skies, the hospitality of animals, the astonishment of shepherds, the astonishment of the Magi. Without this mystic core, the entire event degenerates into a masochistic complacency in being humble or a sadistic drive to show the power of the Cross.[38]

Immersion in the christic event *is* humbling because it is a power not determined by one's particular individuality: Christ is a principle of life both transcendent and free. Identification with this principle constitutes an attitude of active, religious nonviolence, participation in the freedom of the spirit.

Awareness of the christic principle involves a new Christian self-consciousness. Being Christian no longer entails identification with the religio-political *imperium* of Western civilization, Christendom, or with the superiority claims of a particular institutional religion, Christianity. Panikkar calls this identification with the fundamental christic fact "Christianness," a path of personal religiousness, "emphasizing the personal spiritual path, the discovery of the kingdom of heaven, the pearl, the wholeness of the Mystical Body, the communion with the divine, the interior, historical, and at the same time cosmic and transtemporal Christ."[39]

---

36. CTS, 14.
37. CTS, 14.
38. CTS, 17.
39. MCU, 113.

Christianness, as this path of personal religiousness, involves an "experience of the life of Christ within ourselves, insight into a communion, without confusion, with all reality, an experience that 'I and the Father are One,' that labels do not matter, that security is of no importance, and that reflection also is a secondary source (although a primary tool)."[40] Experience of the christic principle leads to a recognition of one's identity as participation in the non-dual character of the cosmotheandric Reality. This mystical foundation of religious life as identification with the activity of the christic event does away with the search for any absolute religious center, with the importance of particular labels for religious identity, and with the finality of any inquiry based primarily on discursive inquiry, any Christo*logy,* or ecclesio*logy,* any theo*logy,* any *logos* that does not transcend itself in experiencing the unity within diversity.

Panikkar concludes his essay in *The Myth of Christian Uniqueness* with a personal "interpretation of Christ in a theoanthropocosmic vision":

> The mystery that is at the beginning and will be at the end, the alpha and omega by and through which all has to come into being, the light that enlightens every creature, the word that is in every authentic word, the reality that is totally material, completely human, and simply divine, which is at work everywhere and elusively present wherever there is reality, the meeting place at the crossroads of reality where all realms meet, that which does not come with fanfare and about which we should not believe that it is here or there, that which we do not know when we perform a good or an evil action and yet is "there," that which we are — and shall be — and which we were, that symbol of all reality not only as it was or is, but as it still shall freely be also through our synergy, is what I believe to be the Christ.[41]

Christ, the christic fact, christic event, christic principle: the Christ is *the* mystery, the ground of being, consciousness and creative activity, the principle of being which transcends finite mathematics and linear geometry, the source of the transformative power which is the core of all reality and the dynamism of its each and every manifestation. Panikkar insists that focus on the christic principle does not seek to escape "the scandal of the incarnation and the process of redemption"; history and revelation in history are real, but not the whole of reality ("I do not worship history") — or of revelation. "Just as traditional theology speaks of a *creatio continua,* we could by analogy envision a continuous incarnation, not only in the flesh, but also in the acts and events of all creatures. Every being is a Christophany."[42]

The christic principle is experienced as a relationship in depth with the power which is constitutive of human consciousness, the dynamism immanent in the desire to know and in the development of personal identity in relationship. At

---

40. MCU, 113.
41. MCU, 113–4.
42. MCU, 114.

the same time, this Lord is the power from which the world proceeds, is sustained, and returns. Knowing is empowered, persons grow and are related, and the world is sustained by participation in this principle: this is the cosmotheandric (or theoanthropocosmic) nature of reality. This relationship of participation among God, persons, and the world is non-dual. Non-duality means that such a relation cannot be numerically determined or modeled in linear fashion: it is neither one nor many. In this sense the christic principle is one without a second, but affirms identity *and* difference.

The christic principle is rightly called Christ by Christians, for it is experienced concretely in Jesus. Even for Christians, however, this principle is not limited to the particular qualities of the historical Jesus. Through their commitment to Christ, Christians perceive and affirm the totality of the christic principle (the *pars pro toto* effect). When Christians enter deeply into the religious dynamics of other traditions, they encounter a reality homeomorphically related to Christian experience. The christic principle is not a universal theory; it is always concrete in expression and universal in extension, not exclusively particular or abstractly general.

Speaking of the christic principle, experienced at the heart of Christian life and in-depth contact with other traditions, always invokes a confession of wonder at a mystery, pluralistic in manifestation, which cannot be encompassed by names or traditions. This character of mystery calls for a kenotic attitude, an emptying of self and transparency to the activity of the Spirit, which constitutes intentional participation in the dynamic character of this principle.

RESPONSE

Such an invitation calls for a response. Panikkar's description of the christic principle and of Christianness as a way of authentic religious living requires more than an appreciative summary. Since perception follows the manner of the perceiver, I am responding not as a practitioner of the theological field called Christology, nor as an official representative of a particular Christian theological system, but as a historian of religions whose own lived understanding of Christianity has been decisively converted by study and participation in the religious traditions of India. My own entry into Hinduism has been through Bengal Vaiṣṇavism, the Caitanya devotional movement, as lived in ritual and performance in the Braj region of north central India, especially in the aesthetics of devotional drama, the cultivation of emotional participation in the realm of Kṛṣṇa's divine play.

Panikkar's method and conclusions accord with my own experience in some fundamental ways. Entering deeply into the dynamics of a Hindu text, a drama in performance as much as a sūtra commentary, leads to an encounter with the Lord. For me, as a Christian, that encounter is not different from my long history of encounters, in radiance and darkness, in word and sacrament, in solitude and community, with Christ. But this encounter, while not different from those others, is not the same. My acquired sensibility for the aesthetic emotions required to appreciate the play of Kṛṣṇa in the *rāslīlā* and for the various levels of participation, divine and human, which intersect in this play was deeply rooted in Kṛṣṇa, in the particular qualities of Caitanyaite devotion, in the land of Braj itself, in the cycle of daily and festival *pūja,* and in the distinct personalities of individual temple deities: an experiential non-dualism of self and Lord, of Christ and Kṛṣṇa, that informs and reforms subsequent religious living. Acceptance of some form of non-dualism, dubbed *advaita* or *bhedābheda,* ontological or devotional, represents a sympathy for Panikkar's description of the christic principle.

The experience of living as a participant observer within the dynamics of another religious culture challenged my theological structure, my orthodoxy, far less than it did my way of life, my praxis. What positive affirmation of Christian life is appropriate in a religious environment shared with other traditions? Panikkar asserts that Christianity is not so much a religion distinct from and apart from others, but rather that Christianness constitutes a radical openness to the activity of the Spirit, a deep solidarity with others, a religious way that incarnates itself in each environment to the point of losing itself in bringing clarity and deeper vision to all. This understanding of Christian vocation seems closer to the ministry of Jesus than that of Christianity as institution. In an environment where the shared meal bespoke intimacy and fellowship, Jesus set a daring standard of non-exclusion, welcome, and communion. Christian life struggles to incarnate this radical acceptance and reciprocal welcome: a table fellowship where everyone is welcomed and no one is excluded. What a kingdom of God that is! In the midst of increasing communalism in India and deepening religious strife in so many places, Christianity is not another religion, asserting its own claims against others, playing its role in socio-political activities that violate religious integrity. The task, to which Panikkar has contributed abundantly in his discussion of the christic principle, is to develop further Christianity as a way of life, a Christianness that, having died to its own desire to exclude and dominate, can confront the powers of division and can participate in a shared meal of reconciliation. "Authentic life is neither conserved nor passed on to others, but burned off, lived out, which means constantly renewed, at the risk of death and new birth."[43]

Panikkar's understanding of Christology as the manifestation of the christic principle provides a useful theological environment for conversation about the meaning of Christ, for selecting those issues which most need theological reflection, and for clarifying the incarnate purpose of Christian affirmation, of the lived christic principle. However, even if I am modestly confident to have summarized some of Panikkar's reflection on this Christophany, and even more, if I am convinced that Panikkar's core method and affirmations are constructive contributions to Christian reflection, I find it necessary to raise three important questions about theological method, language, and context.

First, Panikkar's *method* does not constitute a *compelling* theology. There is

---

43. Raimundo Panikkar, *Myth, Faith and Hermeneutics* (New York: Paulist Press, 1979), 157.

no relentless logical structure to which I, or another reader, finally feel compelled to submit. While there is a spirit of theological nonviolence, this is a powerfully *seductive* theology where the theological rules are different. However rigorous the structure of a particular essay may be, the characteristic mode of discourse goes beyond *logos*. Panikkar is weaving a pattern of symbol and language which becomes in time familiar, sometimes delightful, but ultimately necessary to continue the conversation. A reviewer[44] may well sense the importance of "cosmotheandric" but despair of uncovering its root meaning, not to mention the resonance which links the term to an evolving pattern of thought and the history of this discourse. Panikkar's use of language and symbol is effective; the attentive reader is caught in a web of meanings which establish creative connections where none seemed possible. Whence comes the charm of seductive theology? What standard of allure renders it authentic? What constitutes "just and fair play" in seductive theology? If the circumstances are right, I am quite willing to be seduced, but I would like to know a little more about the game we are playing.

This same development of *language* and symbol presents a related set of problems. It would be impossible at any one point to explain anew the entire network of terms and images which serves to define Panikkar's theology. The scope of his writings is vast, his output daunting: in languages, topics, even fields of inquiry. Is there a cumulative point from which the pattern can be grasped, the weave understood? What could be said without *homeomorphic, ontonomy, cosmotheandric, pars pro toto, Christianness,* and the *christic principle?* The grasp of Panikkar's ideas is also dependent on the weaving of images of entwined geometric strips, water and drops and oceans, rivers and waters and clouds, mountains and paths, rainbows and colors and white light, standing within or without, and a reflecting play of mirrors. His theology is constituted by these neologisms and made-to-order symbols. More recent essays presuppose earlier exercises through brief reference to problems treated previously and elsewhere. If some of Panikkar's essays have a tone of intellectual autobiography, the notes more and more seem to establish a sort of auto-bibliography, a cycle of materials that must be invoked to understand the present work. Let me borrow another image: each point on the circumference (the surface of the wheel) requires the others for structural coherence; how does one move toward the center (the hub of the wheel)? Is there a certain self-referential bondage to Panikkar's work — book to essay, term to term, image to image — a coherence and clarity that reflects only on itself? Worst of all, does this mode of discourse itself involve the meta-system or meta-theology which Panikkar seeks to avoid when that is proposed by Leonard Swidler and others?

My final issue is about initiation. The christic principle, that participation in the life of God, presumes a confession of wonder and flaunts a mystical qual-

---

44. See Johannes Verkuyl's comments on Panikkar ("through a kind of 'cosmotheandrism,' whatever that may be...") in his review of Leonard Swidler, ed., *Toward a Universal Theology of Religion* (Maryknoll, N.Y.: Orbis Books, 1987) in *International Review of Missionary Research* 12 (July 1988), 137–38.

ity. The one who is the being of all being, the consciousness in all knowing, and beyond all telling, the bliss tasted in each joy: this one we have come to know in the depths of ourselves. How are theologians to respond? Various traditions would prescribe meditation and prayer, chanting and dancing, deep feeling and an artist's loving expression. A sincere struggle with Panikkar's theological method and religious language implies that being scholars and theologians is a religious path with its own rites of initiation, its disciplines of purification and prayer, its worship and ecstasy. Where is the place for the mystic in the groves of academe, for prayer in graduate theological education? What form of prayer is needed to engage in reflection on the christic principle, what *sādhana* to cooperate in its incarnation?

Despite these concerns and perceived limitations, I am grateful to Raimon Panikkar for providing a context in which the understanding of Christian life, Christianness, can be deepened. I have tried to show how the christic principle illustrates the development of his Christological thought. I first encountered the writings of Raimon Panikkar in 1972 through two short books, published in Italian,[45] which so interested me that I translated them for my own spiritual reading and to share with friends. I am happy that I continue to be seduced by his theological work, challenged by his re-creation of religious language, and moved to prayer.

---

45. Raimundo Panikkar, *La Gioia Pasquale* (Vicenza: La Locusta, 1968); and *La Presenza di Dio* (Vicenza: La Locusta, 1970).

9

Faith in Jesus Christ in the Presence of Hindu Theism

DANIEL P. SHERIDAN

EXERCISES ON RAIMON PANIKKAR'S BRIDGE OF DIALOGUE

Lumen Ex Lumine — Lumen Ad Lumen.

There is probably no contemporary writer in the area of interreligious discussion who has such uniquely personal style of thinking and reflection as does Raimon Panikkar, and who puts it to such exquisite use. This engaged, nuanced, and idiosyncratic style of thought causes his writing to be very difficult to interpret and yet also makes the attempt extremely productive. As Ewert Cousins states: "His sentences are like entrances to the shaft of a mine, drawing the reader to treasures below. Dynamic with playfulness and power, full of bubbling joy and cascading energy, it covers a breathtaking range — encompassing many disciplines, the entire globe, and the sweep of history."[1] The extent and breadth of Panikkar's writing, as well as the length of his career, make it difficult to summarize his position. He admits that he has changed some of his judgments. However, each work is valuable in itself, especially *The Unknown Christ of Hinduism,* which Panikkar revised seventeen years after its first publication.[2] *The Unknown Christ of Hinduism,* as well as some of his latest essays, will be the focus of this study on a Christian theology of Hindu theism.

Daniel P. Sheridan is Professor of the History of Religions and Assistant Vice President for Academic Affairs at Loyola University, New Orleans. He is author of *Advaitic Theism of the Bhagavata Purana* and numerous articles in *Journal of Dharma, Anima, Indian Philosophical Annual, Purana, Journal of Religion, Journal of Religious Studies,* and *Cross Currents.*

1. Ewert Cousins, "Raimundo Panikkar and the Christian Systematic Theology of the Future," *Cross Currents,* 29 (Summer 1979), p. 141.
2. Raimundo Panikkar, *The Unknown Christ of Hinduism,* completely revised and enlarged edition (Maryknoll, N.Y.: Orbis Books, 1981).

The profoundest tribute I am able to pay to Raimon Panikkar is that I have read and listened to his writings and his thought, struggled with them, and been encouraged from them to be engaged as a Christian with the worlds of Hinduism. Part of this tribute includes my disagreement with several of his basic insights, approaches, and conclusions. I sometimes want to speak where Panikkar wishes to remain silent, and to listen where he wishes to speak. I want to affirm where Panikkar wishes to dialogue. I prefer the kataphatic *bhaktimārga*, path of love, as an interreligious catalyst, instead of Panikkar's choice of catalyst of the apophatic *jñanavā*, path of knowledge.[3]

I would like to compose this essay without getting involved in the seemingly endless debates about the terms *dialogue, exclusive, inclusive, uniqueness, pluralist* and *universal.* Is it not rather surprising that exponents of dialogue are so guilty of using a rhetoric of preemptive persuasion? If there are many ways to the center, or even many centers, there are certainly many ways to be ecumenical. As Panikkar says, "We cannot prescribe from one single perspective what the other Christian views should be. This would amount to establishing ourselves as the ultimate criterion for Christian identity."[4] Although there certainly is an ultimate criterion for Christian identity, the history of Christianity suggests that in order to establish it something more than rhetorical overkill is needed. A fideistic solipsism may be in order. As a Christian, it is time to speak for oneself, and only oneself.

Of course, there is an irony here. At least on the Christian side, there is the ecclesial dimension to faith whereby it is more accurate to say "we believe" than "I believe." There is also the community of scholarship conducted according to critical canons whereby what one person thinks is shaped by many others. These two publics both need to be served by the individual, are present in the individual, and shape an individual person's thought. Yet, as Panikkar has so often emphasized, the community of the faith and the community of scholars are neither symmetrical, identical, nor separable. They both impinge on the individual. Scholarship separated from religious engagement must be used carefully. Moreover, the phenomenological *epoche* practiced in certain forms of critical scholarship is religiously barren: "To exclude my religious convictions from religious dialogue is like renouncing the use of reason in order to enter a reasonable encounter. . . . Dialogue must proceed from the depths of my religious attitude to these same depths in my partner."[5]

I sometimes refer to myself as being both a Christian theologian of religions and a historian of medieval Hindu theism, "without mixture and without separation." The possibility of a personal identity with such disparate elements has now become a theological datum itself, requiring a theology of religions

3. Raimundo Panikkar, "Indology as Cross-Cultural Catalyst," *Numen*, 18, no. 3, pp. 173–79.

4. Raimundo Panikkar, "The Jordan, The Tiber, and the Ganges: Three Kairological Moments of Christic Self-Consciousness," in John Hick and Paul Knitter, eds., *The Myth of Christian Uniqueness: Toward a Pluralistic Theology of Religions* (Maryknoll, N.Y.: Orbis Books, 1987), p. 111.

5. Raimundo Panikkar, *The Intrareligious Dialogue* (New York: Paulist Press, 1978), p. 50.

informed by critical scholarship. This "hypostatic" identification will help to explain why I do not think that Panikkar has produced a Hindu-Christian theology or a Christian theology of Hindu theism, although he has gone quite far toward the latter. This, however, does not mar his achievement. It is not even clear that he would want to do either, given his stringent requirements that such a theology be neither supracultural nor supercultural, but rather trans- or cross-cultural.[6] It is clear that Panikkar would never settle for a casual, or overly general, use of a word like *theology,* or of a misleading parallelism like *Hindu-Christian.* It is part of the joy of reading him that he would immediately begin to unpack the words, to unveil unexpected nuances of their etymologies, their semantic range, and especially their deeper import.

Panikkar is a personal combination of an engaged experiencer of the realities of other religions, a scholar of religions, and an extremely able synthetic philosopher, "carefully mixed and carefully separated." He is a Christian and verges on being a theologian. For Panikkar, as for myself, the fact of each person's particular union/juxtaposition of elements is not a cause for a diagnosis of schizophrenia. It is a result of the peculiar nature of the culture in which we live. Contemporary, modern culture subsumes and sublates what in the past was a great variety of discrete human cultures and religions. We live in a culture that does history, is aware of other cultures, seeks to understand them, even to live within them, all the while critically aware of itself both through our individual self-consciousness and through the canons of scholarship. Hence the hermeneutical "exercises" that Panikkar has produced are very helpful prologomena for a Christian theology of relationship to certain facets of Hinduism. The exercises are not such a theology but, in Panikkar's word, "theologoumena."[7] However, I do walk with Panikkar through these exercises, find them richly rewarding, and then go in theological directions that I do not think he would wish to go in, but directions that I think he would respect, because they are informed by critical scholarship and by the religious engagement of Christian faith. I do not attempt a "universal theology of religions," or "pluralist theology," but rather a theology of the relationship of Christian faith to certain dimensions of Hinduism.

Panikkar makes a fundamental assumption, which I consider penultimate rather than ultimate, about a reality that I consider may be penultimate rather than ultimate: "The *ultimate* religious *fact* does not lie in the realm of doctrine or even in individual self-consciousness."[8] This is true, but neither does the ultimate religious fact lie somewhere other than in the encounter of some individuals with what they consider the ultimately real, if the ultimately real allows the encounter. Doctrine is the means of communicating that encounter, when it occurs, to others. Doctrine thus may also be the proximate occasion of, and means to, the encounter for many who have not experienced the original

---

6. See Raimundo Panikkar, "Can Theology Be Transcultural?" in Paul Knitter, ed., *Pluralism and Oppression: Theology in World Perspective* (Lanham, Md.: University Press of America/College Theology Society, 1988).

7. Panikkar, "Can Theology be Transcultural?," p. 20.

8. Panikkar, *The Intrareligious Dialogue,* p. 57.

encounter itself. Doctrine may be abused, but its proper use vindicates its function. It may also be true that the encounter with the ultimately real need not be universally "experiencable" in order for the ultimately real in its own order to be universally efficacious. To say otherwise would be a further assumption, either gratuitous or in need of a substantial defense. Panikkar goes on:

> The ultimate religious fact can — and may well — be present everywhere and in every religion, although its "explication" may require varied degrees of discovery, realization, evangelization, revelation, hermeneutics, etc. And this makes plausible that this fundamental — religious — *fact* may have different names, interpretations, levels of interpretations, levels of consciousness and the like, which are not irrelevant but which may be existentially equivalent for the person undergoing the concrete process of realization.[9]

I accept the assumption with these provisos: (1) This assumption is really a central judgment in Panikkar's philosophy of religious encounter. (2) The fact that "the *ultimate* religious *fact* . . . can — and may well — be present everywhere and in every religion" does not mean that it *must* be present everywhere and in every religion. The ultimate religious fact may not be present.[10] As Panikkar states: "Religions may be incommensurable with each other despite some possible common traits. Each religion is unique with the uniqueness of every real being."[11] However, he then goes on to say that each "one represents the whole of the human experience in a concrete way," as if every individual real being were an instantiation of all the possibilities of being. This seems to be an a priori judgment, and thus my next proviso. (3) There are both a priori and a posteriori elements in a judgment of presence or absence. There would need to be an a priori reason, prejudgment, or belief in order to make the a posteriori judgment of a presence or an absence of the "ultimate religious fact."[12] (4) One may have an a priori reason or belief that would consider what Panikkar considers *ultimate* to be *penultimate*. As such it would be the basis for making different kinds of judgments that Panikkar himself makes.

With these provisos, it is still a very useful exercise to follow Panikkar's thinking on the relationship of Christianity to Hinduism based on an existential encounter of the two within our own selves. Below, "On the Bridge to the

---

9. Ibid.

10. See Daniel P. Sheridan, "The Silence of God in Early Buddhism," *Studies in Formative Spirituality* I, no. 2 (May 1980).

11. Panikkar, "The Jordan, the Tiber, and the Ganges: Three Kairological Moments of Christic Self-Consciousness," p. 112. See also Daniel P. Sheridan, "Distinct by God's Word: Diversity and the Theology of Religion," *Journal of Dharma* 13, no. 2 (April–June 1988).

12. See Karl Rahner, *Foundations of Christian Faith: An Introduction to the Idea of Christianity,* trans. William V. Dych (New York: Seabury, 1978), p. 321: "It is of course a further question, and one which ultimately can be answered only in an a posteriori way by the history of religion, if we ask whether and to what an extent, and how explicitly or implicitly this anticipation of the absolute savior by faith's memory is demonstrable in mythology or in history. . . . At this point the dogmatic theologian has to hand the question over to the historian of religion and to his Christian interpretation of the history of religion."

Transcendent," I will examine what Panikkar has written on the relationship of Christianity to Hinduism; in "Theology: The Knowings of the Visions of the Eyes of Faith," I will explore a Christian theology of relationship to Hindu theism moving forward from Panikkar's thought; and in "A Christian's View of Krishna with the Eyes of Faith That See Jesus Christ," I will propose some possible affirmations about Krishna that a Christian may make.

ON THE BRIDGE TO THE TRANSCENDENT

We reply that Brahman is known.
Brahman, which is all-knowing and endowed with all powers,
whose essential nature is eternal purity, intelligence, and freedom, exists.[13]

Panikkar builds a bridge from Christianity to Hinduism, or at least to certain forms of Hinduism; in particular, and more precisely, to certain texts of Hinduism and to the experiences and insights that underlie these texts. So far the bridge has been chiefly of use to Christians. For a variety of reasons Hindus tend to ignore this bridge and others like it.[14]

In *The Unknown Christ of Hinduism* Panikkar proposes that Christ is the point of encounter between Christianity and Hinduism, and conversely that the point of encounter should be Christ. The point of encounter between humans and the divine is Christ, and the point of encounter between Christianity and Hinduism is Christ. The question is whether the point of encounter between Hindus and what they consider the ultimate reality is also Christ. If such encounters take place, they would be mutually implicative. Thus an encounter between Hinduism and Christianity would also be a mutual encounter of each with Christ. Also there might be an encounter of Christianity with Hinduism, but not necessarily of Hinduism with Christianity. This too would be an encounter with Christ. Such an encounter, if it takes place at the point of reality that Christians call Christ, would produce "interpenetration, mutual fecundation — and a mutation in the self-interpretation of these selfsame religious traditions."[15] Thus the meeting of the two religions in the persons of their adherents would not be a merely sociological phenomenon. At a deeper level, it would be an encounter with Christ on both sides of the encounter. For Christians, at least, it would be a new place or point of encounter with the reality, Christ, that is the heart of their faith. The encounter takes place in persons of deep human honesty who are open intellectually in their search and who are loyal to their own religious faith and

---

13. George Thibaut, trans., *The Vedānta Sūtras of Bādārayana with the Commentary of Śaṅkara,* Part I (New York: Dover Publications, 1962 [1890]), p. 14, I.1.1.

14. See the analysis and discussion of Kana Mitra, *Catholicism-Hinduism: Vadāntic Investigation of Raimundo Panikkar's Attempt at Bridge Building* (Lanham, Md.: University Press of America, 1987), pp. 125–26: "Most Hindus are not aware of Panikkar, and the few that know of him are not acquainted with his thought in depth.... They are suspicious and not without reason." See also Panikkar's own discussion of this point in *The Unknown Christ of Hinduism,* pp. 9–10.

15. Panikkar, *The Unknown Christ of Hinduism,* p. 35.

tradition. Two faiths and traditions meet in such persons, and a common reality underlies the faiths and the traditions, and their encounter.

The point of encounter is not a doctrine. Instead, it is existential, or "ontic-intentional."[16] The point of encounter is a reality in its own right over and above the fact that it is a point of encounter. The point of encounter occurs in human beings. The point of encounter where they meet is the ontic reality intended by both Hinduism and Christianity. Thus Panikkar proposes that there is a common ontic reality, called by different names, found in Hinduism and Christianity: "Neither will contest that the 'ontic intentionality' is the same in both religions: the greatest possible oneness with the Absolute."[17] In my view, the equation of two different traditions' superlative achievement, "the greatest possible oneness with the Absolute," is an impossible a posteriori judgment to make. As an a priori judgment made on the basis of Christian belief, there may be good reasons to accept it. Thus the common intended ontic reality is Christ of whom Christians have "the *gnōsis* that God is Trinity and our union is with God in Christ."[18]

Christians have a single term for this reality, Christ. Christ is the reality that partakes of both God and the human and as such can be the point of encounter between God and the human. It is precisely such a Christ that Panikkar states is the point of encounter between Hindus and Christians who encounter each other at the deepest religious level of their traditions. Thus the point of encounter between God and humans is also the point of encounter between humans of the two different religious traditions of faith. This latter encounter, a link between Hinduism and Christianity, phenomenally is a human endeavor, but theologically "we might also say that on a higher plane there is no link from below between these historical entities — only one from above, inasmuch as the truly transcendent call manifests itself as an immanent longing in all."[19]

Hindus, who participate in a religion (or group of religions), which sociologically is not as centered as Christianity with its central figure of Christ, do not have such a single term for this reality. Yet they do intend and propose such a reality and have met it many times and in many ways. Panikkar suggests the Hindu name Rama as a possible homologue to Christ: "Rama in fact is totally human and totally divine, Rama is material and spiritual, temporal and eternal."[20] Other Hindus would propose Siva or Krishna. They intend the ontic reality that is the point of contact between humans and the divine, regardless of how it was named, and Hindus take the many names for granted: "One is he whom the sages call by many names."[21] Thus what Panikkar proposes as "unknown" is the Christ known by Christians and not known by Hindus, under that name, and not known by Christians as being present in the ontic intentionality of Hinduism. The unknown Christ of Hinduism is the Christ hidden from

---

16. Ibid., p. 36.
17. Ibid.
18. Ibid.
19. Ibid., p. 96.
20. Ibid., p. 38.
21. Ṛg Veda I. 164. 46. The translation is Panikkar's.

Christians and Hindus but known by both in their separate traditions: "In the wake of St. Paul we believe we may speak not only of the unknown God of the Greeks, but also of the *hidden Christ of Hinduism* — hidden and unknown and yet present and at work because he is not far from any one of us."[22] This analysis has been from the viewpoint of Christianity. The reverse kind of analysis could well be made by Hindus, and has been made, with the same kind of consistency. Then, for example, the subject to be studied would be the unknown *Īśvara,* Lord, of Christianity, etc.

But why is this common intended ontic reality Christ, the Son, rather than the Father, the Godhead?[23] This specific identification is a crucial turn in Panikkar's analysis, since an identification of the common intended ontic reality as God, meaning the Father, would possibly bypass entirely the Christian teaching and experience of God as triune. If the common intended ontic reality is Christ, a trinitarian dimension unfolds. If it is not, then the Christian teaching of three persons might be subject to the rule of parsimony, that is, might seem to be gratuitous assertions. If there is no "economic" trinity in the other tradition, there might be no need for it in the Christian tradition. However, for a Christian to reflect about Christ is to reflect about the triune nature of God. This is subject to test in the encounter with another religion.[24] To find Christ rather than simply God in the initial stage of an encounter with another religion is to begin to discover an unknown trinity. Panikkar's *The Unknown Christ of Hinduism* is as much, if not more, a theology of the Trinity than a christology. Although Panikkar has also written a work explicitly focused on the Trinity, namely, *The Trinity and the Religious Experience of Man,*[25] I find this other work on the Trinity less satisfying because it is more abstract and philosophical, whereas *The Unknown Christ of Hinduism* is more theological and focused on Hinduism. In the latter, Panikkar, having made the theological judgment that the intended ontic reality that Christians call Christ is found in Hinduism, must also affirm the presence of the Father and of the Spirit in Hinduism. The three are inseparable. However, thus far the argument is a priori. It must move to the a posteriori.

Panikkar must thus explore the nature of what Hindus consider the ultimate religious fact on their terms, that is, in terms of Brahman. He turns to the Hindu school of Vedānta and its central text, the *Brahma Sūtras* of Bādārayana, *the Sūtras on Brahman.* The result is an extended and rewarding commentary on *Brahma Sūtras* I.1.2: "Whence the origin etcetera of this." The meaning of

---

22. Panikkar, *The Unknown Christ of Hinduism,* p. 168.

23. It may be that Panikkar's analysis here will turn out to be a very preliminary reconnaissance at only one point in the vastly variegated spectrum of Hindu positions. For example, an analysis of Madhva's (1238–1317 C.E.) theology may uncover an "unknown" Father: "Narayana, he whose only body is the plenitude of perfections, who is exempt from defects, who is supremely attainable through the totality of the sacred words, who gives to this world origin and all other states, whose excellence makes him the object of worship, who is always most dear to me, — I adore him, moved by intense devotion" (*Anuvyakhyana* of Madhva, Prologue 1).

24. See Daniel P. Sheridan, "Grounded in the Trinity: Suggestions for a Theology of Relationship to Other Religions," *The Thomist* 50 (April 1986).

25. Raimundo Panikkar, *The Trinity and the Religious Experience of Man* (Maryknoll, N.Y.: Orbis Books, 1973).

this Sūtra fleshed out is "Brahman is that from which all things come forth, into which they will return and by which they are maintained."[26] Panikkar's commentary is an excellent Indological study of the Sūtra, unfortunately little noticed by Indologists.

A very real knowledge of Brahman is given by Brahman as the grace of the desire to know Brahman, *a desiderium naturale,* either directly or through scripture. Sūtra I.1.1 states: "Then therefore the desire to know Brahman." Included inherently in this desire to know that which is yet unknown is a concurrent knowledge of the contingency of the world and of ourselves. Neither the world nor ourself is its own cause. Hence Brahman is "that from which the origin, etcetera of this." But is Brahman, "that from which the origin, etcetera of this," identical with God? In the context of Vedānta, the question is, is Brahman identical with *Īśvara,* the Lord? Vedānta divides on this point into non-theist and theist schools. Panikkar, basing himself on the non-theist analysis, states: "We could say that Brahman and God are, as it were, *materialiter* the same reality, but *formaliter* different. They point to the same reality, but from two different points of view.... God and Brahman are not just two perspectives of the 'same thing,' because both God and Brahman include the respective 'perspectives.' ... In the final analysis I am not proposing a synthesis but suggesting an understanding."[27] In many of the schools of Vedānta there is at least a formal distinction drawn between Brahman and *Īśvara,* so that Brahman is seen as impersonal and so that *Īśvara* is seen as personal. Further, the impersonal represents the transcendent better than the personal, and thus the two are represented as distinct.

There is a further question according to Vedānta: Is that from which the whole world proceeds Brahman in an absolute manner? Here Panikkar discerns the same movement that Christian Thomistic theology makes on a similar question regarding God's relation to that which is created. Would the cause of the world be transcendent enough, if it is indeed *cause* of the world, to be the transcendent Brahman? He states: "If without due discrimination we make Brahman responsible for the World, if we, as it were, tie Brahman to the World, then it appears difficult to maintain the transcendence, the absoluteness of Brahman."[28] If Brahman is essentially the cause of the world, Brahman is not transcendent enough to be Brahman. If Brahman is so transcendent as to be utterly beyond being a cause, Brahman would then be a superfluous concept in a discussion of the cause of the world. Some Vedāntins and some Christian Thomists are of the judgment, rightly, that "the relation of God as First Cause to the World is not a *real* one, that the reality of the effect and its variations do not affect the simplicity and independence of the cause, that divine causality is precisely of a unique type that results in a dependence that is only one-sided."[29] A real relation would imply that there is an accident, the relation to the created, in God, or would imply change in God. The result is a doctrine of the relation of God and the world,

---

26. Panikkar, *The Unknown Christ of Hinduism,* p. 108.
27. Ibid., p. 143.
28. Ibid., p. 145.
29. Ibid.

or of Brahman and the world, that is neither dualism nor monism. This is found in some forms both of Vedānta and of Christian philosophy. The lack of a real relation between God and the world and between Brahman and world is crucial for Panikkar's interpretation.

Panikkar sees the Vadāntic concept of *Īśvara* or Lord, i.e., God, as the point of Brahman's relation to the world and as the personal aspect of Brahman. *Īśvara,* according to Panikkar, while maintaining all the proper distinctions and differences between Vadāntic thought and Christian thought, "points towards the Mystery of Christ, who, being unique in his existence and essence, is as such equal to God. He is not *the* God, but *equal* to him, Son of God, God from God."[30] In the subtleties of Vadāntic dialectic, leaning toward the great commentator Śaṅkara's (ca. 788–820) interpretation, Panikkar discerns the Father and the Son. The Godhead/Father, without any loss in transcendence, is the basis for the Son from which source the world springs: "All things came into being through him and without him not one thing came into being" (John 1:3). Brahman, without any loss in transcendence, in an extremely close homology (much closer in fact than it seems), is the basis of *Īśvara,* "that from which the origin etcetera of this world." The "that" of the "that from which the origin etcetera of this world" is the Logos, Christ, God from God, *lumen ex lumine.* "Thus Christ (Īśvara), one with the *real* World is — shall be, if we include time — one with God the Father so that God may be all in all and nothing remain beyond or besides or behind him."[31]

Panikkar's trinitarian insight into Vedānta moves beyond his notion of a homomorphic equivalent, the approximate equivalence of points in two different systems. The triune God in the second person, the Christ, is the point of encounter between Hinduism and Christianity because the Christ, the *Īśvara,* is the point of encounter of the Hindus with Brahman, the Father. "Ultimately, we have but one comment to make: *that from which this World comes forth and to which it returns and by which it is sustained, that is Īśvara, the Christ.*"[32] Certainly this Christ is both known and unknown to the Hindus, and is known, and has been unknown, to the Christians. It is now known to the Christians who care to know. Panikkar's is not just brilliant dialectic, not just the discovery of a "vestige," but a Christian theological insight that needs no further adjective: "I am not proposing a synthesis but suggesting an understanding." This is a Christian understanding that is on the verge of becoming a Christian theology of the relationship of Christian faith to Hinduism. Of course, it is not a Hindu theology or a Hindu-Christian theology.

Although Panikkar's main emphasis here is on Christ and then on the Father, where Christ is there is also the Father, and where the Father and the Christ are, there is unknown Christ, although Panikkar says little of the Spirit. In fact, the Father is even more unknown because his unknownness is essential to the

---

30. Ibid., p. 160.
31. Ibid.
32. Ibid., p. 162.

Father's being while the being of the second person is precisely to be known in the relations between God and the world. The Son's unknownness is an accident, while the Father's is in some way essential. This unknownness of the Father will be taken up in Panikkar's later work, *The Silence of God: The Answer of the Buddha.*[33]

What was only hinted at in *The Unknown Christ of Hinduism,* an apophatic experience and intuition of the Father's distant, transcendent presence/absence, will be further developed by Panikkar in his later work. As Ewert Cousins has noted, there is a strong affinity of Panikkar's developed trinitarian theology with Greek theology and the theology of the Franciscan school. "His chief point of originality is his notion of the silence of the Father, which is derived from his immersion in the strong apophatism of Buddhism."[34] Panikkar's trinitarian judgment of the presence of Christ/Son in Hinduism is profoundly Nicaean, and brilliantly orthodox, but with Cousins I have questions about his christology.[35]

The problematic area is the incarnation. Panikkar rightly observes:

> The predominantly Semitic mentality of Christian theology will reach the intelligibility of the ultimately ungraspable Mystery ascending to it from its concrete and visible manifestation: Jesus Christ. Thus, once the identification is made, it will with great difficulty proceed in the opposite direction; if Jesus Christ is the Mystery, any other name or real manifestation of the Mystery will appear inadequate because it contradicts Christian understanding.[36]

Precisely because of this difficulty, Panikkar searched for the unknown Christ. But in doing so he sees a division in Jesus/Christ that other Christians do not see:

> I have tried to show in this book that though a Christian believes that "Jesus is the Christ" as more than an abstract affirmation, i.e. as an expression of faith, this sentence is not identical to "the Christ is Jesus." Similarly, I have maintained that the assertion "Christ is the Lord" cannot simply be reversed. It is not necessary, in fact, that the Lord be named Christ or acknowledged by this title, because the saving name of Christ is a supername, above every name.[37]

This does not seem to be an adequate expression of my faith in the concrete actuality of Jesus. Here is where individual Christians should speak for themselves.

---

33. Raimon Panikkar, *The Silence of God: The Answer of the Buddha* (Maryknoll, N.Y.: Orbis Books, 1989 [1970]).

34. Cousins, "Raimundo Panikkar and the Systematic Theology of the Future," p. 148.

35. Ibid.: "I believe his Christology has not reached the mature crystallization of his Trinitarian theology."

36. Panikkar, *The Unknown Christ of Hinduism,* p. 52.

37. Ibid., p. 14. See Raimundo Panikkar, "The Meaning of Christ's Name in the Universal Economy of Salvation," in M. Dhavamony, ed., *Evangelization, Dialogue and Development, Documenta Missionalia* (Rome: Università Gregoriana Editrice, 1972).

It took several centuries to work forward from Nicaea's (325 A.D.) classic trinitarian understanding of the Son as God from God, light from light, one in being with the Father. The Nicaean understanding and experience of the triune nature of God struggled for several centuries to find an adequate understanding and experience of the Son's relationship to Jesus of Nazareth, died and risen for human beings. On the road to Chalcedon (451 A.D.)[38] lay Apollonaris, Nestorius, Cyril, and Eutyches. Chalcedon discerned and affirmed an orthodox christology in the orthodox trinitarian faith of Nicaea: from the moment of the incarnation, the humanity of Jesus is inseparable from the divinity of the Son; there is one person in two natures, which are united unconfusedly, unchangeably, indivisibly, inseparably. In my judgment, if Christ is discovered in the encounter with Hinduism, that Christ should be the Christ affirmed both at Nicaea and at Chalcedon. Why? Is the judgment upon which such an affirmation is made possible?

Although so many in the present world of theology have their doubts, and see too incarnational a christology as an obstacle to dialogue and to an adequate theology in our intercultural world, I see no obstacle in a Chalcedonian basis for a Christian theology of relationship to Hinduism. (Besides that is my faith/belief.) This judgment is made a priori on the ground of Christian faith, and should be open to the same kind of a posteriori discernment that Panikkar conducted in *The Unknown Christ of Hinduism*. If a Nicaean Christ can be discerned in Hinduism, why not a Chalcedonian Christ?

THEOLOGY: THE KNOWINGS OF THE VISIONS
OF THE EYES OF FAITH

Let us suppose I have grasped the basic belief of a Vaishnava and therefore share it; in other words I can honestly affirm what an orthodox Vaiṣṇava believes. Does this mean I have deserted my original religious position? Are the two beliefs not essentially irreconcilable? Either I believe in Krishna or I believe in Christ. Either I am a Christian and declare Jesus as the Savior of mankind, or I follow Krishna and acknowledge him as the true Savior of mankind. Is it not a double betrayal to try to reconcile these two beliefs, which conflict at every point? Can we find any way out of this dilemma?[39]

In "Faith and Belief: A Multireligious Experience" Panikkar proposes that a distinction between belief and faith can help resolve the dilemmas of "Are the two beliefs not essentially irreconcilable? Either I believe in Krishna or I believe in Christ?" Beliefs are "translations into a given language understandable in a given tradition, of something that outsoars all utterance."[40] More profound

---

38. From the point of view of Eastern Orthodoxy, the road continued until Constantinople III in 680–681 A.D.

39. Raimundo Panikkar, "Faith and Belief: A Multireligious Experience," *The Intrareligious Dialogue* (New York: Paulist Press, 1978), p. 10.

40. Ibid., p. 7.

than the horizontal level of beliefs, there may be a vertical convergence of faith, common to many, which "is a simple, vital act which needs only a minimum of intellectual explicitness...has no fixed points, no adequate intellectual expression, and can only be imperfectly translated into human words."[41] Such a faith is naked. It can separate itself from its expression in a particular tradition's expressed beliefs because those expressions are always inadequate. Because faith can separate itself from beliefs, it can enter into another's belief to reach for that other's faith. This is a new religious experience that can be expressed as a belief. This new belief can be added to former beliefs. Whatever the horizontal encounter of beliefs may come to, for Panikkar, the encounter of persons of faith is vertical and convergent. It "is the connection with the beyond, however you choose to envision it."[42] The answer to the dilemma of "Either I believe in Krishna or I believe in Christ" lies in the level of beliefs. Panikkar in this essay chooses to bypass it. He affirms of faith: "The act of faith is not only transcendent, uniting us with what surpasses us, but also transcendental. It exceeds all possible formulations, and it makes them possible because it precedes them. Faith is a constitutive human dimension."[43] Panikkar is trying to avoid any simplistic reduction. "Faith cannot be equated with belief, but faith always needs a belief to be faith. Belief is not faith, but it must convey faith. A disembodied faith is not faith."[44] Although it is not clear to what an extent there may be a differential in the way beliefs express a single experience of faith, on the level of faith there is no dilemma, no need to choose between Christ and Krishna.

There is still the question of the level of beliefs, and it would be at that level that the theology of relationships of faith in Jesus Christ to other religions must take place. I have just used the term *faith* in a way different from that which Panikkar proposes. I am not distinguishing so sharply the nakedness of faith. Panikkar several times cites Thomas Aquinas on this point: "*Actus credentis non terminatur ad enuntiabile sed ad rem* — the act of the believer does not end at the formulation, but in the thing itself."[45] An interesting thing happens, however, when the *res* is a *persona* intended as an ontic reality, when the *significatus* is the Jesus Christ of Christian faith. Then something more needs to be said about faith and belief.

Faith, as Panikkar understands it, is an act that intends an ontic reality that underlies all that is and that is sufficient unto itself apart from all that is. Such an act is both subjective, as a human act, and objective, as an act that truly reaches to what it intends. Faith is certain that it reaches what it intends not from having grasped the intended but instead from having been grasped by the intended. However, this grasping is itself an *enuntiabile*. The act of believing does not search for the intended; it is the reaching of the intended itself be-

---

41. Panikkar, *The Unknown Christ of Hinduism,* p. 60.
42. Panikkar, "Faith and Belief: A Multireligious Experience," p. 18.
43. Ibid., p. 21.
44. Ibid., p. 18.
45. Cited in Raimundo Panikkar, *Myth, Faith and Hermeneutics: Cross-Cultural Studies* (New York: Paulist Press, 1979), p. 6.

cause the intended allows itself to be reached. The act of believing knows while it is intending and knows what and whom it has intended. As Hans Urs von Balthasar notes:

> The formula *fides quaerens intellectum* [faith seeking understanding] does not fully correspond to what we find in the Scriptures. Here we do not find the gnōsis [knowledge] of faith presented as searching and tentative (which would make it somehow uncertain), but rather as solid and all-encompassing at bottom, a knowledge which needs no further instruction so long as it remains faithful to the principle which enlightens it.[46]

Quaerens (seeking) must inseparably be joined in faith with *inveniens* (finding). Faith always has a gnoseological component. There is a circumincession of *pistis* (faith) and *gnōsis* (knowledge). If we have discovered the unknown Christ of Hinduism, we have turned the unknown into the known in an act not divorced from the act of faith. The act of faith should not be disengaged from the experience of insight, from understanding, and from the co-inherent knowing of that which is intended.

Faith has eyes. Its seeing is a knowing. The Christian believer in a single act may know Jesus Christ.[47] The believer in known Jesus Christ knows that from which all things have come forth, into which they will return and by which they are maintained, has become incarnate, died, been buried, and risen, and will return again. Without discussing the complexities of the language used here, I believe that Jesus Christ, in a Chalcedonian sense,[48] is co-present, truly real in my present moment as well as in any moment when I may encounter one of the religious realities of Hinduism. This is an antecedent and a priori judgment. A Christian theology of relationship to the forms of Hinduism begins here with the a priori, but such a beginning is utterly inadequate in an age of interreligious encounter and of the scholarship of the history of religions. It is also inadequate on its own grounds. As Panikkar has shown in *The Unknown Christ of Hinduism,* Christ is the point of encounter between Christianity and Hinduism. A theology of relationship to another religion cannot be content with the "unknown." Once the unknown comes into view, when one knows that one does not know, or in this case, when one knows that Christ is present, but not the how and the why: "Then therefore the inquiry into Brahman." The type of investigation Panikkar has made into the understanding and experience that underlie Bādarāyana's *Brahma Sūtras,* or any Hindu text, must continue. The question "Either I believe in Krishna or I believe in Christ" becomes: what do the eyes of faith in Jesus Christ see when they see Krishna?

---

46. Hans Urs von Balthasar, *The Glory of the Lord: A Theological Aesthetics. Volume I: Seeing the Form,* translated by Erasmo Leiva-Merikakis (San Francisco: Ignatius Press, 1982), p. 136.

47. I say "may" because other Christians will not affirm what I am affirming here. I will not speak for them.

48. "He is of the same reality as God as far as his deity is concerned and of the same reality as we ourselves as far as his humanness is concerned" (Decree of Chalcedon, in John H. Leith, *Creeds of the Church* [Atlanta: John Knox Press, 1973], p. 36).

A CHRISTIAN'S VIEW OF KRISHNA WITH THE EYES OF FAITH THAT SEE JESUS CHRIST

> *Sister, I had a dream that I wed*
> *the Lord of those who live in need:*
> *Five hundred sixty thousand people came*
> *and the Lord of Braj was the groom.*
> *In dream they set up a wedding arch;*
> *in dream he grasped my hand;*
> *in dream he led me around the wedding fire*
> *and I became unshakably his bride.*
> *Mira's been granted her mountain-lifting Lord*
> *from living past lives, a prize.*

— Mirabai[49]

The identity of the persons and of the traditions of which they are part will emphatically influence the quality of a religious encounter. In *The Unknown Christ of Hinduism* Panikkar chooses an encounter with the *jñanavāda* (path of knowledge) forms of Hinduism. The results were profound *theologoumena* for a Christian theology of that form of Hinduism wherein the presence of Christ as "that from which the origin etcetera of this" was affirmed. What if the point of encounter were with the rich Hindu tradition of *bhaktimārga,* the path of those who love God?[50] What if one of the persons taking part in the encounter were from the Christian tradition of loving God? The types of affirmations made will be somewhat different from the types of affirmations made after an encounter with *jñanavādins.*

Mirabai was a sixteenth-century Hindu woman who loved God with her whole heart, mind, soul, and strength.[51] This is clear from a reading of the poems/hymns ascribed to her. If they are by more than one person, then there are several lovers of God with whole heart, mind, soul, and strength. She was part of a movement of Hindu *bhaktas,* lovers of God, who emphasized the gloriously concrete manifestations of God's presence in the world and among human beings. This *saguna* (with attributes) school imaged God in its poems and in its inner experiences as personal. God was personally Krishna and Krishna was personally God. Mirabai's poetry in the Braj dialect of western Hindi is close to a folk idiom far from the dialectical niceties of the great Sanskrit *acaryas* (teachers) of Śaṅkara, Ramanuja, and Madhva.

According to the legend Mirabai from the time she was a little girl wanted to have Krishna for her husband. Krishna is the full avatar of God, who long ago had been a cowherder in Vrindavana, attracting the amorous attention of all

---

49. John Stratton Hawley and Mark Juergensmeyer, trans., *Songs of the Saints of India* (New York: Oxford University Press, 1988), p. 137.

50. See Daniel P. Sheridan, "Stations Keeping: Christ and Krishna As Embodied," in *Cross Currents* 38, no. 3 (Fall 1988).

51. See A. J. Allston, *The Devotional Poems of Mirabai* (Delhi: Motilal Banarsidass, 1980).

the local women since he, as the manifestation of God in the form of a human male, was the most attractive human male who had ever lived. No ordinary male could compete with Krishna's attraction. Mirabai loved Krishna under the title of Giridhar, "Lifter of the Mountain." The story is that the young Krishna had held high in the sky Mount Govardhan as an umbrella in order to protect the cows and cowherders of the area from the stormy hatred of the rain-god Indra. Mirabai had a personal image of Krishna in this form.

Unfortunately, Mirabai did not have control of her marital destiny and was married to a princely Rajput. She spent the rest of her days in the tense situation of truly loving Krishna while belonging to another. An attempt was made to poison her while worshiping Krishna. To no avail. She eventually traveled to Vrindavana to be close to the places that commemorated Krishna. These places were much more than mere memorials. The memories were alive; Krishna was present. The legend states that at the end of her life Mirabai was drawn into an image of Krishna at his city of Dvaraka and never seen again. At the core of her legend is a defiance of the ordinary conventions of everyday life and a fierce love for her true husband, Krishna. A literary critic would say that her love for Krishna lives in her poetry.

> Go to where my loved one lives,
> go where he lives and tell him
>> if he says so, I'll color my sari red;
>> if he says so, I'll wear the godly yellow garb;
>> if he says so, I'll drape the part in my hair with pearls;
>> if he says so, I'll let my hair grow wild.
> Mira's Lord is the clever Mountain Lifter:
> listen to the praises of that king.[52]

The living memory and the tradition of reciting her poetry as acts of devotion to Krishna mean that these poems themselves can be the point of encounter for a Christian with this form of Hinduism. In this encounter must one choose between Christ and Krishna? No. But then what judgment will one make? I think that the positive affirmations need to be carefully formulated. One does not need to say too much. On a priori grounds the Christian affirms the presence of Christ wherever God is loved. But in a sense the question is not about the presence of Christ but the presence of Krishna.

The question of the presence of Krishna is the question of what type or degree of intended ontic reality is to be given to him by an outsider, the Christian who encounters Krishna in Mirabai's poetry. That God is being loved when Mirabai's poetry is prayed is without doubt. The poems can be prayed as poems of devoted love for God. The language of loving God is always stretched to language's limits. Yet *caritas capax verbi,* as the loving descriptions of innumerable lovers manifestly prove. The metaphors used in such love language need to be taken seriously, never underestimated or undermined. They carry an

---

52. Hawley and Juergensmeyer, *Songs of the Saints of India,* p. 138.

overload of meaning and of ontic intentionality rather than an underload. God is really being loved in the person of a Krishna who is real in ontic intention, even if the form of the intention is only imaginative.

Mirabai directly address Krishna; she uses the first person. Need the reader's or the reciter's intention be merely literary? No. The vicarious participation of the Christian reciter is invited not merely by the poems' literary conventions but also by the subject matter where a divine subject is intended. Based on an a priori believing judgment, Christ, incarnated in Jesus of Nazareth, the manifestation of the Godhead/Father, is being intended, both as known to the Christian and unknown to the Hindu under that name, in the Christian reader's appropriation of Mirabai's love for the Lifter of the Mountain. Krishna is directly intended in at least the real intention of the imagination. Such an intention truly reaches the Triune God. It is true that the totality of God cannot but be loved in any love, and in any love for God, *das Ganze im Fragment*. Krishna takes on a sensate form in the imagination of the lover, and is truly lovable. "The perfection of charity is in the perfection of the capability of the lover to love and in the lovableness of the subject who is the object of love."[53]

Panikkar's insight would be right in the context of love for God:

> Religions may be incommensurable with each other despite some possible common traits. Each religion is unique with the uniqueness of every real being.... This very incommensurability, like that of the radius with the circumference, does not preclude the fact that each religion may be a dimension of the other in a kind of trinitarian *perichorēsis or circumincessio*. Each one represents the whole of the human experience in a concrete way.[54]

Every individual love is unique with the uniqueness of real being. The subject, the object who is also subject, and the love each carries a uniqueness, absolutely irreplaceable, and yet made common by the movement of God's Spirit. Each is centered on God's triune being, and multiplied by that threefold being. There is enough subjectness in the subjectivity or subjectivities of God's persons to supply the center of the myriad loves in the incarnate human order. God's triune reality with the Word incarnate in Jesus is present all the more when the human lovers turn to God, whether instantiated to the lover as Jesus, with all that such loving faith intends, or as Mirabai's Krishna, with all the concrete actuality Krishna had for Mirabai, or as a Hindu reciter's Krishna, with all the participated concrete actuality Krishna may have for the Hindu reciter of Mirabai's poems, or as a Christian reciter's Krishna, with all the uniqueness and concrete reality such a Krishna may have. A protective Krishna, in some form of intentional ontic actuality, really lifts the mountain of Govardhan over the head of the Christian who sees Krishna with the eyes of the faith that sees Jesus Christ.

---

53. Sheridan, "Stations Keeping: Christ and Krishna As Embodied," p. 337.
54. Panikkar, "The Jordan, the Tiber, and the Ganges: Three Kairological Moments of Christic Self-Consciousness," p. 114.

I do not know fully what the relation of Christ is to Krishna in an a posteriori sense. As a relation in the understanding Christ and Krishna may be analogized and homologized, and thus both are real in that sense. In contrast to a mental universe of intentionality, the questions arise as a relation in actual reality: Is there a Christ? Is there a Krishna? Who is Christ? Who is Krishna? The Christian knows through an active knowing and loving faith who Jesus Christ is and how actual he is. *Pistis* includes *gnōsis*. Both are subsumed in love. Krishna was intentionally actual for Mirabai in a similar order of loving intentionality. But who is Krishna? Given the kinds of reflection made so far in this study, and walking with Raimon Panikkar, there is no need to affirm that Krishna does not exist in at least some of the orders of intentionality that Hindus intend, and these orders vary. The Christian may affirm the judgment that Krishna exists, and thus may be loved. This judgment implies no diminution of the affirmations of Nicaea and Chalcedon about Jesus Christ.

Is Krishna Jesus Christ? Yes, I would say that Krishna is Jesus Christ, but in no simple way. The affirmation, however, is simple, no matter how complex the understanding. Can Krishna be loved by a person of the faith that sees Jesus Christ with the eyes of faith? Yes.

PART III

Praxis

10

Panikkar's Hermeneutic of Myth

BETTINA BÄUMER

> *Communion in the same myth is what makes tolerance possible.*
> — Raimon Panikkar[1]

If we take Panikkar's understanding of *myth* seriously, the title of this paper seems to be a contradiction, for he says clearly that myth is a reality that cannot be subjected to a hermeneutic, that cannot be reduced to any kind of *logos*. Any such attempt would amount to killing myth as myth, and would at best create mythology. It is not my intention to write Panikkar's mythology by exposing his own myths! He calls myth a symbol, not a concept, since a symbol is polysemic and myth is multidimensional. More important, myth in Panikkar's understanding is transparent; thus we do not see (a) myth, we see through (a) myth. The proper attitude is thus one of participation, of sharing, of communion in our myths. The approach is not reflective analysis but faith, which means accepting myth as a living reality and not as a dead object. Let us then try to discover Panikkar's symbol by a process of communion and dialogue.

We know that most of the tensions and clashes in our present world are clashes between different myths of which the respective groups — people, nations, religions — are not aware. It is here where Panikkar's approach has even far-reaching political and social consequences, where, instead of hardening and objectifying myths, it is dialogue which is required. But this will become clearer as we go along with Panikkar's thinking.

From the outset we have to distinguish between two levels of myth in Panikkar's language: The first is more philosophical, implying a strong anthropological dimension, and to which he has given a new coloring. To distinguish

Bettina Bäumer is a Fellow of the Indira Gandhi Center for the Arts and Director of the Alice Bonner Foundation in Varanasi, India.

1. R. Panikkar, *Myth, Faith, and Hermeneutics* (New York: Paulist Press, 1979), p. 32. Hereafter MFH.

it from concrete myths he calls it *mythos*. The second is what historians of religions understand by myth(s), which he calls *mythologumenon*. There is no doubt a link and an inner relationship between these two concepts, the second being, so as to say, the manifestation of the first, but this continuity is not always obvious in Panikkar's thought. His preference seems to lie with the first aspect, to which we shall direct our attention.

The main reason for Panikkar's discovery of myth in the first sense is his dissatisfaction with the predominance of rationality — *logos* or *ratio* — in Western thought, including modern scientific developments. He discovers the traditional belief in the universality of reason to be a myth! In other words, the myth of enlightenment, which has not yet lost its power — that humanity will solve its problems by becoming more reasonable — has to be thoroughly demythicized. The problem arises within the Western tradition, where a certain dissatisfaction with rationality can be felt, but more acutely in the meeting of cultures, one of the salient features of our time, and of which Panikkar is one of the most important prophets. The so-called dialogue between cultures has mostly been, and still is largely in philosophical and scientific circles, a Western monologue,[2] where political colonization has been replaced by a scientific-technological one. Even today serious European thinkers are hard to convince that for example, in India there is something like philosophy,[3] let alone science. All this is due to the domination of rationality. It is here that Panikkar proposes another paradigm of human understanding, another approach to reality, which he calls myth. Whether myth was the best term to choose is debatable, but it has certain advantages which we shall discover as we try to understand Panikkar's conception.

For centuries, starting from the Greek philosophers myth and the mythical have been ridiculed in Western thought, especially by Christian authors, being almost synonymous to obscurantism, irrationality, superstition, and so on.[4] There has been a complete reappraisal in the romantics and in the twentieth century. For some authors the new positive approach passed through the Greek world (W. F. Otto, K. Kerenyi); for others, through a wider perspective of the history of religions (the outstanding figure being M. Eliade); for still others it was a philosophical rediscovery (M. Heidegger, H.-G. Gadamer, and others), often through the medium of poetry and art. In theology, the rediscovery of the patristic reinterpretation of Greek myths by Hugo Rahner broke new ground,[5] though the main discussion was dominated by the theme of demythicization. Panikkar's discovery of myth is related to all these interpretations and partly influenced by

---

2. See W. Halbass, *Indien und Europa: Perspektiven ihrer geistigen Begegnung* (Basel: Schwabe, 1981).

3. See R. Panikkar, *Śataspathaprajñā: Should We Speak of Philosophy in Classical India?* (unpublished paper).

4. See the rich bibliography given in A. Horstmann, "Mythos, Mythologie," in *Historisches Wörterbuch der Philosophie*, ed. J. Ritter and K. Gründer (Basel: Schwabe, 1971), pp. 316–18.

5. H. Rahner, *Griechische Mythen in christlicher Deutung* (Zurich: Rhein-Verlag, 1996 [1957]).

them, and yet it stands out as a unique contribution to the ongoing discussion on myth.

In fact, much of Panikkar's work on myth originated in the context of the colloquia organized by E. Castelli in Rome in the sixties, which were centered around these themes.[6] However, we are not trying here to situate Panikkar's understanding of myth in the historical context, studying the influences of other thinkers or his reaction to them. Whatever his position within the history of ideas in the West, we must not forget his Indian source. Indian philosophy, unlike its Western sister, has never discarded its own myths as "stupid";[7] instead, it has elaborated and reinterpreted them.

In this context we should mention that myth is not only a counterpart of *logos* or rationality, but is also a counterpart of history. Panikkar reacts from an Indian and generally Asian point of view to the Western "myth of history." By declaring the European belief in the sole validity of history as criterion of reality a myth, he commits an unforgivable sin in the eyes of Western and Christian thinkers. This is precisely the point where the East-West dialogue becomes vital: If historicity remains the sole criterion, there is no hope of a possible understanding between cultures.[8]

But let us proceed with Panikkar's understanding of myth. Linking the two above-mentioned dimensions of myth, he writes:

> A living myth does not allow for interpretation because it needs no intermediary. The hermeneutic of a myth is no longer the myth, but its *logos*. Myth is precisely the horizon over against which any hermeneutic is possible. Myth is that which we take for granted, that which we do not question; and it is unquestioned because, de facto, it is not seen as questionable. The myth is transparent like the light, and the mythical story — *mythologumenon* — is only the form, the garment in which the myth happens to be expressed, enwrapped, illumined.
>
> Myth is not the object of thought, nor does it give food for thought. Rather it purifies thought, it bypasses thought, so that the unthought may emerge and the intermediary disappear. Myth is the salutary fasting of thinking (sic!); it liberates us from the burden of having to think out and think through everything and thus it opens up the realm of freedom: not the mere liberty of choice, but the freedom of being. When the thinking has not yet landed on the thought so that it cannot yet know what is being thought in the thinking, we are still in the domain of the myth.[9]

---

6. See E. Castelli, ed., *Demitizzazione e morale* (Padova: CEDAM, 1965); *Mito e fede* (Padova: CEDAM, 1966); etc.

7. See A. B. Keith about the cosmogonic myths in the Brāhmanas: "The details of these stupid myths are wholly unimportant" (quoted in F. Staal, *Agni,* vol. 1, p. 116).

8. See *Cultures and Time* (Paris: UNESCO, 1976) with the article by R. Panikkar, "Time and History in the Tradition of India: *kāla and karma,*" with an appendix by B. Bäumer, pp. 63–88; see also the Introduction by P. Ricoeur.

9. MFH, pp. 4–5. This may also be compared with J. Krishnamurti's idea of "the freedom from the known."

Myth is not intelligible, but the very horizon of intelligibility; myth "is the very foundation of all communication; it is the horizon you accept without question and that makes possible a certain communion, the condition for any subsequent communication."[10] Myth is thus the "undifferentiated magma";[11] it is not an object of thought but rather a "human organ" with which we apprehend reality.[12] "Man cannot live without myths,"[13] or rather, without myth as a fundamental, largely unconscious or subconscious dimension of human existence and perception of reality. It is important, however, that Panikkar carefully avoids a psychological language, although he points to the psychological implications of his theory. Thus *mythos* preserves its double meaning, uniting the subjective and the objective, the individual and the collective, if these terms are not over-stressed. The domain of myth is darkness over against the often overexposed light of reason.[14] Myth is not a particular content, but the intentionality, as well as the silent presupposition out of which we live.

The nature of myth, however, implies a positive as well as a negative side. The positive is that myth is inexhaustible, that is, it is not subject to reason and to our space-time way of thinking. The negative is the danger of obscurantism, of being the victim of our own presuppositions and preconceptions without being aware of them, and thus projecting them on our perception of reality. Panikkar accepts this negative aspect of myth and admits that the *logos* has a necessary corrective function. The two possibilities of overcoming the obscuring power of myth are *dialogue* on the one side and *demythicization* on the other. Myth in this sense can be collective, concerning a whole culture or civilization, or individual, as my own set of tacit assumptions and beliefs. Our myths are a complex combination of both; they are multilayered and contain both, positive as well as negative aspects.

It may be useful to illustrate the positive aspect of myth by two Indian examples. A poetic illustration of Panikkar's understanding of myth can be found in a poem by Rabindranath Tagore:

I woke and found his letter with the morning.
I do not know what it says, for I cannot read.
I shall leave the wise man alone with his books,
I shall not trouble him, for who knows if he can read what the letter says.

Let me hold it to my forehead and press it to my heart.
When the night grows still and stars come out one by one I will spread it
  on my lap and stay silent.
The rustling leaves will read it aloud to me, the rushing streams will chant
  it, and the seven wise stars will sing it to me from the sky.

---

10. MFH, p. 399.
11. MFH, p. 400.
12. Cf. MFH, p. 345.
13. MFH, p. 345.
14. MFH, p. 39.

I cannot find what I seek, I cannot understand what I would learn; but this unread letter has lightened my burdens and turned my thoughts into songs.[15]

Is not the wise man — the pandit, the professor, the scientist — the human *logos* and the unread letter the *mythos?* The "unread letter" has to be "read" or approached by other means than those of the *logos* — and Tagore hints at those means, a silent communion with reality. The *logos* could not teach the *illiterate* receiver of the letter what he would like to learn. For receiving the full content of the letter he may even have to renounce "understanding" it. Had he trusted his *logos* alone, the beauty and the mystery of the letter would have evaporated. It would have lost its transforming power.

The second Indian example relates to one of the sages of the twentieth century, Sri Ramana Maharshi, who received his enlightenment at the age of sixteen and in subsequent years became fully established in the experience of nonduality (*advaita*). He was irresistibly drawn to a holy mountain, Arunachala, in whose caves he lived. Arunachala became his "guru" and the symbol for the immutability of Being, and the object of his passionate love. Arunachala had a long history and myth behind it which contributed to his power of attraction for Ramana. What is important for our understanding of myth is that Ramana never denounced the myth of Arunachala, even though he attained a state of enlightenment which, we would think, did not require any myth as support, which transcended faith or belief in any myth. It is certainly possible to reduce his experience to its *logos-* content of pure *advaita,* but he would not be Ramana Maharshi without the myth of Arunachala.

In Panikkar's thought there is a balance among three dimensions which he calls the "threefold gift and task of philosophy" and which form a — tantric or trinitarian — triangle:[16] *mythos, logos, pneuma. Mythos* stands for the unthought, *logos* for the thought, and *pneuma* for the unthinkable. It is only a harmonious integration of these three dimensions that can overcome the onesidedness of thinking. Let us first consider the *mythos-logos* pair.

MYTHOS AND *LOGOS*

The specific nature of myth is best brought out by contrasting it with its complementary/opposite notion: *logos.* Panikkar repeats time and again that these two "human organs of apprehension" of reality belong together. "*Mythos* and *logos* are two human modes of awareness, irreducible one to the other, but equally inseparable."[17] The *logos* grasps with the intellect, it objectifies, whereas *mythos* is a way of participation in reality,[18] therefore related to ritual, to sacred

15. From: "Fruit-gathering," in *Collected Poems and Plays of Rabindranath Tagore,* (London, Macmillan, 1973), pp. 177f.
16. MFH, pp. 342ff.
17. MFH, p. 100.
18. Cf. *Le mystère du culte dans l'hindouisme et le christianisme* (Paris: Cerf, 1970), pp. 180f.

action. Their common root is their relation to language; both are modes of language, the *logos* developing into rational speech and discursive thinking, and *mythos* representing prerational forms of language.

> They represent two aspects of the Word, the first (myth) being the word expressing thoughts (as realities), the second (*logos*) being the intelligent act.... *Logos* denotes the word in relation to the subject which thinks and speaks: that which is spoken and calculated. What *mythos* stands for first of all "is precisely not the word expressing that which is thought, but expressing that which is real."[19]

In short, the *logos* stands for the thought whereas *mythos* stands for the unthought, for that which is irreducible to thinking.

> The *logos* must not be abolished, superseded or given up in favor of irrationalism, emotionalism, fideism or some other rebellions, all one-sided. In philosophy the *logos* plays an irreplaceable double role: that of illuminating, clarifying, and that of critiquing, testing, controlling. If anything contradicts the *logos,* it cannot be accepted.[20]

However, the history of philosophy and theology in the West has almost led to the tyranny of the *logos,* understood as *verbum mentis,* leading to what Heidegger calls "forgetfulness of Being," and suppressing all other forms of apprehension of truth, suppressing even the original character of *logos* as symbol and sacrament.[21] Therefore Panikkar stresses the other two dimensions of *mythos* and *pneuma. Mythos* is the inexhaustible source of *logos,* and there is a continuous process flowing from the source, the unthought, to the expression, the thought. However, the process does not end with the *logos:* "The procession from *mythos* through *logos* to *pneuma* is endless. Precisely this pneumatic dimension guarantees the constant openness into which we may take a step forward."[22] *Pneuma* stands for the unthinkable, and like *mythos,* it cannot be made an *object* of the *logos,* of thought or reason. In this sense, *mythos* may be called pre-*logos* and *pneuma* post-*logos.* Just as in the simile of the Kena Upaniṣad, the moment Indra tries to grasp Brahman, it vanishes, similarly both *mythos* and *pneuma* vanish if the *logos* tries to grasp them.[23]

The metaphor of darkness and light is quite illustrative of the relationship between *mythos* and *logos:* "The illuminating 'light' of reason indeed destroys the 'obscurity' of myth."[24] However, "darkness" is not meant in an absolute sense, but rather as the (invisible) source of light: "You cannot look directly at

19. Ibid., pp. 181–82. The last quotation is from W. F. Otto, *Theophania — der Geist der altgriechischen Religion* (Hamburg: Rowohlt, 1956), p. 23.

20. MFH, p. 343.

21. Cf. *Le mystère du culte,* pp. 174ff.

22. MFH, p. 347.

23. Cf. Kena Up. 3–4. It would be interesting to read the simile in this light: When the male gods Agni (fire), Vāyu (wind) and Indra failed to grasp the mystery of Brahman, it is a woman, the goddess Umā, who reveals it to them.

24. MFH, p. 39.

the source of light; you turn your back to it so that you may see — not the light, but the illuminated things. Light is invisible. So too with the myth."[25] Though there is an apparent contradiction in this metaphor — Is myth darkness or light in itself? — the meaning is clear. The light of the *logos* illumines the objects, but light would not be such without darkness.

"All human culture is a texture of myth and *logos.*"[26] Cultures which have preserved their ancient and primordial myths in one form or another often have a more balanced relationship between the two, whereas cultures which are dominated by the *logos* and which have suppressed their ancient myths become more vulnerable to new and unconscious myths. "The myth-*logos* relation is so deeply anchored in human reality that even so-called developed countries have built formidable ideologies only on one front, exposing their flank, as it were, to infiltration by other myths. It is thus that even ideologies end by turning into myth. And so they become tolerable."[27] This phenomenon is particularly important in an analysis of our cultural situation in the West where, under the cover of rationality, a number of new myths have sprung up.

MYTH AND LANGUAGE

It is generally admitted that "myth is an expression of the sacred in words," though its language is different from other types of descriptive or analytical language. "In communicating the sacred, a myth makes available in words what by no other means is available, and its words are different from other words.... The language of myth does not induce discussion; it does not argue, but presents."[28] Panikkar stresses the dimension of silence. However, it cannot be an absolute silence but is so to speak, the silent dimension of language itself. "Man knows through the *logos* that he unearths from myth and that still remains in myth. *Mythos* is the second dimension of speech itself, the silence between the words, the matrix that bears the words."[29] It is precisely this dimension of silence between the words which calls for innumerable interpretations and thus makes myth inexhaustible. A rational statement is exhausted once it is understood — a myth can allow as many interpretations as there are human situations. That is what "allows the continual passage from *mythos* to *logos,* and the constant 're-sourcing' of the *logos* in new *mythoi.*"[30] Here Panikkar's hermeneutic of myth as silence agrees with his idea of the Word born out of silence.[31]

However, this generalization of the concept of myth carries the danger of overlapping with the silence of the *pneuma,* the third dimension of philosophy. The difference could be described in this way: *pneuma* is the unthinkable and

25. MFH, p. 4.
26. MFH, p. 32.
27. Ibid.
28. See Kees W. Bolle, "Myth," in *The Encyclopedia of Religion,* ed. M. Eliade, vol. 10, pp. 261–262.
29. MFH, p. 344.
30. MFH, p. 100.
31. Cf. "Silence and the Word," in MFH, pp. 258ff.

thus unspeakable silence, whereas *mythos* is the "spoken unthought." *Mythos* speaks, but out of the deep ocean of pre-thinking. It is this dimension which has tempted psychological hermeneutics of myth of all schools, whether in the light of Freud or of C. G. Jung's "collective unconscious." But Panikkar avoids carefully any purely psychological approach. The reason he does not fall into the trap of psychological interpretations is his "golden rule of hermeneutics," i.e., that the interpreted thing (tradition, person, culture, text) has to recognize itself in the interpretation.[32] Most psychological interpretations of myths do not follow this rule but rather some preconceived model.[33]

Coming back to the relation of myth and language, which concerns the second aspect of myth (*mythologumenon*), Panikkar agrees with K. Kerenyi that the proper approach to the myth is *mythos legein* over against mytho-logy, i.e., the telling of a myth and not its phenomenological analysis.[34] In this telling there is participation.

Whether we call it silence or the original Word, in any case the language of myth is *sui generis;* it cannot be identified with the language of poetry, much less that of science. It is close to the original power of the Word, which is one of Panikkar's main theological concerns. Here one may raise a critical question: If the triangle *mythos-logos-pneuma* is to exhaust the dimensions of philosophy, does it imply that any non-rational language has to fall under the category of *mythos?* Apart from poetry, not every sacred language is mythical, and it would not be appropriate to include, for example, the whole dimension of *mantra* or of mystical language or even of parable under the category of myth, though these aspects of language also share the characteristics of the "unthought" in Panikkar's terminology.[35] The danger of stretching one concept too far is that it loses its specificity.

THE MYTH OF THE OTHER: DIALOGUE

Just as we cannot see our own back without the help of a mirror, or hear our own dialect except with a tape recorder, we cannot be aware of our own myth, i.e., our silent presuppositions or convictions, except in dialogue. It is the other, the partner in dialogue, who can uncover our myths. We cannot live without myths, as we have seen, just as we cannot live without our shadow.[36] According to Panikkar, the only way of overcoming our personal and cultural misunderstandings, of becoming aware of our unreflected assumptions, is an open dialogue between persons, cultures, religions, and philosophies. Becoming aware of our myths may lead to their demythicization, to their transformation,

---

32. See MFH, p. 105; see also p. 427 for the overcoming of the psychological level.

33. A typical and extreme example is W. Doninger O'Flaherty's interpretation of puranic myths, e.g., *Asceticism and Eroticism in the Mythology of Siva* (London, New York: Oxford University Press, 1973).

34. Cf. K. Kerenyi's contributions in the volumes edited by E. Castelli.

35. On the hermeneutic of parable, see *Le mystère du culte,* pp. 182ff.

36. See Peter Schlemihl's highly symbolical story by A. Chamisso.

modification, strengthening, or even disappearance, as the case may be. Here dialogue can hurt (people are more attached to their myths than to their conscious convictions) as well as liberate; in any case it will purify those very convictions.

Panikkar maintains that dialogue is possible on the basis of myth, whereas the *logos* only leads to dialectics. This has to do with the question of pluralism and tolerance.[37] It is the dimension of myth which makes pluralism possible — and tolerable.

DEMYTHICIZATION, REMYTHICIZATION, TRANSMYTHICIZATION

Without going into the history of demythologization/demythicization with its philosophical and theological implications, we have to mention it in the context of Panikkar's understanding of remythicization. Demythicization comes out of dissatisfaction with myth — or rather with a particular myth, mainly in the content of biblical exegesis. The danger of demythicization is, however, replacing the old myth with our (new) *logos,* and the question is whether this procedure is able to save the context of a text, or whether it kills it. Panikkar discovers in this method the Western, technological tendency to change and cultivate the externals, the object, instead of cultivating the subject and making it capable of receiving the content. In the case of demythicization "one does not ask Man to become receptive or flexible, rather one demands a technical translation of the message so that it can be well understood."[38] Instead of changing the text, the receiver should be transformed.

On the other hand, demythicization often overlooks the necessity of truth to be incarnated, and it is precisely myth which incarnates it, not *logos.*[39] What happens in the attempt at demythicization is not a total emptying of the myth but a transformation into another myth, which Panikkar calls either remythicization or transmythicization. This has to do with the fact that "thought demythologizes, but life is mythopoietic."[40]

> Demythicization is necessary once one is unhappy with his "myth" because the *logos* has already replaced it; but each demythicization brings with it a remythicizing. We destroy one myth — and rightly so if that myth no longer fulfills its purpose — but somehow a new myth always arises simultaneously. Man cannot live without myths.[41]
>
> It should be stressed here that myths do not need to be overcome. When we overcome one myth, another creeps into its place, though perhaps at a deeper level. The process of demythicization so popular nowadays is

37. See "Tolerance, Ideology and Myth," in MFH, pp. 20ff.
38. *Le mystère du culte,* p. 173.
39. Cf. ibid.
40. MFH, p. 218.
41. MFH, p. 345.

really the dynamic of *trans*-mythicization, a kind of mythical metamorphosis where obsolete and anachronistic myths yield to more modern and up-to-date myths. Obviously, these new myths, like the old myths for those who believed in them, are not seen as myths by the new believers.[42]

This is Panikkar's important contribution to the whole discussion on demythologization, i.e., that a total demythicization is neither possible nor desirable, and that the whole mutation we are witnessing at present is also a process of transmythicization. Not by chance also many old myths are being resurrected and gain new significance today in this late twentieth century, with the rediscovery of shamanism, occult and esoteric traditions — whatever may be the interpretation and use that is made of them. At any rate, we are witnessing a major process of remythicization.

MYTH AND EXPERIENCE

Whereas some thinkers understand myth as the opposite pole of experience — here in the sense of ultimate or mystical experience — Panikkar links the two. For him, the very fact that ultimate experience is irreducible to anything else and cannot be subjected to logical analysis, i.e., to the *logos,* makes for its "mythical character."[43]

Any experience, — sensory, intellectual or spiritual — in fact functions as a myth. To begin with, it performs the same role and presents the same structure. Myth, like experience, enables us to stop somewhere, to rest in our quest for the foundations of everything. Otherwise there would be a *regressus ad infinitum.* You cannot go beyond a myth, just as you cannot go beyond experience. If you could, you would lose both the myth and the experience.

Another common feature is that:

In myth as in experience there is no distance between the subject and the object. You are in the myth as you are in the experience, you live in them, or rather you live them.[44]

Apart from their similar structure, experience itself is a kind of myth: "The myth of the experience is another more subtle form of the myth of heaven and the celestial paradise. It is a sublimated form of the myth of the ultimate."[45]

Panikkar's intention in upgrading and reevaluating both myth and experience is clear: integration of dimensions of reality and human experience which cannot be suppressed by the *logos.*

We might ask what this highly speculative notion of myth has to do with concrete myths or *mythologumena* known to us from the history of religions but

---

42. MFH, p. 298.
43. MFH, p. 296.
44. MFH, pp. 296f.
45. MFH, p. 298.

also within Christianity. Panikkar has interpreted a few myths from the Indian tradition and a few Christian ones. The selection itself is significant. As Peter Slater says: "He doesn't tell stories!...I have come across only one sustained discussion of a particular myth in his writing, and even then the focus of attention is more on abstracting philosophical-religious insight than on delineating the structure of the story as such."[46] From the selection of Hindu myths itself "it is evident in all that he writes that Panikkar's master story or basic myth is a Christian one."[47] Apart from avoiding the pitfall of mytho-logy, as we have seen, we do not find any attempt in his work of interpreting the whole complexity of, for example, Hindu myths. If myth in his understanding is that with which we identify ourselves, then he has surely chosen those myths in which he can find himself also as a Christian: Prajāpati and Śunaḥśepa.[48]

Generally we can say that we find two approaches: The first is the interpretation of ancient and primeval myths in the light of our present existential situation; the second is a creative remythicization which sometimes assumes powerful prophetic dimensions.

The best example for such a prophetic myth is his reinterpretation of the Tower of Babel.[49] His real strength seems to lie in this kind of recreation of ancient myths, taking them out of their monocultural context and inserting them into the pluricultural context of our present world.

In the history of a single tradition itself myths have been revived and reinterpreted periodically according to the needs of the people in a given situation. Obsolete myths have been simply dropped and have fallen into oblivion. This process is still going on, and Panikkar's contribution seems to lie more in this creative use of myths than in their interpretation.

Regarding interpretation, Panikkar actually finds himself between the two positions which he describes: The first is the traditional attitude, which is concerned with the *legein* of the myth, with its retelling, without feeling the need of a hermeneutic, precisely because the meaning is obvious to those who live in this tradition. The second starts from a certain distance, historically or culturally, and therefore requires an interpretation. Here is how Panikkar tries to find a middle way:

Is it possible to make a hermeneutic of a myth as myth? Do we not

> condemn our own effort, since we are trying precisely to interpret this
> myth? Do we kill the myth by interpreting it? My reply here must be as
> carefully nuanced as it is sincere. The moment someone feels the need
> to interpret a myth he cannot, by this very fact, accept it without his in-
> terpretation. But then myth has crossed over from the invisible horizon
> to the visible object, from the background canvas to the figure in relief,

46. Peter Slater, "Hindu and Christian Symbols in the Work of R. Panikkar," *Cross Currents,* 29 (1979), p. 172.

47. Ibid., p. 174.

48. See "The Myth of Prajāpati," MFH, pp. 38 ff.; and "Śunaḥśepa, a Myth of the Human Condition," MFH, pp. 98ff.

49. *Cross Currents,* pp. 197ff.

from the context to the text. When we cease to believe *the myth*, when it no longer "goes without saying," we try to believe *in* it by means of our interpretation. But in so doing we distance ourselves from it; the myth is no longer connatural to us, transparent. Its interpretation inter-poses itself between the myth and us. Was Socrates not condemned to death for daring to interpret myth?[50]

This is an honest confession about his own predicament when he interprets Indian myths, but this predicament is not only embarrassing — because he is no longer a part of the tradition — it also contains the seeds of a creative "reading" of the myth which a traditional commentator is not able to give because he lacks the distance. Whether or not we are convinced of the outcome of such an interpretation, we have to admit that such a method is legitimate — as long as it respects the "golden rule of hermeneutics" and does not do violence to the story. The question is precisely this:

> Can we present this myth in such a way as to express the deep convictions, the horizon, of the culture that gave it birth, and at the same time discover it as a sacred history able to offer to other cultures a guidepost to where they may find a thinking deeper, or even fresher, than their own? Has this myth a transcultural value, and consequently a role to play in the encounter and eventual enrichment of human traditions?[51]

The "middle way" to which Panikkar aspires in the interpretation of a myth should combine a careful listening to what the myth has to tell, before we project our own questions, and an existential search for meaning in the myth, not to talk about the "objective" methods of philology and history, to situate the myth in its proper context. But it would lead us too far to exemplify these questions in the case of one of Panikkar's myths.

If mytho-logy, "that hybrid and even self-contradictory science,"[52] is not appropriate because it, so to say, destroys what it wants to preserve, the proper approach to myth is mytho-phany. It requires not the "masculine" *logos,* but the "feminine" *phantasia,* which lets the myth literally "shine through" and lets it be. Therefore myth is related to ritual and contemplation. Finally, it is related to Panikkar's ideal of a "second innocence": If the primordial myths in their own context may represent the "first innocence," their rediscovery in our technological age may help us to find that new innocence which allows Being to shine through. Panikkar's "symbol" of myth is certainly an important contribution toward that necessary integration and participation in the total reality. Its application in the interpretation of our own myths and those of other cultures should be further developed to make possible the authentic re-sourcing of our thinking, which alone will contribute to an understanding among cultures.

---

50. MFH, p. 132.
51. MFH, p. 134f.
52. MFH, p. 39.

11

Cosmic Confidence or Preferential Option?

PAUL KNITTER

The title of this essay is meant to be a respectful, and I hope helpful, twist on the title of Raimon Panikkar's contribution to a 1984 conference on "A Universal Theology of Religion." Uncomfortable with the content and direction of the conference, Panikkar delivered his remarks under the title "The Invisible Harmony: A Universal Theory of Religion or a Cosmic Confidence in Reality?"[1] In what follows I will suggest that just as Panikkar had reason to remind his colleagues that all "universal theories of religion" are dangerous and therefore must be controlled and grounded in a cosmic confidence, so he, too, needs the reminder that such a cosmic confidence is inadequate (and perhaps dangerous) unless directed by and rooted in what Christians would call a preferential option for the suffering victims of this suffering earth.

To clarify the contents of this reminder and why I think it is important, even urgent — and to enable Panikkar to state whether he would agree — I will first summarize the content and validity of Panikkar's criticism of universalist or pluralist theories; then, after pointing out what seem to be the limitations and dangers of Panikkar's criticisms, I will try to state how his position might be enhanced or clarified by grounding "cosmic trust" in a preferential option for victims.

Paul Knitter is Professor of Theology and Director of Peace Studies at Xavier University, Cincinnati. He is author of *No Other Name?, One Earth — Many Religions*, and *Jesus and the Other Names*. He is General Editor of the Orbis Books series Faith Meets Faith and is active in the quest for peace and justice in Central America.

1. "The Invisible Harmony: A Universal Theory of Religion or a Cosmic Confidence in Reality?," in *Toward a Universal Theology of Religion*, ed. Leonard Swidler (Maryknoll, N.Y.: Orbis Books, 1985), pp. 118–53. (Hereafter IH.)

PANIKKAR: A MAVERICK PLURALIST

The contemporary discussion about a theology of religions and interreligious dialogue gravitates around the thorny question of whether or how religious persons can move from an *inclusivist* model, which recognizes the possible value and truth within all religions but holds up one's own truth as normative and inclusive of others, to a *pluralist* model, which recognizes a possible "rough parity" and mutual validity of many religious paths. Inclusivists affirm the value of the many but hold also to the value or necessity of one norm or ultimate expression of truth; pluralists, in order to affirm the value of the many, are wary of any one, ultimate norm of truth. From his inclusion in a recent assemblage of pluralist proposals, one might say that Panikkar has clearly pitched his tent in the pluralist camp.[2] But from the content of his contribution to that assembly and from his more recent efforts to distance himself from its public image,[3] it would be more exact to say that Panikkar is the "gallus cantans extra chorum" (the rooster crowing out of tune), or, to switch images, that Panikkar's tent is on the edge — or even on the outskirts — of the pluralist camp. He is a pluralist, but a maverick or gadfly pluralist. Taking his place with those who are seeking new and more pluralistic models for understanding the world of many religions, he warns his fellow-seekers that they are going about their search either in false directions or with a lack of sufficient resolve.

Panikkar is a *radical pluralist.* This is what makes him different from, and what fires his criticism of, many of his fellow pluralists. They aren't radical enough. They affirm pluralism but don't carry through; they don't realize the implications and the demands of what they are affirming. Panikkar would chide colleagues such as Leonard Swidler, Wilfred Cantwell Smith, John Hick, Gordon Kaufman, and myself for not taking pluralism seriously enough. Too many pluralists — especially those with first-world, capitalist, liberal backgrounds — eagerly hoist the flag of pluralism only to mount it on the secure foundation of some particular system or world view that they assume to be universal. For most pluralists, in Panikkar's estimation, "manyness" is too messy; and so they try to clean it up or unify or reduce it to some particular framework. Panikkar will have none of this. Pluralism must be kept unadulterated and accepted for what it is. It must be embraced and lived and suffered through before any kind of possible unity or intelligibility can begin to be proposed or fashioned. To grasp and feel the impact of this challenge, we can briefly review Panikkar's reasons for making it.

---

2. *The Myth of Christian Uniqueness: Toward a Pluralistic Theology of Religions,* ed. John Hick and Paul F. Knitter (Maryknoll, N.Y.: Orbis Books, 1987).

3. "The Jordan, the Tiber, and the Ganges: Three Kairological Moments of Christic Self-Consciousness," in *The Myth of Christian Uniqueness,* pp. 89–116. (Hereafter JTG.) See his "distancing" letter to the editor in *International Bulletin of Missionary Research* 13 (1989).

Grounds for Panikkar's Radical Pluralism

1. *Philosophical-Political:* In many ways, Panikkar's criticisms of Christian proposals for a "pluralist" or a "world" or a "universal" theology of religions echoes the anti-foundationalist critique in modern philosophy.[4] For Panikkar, historical relativity (which, he continues to point out, does not mean historical relativism) is a reality that can be denied only with a violation of one's integrity. There is no way to crawl out of our particular historico-cultural skins and assume an astral body by which we can float above all cultures and religions in order to compare or pass judgment on them. Therefore, there can be no such thing as a comparative philosophy or a science of comparative religion, simply because "the necessary standpoint from which the comparison is to be made already belongs to a definite philosophical [or religious] view." There is no one philosophical or religious *metron* by which various religious traditions can be "justly and truly measured."[5]

But if all that sounds like a typical Western, liberal perspective, Panikkar underlines and broadens it through his third-world experience; he roots his "historical consciousness" of relativity in his "hermeneutical suspicion" of ideology. Simply stated: "A universal theory of religion is loaded with political overtones" — that is, it bears a "latent will to dominate."[6] An "anonymous imperialism" can lurk not only behind the inclusivist theories of "anonymous Christianity," but also within the more recent, liberal proposals for a pluralist theology of religions. If it is true that every theory presupposes and is meant to maintain a particular praxis, Panikkar suggests that many of the new universal theories of how the different religions can contribute to a world theology or learn to speak a common religious Esperanto are nurturing, most likely contrary to their own intentions, the Western praxis of dominating other cultures or of maintaining, under the cloak of a "global theology," the present status quo of widespread inequality. History shows that the West has a genetic need to herd manyness into the corral of unity — a corral of its own construction. Panikkar calls this the West's "colonialistic cultural monoformism."[7] While he sees it clearly expressed in Boethius's "Everything that exists, exists therefore because it is one," he can also point a taunting finger at Christian attitudes: "The 'once and for all' of the Christian event (see Heb. 7:27) and its claim to universality are perhaps the clearest manifestation of this [colonialistic] spirit."[8]

---

4. Richard Rorty, *Philosophy and the Mirror of Nature* (Princeton: Princeton University Press, 1979); Richard Bernstein, *Beyond Objectivism and Relativism: Science, Hermeneutics, and Praxis* (Philadelphia: University of Pennsylvania Press, 1983); George Lindbeck, *The Nature of Doctrine: Religion and Theology in a Postliberal Age* (Philadelphia: Westminster Press, 1984); Francis Schüssler Fiorenza, *Foundational Theology: Jesus and the Church* (New York: Crossroad, 1984); and most recently and lucidly, William C. Placher, *Unapologetic Theology: A Christian Voice in a Pluralistic Conversation* (Louisville: Westminster/John Knox Press, 1989).

5. JTG, p. 103.

6. IH, p. 136.

7. IH, p. 136; see also pp. 120–24.

8. IH, pp. 120–21.

2. *Metaphysical:* Panikkar's philosophical-political reasons for affirming a radical pluralism are grounded even more deeply and firmly in his theological metaphysics. For Christians, "The mystery of the Trinity is the ultimate foundation for pluralism."[9] Just as experience of and belief in the Trinity affirms a radical, irreducible pluralism within the Godhead, so too it affirms a similar pluralism as the very stuff and dynamic of finite reality. Divine pluralism *ad intra*, makes for finite pluralism *ad extra*. This means that "reality itself is pluralistic — that is, incommensurable with either unity or plurality." Therefore, just as God cannot be reduced to a unity that would remove irradicable differences, so too the world of religions forbids a notion of unity that would do away with differences among the religions. "Pluralism does not allow for a universal system. A pluralistic system would be a contradiction in terms. The incommensurability of ultimate systems is unbridgeable. This incompatibility is not a lesser evil... but a revelation itself of the nature of reality."[10]

Panikkar's metaphysical perspective includes and is clarified by a polarity of, yet subordination between, consciousness and Being, Spirit and Word. Simply stated, consciousness is not coextensive with Being; *Pneuma* is always a few (even myriad!) steps ahead of *Logos.* "Spirit... cannot be reduced to logos, vāc, mind, consciousness, cit. Consciousness is Being, but Being does not need to be only Consciousness."[11] Reality — not just divine but also finite — is, therefore, essentially opaque. This opaqueness has to do, for Panikkar, with the profound and pervasive *freedom* that characterizes being. What is free can never be captured with the mind; the Spirit will always blow where she will, when she will. "If the Logos is the transparency of Being, the Spirit is, paradoxically, its opaqueness. The Spirit is freedom, the freedom of Being to be what it is. And this is, a priori as it were, unforeseeable by the Logos."[12]

All this is not "good news" for the Western mind, for which "verum et unum convertuntur" ("the true and the one are convertible"), for which, therefore, the "true" must be fit and "com-prehended" in the one and therefore "understood" by the *Logos.* So it was that the "divine darkness" of Gregory of Nyssa never really played very well in the West and would become the "dark night of the soul" for John of the Cross.[13] So too did the principle of non-contradiction reign supreme over Western epistemology and metaphysics; it was the tool by which Being was forced to submit to consciousness. "The (epistemological) principle of non-contradiction becomes here the ontic principle of identity."[14]

This resolute affirmation of radical pluralism marks a shift in Panikkar's earlier views of the absoluteness and finality of Christianity. Today, on the one hand, he reaffirms absolute claims, for this is what the pluralism and incommensurability of religions really mean: that each religion will make its absolute

---

9. JTG, p. 110.
10. Ibid., pp. 109–10.
11. IH, p. 129.
12. JTG, p. 109; see also IH, p. 145.
13. IH, p. 123.
14. IH, p. 130.

claims that cannot be neatly reconciled with that of others. "Pluralism has to do with final, unbridgeable human attitudes."[15] But, on the other hand, Panikkar is calling on Christians to recognize the absolute claims of other religions. Christianity, in its own self-understanding and in its attitudes toward other traditions, is no longer the "only absolute." Pluralism means there are many absolutes, which are not simply to be stoically tolerated but happily embraced. No longer can Panikkar claim, as he did in the first edition of *The Unknown Christ of Hinduism*, that Christianity is "the end and plenitude of every religion."[16] Now he holds that every religion must "give up the pretense to monopoly of what *religion* stands for."[17] The pluralism of religions, Panikkar is convinced, won't go away. Christians must abandon their eschatological dreams of gradually and finally including all other faiths under their own religious umbrella.

Cosmic Trust

But if Christians — or any religious persons — must abandon their dreams of inclusion, they need not and should not give up their dreams of relating to and therefore changing other religions. Here we come to the "flip side" of Panikkar's radical pluralism — its other pole. Earlier we heard him announce that radical pluralism is "incommensurable" with either final unity *or* utter *plurality*.[18] To hold that pluralism cannot be reduced to plurality would seem to mean that the incommensurability of religions does not, paradoxically, make for an ultimate mish-mash of religions — a cacophony of religious voices. Panikkar believes that despite — or because of — their incommensurable differences, religions — often and significantly and necessarily — can make music rather than noise together. Within the pluralism of religions there is a dynamic basis for relationality and discourse and cooperation. It seems that while Panikkar questions whether the "verum et unum convertuntur," he would affirm that "verum et bonum convertuntur" ("the true and the good are convertible"). If the "truths" of the various religion cannot be reduced to "one," it is still "good" that they exist and that they interrelate. How does Panikkar know this? He doesn't. He *trusts* that this is so.

---

15. IH, p. 125.

16. R. Panikkar, *The Unknown Christ of Hinduism* (London: Darton, Longman and Todd, 1964), p. 24. See also *The Trinity and the Religious Experience of Man* (Maryknoll, N.Y.: Orbis Books, 1973), p. 55.

17. R. Panikkar, "Have 'Religions' the Monopoly on Religion?" *Journal of Ecumenical Studies* 11 (1974), p. 517. It seems that the turning point at which Panikkar moved away from direct or indirect claims for the finality of Christianity was signaled in his "Christianity and World Religions," in *Christianity* (Patiala, India: Punjabi University, 1969), pp. 78–127, and then carried out in "The Category of Growth in Comparative Religion: A Critical Self-Examination," *Harvard Theological Review* 66 (1973), republished in *The Intrareligious Dialogue* (New York: Paulist Press, 1978), pp. 53–73, and in *Salvation in Christ: Concreteness and Universality, The Supername* (Santa Barbara: privately published, 1972) and especially in the second edition of *The Unknown Christ of Hinduism* (Maryknoll, N.Y.: Orbis Books, 1981). See Paul F. Knitter, *No Other Name? A Critical Review of Christian Attitudes toward World Religions* (Maryknoll, N.Y.: Orbis Books, 1985), pp. 152–57.

18. JTG, p. 109.

Panikkar admits that this trust impels him to search for (not to prefabricate) a "universal myth" that will sustain a "universe of discourse." This myth will have to be discovered and fashioned in the very process of conversation, but it will be one that sustains and makes possible the very conversation that creates it. We need such a myth and such a trust, for although we today recognize that religions are separated by incommensurabilities and do not have any common foundations or norms, we still cannot eradicate the inherent feeling that we can and must speak to each other and that "my truth" can also become "your truth." "The human mind can work only if it assumes that what we consider to be the case is in fact, at least to some extent, the case for others as well as for ourselves.... We require an intentional universality within a certain myth — a certain cosmology, one could also say, a universe of discourse."[19] Such a discourse, because it takes shape within incommensurabilities and without a final norm, will always be messy and will never be finished. It will be a discourse or music of "discordant concord" that eschews both final agreement and rampant disagreement. "Concord is neither oneness nor plurality. It is the dynamism of the Many toward the One without ceasing to be different and without becoming one, and without reaching a higher synthesis.... Neither many nor one, but concord, harmony."[20]

Panikkar's existential trust that such discourse is *possible* is based on his pragmatic assessment that it is *necessary*. If this world is going to work, it will be because human beings, in cooperation with that which is more than human, make it work; but they can make it work only if they speak with and cooperate with each other. So the incommensurabilities of religions must be bridged by a "common struggle for an ever better shaping of reality," which in turn is shorn up by a "basic belief [trust!] in the human project, or rather in the worthwhile collaboration of humans in the overall adventure of being."[21] We find ourselves believing and trusting that despite our utter differences we can join hands and minds in saving and enhancing our shared universe.

But what is the deeper basis for this ability to hope against hope and to believe in the possibility and value of such discourse? Here Panikkar reveals the religious and therefore apophatic basis for his trust, which he suggests is a basis shared by all. The trust he is talking about constitutes "one and the same fundamental religious attitude," which he holds is "a basic human attitude.... It is an attitude of trust in reality."[22] So, in the end, Panikkar — cautiously, hesitantly, apophatically — does hold to "something in common" at the basis of or ahead of the meeting of religions. While warning that his viewpoint "does not stand for the transcendent unity of all religions in an unqualified way," he does admit that "it goes in this direction."[23] In Panikkar's more speculative and

---

19. "Chosenness and Universality: Can Christians Claim Both?" *Cross Currents* 38 (1988), p. 321; see also IH, p. 124.
20. IH, p. 145.
21. IH, p. 143, see also p. 148.
22. IH, p. 137.
23. JTG, p. 92.

theological imagery, what is common to all the religions is what he terms the "theanthropocosmic reality" — the given unity-in-difference between the Ultimate, the Human, and the Cosmic — the nonduality between the Divine and the Human-Material.

More specifically, in the universal discourse of religions this theanthropocosmic reality is activated through the *Pneuma*. For all practical purposes, Panikkar can boldly suggest (or trust) that there is a common Spirit pulsing or seeking to take form within the pluralism of religions, for he states that the "hope ... that human conviviality makes sense, that we belong together, and that together we must strive" is not simply a human "option" but "an instinct, the work of the Spirit." It is a "cosmic confidence ... in the Spirit ... which allows for a polar and tensile coexistence between *ultimate* [that is, incommensurable] human attitudes, cosmologies, and religions."[24] And when Panikkar seeks to say more about the content of this animating Spirit, he resorts not to *Logos* but to praxis. To be borne by the same Spirit, to share in the same trust, is to share not in a common "theory" or plan but in a shared "agon" or struggle or "pathos": "One animus does not mean one single theory, one single opinion, but one aspiration (in the literal sense of one breath) and one inspiration (as one spirit). Consensus ultimately means to walk in the same direction, not to have just one rational view."[25]

Panikkar does not, for the most part, spell out just what this "agon" or struggle aims at or the direction it is moving in — which leads us to examine what might be the limitations or dangers of his inspiring proposal.

LIMITATIONS AND DANGERS

In pointing out what appear to be inadequacies and dangers, I am referring to what Panikkar has said and written rather than to what he is doing — to his theory rather than his praxis. And I am pointing not so much to what his theory *contains* and to what I think is *missing* in it. My proposals intend not to correct what is false but to complement what is incomplete. Such is the spirit and intent of the criticisms that follow.

In so stressing the utter differences between the religions, in warning that no religion can ever really cross the gap of ultimate positions and so stand in judgment over another religion, in the constant admonitions that if there is any possibility of unity and conversation among religious believers it will not be on the basis of a shared *Logos* but only through the mystical movings of the Spirit — in such insistence on diversity and on non-noetic foundations of conversation, Panikkar is either encouraging or permitting a bourgeois mystical understanding of religious pluralism and dialogue.[26] His notion of radical plu-

---

24. IH, p. 148; JTG, p. 110.

25. IH, p. 147.

26. Such dangers are also lurking in Panikkar's imagery of the religions of the world as rivers that do not meet here on this earth in their form as water but only "in the skies" after they have been "vaporized" (see JTG, p. 92).

ralism might lead participants in dialogue to simply delight in diversity without ever really "judging" the differences. To clothe pluralism with a kind of onto-logical ultimacy, as Panikkar does, can all too easily create the temptation, in David Tracy's opinion, "to enjoy the pleasure of difference without ever com-mitting oneself to any particular vision of resistance or hope." For Tracy, this is "the perfect ideology for the modern bourgeois mind."[27]

Participants in interreligious dialogue can be so swept away with diversity and with incommensurability that they miss the broader context of their conver-sation — the broader context of religious experience and commitment. Religious conversations, like so much of religion itself today, tend to become "other-worldly." Indeed, look at the context and constitution and topics of most of the "interreligious encounters" that are proliferating today: so often they take place among white, middle-class males, on the mountaintops of the academy or monastery or ashram, far removed from the valleys of hunger and oppres-sion. Not to oversimplify, but the Marxist critique might well apply to much of contemporary interreligious dialogue: its participants seek to understand each others' worlds (but only partially and inadequately), not to change each others' worlds.

Panikkar, I know, is sensitive to such warnings. And yet, to respond to them, he must say more than he has so far. In order to show how his position is one of "relativity" and not of "relativism," he must make clearer how he can come to discern between what is "true and false," "good and evil." While he rightly in-sists that the diversity of religious experience is infinite, does that mean that *all* religious views can contribute to the dialogue? Are there ever situations where Panikkar would have to exclude someone from the table of dialogue? More specifically, it does not seem that Panikkar has sufficiently laid out the criteria — or the procedure — by which he can confront and oppose what seem to be the *intolerables* that are present within our contemporary world. I, and many others, find ourselves morally constrained to declare intolerable such real-ities as needless starvation, oppression of some human beings by others, torture, and economic injustice that destroys both human and planetary life. Often such intolerables are promoted or condoned by religion.

For many people, unless in our interreligious conversations we are able to confront and pass judgment on such intolerables, the dialogue itself becomes immoral. It is exposed to the Marxist criticism of promoting opium rather than responsibility. And as Kenneth Surin has pointed out in his "materialist critique" of modern notions of religious pluralism and dialogue, when promoters of inter-religious dialogue are oblivious of such gross human and ecological sufferings and injustice, or when they are not able to take any kind of a moral position be-fore them, they become, willy-nilly, anonymous agents of the ideology of first- and second-world powers to hold hegemony over the world. To proclaim "peace

---

27. David Tracy, *Plurality and Ambiguity: Hermeneutics, Religion, Hope* (New York: Harper & Row, 1987), p. 90.

amid diversity" when there is really "inequality and oppression amid diversity" is to turn pluralism or dialogue into an ideological weapon.[28]

Panikkar, especially in his recent writings, is aware of such moral imperatives and of the dangers of being ideologically co-opted by the powers that be. And so, after arguing that we cannot judge another culture or religion on the basis of our own always-culturally-limited perspectives, he adds: "This is an epistemological statement. I am in no way saying that the Aztecs did well in performing the human sacrifices they did, just as I am not saying that some countries today do well in trading arms or in building atomic arsenals."[29] And, after announcing that given the lack of common moral criteria we have "to trust even what we do not understand or approve of," he adds, "unless there are positive and concrete reasons to fight what we discover to be evil or error."[30] Therefore, to the question whether one must give up any critical stance in one's notion of pluralism, he responds resolutely, "Far from it." "We cannot postpone to an eschatological happy ending the solution of antimonies.... By that time ... millions of our fellow beings will have already starved to death or been killed in fratricidal war."[31]

But in recognizing the need for critical stances, he does not elaborate on how such stances are to be found, or what are the "positive and concrete reasons" for determining "evil" or intolerables. Here, I suggest, is one of the "softest" areas of Panikkar's otherwise challenging vision of interreligious dialogue. His appeal to a "cosmic confidence," by itself, doesn't do the job of enabling one to take critical stances and enter the difficult arena of not only understanding but also of confronting and opposing each other.

In the remainder of this essay I would like to expand on what I think are some of the hints that Panikkar has given in recent writings as to how his cosmic confidence might receive more of a this-worldly and ethical grounding. After recognizing the chasm-like differences between religions and the lack of any bridges between them, Panikkar proposes that if there is any material out of which bridges might be built, it must be earthly — that is, concerns for the welfare of life-on-earth and how to make this world a more habitable garden for all species: "The symbol here is *earth* — that is, secularity (saeculum), or the kingdom of justice here on earth, which entails the readiness to collaborate with all others, even if we disagree with them."[32] In one of his most recent essays, he becomes even more specific concerning what in the "saeculum" might be the crosscultural common matter for bridging differences and enabling mutual understanding and collaboration: the *anawim* or poor of this world. In the victims of this world, in those who for the most part have been

---

28. Kenneth Surin, "Toward a 'Materialist' Critique of 'Religious Pluralism': A Polemical Examination of the Discourse of John Hick and Wilfred Cantwell Smith," in Kenneth Surin, *The Turnings of Darkness and Light* (New York: Cambridge University Press, 1989).

29. IH, p. 129.

30. IH, p. 148.

31. IH, pp. 137, 126.

32. JTG, p. 102.

cast out from or marginalized within their individual cultures, we find a reality that "transcends the boundaries of one particular culture and can be called crosscultural."[33]

> The poor are precisely those who have not "made it" in any culture; they remain at the bottom-line. They are undifferentiated, not culturally specialized. They are crosscultural, for they are found in all cultures. Concern for brahmins or rabbis, scientists or saints, white people or only free citizens requires certain cultural options, but concern for the poor demands a crosscultural attitude. The poor are always with us, in every culture.[34]

In its concern for the poor, then, Christianity or any religion can make crosscultural claims and can encounter other religions on shared ground. As far as I know, Panikkar has not developed how this commitment to the *anawim* can be related to and provide a hermeneutical foundation for his cosmic trust.

A SHARED PREFERENTIAL OPTION FOR VICTIMS AS THE BASIS FOR INTERRELIGIOUS DIALOGUE

I am suggesting how Panikkar might give greater content and practicality to the "universal myth" that he is searching for and which he hopes will provide the context for a more effective encounter among the religions. He warns that such a myth "cannot be concocted" and must emerge from the conversation, that it will have to be "polysemic and irreducible to one interpretation" and not supportive of any "particular theory."[35] I propose that such a myth might be described in terms of the Christian notion of *soteria* — human well-being in this world. Such a concern for human and ecological well-being, focused in those whose well-being has been most severely destroyed or threatened (the *anawim*), seems to be emerging out of the present-day encounter of religions; it is clearly polysemic in that it is open to multiple understandings and symbolic images (kingdom, nirvāṇa, *moksha*), while it is unable to be captured in any one theory (communism, capitalism, historicism).

The Kairos Confronting All Religions

Declarations that the human project and this planet earth today face threats that have never before existed — or never existed with such intensity — are no longer coming only from visionaries suffering from apocalyptic fever; today we hear such warnings from scientists, philosophers, even economists and politicians. They point to realities that are recognized internationally and crossculturally and that individuals can deny only at the cost of their own

---

33. "Can Theology Be Transcultural?" in Paul Knitter, ed., *Pluralism and Oppression: Theology in World Perspective* (Lanham, Md.: University Press of America, 1991), p. 12.
34. Ibid.
35. IH, p. 124.

moral integrity and the welfare of their children: on the humano-social level, the specter of poverty, starvation, malnutrition caused not by "natural forces" but by human choices enfleshed in political-economic systems; on the international level, the horror of wars that can devastate and have devastated vast portions of civilian populations and that, if launched with the ever-growing nuclear arsenal, can destroy the world as we know it; on the ecological level, a world *already* being destroyed and sacrificed on the altar of commerce and consumerism.

The reality of such widespread and for the most part needless suffering both of humanity and of the earth, together with well-founded fears for the very existence of humankind and the planet, has created, among many other things, what can be called a new "hermeneutical kairos" for interreligious encounter. By this I mean a situation that casts both its shadows and its lights on all corners of the globe and in doing so makes a new encounter of religions both *necessary* and *possible*. I call it a *kairos* because it is a unique constellation of events that constitutes both new opportunities and responsibilities; it is *hermeneutical* because it enables followers of different religious paths not just to feel the need for each other but to talk to and understand and engage each other as never before. Perhaps it is close to Panikkar's envisioned "universal myth." As he has said, Peace (understood not just as the absence of war but as the "tranquility of order" among persons and with the earth) is becoming the universal religious symbol and ideal common to all traditions.[36]

Today our world-shaking state of confusion and conflict has brought forth concrete questions, dangers, problems that, willy-nilly, are confronting and demanding responses from all religions. They are questions that transcend cultural and religious differences, and if they don't require the religions to look at each other, they certainly require them all to look in the same direction. They touch *all* religions because they are the kind of questions that not only demand immediate attention but that cannot be answered, so it seems, without some kind of transformation of the human species, without some kind of new vision or new way of understanding who we are as humans and how we are to live on this dizzying, threatened planet. In calling for a clarification of ethics and fundamental values and for a radically different way of viewing our world and acting in it, in confronting the limits of the human condition as we know it, these issues are *religious* questions — questions that every religion either has tried to answer, or will want to answer, or will be required to answer.

The religions of the world, therefore, can seek to bridge their incommensurabilities and to discover some common ground by embracing a shared concern and commitment for the welfare of this world. This will give further substance to Panikkar's notion of the "saeculum" or of "peace" as symbols that can hermeneutically link various religions. But is this suggestion still another form of "anonymous imperialism"? Is this an imposition of Western or Christian concerns for this world on other religions?

---

36. R. Panikkar, quoted in R. Rapp, "Cultural Disarmament," *Interculture* 89 (1985), p. 29.

My proposal that interreligious encounter be based on a shared preferential option for the victims of this world is itself based on the hypothesis — better, I should say "trust" — that there is what might be called a soteriocentric core within all religious traditions. In the words of Gordon Kaufman, this means that "every religious tradition promises salvation in some form or other, i.e., promises true human fulfillment, or at least rescue from the pit into which we humans have fallen. Every religious tradition thus implicitly invokes a human or humane criterion to justify its existence and its claims."[37] Aloysius Pieris, on the basis of his broad knowledge of Asian religions, is even more forceful in his affirmation that at the heart of *homo religiosus* there is a "revolutionary urge...to generate a new humanity."[38]

In making such claims I do not naively imply that every follower of every religion brims with such this-worldly concern. One has only to look at many Christians to disabuse oneself of such naiveté. I am suggesting, however, that within the Sacred Scriptures and the mainstream traditions of what are called the world religions (but I would not exclude the tribal religions), there is a concern and a commitment — expressed in vastly different ways — to promote human well-being and betterment in this world. Therefore, within all the world religions, we can find *some* — I would make bold to say, *many* — believers who would not only willingly endorse but eagerly embrace what we are calling a salvation-centered (or this-worldly) basis for interreligious dialogue.

In the terminology of Bernard Lonergan, a common preferential option for the victimized and marginalized would constitute a "common conversion" preceding and nurturing the interreligious dialogue. Lonergan, with others, holds that religious believers need to be authentically converted before they can genuinely talk to and understand and appreciate each other.[39] But in calling for a preferential option for the poor, I am speaking not of a religious conversion in the usual sense of the word, but of a religious conversion in an implicit sense — a conversion and commitment to the victims, the oppressed, the struggling poor. (Christians would hold that such a conversion to those who are suffering is at least an implicit religious conversion because of the Mystery that addresses and claims us through our suffering neighbor.) Such a conversion and such a preferential option to respond to the human and ecological suffering that crisscrosses our cultures and religions would form the starting point, the basis, the heuristic for interreligious cooperation and conversation. And so, Panikkar's "cosmic trust" — or, the "agon" and "pathos" that he thinks animates religious conversations — would receive a grounding and a direction that would integrate its mystical content with concrete prophetic concern.

---

37. Gordon D. Kaufman, *The Theological Imagination: Constructing the Concept of God* (Philadelphia: Westminster Press, 1981), pp. 197–99.

38. Aloysius Pieris, *An Asian Theology of Liberation* (Maryknoll, N.Y.: Orbis Books, 1987), p. 108.

39. Bernard Lonergan, *Method in Theology* (New York: Herder and Herder, 1972), pp. 118–19; see also, pp. 267–81.

HOW DIALOGUE BASED ON A PREFERENTIAL OPTION WOULD WORK

It has often been said that the first step in dialogue is to listen rather than to speak — to try to understand others before we try to share our ideas with them. A dialogue based on a shared preferential option for victims would certainly agree with this, but it would want to clarify what it means to "listen to" and how one can go about "understanding" others. It would urge that an essential element — I almost want to say a primary element — in understanding others, and in enabling them to understand us, is to *act* with them. By this I mean that dialogue must also include — ideally, it should begin with — some form of shared praxis that is based on shared concerns and shared efforts to confront common problems. Of course this is not the only way to understand others. But the other ways — talking, studying, praying/meditating together — are in a sense incomplete without this shared praxis. More, I am suggesting that the other ways of understanding each other can be enhanced and made more effective if based on shared praxis.

This suggestion reflects the "method" of liberation theology. Liberationists tell us that theology, as a reflective effort to understand and unlock the ever-new treasures in the Word of God, is always a "second step." The first step — the essential key to the treasure-chest of God's Word — is *liberative praxis;* that is, efforts, in whatever form, to love our neighbors by responding to their suffering and removing the causes of that suffering. On the basis of such a human commitment we can take up the Word of God and hear and feel and be challenged by insights we had not been aware of before.

This same insight can be applied to, and become an essential ingredient in, an interreligious dialogue. Besides — ideally, before — listening to each other's religious beliefs, or exploring each other's scriptures, or sharing prayer, we must share with followers of other religions a preferential option for the oppressed and suffering. Our dialogue, in other words, will be based on a common "conversion" of differing religious believers to the common horror that faces us all: human or ecological suffering. Naturally, such suffering will be found in different forms according to our differing socio-political contexts. Certainly, however, in every life-context there will be areas of suffering or injustice that all religious persons will be able to recognize in common. If we can't find them, then all we have to do is turn to and listen to the marginated of our particular society. Among representatives of differing religions, therefore, a "joint agreement" can be reached that as religions persons they want to bring "salvation" or "cessation" to the suffering that plagues our society. Naturally, each religion will have differing views of what is to be done. That provides the "matter" for dialogue. But the problems are common, and so is the commitment.

Of course, not all followers of other religious traditions will feel or share this concern for human suffering (just as not all Christians do). But, as stated above, there are growing numbers of believers within all religions who are sensing their need to respond, as religious persons, to the "signs of the times" as those signs are clearly traced in the economic injustice, nuclear threat, and ecological devastation that are part of our world today. With such believers, who have been "converted" to the victims of the world, religious dialogue can be carried on most profitably. This is not to exclude dialogue with other believers who don't share such concern; yet I am suggesting that such salvation-centered dialogue should be a priority, both because of the urgency of the issues and because of the promised fruit of understanding and unity resulting from such an approach.

But such shared praxis will lead, naturally and spontaneously, to *shared reflection*. (In more technical terms, praxis can never stand by itself but must be integrated with theory.) Having acted together, having shared in a conversion to the victims, having experienced the frustrations and the joys, the fears and the hopelessness of working to transform local or international structures of injustice and oppression — we will come together to both speak with and sustain each other. We will want to give an explanation for the hope that is within us — that is, to let those of other religious traditions see what it is that impels and directs us in our liberative praxis. And we will want to hear from them about the hope and vision that animate them. Here the experience of the base Christian communities can become real in interreligious communities of dialogue; just as the prior praxis of justice and commitment to the poor has enabled Latin American communities to find "new ears" by which to hear and rediscover the meaning of the gospels, so too can a shared preferential option for the suffering enable us not only to hear but also to speak to others perhaps more effectively than ever before. We will be able to hear the words or explanations of others with new ears. A shared liberative praxis and commitment to the suffering become, in other words, a *common hermeneutical ground* on which followers of different religious traditions can share the meaning of their symbols and beliefs and rituals in a more effective and challenging manner than in the past.

But such a dialogue will provide new possibilities not just for understanding each other. We will also be able to see and deal with our differences; we will be enabled to confront and tell each other where we think the other is wrong. But — and this is a big "but" — the criterion for doing so will not be some doctrinal or absolute truth; it will not be an imposition of clearly defined and pre-given Christian viewpoints. Rather, it will be the criterion of human well-being — what does or does not promote the removal of starvation and oppression, what does or does not foster life. Clearly, such a criterion is not already neatly and absolutely given. There will be differing views on what it contains and how it is to be applied. But it is a practical criterion — something we can work with *together*. In our shared liberative praxis and in our shared reflection we have to discover together what makes for human well-being. That task, Christians would say, is never fully accomplished.

But if our criterion for judging what is true or false, good or bad, is no longer "Is it in the Bible or the Upaniṣads or the Koran?" but rather "Does it remove human suffering and promote life?" — if this is our criterion, then we cannot apply it without listening to the poor and the victims. The oppressed, the marginalized, those who in the past "didn't count" must also have a voice in a soteriocentric dialogue; they must speak with and to the so-called experts. It is their voice and their experience — much more than that of exegetes, theologians, popes, or even mystics — that will tell us what in our religious beliefs and practices promotes human well-being and thus what is faithful to our scriptures.

If such a soteriocentric dialogue seems somewhat idealistic and difficult to achieve, we can suggest a concrete means for its realization, a means that is already being applied in countries of Asia. Asian Christians such as Aloysius Pieris, Michael Amaladoss, Felix Wilfred, Sebastian Kappen, and the late Michael Rodrigo are coming to the realization that what is needed in their interreligious context are not only base Christian communities, but *base human communities.*[40] The primary requirement for participating in such communities is not commitment to Christ, but rather religious commitment to *soteria* — to the struggle for justice and life. Members belong to different religious traditions and bring their respective religious symbols and hopes to implementing and sustaining that commitment to human well-being. Just as in base Christian communities of Latin America, members of the base human communities *act* together and then *reflect*, and where possible pray and meditate together. So action and reflection no longer take place in separate religious camps, but *together* — Buddhists, Muslims, Hindus, Christians acting and reflecting and explaining their scriptures *together*. As Pieris describes his experience, members of such communities are discovering a new heart for each other: "Here [in these base human communities] co-pilgrims expound their respective scriptures, retelling the story of Jesus and Gautama in a core-to-core dialogue that makes their hearts burn (Luke 24/32)."[41]

Panikkar is entirely correct in warning us against universal "theories" of religious pluralism or too facile methods for religious dialogue. And he does well to balance this warning with his proposal that unless there is a shared "cosmic trust" in the value of our differences and the prospects for learning from and cooperating with each other, our conversation will be impossible. Yet I suggest that, by itself, Panikkar's image of cosmic trust is still too general or too mystical. It can be, and needs to be, grounded and inspired by a shared preferential option for the suffering and the victims of this world. Through such an option, religious persons will be better able to say to themselves and to their dialogue partners, "Scio in cui credidi" — "I know in whom/what I have trusted" (2 Tm 1:12).

---

40. Sebastian Kappen, "Toward an Indian Theology of Liberation," Felix Wilfred, ed., *Leave the Temple* (Maryknoll, N.Y.: Orbis Books, forthcoming); also Michael Amaladoss, "Liberation: An Inter-Religious Project," also in Wilfred, *Leave the Temple;* Michael Rodrigo, "Buddhism and Christianity: Toward a Human Future: An Example of Village Dialogue of Life," paper at Buddhist-Christian Conference (Berkeley, California, August, 1987).

41. Aloysius Pieris, "Jesus and Buddha: Mediators of Liberation," in Hick and Knitter, *The Myth of Christian Uniqueness,* p. 175.

12

The Eco-Technological Issue
Toward a Liberating Production Theology
ENRIQUE DUSSEL

Raimon Panikkar has tackled the "technological issue" several times.[1] We would like to rethink this theme from the situation in Latin America and in the peripheral countries, as the contradiction is much clearer here. Indeed, these countries need, on the one hand, a speedy "development" in order to escape shortages, hunger, and misery. But, on the other hand, that very same development propels into the foreground, in a much sharper way than in the developed countries, the ecological issue, the problem of the destruction of the natural milieu and traditional life, which has created over centuries — if not millennia — a balance between the human race and Mother Earth. Is it contradictory to attempt at the same time development and ecological conservation? Must one remain underdeveloped, exploited, and oppressed in the name of defense of nature? These are serious, real problems, relevant issues lying at the very heart of the revolutionary situation of the Third World.

Enrique Dussel is author of more than forty books, including *A History of the Church in Latin America: Colonialism to Liberation, The Invention of the Americas: 1492,* and *The Underside of Modernity: Apel, Ricoeur, Taylor, and Rorty*. A founding member of the Ecumenical Association of Third World Theologians, Professor Dussel serves as President of the Commission on Studies for Church History in Latin America.

Dussel is translated here by Adolfo Abascal-Jaen and Albert Lepiece.

1. See, among others, R. Panikkar, *Técnica y tiempo* (Buenos Aires: Columba, 1967); "Some Theses on Technology," *Logos* 7 (1986), pp. 115–24; "Some Supplementary Theses on Technology," (unpublished, 1987); "Ecology from an Eastern Philosophical Perspective," *Monchanin* (Montreal) 50 (1975), pp. 23–28; "Alternatives to Modern Culture," *Interculture* (Montreal) 77 (1982), pp. 2–4; *Worship and Secular Man* (Maryknoll, N.Y.: Orbis Books, 1973); *Blessed Simplicity* (New York: Seabury Press, 1982).

THE "NO" TO TECHNOLOGY

Panikkar, like Heidegger,[2] is clear in his "no" to technology *as such* — in its essence. Technology is a "mathematical" rationalization of reality: the tyranny of quantity over quality;[3] it manages to exert a total hegemony over Western civilization as "technocracy." Technology is neither neutral[4] nor readily universal: "The universalization of technology implies the Westernizing of the world and the destruction of the other cultures that rest on visions of reality that are incompatible with modern Western presuppositions of technology. Technology is therefore not neutral."[5]

In fact, technology is not autonomous from the human being.[6] It is the primacy of what is mechanical — and of machines — over the human being. But, at the same time, and paradoxically, it is an affirmation of the "anthropocentrism" ("homocentrism") that destroys nature. It asserts "objectivism" versus the subjective and ethical existence of the person. The time and space of technology cancel, annihilate, despise the time, space, and rhythm of human — organic, cultural, historical — life. The inertia of matter destroys the "soul." Technology supposes a certain epistemology, a manipulating nominalism: "quantifiability."[7] It is the triumph of instrumental reason: control, instrumentalization, bureaucratization.

THE "YES" TO TECHNOLOGY

As Panikkar has told me, one has to distinguish between technology and technique. The first refers to the modern and scientific use of technique — with all its attendant dangers. But technique — the Greek word *tekhnè* must be understood as a creative attitude of the human being who transforms nature without destroying it but rather respecting its rhythm, its timing, its balance — is an organic integration with the cosmos:

> Technique is always of the order of *tekhnè,* technology introduces into *tekhnè* an essential mutation. Technique is an art . . . wherein the human mind embodies itself into matter to produce an artifact (pottery, music, poetry, a building, etc.). . . . In one sense, technical activity is human activity that modifies the material world by establishing a new symbiosis with

2. See Friedrich Dessauer, *Streit um die Technik* (Freiburg: Herder, 1959); Joseph Sadzik, *Esthétique de M. Heidegger* (Paris: Ed. Universitaires, 1963). For another view on the subject, see Carl Micham and Robert Mackey, *Philosophy and Technology* (London: Macmillan, 1972), bibliography, pp. 379–89. See also Enrique Dussel, *Filosofía de la producción* (Bogotá: Nueva América, 1984); idem, "Ecologico-cultural Ethic," *Etica comunitaria* (colección Cristianismo y Sociedad=Teologia e Libertação) (Ediciones Paulinas, 1986). There are translations of this last work in Portuguese (Vozes), English (*Ethics and Community* [Maryknoll, N.Y.: Orbis Books]), and German (Patmos).

3. Panikkar, "Some Theses on Technology," pp. 115ff.

4. Ibid., pp. 117ff.

5. Ibid., pp. 117–18.

6. Ibid., p. 118.

7. Ibid.

Man. When this activity is institutionalized, it belongs to human affairs, and hence to culture, which consists in cultivating not only the earth but also all that contributes to the enrichment of human life.[8]

THE DILEMMA

The difficulty begins when society as a whole, and the Third World in particular, wonders: What is the solution, using or forgoing technology? One could possibly dream in a romantic or utopian way of a zero rate of development. But can the poor and miserable countries without means of feeding, clothing, and housing their populations leave technology aside in their projects of liberation and development, projects of satisfying basic needs?

Panikkar puts the question as follows:

It becomes difficult, often impossible, not to collaborate with the sons of men in the building up of the earthly city. . . . This does not prevent us from being conscious of what we would like to call Samson's vocation: getting involved, mixing with the others, collaborating and pulling everything down, because there is no other means of building up the extra-temporal kingdom than to exhaust the potentialities of the temporal kingdom.[9]

But in the impoverished, underdeveloped, and exploited world of the periphery, Samson would not find a palace to pull down, only people in need of tilling the land for food, of weaving clothes to face the cold, of using technology to build houses.

Panikkar raises this objection:

One may say that non-technological Man was subject to cold, epidemics, floods, seasons and such. The answer to all that is that *tekhnè* can solve the majority of these problems and that there is no need of going back to some primitivism, that no form of romanticism can justify. The point is to discover the meaning of life and the nature of human joy, and seek to determine whether in this respect technology has brought us forward or backward.[10]

Moreover — and it is relevant today, at the end of the twentieth century — we are made aware by the ecological movements of the deadly risk for the human race entailed by the destruction of Mother Earth. It is simply a matter of suicide: nature's death is our death. And it is sure that technology is the major instrument of ecological destruction. Here too we reach an impasse: a sharp "no" to technology as destructive power, and a mistrustful, hesitant "yes" to the positive potentiality of that instrument; a "return" to the cultures, civilization, or to the organic and balanced *tekhnè* of the pre-modern human being. But are such

---

8. Ibid., p. 115.
9. Panikkar, *Técnica y tiempo,* pp. 36–37.
10. Panikkar, "Some Theses on Technology," p. 119.

returns actually possible? Who is going to defend — and with what means — those nice utopian experiments, which are impossible as viable alternatives for the millions of famished people of the peripheral, underdeveloped, and exploited world? The ecological movement is right in its diagnosis, but it is caught in an impasse as far as a concretely applicable alternative is concerned.

TECHNOLOGY AS TECHNOLOGY, AND TECHNOLOGY AS CAPITAL

The implicit argument in the sharp and essential "no" to technology — of the movement of ethical affirmation — would seem always to reach the same point: technology, both in a capitalist society and in a socialist society (where there exists a "technologistic" spirit of ecological destruction, although in a different way) comes out with the same effects. However, it is possible that modern capitalist technology raises critical issues for different reasons from those in socialist countries. The fact that technology, both in capitalism and in existing socialism, has developed in such a way that it destroys nature and rules over humans has nothing to do with its essence but only with two historical paths of its possible developments. There has been confusion between the essence and the possibilities of technology *as such,* on the one hand, and the development of technology in capitalism and in existing socialism, on the other. This confusion leads to saying "no" to the essence of technology, a "no" that has nothing to do with the human possibilities of technology. I think that this is due to a certain limitation or blindness at the analysis level. I should like to limit myself to pointing out another path (which, within the limits of this work, I shall not cover completely).

When one speaks of modern or European technology or of overdeveloped society, one always means technology such as it has been subsumed by capital in its own movement. Should this ontological aspect be left in the shade, one leaves aside the transubstantiation of *tekhnè* into technology.

In all pre-capitalist systems, *tekhnè* or the instrumental totality — comprising material objects as well as science as a theoretical instrument — was confined to a secondary area, even if it was determinant in many aspects. Darcy Ribeiro has shown technico-instrumental conditioning in universal history.[11] The use of the horse introduced a much speedier vehicle than those known before. The introduction of iron into weaponry and agricultural tools — a food revolution and consequently a demographic explosion — resulted in migrations of warriors. Using horses and iron is subjacent to the Indo-European invasions and to the organization of the first states and empires. But those developments never got anywhere near to technology under the reign of capital.

If capital is the movement (*kinèsis* in the Aristotelian sense) of the economic value in the process of valorization (even unto profit), technology will be an essential moment of its own being. Capital reaches a relative surplus-value or

---

11. Darcy Ribeiro, *El proceso civilizatorio* (Caracas: Universidad Central de Venezuela, 1970). See Eugene Ferguson, *Bibliography of the History of Technology* (Cambridge: MIT Press, 1968).

increase in exploiting the living labor thanks to machinery — that is, science and technology — which increases the productivity of this living labor. More value is produced over the same time or the same value in less time. The "saved" time of living labor is the "surplus-value" produced, which will later be realized as "profit."[12]

Technology as an Instrument for Life

As such, *tekhnè* — in its preindustrial (pre-capitalist) meaning — and technology can be interpreted positively as a means for life: "Technology presents itself to us as the activity of the human being in front of nature, the immediate process of production of life."[13]

Technology, according to its anthropological and ethical definition — and not technology as we know it today — is a mediation toward life:

> I would have objectified my individuality and its peculiarity in my production, I would thus have had a double enjoyment; during the activity, by experiencing an individual vital expression, and, in contemplating the object, the individual joy of knowing that my personality is an objective power. Work would be an expression of free life and thus enjoyment of life.[14]

Technology as Capital: A Valorization Instrument

In a text of major anthropological and ethical importance — and also theological, as will be shown later — it is said:

> Even if it is only in the machine (read: in technology) that capital gives itself its adequate form as use-value in the production process, this does in no way mean that this use-value — the machine as such — is the capital or that its existence as a machine is identical to its existence as capital.[15]

It is a fundamental ontological problem. Technology in itself, in its essence, is a means for human life. It is intrinsically valuable and not ambiguous, as Heidegger pretends. But, when it is subsumed by the economic value as its mediation to reach a greater surplus-value, a greater *profit,* then technology is perverted, loses its essence, is corrupted. It is no longer a means of life but rather for death. It is here — and not earlier — that a "no" has to be said to technology. Actually, with technology, capital has also assumed the human person, the "living work," as a mediation for profit. It is only here that technology

---

12. See Karl Marx, *Cuaderno histórico-tecnológico, London 1851,* trans. and intro. Enrique Dussel (Puebla: Universidad de Puebla, 1983). On the technological issue in Marx, see Enrique Dussel, *La producción teórica de Marx: Un Comentario a los Grundrisse* (Mexico: Siglo XXI, 1985), and *Hacia un Marx desconocido: Un comentario a los Manuscribos del 61–63* (Mexico: Siglo XXI, 1988). I am preparing a third volume with a long chapter on technology.

13. Karl Marx, *Kapital* 1, ch. 13 (*Marx-Engels Werke*) vol. 23 (Berlin: Dietz, several editions), p. 393, note.

14. *Paris Notebooks (1844)* (*MEGA* 1, 3 [1932]), pp. 546–47.

15. *Grundrisse* (Berlin: Dietz, 1974), p. 585.

is transformed into an anti-ecological structure. But, in truth, it is no longer technology but its new substance, its new essence: capital.

What is questioned, then, is not technology or science *as such;* it is their alienation (their destitution and corruption, the negation of their essence) when they are assumed by capital. Capital, the movement of economic value (as money, means of production or utilized living labor, product, merchandise, and, again, as money) goes through the metamorphosis of its determinations, of its moments. Capital is the movement of the life of economic value (a thing) to which the living person is immolated. It is a holocaust offered to an anthropophagic idol. Technology becomes an instrument of torture, of mediation that imprisons living labor and has it work at its own rhythm, in its materiality, under its control. Technology, *as capital,* is an anti-human monster.

In the nineteenth century, long before any theoretical critique of technology, machines were destroyed by workers. We could say that in the judgment against technology, something like an ideological misformation happened. The sheer *appearance* of the "technology of capital" was attributed to the *essence* of technology and, by negating this one in its essence, one negates the alternative — a just use of technology.

In an ontology of technology, it would be necessary to show how today's technology is the sheer phenomenon or appearance of the inner being of capital. Thus, technology "as capital" is the negation of the essence of technology — mediation for more human life. In capital, technology is a means or instrument to increase surplus-value production, that is, profit. If a technological invention does not yield immediate profit, it will not be put into operation, will effectively not exist. In the history of current technology, the only real inventions are those which are subsumed by capital. Consequently, technology can objectively destroy the human being, for it is assigned a goal which is alien to that human being. Such is the perverse — ethically and ontologically — sense of technology or science.

Development of Third-World Countries and Eco-Technology

The poverty of the peripheral underdeveloped countries, which has increased enormously recently, and will do so even more in the coming decades, is produced by the exploitation of the capitalist system. The dependent capitalism of the peripheral countries — with its national bourgeois class that oppresses the poor and unjustly extracts exchange-value — transfers exchange-value to the capital of the rich and developed countries. This constitutes a gigantic mechanism of extraction of life, which in turn generates the death of nature and of humans. The exchange-value (gains) of the peripheral capital (Third World) passes over to the global capital of the central countries (USA, Federal Germany, Japan, etc.) thanks to the profits of the transnational corporations, the banks with their fictitious credits, and monopoly prices. Capital and interest must be paid to the banks not just with printed money notes, but with products in which human life is objectified: exchange-value. The monopoly prices are fixed under their exchange-value for the products of the poor countries and over this value for the products of highly developed countries. It is thus a theft of human life objectified in the exchange-value extracted.

But, besides the theft of human life — theft of exchange-value, which is the reason for the poor's poverty — the ecological value of nature is also destroyed. The ecological value of the human being is not only destroyed through economic exploitation but also in the devaluation of human life in the Third World. The urban catastrophes (Mexico, Calcutta) are products of economic exploitation — industrial wastes, vehicle fumes, etc. — that provoke a contamination of water, air, and ground. Capital destroys simultaneously the earth and the human being. This destruction is not the work of technology as such, but of technology as used and developed by capital (or by existing socialism, which is not the kind of socialism to be put to work in the Third World). This means that technology, as we know it, is not what it could be at the service of the human being. The perverse development of technology in the hands of capital has produced absolutely inhuman instruments, articulations, and theories. But negating those technological developments does not invalidate in any way technology as such. The automobile, as we know it, is a harmful product, a disproportionate and irrational means of transport. It spends too much nonrenewable energy in order to transport little weight; it needs too much space; and so forth. But there could be an electric solar car. This car would be an ecologically harmless means of transport. But it would bring in fewer gains to the automotive corporations, and therefore this development has not taken place.

Intrinsically, technology has a value from the ecological viewpoint (ecological value, use-value), for it results in saving human labor. Technology does not add exchange-value to the products, but it saves work by reaching the same use-value (ecological value) with less exchange-value (economic value). From an anthropological viewpoint, it allows sparing human life, and this constitutes its ethical value: technology, as such, is "good" from the ethical standpoint. Saving human work *for life* means that the person can work less or produce more in the same time. But if technology is in the hands of capital, the saving of human life is accumulated into capital gain instead of objectifying this boon as a decrease in human work. This is why technological discoveries have not directly benefited humankind, but rather capital. Technology has only secondarily benefited humankind through the means of the technological monsters built by the profit-minded logic of capital without the least humane intention. Marx called this "the civilizing power of capital."

It follows, then, that in the impoverished and exploited Third World, the first essential and irreplaceable task, after the revolution, is the use of technology in favor of the human being. "After the revolution" because before it any technological development in the hands of capital is a factor of a greater exploitation and of a greater destruction of the environment. One cannot go back to building roads with shovels, because bulldozers would allegedly be perverse technology, any more than one can go back to counting on one's fingers because computers would enslave the imagination. Technology, as a means or instrument to save and develop human work by bringing in more strength, more precision, more speed (quantitative increases, of course) can serve the human person and development. This is an inescapable and fundamental challenge.

It must be an "eco-technology," a "techno-ecology," an ecological technology that develops the productive potentialities of the human being while preserving nature and allowing for its development. Two poles must be maintained: on the one hand, the defense and development of nature; on the other hand, the development of a technology for life and justice, in order to feed the hungry, provide drink to the thirsty, clothe the naked, house the homeless, and restore the sick to health.

TOWARD AN ECO-TECHNOLOGICAL AND ECONOMIC THEOLOGY

The theological question that unifies our theme is the sacramental question. It articulates person-nature relations, the person-technological means relations, and time spent with other persons — all in the context of an economy that governs the relation between persons through the production of work on nature with tools. The sacrament is a material good — water, bread and wine, oil — that bestows God's grace.

The eucharistic bread is first wheat — fruit of the earth, sun, water, vegetative life. But it then becomes flour — fruit of the work of the peasant, the transporter, the miller. Finally, it is bread — fruit of the work of the baker, the distributor. It is actually a total synthesis of the evolution of life on earth since the creation of the universe and of all the existing technologies — from the plow to the truck and the computer. A synthesis of the history of creation, of the life of humankind — all in a simple piece of bread! When the celebrant says, "We offer you this bread, fruit of our work and of the earth," he refers to this ecological, technological, and economic synthesis. The theological status of technology is sacramental and its locus in the believing praxis is liturgy: celebrations, joy, feast, banquet of the Kingdom.

In those conditions, artistic and spiritual creation — art and science, and let us add prayer and mystical contemplation — would be the fundamental human activity. What is important to us here is to show the anthropological and ethical meaning of technology; it is a mediation toward free time, free from material coercion in order to attain to the supreme human goals. Technology makes possible the existence of bread as surplus for the sacrifice (given that one can only offer or make an offering of what is not absolutely needed to satisfy basic needs) or, even more, it is a mediation toward the free time of feasting, of liturgy.

The development of the Third World, impossible without technological mediation, must go further than the capitalist system in a non-Stalinist mode of socialism. This development is the condition to celebrate the eucharist in those countries. The bread offered in sacrifice must be the bread of justice — which is also economic justice — "good" technological bread — product of a *tekhnè* — bread in surplus of what is needed to live. The eucharistic feast cannot be celebrated if there is hunger:

All the believers shared their belongings with one another. They would sell their property and possessions and distribute the money among all, according to what each one needed. Day after day they met as a group in the Temple and met in their houses for the breaking of bread (Acts 2:44–46).

The liberation of the human being today requires the liberation of technology as a fundamental moment. It is a liberation of technology as a moment of capital — as its instrument, an instrument of death, an anti-ecological and anti-human instrument. Thus, technology ethics deals neither with the moral issue of respecting the property of inventions nor with that of devoting oneself to science or to technology as one would to a religion, nor again with that of deceiving a colleague, and so forth. The ethical — and theological — issue par excellence of technology today is that which discovers, in the first place, the sad and destructive function of technology as a mediation for the extraction of surplus labor, as a means of extracting life from the living work of the worker of the poor countries. Second, this ethics of the liberation of technology must create conditions for the production of a technology as a mediation for human life, for the respect of nature and the development of conditions of decent living for the poor, the exploited, the oppressed. It is the liberation of technology so that it may produce the eucharistic bread.

If technology is not liberated on behalf of the human being, the human being will go on being immolated to the Fetish, to the Idol, through its materiality as a machine, as technology, and thus:

All surplus labor, which humankind can obtain as long as it exists, belongs to capital according to its inbred laws. *Moloch.*[16]

---

16. *Kapital* III, ch. 24 (*Marx-Engels Werke* 25), p. 378.

13

Methodological Foundations for Interreligious Dialogue

DAVID J. KRIEGER

It is one of the essential characteristics of our time that the borders between cultures and religions are disappearing. The existential risk and the intellectual burden of interreligious dialogue is, therefore, not merely the personal adventure of privileged individuals, but the very condition determining all relevant theology today.[1] Raimon Panikkar poses the problem of the encounter of religions in the following way:

David J. Krieger teaches at the University of Luzern, Switzerland, and directs a research project on interreligious environmental ethics financed by the Swiss National Science Foundation. He is founder of the Institut für Kommunikationsforschung in Meggen, Switzerland, and author of *The New Universalism, Fundamentalismus — Prämodern oder Postmodern*, and *System, Kommunikation und Konstruktivismus*.

1. Karl Rahner bases his dogmatic theology of the non-Christian religions in "Christianity and the Non-Christian Religions" (see *Theological Investigations*, vol. V [Baltimore: Helicon, 1966], pp. 115–34) on precisely this fact. The following sentences do not appear in the English translation and are therefore offered here in my translation. They are found on page 137 of the German text. "Earlier another religion was practically also the religion of another cultural circle, a history with which one communicated only on the edge of one's own history. Today it is different. There is no Western culture enclosed within itself any more, no Western culture at all, which could consider itself simply as the center of world history....Today everyone is everyone else's neighbor, and therefore determined by the global communication of life-situations: Every religion which exists in the world is, as all cultural possibilities and realities of other men, a question and a possibility offered for all." In order to get an idea of the magnitude and significance of the historical shift which occurred within the first half of the twentieth century, one need only compare the above statements to the cultural isolationism in which Ernst Troeltsch ended forty years earlier (see "The Place of Christianity among the World-Religions" in *Christian Thought: Its History and Application*). For Troeltsch, "the only religion that we can endure is Christianity, for Christianity has grown up with us and has become a part of our very being" (p. 25). "But this does not preclude," he continues, "the possibility that other racial groups, living under entirely different conditions, may experience their contact with the Divine Life in quite a different way, and may themselves also possess a religion which has grown up with them, and from which they cannot sever themselves so long as they remain what they are" (p. 26). Religious truth is bound to its particular historical and cultural setting and there can be no real encounter or dialogue between such mutually inaccessible realms. "The various racial groups can only seek to purify and enrich their experience, each within its own provence and according to its own standards" (pp. 27–28). "There can be no conversion or transformation of one into the other" (p. 30).

To be sure, each tradition, seeing itself from within, considers that it is capable of giving a full answer to the religious urge of its members and, seeing other traditions from outside, tends to judge them as partial. It is only when we take the other as seriously as ourselves that a new vision may dawn. For this we have to break the self-sufficiency of any human group. But this requires that we should somehow have jumped outside our own respective traditions. Herein seems to lie the destiny of our time.[2]

How can we consciously accept this destiny and approach the encounter of religions with methodological adequacy? Much of Panikkar's published work is primarily concerned with the concrete dialogue between Christianity and Hinduism. Still, there are important methodological reflections throughout these works, as well as major essays dealing specifically with methodological issues. Drawing upon these various sources, I will attempt a systematic *reconstruction* of Panikkar's method for conducting interreligious dialogue.[3] To state the result at the outset, the method will be found to consist of seven steps:

1. One begins with a faithful and critical understanding of one's own tradition — an understanding won with historical-critical, philological and phenomenological methods.

2. In the same way, an understanding of another tradition is acquired.

3. This understanding becomes conviction.

4. An internal, *intra*religious dialogue begins between the two convictions.

5. The internal dialogue becomes an external, *inter*religious dialogue with representatives of the other tradition.

6. Steps 1 through 5 are presupposed for all partners in the dialogue.

7. New interpretations are tested for their "orthodoxy."

In the following discussion I will be primarily concerned with presenting a *method* not only specifically for interreligious dialogue, but also for intercultural encounter in general. The focus upon method necessarily implies a certain narrowness of vision with respect to the full body of Panikkar's thought. To a certain extent the entire philosophical and theological "system" which surrounds and, to a certain extent, grounds Panikkar's method must be neglected. I will also not attempt to answer the historical question concerning the development of his thought.

Panikkar places certain "indispensable prerequisites" at the beginning of the encounter of religions:

2. See Raimundo Panikkar, *The Unknown Christ of Hinduism,* revised and enlarged edition (Maryknoll, N.Y.: Orbis Books, 1981), p. 34.

3. The following discussion draws heavily upon material published in my book *The New Universalism: Foundations for a Global Theology* (Maryknoll, N.Y.: Orbis Books, 1991). See also "Communication Theory and Interreligious Dialogue," *Journal of Ecumenical Studies* 30:3–4 (Summer-Fall 1993), pp. 331–53.

a deep human honesty in searching for the truth wherever it can be found; a great intellectual openness in this search, without conscious preconceptions or willingly entertained prejudices; and finally a profound loyalty towards one's own tradition.[4]

Already we have here the first two steps of the method any interreligious dialogue must follow. The first step consists in obtaining a faithful and critical understanding of one's own tradition; the second step requires that one acquire a similar understanding of another tradition.[5]

In order to clarify the procedures by which this is to be accomplished, Panikkar proposes to view the problem of intercultural understanding in terms of three kinds of hermeneutics: "morphological," "diachronic," and "diatopical."[6] If we take the three kinds of hermeneutics which Panikkar describes as *levels of human communication,* then Panikkar's diatopical model allows us to distinguish *three levels of discourse* upon which communication may take place. First, *within* a culture, tradition, world view or religious understanding is achieved by means of a first level of discourse, which Panikkar calls "morphological" hermeneutics. This refers to that language in which we make assertions about matters of fact in the broad sense. This is everyday language, the normal language in which we communicate and coordinate our practical as well as theoretical concerns. Whatever we say in this language is meaningful by reason of being either true or false according to commonly accepted criteria of truth and validity. These criteria form the life-world horizon, the set of taken-for-granted truths about reality which constitutes our "world." Within this horizon of shared criteria, methods according to which we handle statements claiming to be true and meaningful may be called methods of verification.

When systematically developed, first-level discourse becomes the well-known methods of *argumentation* — formal, empirical, historical-critical and phenomenological — in which scientific inquiry is conducted. Panikkar refers to this form of understanding as "morphological hermeneutics," for it is by means of these methods that the distance which separates us from understanding that which is strange or unknown within a given world horizon, whether a natural phenomenon, a text, a work of art or a social institution, is overcome.

Morphological hermeneutics, therefore, mediates understanding *within the same cultural and historical context* as the interpreter. To take an example from everyday life, an expert explains the proper use of a computer to someone from his own culture who has a similar general education. He may presuppose a common language and a shared form of thinking and even a common world view. It is presupposed that the person who is seeking information about the computer already knows, at least to a certain extent, what a "computer" is, what a "machine" is and what one does with such things.

---

4. Ibid., p. 35.
5. Ibid., p. 67f.
6. See R. Panikkar, *Myth, Faith and Hermeneutics* (New York: Paulist Press, 1979), p. 8f.

The problem of explaining, understanding and discovering truth becomes very different, however, when it is a matter of obtaining information about something from the past, from a culture which lies far distant in time, say, a text or artifact from ancient Rome or Greece. We can no longer presuppose a common language or world view. The world has changed, and the context in which the text originally was written or the artifact produced no longer immediately determines our view of the world. Understanding now requires that the context itself be reconstructed and mediated with our present-day context or life-world horizon. This is a task which must be carried out upon a different level of discourse; namely, a discourse which, since it cannot appeal to common criteria of truth or meaning, must itself express these criteria and thus "set boundaries" for our life-world horizon.

We may speak of this second-level discourse as *boundary discourse.* Panikkar here speaks of "diachronic" hermeneutics, because the task is to overcome alienation of meaning *caused by temporal distance.* Diachronic hermeneutics, or second-level boundary discourse, articulates itself as the retrieval of founding texts and events. Consequently it is concerned to define and preserve *one* specific cultural tradition (e.g., Western culture). The understanding it expresses by mediating horizons of meaning constitutes the historical continuity and cultural identity of a "tradition." As a systematically developed method of inquiry, boundary discourse becomes historical hermeneutics or dialectic.[7]

Both morphological and diachronical hermeneutics may be applied in the attempt to understand another culture, as, for example, is the normal procedure in ethnology, anthropology and history and their respective applications in the science of religions. Nevertheless, says Panikkar, they are not sufficient to overcome the radical distance which separates different cultures from one another. For this reason, still another form of hermeneutics and thus a higher level of discourse must be postulated wherein these disciplines will be able to go beyond their present methodological limitations. Only upon the basis

---

7. See ibid., p. 9. Panikkar's relation to dialectics is ambiguous. On the one hand, he seems to limit its usefulness to the reconstruction of meaning in history, that is, within the history of one particular culture — this is history as seen from the point of view of a particular people; it is "their" history. Nevertheless, he himself employs dialectical constructions without restricting their scope; see, for example, "*Colligite Fragmenta:* For an Integration of Reality" in *From Alienation to At-Oneness,* Proceedings of the Theology Institute of Villanova University, ed. F. A. Eigo (Villanova, Pa.: Villanova University Press, 1977), pp. 19–91. Here Panikkar speaks of "three kairological moments" in the "unfolding of consciousness" (p. 35ff.). But since dialectical reconstructions of this sort necessarily presuppose an evolutionist or developmental scheme, it is difficult to apply them in the intercultural encounter, wherein each culture sees itself as the peak of historical evolution. Eric Voegelin (see *The Ecumenical Age,* vol. IV of *Order in History* [Baton Rouge: Louisiana State University Press, 1956 ff.]), calls all such developmental reconstructions of history into question when he admits that his original project of conceiving history as "a process of increasingly differentiated insight into the order of being in which man participates by his existence" (p. 1) could not be carried out because of "the impossibility of aligning the empirical types in any time sequence at all that would permit the structures actually found to emerge from a history conceived as a 'course'" (p. 2). This would also seem to preclude the possibility of any scheme of dialectical development the moment the one-sided perspective of a given culture is abandoned.

of a discourse which opens up a *horizon of encounter* within which radically different traditions may "co-respond" with one another does intercultural understanding become possible. Interreligious understanding, therefore, goes beyond the mere preservation of a tradition and acquires the character of a founding *event*. For, at a certain point, there occurs an appropriation of a *new horizon* of taken-for-granted truths, a new "myth," as Panikkar would say.

Such understanding is necessarily different from merely acquiring new information about something in the world. It cannot, therefore, be carried out upon the level of argumentative discourse, that is, by means of historical or phenomenological comparison of beliefs. Furthermore, it cannot limit itself to the continuity of a single historical tradition and the retrieval of its founding texts or events, as does the second level of boundary discourse or diachronic hermeneutics. It is for this reason that Panikkar has introduced a "third moment" into hermeneutics:

> There is . . . a third moment in any complete hermeneutical process and the fact that it has often been neglected or overlooked has been a major cause of misunderstandings among the different cultures of the world. I call it *diatopical* hermeneutics because the distance to be overcome is not merely temporal, within one broad tradition, but the gap existing between two human *topoi,* "places" of understanding and self-understanding, between two — or more — cultures that have not developed their patterns of intelligibility or their basic assumptions out of a common historical tradition or through mutual influence. To cross the boundaries of one's own culture without realizing that another culture may have a radically different approach to reality is today no longer admissible. If still consciously done, it would be philosophically naive, politically outrageous and religiously sinful. Diatopical hermeneutics stands for the thematic consideration of understanding the other without assuming that the other has the same basic self-understanding and understanding as I have. The ultimate human horizon, and not only differing contexts, is at stake here.[8]

If diatopical hermeneutics is to be possible the "ultimate human horizon" is and must always remain a horizon of *encounter* rather than a horizon of *indifference* and *exclusion* as presumed by first-level discourse and projected by second-level discourse. The phenomenology of religion, for example, has its function in the identification and preliminary clarification of religious phenomena, but not in actually carrying out the dialogue between religions because, as first-level discourse, it operates within a horizon of phenomenal *indifference,* or givenness, which precludes the radical *discontinuity* among different religious traditions.[9] This is also true, according to Panikkar, for the philosophy of reli-

---

8. See Panikkar, *Myth, Faith and Hermeneutics,* p. 9.

9. See R. Panikkar, "Epoché in the Religious Encounter," *The Intrareligious Dialogue* (New York: Paulist Press, 1978), pp. 39–52, for a discussion of the limitations of phenomenology in the interreligious dialogue. Panikkar understands *epoché* to mean "putting aside one's personal religious convictions, suspending judgment on the validity of one's own religious tenets;

gion.[10] Philosophy of religion operates, along with theology, upon the second level of discourse, which is concerned to establish criteria of meaning and truth as the encompassing boundary of a particular context of interpretation.

From the methodological point of view, the first two levels of discourse together with their respective systematic methods of inquiry are not able to appropriate constructively the moment of *praxis* which necessarily accompanies interreligious understanding, namely, the moment of becoming *convinced* of the truth of the other religion or world view as a new possibility for one's own life. Although it is certainly *necessary* to study another religion or culture with all the methods which the various sciences place at our disposal before a meaningful dialogue can take place, it is not *sufficient*. This follows from the fact that the understanding of another culture or religion inevitably brings with it the disclosure of an entire world of meaning and value which includes new possibilities for human existence. The disclosure of such a world of meaning implies becoming convinced of its truth. Understanding upon this level is itself a "religious" event, which in turn implies that we experience, with respect to the other religion, what can only be called a *conversion.*[11]

Of course this can and must be said for second-level boundary discourse also. To set the boundaries of a life-world is not to make assertions which may be either true or false according to given criteria, for boundary discourse expresses or "sets" the criteria. Here also the pragmatics of discovering truth consist not

in a word, bracketing the concrete beliefs of individual allegiance to a particular confession" (p. 42). Although he admits that such a methodological device has its place "in the introductory stage" of "getting to know a particular religiousness by means of unbiased description of its manifestations," he nonetheless finds it "psychologically impracticable, phenomenologically inappropriate, philosophically defective, theologically weak and religiously barren" when applied to the interreligious dialogue (p. 43). It is *psychologically impracticable* because "I cannot act ... *as if* I did not believe in these tenets" (p. 45); *phenomenologically inappropriate* because "it is a methodological error to leave outside the dialogue an essential part of its subject matter" (p. 47); *philosophically defective,* first, because the bracketing of ultimate convictions would imply that "there is no *doer* left to perform such a maneuver," and second, because philosophical encounter "requires a sincere and unconditional search for truth and there can be no such search if my truth is removed from the sight of my partner" (p. 48); *theologically weak* because it would imply that faith is "a kind of luxury" (p. 48) of "no fundamental relevance for my humanity" (p. 49); and finally, the *epoché* is *religiously barren* because it would "delete at a stroke the very subject matter of the dialogue" (p. 49), namely, religion. Panikkar concludes: "The peculiar difficulty in the phenomenology of religion is that the religious *pistema* is different from and not reducible to the Husserlian *noēma*. The *pistema* is that core of religion which is open or intelligible only to a *religious* phenomenology. In other words, the belief of the believer belongs essentially to the religious phenomenon.... This being the case, the *noēma* of a religiously skeptical phenomenologist does not correspond to the *pistema* of the believer. The religious phenomenon appears only as *pistema* and not as mere *noēma*" (p. 51).

10. See "The Category of Growth in Comparative Religion: A Critical Self-Examination" in Panikkar, *The Intrareligious Dialogue,* pp. 53–75, especially p. 67, where Panikkar again emphasizes that "to elaborate a Philosophy of Religion we need to take religions seriously and, further, to experience them from within, to believe, in one way or another, in what these religions say.... Religions are not purely objectifiable data; they are also essentially personal, subjective.... Without that belief no philosophy of religions is possible."

11. For a forceful and convincing presentation of this view of understanding other religions see the methodological studies of M. Eliade in *The Quest: History and Meaning in Religion* (Chicago: University of Chicago Press, 1969).

in procedures of verification but in processes of initiation, socialization and conversion. But the experience of conversion on the second level of discourse is limited to establishing the cultural identity and historical continuity of a single tradition to the exclusion of all others. Therefore, it is necessary to postulate a third level of discourse where conversion is not exclusive.

It is precisely this requirement which the various scientific disciplines cannot fulfill. The empirical sciences are bound to methodological abstinence from value judgments, whereas the hermeneutical and dialectical sciences are bound to a confessionally exclusive closure of the horizon of meaning which projects specific criteria as absolute.

In order, therefore, clearly to bring out the implications of the problem of understanding on the level of interreligious encounter and also to explain what is involved in diatopical hermeneutics, Panikkar puts forth the following provocative thesis: "To understand is to be convinced."[12] This refers to the way in which truth is discovered on the level of a discourse that does not presuppose common, taken-for-granted criteria of meaning and validity. What is said within first-level discourse is meaningful, as we saw, precisely because it can be either true or false according to given criteria. Upon those higher levels of discourse, however, where it is not a matter of asserting facts about the world but "proclaiming" the very boundaries of the world, language is either meaningful or meaningless and its meaning *is* its truth.

This implies that on the "religious" plane understanding what a statement means is the same as acknowledging its truth. Or, put the other way round, on this highest level of discourse a false proposition cannot be understood at all. Panikkar says, "To understand something as false is a contradiction in itself."[13] This is because "understanding produces conviction."[14] Panikkar summarizes, "In the thesis lies the assertion that one cannot really understand the views of another, if one does not share them."[15]

Before looking more closely at how Panikkar seeks to establish this assertion, let us attempt to make clear just what is at stake. It is asserted that the historical, phenomenological and philosophical methods, with which we hitherto have understood our own and also other traditions, on the one hand, inevitably lead to conviction, whereas on the other hand, because of their ideals of value-free objectivity, they can neither consciously admit nor adequately appropriate the "conversion" which accompanies all understanding. In a non-pluralistic situation characterized by relatively unquestioned agreement on basic values, this moment of conversion does not become explicitly problematical. Methods of understanding which are explicitly or implicitly intended to secure the cultural

---

12. See R. Panikkar, "Verstehen als Überzeugtsein," in *Neue Anthropologie,* ed. by H.-G. Gadamer and P. Vogler, vol. 7 in the series *Philosophische Anthropologie* (Stuttgart: Thieme, 1975), pp. 132–67. This citation is taken from p. 134 and is, as all other citations from this essay, translated by me. Here we are not concerned with the philosophical foundations of the interdependence of truth and meaning which Panikkar postulates.

13. Ibid., p. 136.

14. Ibid., p. 135.

15. Ibid., p. 137.

reproduction of a society are at first unproblematical; that is, they perform an enculturating function more or less adequately and actually do simultaneously bring about understanding and belief in the basic values and truths of a society. We are usually unaware of the fact that we have been "converted" to our own cultural life-world and that such a conversion lies at the basis of almost all our beliefs and convictions.

As soon as this naive unanimity is broken, however, as it is in a radically pluralistic situation, methods of understanding which do not explicitly take the moment of conversion into account become counterproductive. The implicit convictions of the interpreters, as long as they themselves are not raised to the level of methodological awareness, cause polemical distortions and block understanding. What is at stake in this claim, therefore, is the insight that the interreligious encounter requires its own method of understanding which *explicitly* includes the moment of conversion.

Let us now look at how Panikkar establishes his thesis. He offers the following example:

> Granted "A is B" means "Jesus is the Lord" and you, as orthodox Jew would not agree to the statement. Now you go further and say: "M is p," that is, "Christians believe that Jesus is the Lord." You ask yourself: How do they come to believe this? The reason: "M thinks that n is correct," that is, "Christians understand the Jewish messiah to be the Lord and suppose that Jesus is this messiah." You, however, do not believe that n is correct, that is, that Christ is the messiah, although you admit that the messiah is the Lord. You understand clearly that some men consider Jesus to be the messiah and therefore say: "Jesus is the Lord" ("A is B"). But you will object that this is not correct, because the statement is grounded upon a false reading into the facts, namely, the identification of Jesus with the messiah. Although you understand "M is p," you do not understand "A is B," because for you A is not the A which M means (Jesus, the messiah), but A_1 (Jesus, a condemned Jew). This means that Jesus is not the messiah for you so that the sentence "Jesus is the Lord" is for you unacceptable. You understand, therefore, the sentence "A_1 is B" and even "A_1 is not A" — and therefore you cannot perform the spiritual act of saying with meaning: "A is B." You understand what "they" say, and even why they say it, but you do not understand what they understand, and this precisely because you have another understanding of A (namely A_1).[16]

Since it is precisely the human sciences which formulate such sentences, namely, "M thinks that n is correct," or "M says, A is B," this argument shows the limits of a certain kind of scientific method. For if understanding of what the other says depends upon our insight into the truth of his or her statement, then the methodological ideals of value-neutrality and objectivity actually hinder the process of understanding in every situation where a common agreement about

---

16. Ibid., p. 143.

basic convictions cannot be presupposed. Not only is the claim of such methods to be the only ones capable of yielding true knowledge itself unscientific, but such "scientific" ideals of knowledge tend to make interreligious dialogue impossible. In the first place they do not acknowledge other forms of thought as equally valid means of knowing, and in the second place they produce an interpretation wherein the other cannot, as Panikkar says, "find himself":

> We investigate, for example, the customs of some "animistic" tribe and describe them in every detail, whereby we also show the logical connections between them, etc. We are able to reproduce "M is p" almost like a photograph, but if we overlook the other (deeper lying) level, upon which the truth-claim arises, then we do not really attain to the thing which we are describing. In other words: The group M will not be satisfied with our purely phenomenological explanations, which have intentionally placed the question of truth, which to them is the most important question, in "parentheses." This means, "M is p" may indeed seem to me to be so, but the group M will not at all see itself in this statement.[17]

It is in this context that the full significance of *conversion* as the *third step* in the method for the interreligious dialogue becomes clear. Referring to the dialogue between Christianity and Hinduism, with which Panikkar has primarily been concerned, this means:

> A Christian will never fully understand Hinduism if he is not, in one way or another, converted to Hinduism. Nor will a Hindu ever fully understand Christianity unless he, in one way or another, becomes a Christian.[18]

The concept of conversion must be taken seriously. Literally the word, coming from the Latin *convertere,* means "to turn about." It implies a change, which, because it occurs in the dimension of a person's basic beliefs, is a radical change involving the whole person, his or her vision of the world and the entire network of social relations in which the person is embedded. Traditionally, conversion has been confessionally understood in terms of a model of *rejection and acceptance,* that is, as a complete rejection of the "old" view and a similarly total and unquestioning acceptance of the "new." For this reason it has

---

17. See Panikkar, "Verstehen als Überzeugtsein," p. 145. The hermeneutical requirement that the one to be understood must be able to "find himself" in the interpretation was already decisively formulated by W. B. Kristensen: "Let us not forget that there is no other religious reality than the faith of the believers. If we want to make the acquaintance with true religion, we are exclusively thrown on the pronouncements of the believers. What we think, from our standpoint, about the essence and value of foreign religions, surely testifies to our own faith or to our conception of religious belief, but if our opinion of a foreign religion differs from the meaning and the evaluation of the believers themselves, then we have no longer to do with their religion. Not only our own religion, but every religion is, according to the faith of the believers an absolute entity and can only be understood under this aspect" (cited in C. J. Bleeker, "The Phenomenological Method," *Numen* 6 [1959], p. 106–7). This statement has haunted the methodology of the science of religions until today. As we will argue below, the "ghost" will only be exorcised when the possibility of methodological conversion is explicitly acknowledged.

18. See Panikkar, *The Unknown Christ of Hinduism,* p. 43.

become important in the theological rather than the philosophical or scientific traditions.[19]

Biblically, the idea of *metanoia* contains several moments: (1) a *total* disposition which involves the whole person and all of his or her abilities and powers; (2) a *religious* conversion, that is, the complete turning about which someone experiences when he or she gives up an old way of life and returns to a way of life in harmony with God; (3) not only a turning away from the old, but a turning into a *new orientation* for the future, which (4) implies a new and deeper *understanding* of God and God's will; and finally, (5) all the above are seen as a *response* to God's call to reconciliation and his granting of the possibility of salvation through grace.[20] Psychological and sociological studies of conversion experiences yield a scenario of conflict, crisis of meaning and resolution of crisis by means of a personal and social reorientation in which socialization processes, group support and institutional determinants play a decisive role.[21]

Summarizing these various moments, we may understand the methodological concept of conversion — as opposed to the apologetic and exclusive confessional form of conversion — to denote a transformation of one's whole world view — in its cognitive, affective and social dimensions — whereby the *turn away* from an inadequate and incomplete knowledge of truth, the *turn into* a true and valid order and the *turn toward* new possibilities for life and thought are all a function of genuine *communication* between religions rather than the result of an apologetic and defensive conflict.

As we saw, the diatopical model allows us to distinguish between a second and third level of discourse, so that the idea of a methodological conversion, as opposed to an exclusive, confessional conversion, becomes conceivable. Quite apart, however, from the question of whether such an idea is adequately founded philosophically, a question I will take up below, there immediately arises the question of whether it is theologically acceptable. At first sight it would seem that as a step in the method for interreligious dialogue, methodological conver-

---

19. It is my purpose to correct this situation and show that the idea of a methodological conversion must replace the confessional understanding of the event of conversion, and then to show its importance also for a general theory of understanding. In another place (see *The New Universalism* [Maryknoll, N.Y.: Orbis Books, 1991]) I argue that the universality of hermeneutics as well as an adequate theory of communication in the global situation is only conceivable on the basis of *methodological conversion*. This is so because no life-world, no universal horizon of meaning — which is the necessary condition of knowledge of innerworldly matters — is simply "given," rather, it must be appropriated, internalized and made one's own through an *event* personal, social and transcendent, which is most adequately conceived as a conversion, though, of course, not as a confessionally biased, polemical and apologetic conversion, as this term is normally understood. In this sense, conversion lies at the beginning of all knowledge, or in other words, knowledge is always grounded in a conversion. What sort of conversion this is, whether methodological or confessional/apologetic is decisive for the question of whether the knowledge therein grounded will be truly universal.

20. These elements of the biblical idea of *metanoia* are taken from Rudolf Schnackenburg's article "*Metanoia*," in *Herders theologisches Taschenlexikon,* vol. 5 (Freiburg: Herder, 1973), pp. 60–63.

21. See Lewis Rambo, "Conversion," in *Encyclopedia of Religion,* vol. 4, pp. 73–79.

sion brings with it insurmountable theological problems. Must not dialogue be rejected from the very beginning in order to remain faithful to one's own religion? If understanding the other inevitably leads to some sort of conversion to what the other believes, as Panikkar seems to claim, then the dialogue would appear to demand that I be prepared to give up my own faith, which is, of course, neither theologically nor methodologically acceptable.[22]

Panikkar attempts to solve this difficulty by means of a distinction between *faith* and *belief.*[23] Faith is a "constitutive dimension of man." Human existence is such only by virtue of an openness to transcendence, that is, to the absolute and unconditioned. If men and women did not have this possibility of openness toward the transcendent, then they could not distance themselves from the things around them and become aware of themselves as knowers of the world. Humans would not have the ability to become self-conscious at all and thus to become what a human being essentially is. The existential movement beyond oneself, however, must have a direction. This is the absolute as ground of being. For to go beyond oneself means nothing else than that a human being knows that he or she is *not* a thing in the world (see the *neti neti* of the Upaniṣads), but that existence is grounded in the mystery of the absolute and unconditioned.

It is the unconditioned ground of being which the Western Judeo-Christian tradition calls God. The constitutive self-transcendence of human existence is, therefore, nothing other than the ontological relation which a person has to his or her creator, to God. And since it is the relation to God which the Christian tradition has always called faith, Panikkar feels entitled to use the properly theological term faith to denote this constitutive dimension of human existence.[24]

It follows that it is faith, and not, say, a common biological structure or purely natural reason which fundamentally unites humanity and makes communication and communion among men and women everywhere and at all times possible.

Faith, however, must not thereby be confused with *belief,* that is, with

---

22. According to Carl-Heinz Ratschow, for example (*Die Religionen* [Gütersloh: Mohn, 1979]), we can employ the concept of faith "only in relation to God the Father of Jesus, because the relation to God in other religions is only accessible to us from the outside." For "he who has an insight into the devotional relationship to a God, worships this God and becomes His devotee." Therefore, as Christians, we must reject this insight; and this constitutes the "unbridgeable hiatus" and the "unsurmountable difficulty" which accompany every "theological comparison of religions" (p. 123–24). (Translation mine.)

23. This is a constant theme of Panikkar's work. See especially, "Faith as a Constitutive Human Dimension," *Myth, Faith and Hermeneutics,* pp. 188–229; and "Faith and Belief: A Multireligious Experience," in *Intrareligious Dialogue,* pp. 1–23.

24. See Panikkar, *Myth, Faith and Hermeneutics,* p. 190: "Our thesis maintains that if creatureliness can be said to be simple *relation* to God, to the Source or whatever name we give the foundation of beings, faith is another name for the *ontological relation* to this absolute that characterizes Man, distinguishing him from all other beings. If beings as such are nothing but this relation (the creature neither is nor has its foundation in itself), Man is that unique being whose rapport with the foundation becomes the *ontological link* that constitutes him as Man. Thus faith is not the privilege of some individuals or the monopoly of certain defined groups, however large their membership. Faith is not a superfluous luxury, but an anthropological dimension of the full human being on earth."

the many expressions and formulations of faith. As Panikkar puts it, "Faith is not in dogmas, but in the 'thing' expressed in and through them."[25] The "thing" which is here spoken of is "the ever inexhaustible mystery, beyond the reach of objective knowledge,"[26] which, therefore, we can only attain through a "real mysticism" that carries us "beyond — not against — formulae and explanations."[27]

Panikkar finds support for this view not only in philosophical reflection but also in the theological tradition. For Christian theology, it is an axiom that humans can only be saved by faith. The problem thus arises of whether only those who have been reached by the gospel and possess the *explicit* Christian faith may be saved, or whether God, out of his will to save all men, has not given every people always and everywhere an "implicit faith." Further, the ancient praxis of baptizing children could have no possible effect apart from faith — a faith, however, which is not dogmatically formulated or even consciously perceived. According to Panikkar, "Both of these — the doctrinal insufficiency of the ignorant and the doctrinal incapacity of baptized infants" imply that "faith must be something common to Men, whatever their religious beliefs."[28]

If faith is not to be identified with some particular historically conditioned expression, then it must be constituted as indefinite openness, and it must function to ground the possibility that humans can always go beyond whatever conception of them they or their society may have.

It is, therefore, upon this distinction between the universally human and religious dimension of faith, on the one hand, and the various beliefs it gives rise to, on the other, that Panikkar grounds the theological acceptability of the interreligious dialogue once it is admitted that all understanding implies conversion. The significance of this distinction for a methodology of the interreligious encounter cannot be overestimated. We will do well, therefore, to pause here to consider some of its implications.

First, let us note that this distinction enables us to overcome the exclusivist truth-claims of both secular humanism and orthodox theology. Because humanist science confuses faith with belief it must suppress the universality of the religious dimension. This compels it to assign belief to the aesthetic or affective realm of subjective opinion, which in turn allows it to base its own universal claims upon the methodological ideals of value-free objectivity. But, as we saw, scientific method cannot reach the level of knowledge upon which the interreligious encounter takes place. Conversely, because orthodox theology confuses belief with faith, it can only experience the moment of conversion, which all understanding on the interreligious level implies, confessionally and exclusively

---

25. Panikkar, *The Unknown Christ of Hinduism,* p. 52.
26. Panikkar, *Myth, Faith and Hermeneutics,* p. 6.
27. Panikkar, *The Unknown Christ of Hinduism,* p. 59. "Mysticism" here should not be understood as the mere negation of all differences, the "night in which all cows are black" (Hegel), but a pragmatic condition of universal validity.
28. Panikkar, *Myth, Faith and Hermeneutics,* p. 205.

and thus as a threat to saving faith, and not as a transformation, deepening and growth of belief.

A second important result of this distinction, which follows from the first, is that it allows a *horizon of encounter* to be opened up wherein all religions may take their place. For once belief is distinguished from faith, it becomes clear that there exists a certain *similarity* between religions that can be articulated in a third level of discourse which is neither that of the mere comparison of phenomenal similarity nor the apologetic projection of totality based upon a particular system of beliefs, whether orthodox-exclusivist or secular-rejectionist. Religions may thus encounter each other upon the basis of a functional similarity, for they are all expressions of a fundamentally human search for the absolute.[29]

On the one hand, this insight, as already noted, delivers us from the impasse in which the science of religions currently finds itself, for it grounds the possibility of universalistic thinking upon a religious basis, instead of on the basis of the secular ideals of objective, value-free knowledge. On the other hand, it discloses a space of encounter and thus grounds the possibility that the different religions can enter into open and honest dialogue with each other without fearing that the conversion, which dialogue brings with it, will necessarily lead to the loss of saving faith.[30] It therefore serves to free religion from its exclusivistic aspects, its sectarian and confessional character and from an apologetic universalism incompatible with the emergence of a global culture and a universal human community.[31]

Third, it is equally instructive to see what consequences follow for the interreligious dialogue when this distinction is *not* made and dialogue must occur upon a lower level of discourse. If faith is identified with belief, there arise certain *typical deformations* of thought: *exclusivism, inclusivism* and *indifferentism.* All three represent inadequate solutions to the problem of the interreligious encounter. They remain, nevertheless, typical theological approaches to this problem today. It is useful, therefore, briefly to describe these programs in order to see what the interreligious dialogue is *not* before coming back to the question of how the third step of a methodological conversion is to be concretely carried out.

It is important at the outset of this discussion to keep in view the fact that although faith is distinct from its many expressions, there is still no such thing as a pure, expressionless faith:

---

29. This becomes clear when we consider that *as* formulations of faith all religious doctrines are *functionally similar.* See Panikkar, *Intrareligious Dialogue,* p. 22: "I am not suggesting that all beliefs are equal and interchangeable; I am saying that in a certain respect they exhibit the same nature, which makes dialogue, and even dialectics, possible. Moreover, I assert they are generally equivalent in that every belief has a similar function: to express Man's faith, that faith which is the anthropological dimension through which Man reaches his goal — in Christian language, his salvation."

30. Thus is the "unsurmountable difficulty" of all "theological comparison of religions," which, according to Ratschow, *Die Religionen,* condemned all interreligious dialogue to failure, in principle overcome.

31. Panikkar, *Myth, Faith and Hermeneutics,* p. 191.

Faith cannot be equated with belief, but faith always needs a belief to be faith. Belief is not faith, but it must convey faith. A disembodied faith is not faith.[32]

The three theological models for interreligious dialogue mentioned above arise from the different ways of reacting to this fact which are possible upon the second level of discourse.

Second-level discourse, we recall, is concerned with projecting the unity and totality of a life-world horizon, a tradition. On this level there are three possible relations to other traditions. First, our own symbols may be assumed to be the only valid ones and all others are rejected. Second, it is admitted that symbols other than our own are true, but only to the extent that they allow themselves to be integrated into our system of thought and belief. Third, all traditions may be thought to be equally true, but with the proviso that they, for that very reason, should not and cannot have anything to do with one another. All of these positions may be developed into deliberate methodological models or programs. The first represents an exclusivist model, the second an approach which may be termed inclusivism, and the third is indifferentism.

The upshot of this seems to be that we are confronted with a decision:

Either [one] must condemn everything around him as error and sin, or he must throw overboard the exclusivistic and monopolistic notions he has been told embody truth — truth that must be simple and unique, revealed once and for all, that speaks through infallible organs, and so on.[33]

Here the methodological significance of the distinction between faith and belief becomes clear. For only after we have consistently carried this distinction through, not only theoretically but also existentially, will it become possible to "throw overboard" the presupposition of the monological unity, continuity and totality of truth lying at the base of all apologetics and thus overcome these three inadequate programs.

Our step-by-step reconstruction of the method for the theology of religions on the basis of Panikkar's work has so far led through the steps of a critical and faithful appropriation of one's own religion, a similar appropriation of another tradition and then directly into the problem of conversion as an unavoidable step in interreligious understanding. In order to show how such a methodological conversion may be conceived, the diatopical model of communication was used to distinguish between a second and third level of discourse. Second-level discourse, or what Panikkar calls diachronic hermeneutics, articulates religious understanding as an exclusive, confessional conversion. Only upon the third level of discourse — which opens up a horizon of encounter wherein religions may appear as equally valid life-worlds and enter into genuine communication with each other — does the notion of a methodological conversion become

---

32. Panikkar, *Intrareligious Dialogue,* p. 18. This qualifies what was said above about mysticism.

33. Panikkar, *Intrareligious Dialogue,* p. 5.

meaningful. To show that such a notion was also theologically acceptable we appealed to Panikkar's fundamental distinction between faith and belief. We saw that upon the basis of this distinction, to allow our beliefs to undergo transformation does not necessarily imply the loss of saving faith. Finally, we saw what consequences follow upon the failure to make this distinction, namely, the derailing of the dialogue into one or another of the inadequate programs of exclusivism, inclusivism or indifferentism. It remains now to show what that discourse is which claims to mediate radically different systems of belief while maintaining itself within a horizon of faith.

This roundabout way was necessary to put us in the position to comprehend the fourth step in Panikkar's method. For it is not sufficient that I simply allow myself to be converted to another world view. This is only the beginning of the real process of understanding. If the conversion experience is not to derail and become confessionally distorted into one of the inadequate responses to the encounter of cultures and religions discussed above, I must somehow bring the two convictions which I have within myself into harmony with each other. If the experience of conversion is to be sustained and I am not to break under the stress of conflicting loyalties, and the process of understanding is not to be forced back onto the second level of discourse and thus into a defensive, apologetic "jumping-back" or "jumping-over," then there must occur, as Panikkar says, a meeting of the two religions in myself:

> The meeting of two differing realities produces the shock of the encounter, but the *place* where the encounter happens is one. This one place is the heart of the person. It is within the heart that I can embrace both religions in a personal synthesis, which intellectually may be more or less perfect. And it is also within my heart that I may absorb one of the two religions into the other. In actuality religions cannot sincerely coexist or even continue as living religions if they do not "co-insist," i.e. penetrate into the heart of each other.[34]

Accordingly, the fourth step is what Panikkar calls the "intrareligious dialogue," that is, the encounter and co-responding of two convictions in me. This is how the third-level discourse of disclosure becomes concrete. Only at this stage can we begin to speak of dialogue in the full sense of the word:

> The real theological task, if you will, begins when the two views meet head-on inside oneself, when dialogue prompts genuine religious pondering, and even a religious crisis, at the bottom of a Man's heart; when interpersonal dialogue turns into intrapersonal soliloquy.[35]

---

34. Panikkar, *The Unknown Christ of Hinduism,* p. 12.

35. Panikkar, *Intrareligious Dialogue,* p. 10. Also interesting in this connection is Panikkar's answer to the question of whether the interreligious dialogue does not carry with it a certain risk ("Dialogue with Panikkar," p. 22): "A total risk, of dying, and you believe that you may rise again, but you really don't know it. The resurrection is not a trick. There is real religious risk in religious dialogue, if you take the faith or beliefs of all your fellow beings seriously."

My intrareligious soliloquy will have to blend my earlier beliefs with those acquired later. . . . Here an alternative lies before me: Either I have ceased to be a Christian . . . or else I am able to establish a special kind of bond between the two that both religions, at least one of them, *can* acknowledge and accept (I do not say they already *have* accepted it).[36]

The *intra* religious dialogue is, therefore, the place where diatopical hermeneutics actually begins. For it is only when we find ourselves *between* two worlds, two *topoi,* that they become for the first time disclosed and thus questionable. In the encounter with the other which occurs internally, as Panikkar says, within the "heart" of the person, our own myth loses its unquestioned taken-for-granted character and we become aware of its limits and thus also of its possibilities. It is through the other — and this is his or her great service to us — that we become capable of criticizing, renewing and deepening our own world view, a critique which is desperately needed if we are to realize the transcendental movement of faith. In this respect Panikkar writes:

> Dialogue is, fundamentally, opening myself to another so that he might speak and reveal my myth that I cannot know by myself because it is transparent to me, self-evident. Dialogue is a way of knowing myself and of disentangling my own point of view from other viewpoints and from me, because it is grounded so deeply in my own roots as to be utterly hidden from me. It is the other who through our encounter awakens this human depth latent in me in an endeavor that surpasses both of us. In authentic dialogue this process is reciprocal. Dialogue sees the other not as an extrinsic, accidental aid, but as the indispensable, personal element in our search for truth, because I am not a self-sufficient, autonomous individual. In this sense, dialogue is a religious act par excellence because it recognizes my *religatio* to another, my individual poverty, the need to get out of myself, transcend myself, in order to save myself.[37]

It is, therefore, a presupposition of the internal intrareligious dialogue that our traditional symbols can be questioned without reducing them to mere signs and subsuming them under a nonreligious, logical discourse which rejects revelation.

This does not mean, it must be emphasized, that we simply throw our tradition overboard, or that we must give up the idea of a *common language.* Were this the case all dialogue would be impossible. The very task of diatopical hermeneutics is fulfilled and the intrareligious dialogue realized only when a common language arises, wherein the two religions, which previously were perceived to exclude each other, now are seen to complement and mutually fecundate each other. Panikkar describes his program thus:

---

36. Panikkar, *Intrareligious Dialogue,* p. 14.
37. Panikkar, *Myth, Faith and Hermeneutics,* pp. 242–43.

I am attempting to speak a language that will make sense for the follower of more than one philosophical tradition — a risky task perhaps, but necessary if one is to do justice to a cross-cultural investigation.[38]

This claim immediately gives rise to serious questions: Where is such a universal language to be found? And if it could be found, how does it legitimate the claim it makes to speak for more than one tradition? Wherein is such a language grounded, if not in one religion/culture or another? Is a thinking not bound to any specific tradition possible? Would not such a "free-floating," culturally unconditioned thinking suffer from exactly the same illusion Panikkar criticizes in the scientific ideals of objectivity and value neutrality? Do we not in the end have to decide *either* for a universalistic and thus *scientific* thinking, *or* for an inevitably exclusive religious *confession?*[39] Whatever the sought-for universal language might be, it certainly can be neither the allegedly neutral language of science nor the exclusively valid symbols of a particular confessional proclamation.

We must learn to think in and with the symbols of another tradition as with our own. Much depends upon whether we succeed in thinking these symbols together: first, the adequate appropriation of the conversion experience itself; second, understanding the other religion as well as our own (for we can, in the end, only understand our own religion *together* with the other);[40] and finally, upon the success or failure of our attempts to think the two traditions together depends our success or failure in avoiding the programs of exclusivism, inclusivism and indifferentism, and thus preserving the creative tension between faith and belief.

All this leads to the question of how different symbols can be thought together. Panikkar answers:

As an example of what is needed, we may use the notion of homology, which does not connote a mere comparison of concepts from one tradition with those of another. I want to suggest this notion as the correlation between points of two different systems so that a point in one system corresponds to a point in the other. The method does not imply that one system is better (logically, morally or whatever) than the other, nor that the two points are interchangeable: You cannot, as it were, transplant a point from one system to the other. The method only discovers homologous correlations.[41]

---

38. Ibid., p. 381.

39. See Krieger, *The New Universalism,* for a discussion of these questions on the level of a philosophical foundation of the interreligious dialogue as intercultural hermeneutics and a demonstration of the possibility of a universal language as discourse of disclosure.

40. That a faithful and critical understanding of one's own revelation can only be attained through understanding all other revelations is a consequence of the methodological concept of "conversion."

41. Panikkar, *Intrareligious Dialogue,* p. 33.

An example of such an "homologous correlation," or as Panikkar also says, a "functional equivalence,"[42] may be found in *The Unknown Christ of Hinduism.* In this book Panikkar attempts to bring the symbols Christ and Ishvara (the lord) into correlation with each other through an analysis of their "functions" within their respective systems. He constructs the following analogy: *As* Christ constitutes the relation between God and the world in Christianity, *so* in Hinduism, a similar function is fulfilled by Ishvara. We cannot here examine how Panikkar substantiates this "comparison." Rather, let us note that he is uncomfortable with the term analogy. Homology, he will say, is not identical to an analogy.[43] Nevertheless, Panikkar does not wish to dispense with the idea of analogy altogether:

> Now a homology is not identical to an analogy, although they are related. Homology does not mean that two notions are analogous, i.e., partially the same and partially different, since this implies that both share in a "tertium quid" that provides the basis for the analogy. Homology means rather that the notions play equivalent roles, that they occupy homologous places within their respective systems. Homology is perhaps a kind of existential-functional analogy.[44]

What is meant here by an "existential-functional analogy" we may perhaps discover by reflecting upon what is meant by a "system." In systems symbols like Christ and Ishvara have a definite meaning. They function in a certain way and play a "role" which is defined in relation to all the other symbols, practices and doctrines of a religion. The question is whether a system or a religion is completely delimited and defined on all sides, or whether it is not rather the case that religious systems are essentially open, that symbols are never exhaustively interpreted, that their meaning is never completely defined and fixed once and for all. Can and must we not delve always further and always more deeply into the meaning of the revelation which has been granted us? Does not this growth in understanding belong necessarily to religious experience? And is the transformation of religious consciousness not much more than a mere increase of information, but rather, an existential and historical event which not only changes a man or woman but also the "world" in which he or she lives? "At the very least," says Panikkar, "human consciousness is set in evolution"; and with it "the entire cosmos, all creation, reality."[45]

---

42. Ibid., p. xxii.

43. For a thorough discussion of the analogy problem, see L. Bruno Puntel, *Analogie und Geschichtlichkeit I* (Freiburg: Herder, 1969). Although the functional equivalence between Christ and Ishvara looks like a classical *similitudo proportionum,* that is, a relation of relations according to the schema: a/b=c/d, it is not this, for this would degrade both symbols to the level of interchangeable elements in a formal structure. On the other hand, the similarity between Christ and Ishvara is also not a typical analogy *unius ad alterum,* for then Christ and Ishvara would be subjugated to a third, higher moment.

44. See Panikkar, *Intrareligious Dialogue,* p. 33.

45. "The Category of Growth in Comparative Religion," *The Intrareligious Dialogue,* pp. 69–70. Panikkar develops this idea against the background of his "cosmotheandric vision": "I submit

A religious system, therefore, insofar as it is part of a living religion, is not finished and closed, neither in its doctrinal *content* nor in its conceptual *form*. For behind all formulations stands the mystery from which they spring forth. This is the goal of self-transcending faith. This is what third-level discourse of disclosure expresses. Religions, again, are not things which, for example, can be compared in the same way as two organisms in order to see in what respects they are alike or different. Comparison and abstraction to the next higher generic concept is not a reliable method when it comes to religions, cultures and world views.

Neither can we attempt to avoid the problem by apologetically projecting the closure of our own mythological discourse upon all other myths. The discovery of functional similarities, therefore, is neither an objective knowledge about something nor an apologetic proclamation, but rather an existential event, a spiritual praxis and an authentic religious experience through which religious consciousness responds ever more deeply to the mystery of revelation. "Dialogue," Panikkar reminds us, "is not a bare methodology but an essential part of the religious act par excellence."[46]

What makes the discovery of functional similarities possible can be nothing other than the horizon of encounter opened up by the discourse of disclosure, or in other words, the ground of faith. For if it were not possible to discover such correspondences, the human spirit would either suffocate in an exclusivistic ideology or disintegrate into a myriad of little "worlds," none of which would be capable of communicating with the others. But faith, as we saw, is precisely that which keeps human beings open to transcendence and thus guarantees spiritual unity. From the point of view of the discourse of disclosure, that which is revealed in one religion cannot exclude what is revealed in another. From a Western-Christian standpoint, the ground of faith is the one "God" who is present in all religions. In this sense, Panikkar speaks of a "previous homogeneity" or a "certain presence" of one religion within the other:

> If the use of a concept foreign to a given cultural setup is to be made viable, if it is to be successfully grafted onto another system of thought (the Christian for example), it will succeed because it has somehow attained a certain homogeneity with the host cultural and religious world so

---

that the one category able to carry the main burden in the religious encounter and in the further development of religion (and religions) is *growth*. . . . Religious consciousness is something more than an external development of a knowing organ that at a certain moment discovers something of which it was not previously aware. And, since religious consciousness is an essential part of religion itself, the development of this consciousness means the development of religion itself. Secondly, it amounts to more than just a development in personal consciousness; at the very least human consciousness is set in evolution. What develops, in fact, is the entire cosmos, all creation, reality. The whole universe expands. In a word, there is real growth in Man, in the World and, I would also add, in God, at least inasmuch as neither immutability nor change are categories of the divine."

46. Ibid., p. 10.

that it may live there. If this is the case, it amounts to recognizing that its possible use depends on a certain previous homogeneity, on a certain presence of the one meaning within the other framework; otherwise it would be completely impossible to utilize the concept in question. In spite of the heterogeneity between the Greek and Christian conception of the *logos,* for instance, the former had to offer a certain affinity with the new meaning that would be enhanced once it was assumed.[47]

The full realization of such a functional similarity between the central symbols of two religions — in the cognitive as well as existential dimension — implies a considerable rethinking of traditional Christian (and Hindu!) self-understanding. But it is precisely this "mutual fecundation"[48] which is "one of the primary tasks facing theology."[49]

Naturally, the intrareligious dialogue stands or falls with the discovery of those symbols which really are rooted in the transcendent ground of all religions and thus really do correspond with each other over and beyond the socio-historical trappings in which they are clothed. Panikkar does not underestimate the difficulty here, and he is well aware that such symbols can neither be found lying about nor simply invented; they must be *revealed.* This sets a clear limit to all methodology in the sense of prescribed rules of inquiry which guarantee objective knowledge. At this point in the encounter of religions and cultures there are no "controls," and we must admit that understanding is never continuous and progressive, but always discontinuous and surprisingly different from whatever we may have expected. As Panikkar puts it, "the continuation of the dialogue has to produce its own rules and categories."[50]

Supposing now that the sought-for categories and symbols have been found, namely, that the intrareligious dialogue has come to a preliminary conclusion, then the next step is to present this new understanding to a representative of the other religion.[51] At this point the intrareligious dialogue becomes a truly *inter* religious dialogue:

> My partner in dialogue will then judge whether what I have learned . . . is sound or not. I will have to give him an account of my belief and he will tell me whether what I say . . . represents fundamental belief . . . or not.[52]

---

47. Ibid., p. 61.

48. Panikkar, *The Unknown Christ of Hinduism,* p. 163.

49. Panikkar, *Intrareligious Dialogue,* p. 19; also the important programmatic essay "Metatheology as Fundamental Theology," *Myth, Faith and Hermeneutics,* pp. 322–34.

50. Panikkar, *Intrareligious Dialogue,* p. 17. Here Panikkar finds himself in basic agreement with Heidegger's notion of truth as disclosure and Hans-Georg Gadamer's understanding of hermeneutics as not reducible to objective methods.

51. The question of which persons, groups or institutions may be considered representative of a particular religion is, of course, a matter for itself. Most probably this question would have to be answered differently within each tradition. Representative status is also, as we shall see below, not independent of preparedness for interreligious dialogue.

52. Ibid., p. 14.

The criterion of the correctness of my interpretation is the well-known hermeneutical rule that "the interpreted thing can recognize itself in the interpretation."[53] Panikkar writes:

In other words, any interpretation from outside a tradition has to coincide, at least phenomenologically, with an interpretation from within, i.e., with the believer's viewpoint. To label a *murtipujaka* an idol-worshiper, for instance, using idol as it is commonly understood in the Judeo-Christian-Muslim context rather than beginning with what the worshiper affirms of himself, is to transgress this rule.[54]

And in another place he says that,

any genuine "Christian" interpretation must be valid and true, and for this very reason it must also be acceptable to those who are being interpreted; a basic methodological rule for any interpretation. This means that no interpretation of any religion is valid if the followers of that religion do not recognize it as such.[55]

This rule not only firmly excludes reductionistic explanations of religion on the part of psychology and sociology, for example, but it implies that both partners in dialogue must have gone through the same process up to this point. All the steps of the method which have been described up till now must be presupposed for both partners. This is itself an important methodological step. For "there must be *equal preparation* for the encounter on both sides, and this means cultural as well as theological preparations."[56] An exclusivist apologetic approach on either side would, of course, make all dialogue impossible.

Supposing, however, that both partners have gone through the intrareligious dialogue and have entered the interreligious dialogue with "a set of propositions that may answer the requirements of orthodoxy on both sides,"[57] then they must be prepared to accept the judgment of the other whether their new interpretations are *orthodox* or not. This claim to orthodoxy — not to be confused with the distorted orthodoxy of exclusivism! — constitutes the last step in the method of the interreligious dialogue. If I do not succeed, that is, if my new interpretation is not accepted by the representative of the other religion, then I am automatically sent back into the intra-religious dialogue, where I search for another, more adequate understanding.

Here it becomes clear that the method is circular, that the last step leads us back to the first. For in the methodological insistence upon orthodoxy exactly that is realized which was required by the first two steps of the method; namely, the appropriation of a faithful and critical understanding of one's own and of another tradition. "Faithfulness" to one's own and to another tradition is only to

---

53. Ibid., p. 30.
54. Ibid.
55. Ibid., p. 64.
56. Ibid., p. 36.
57. Ibid., p. 15.

be secured by means of the principle of orthodoxy, whereby "critique" of one's own and of another tradition can only be consequently carried through when understanding is no longer a one-sided apologetic for one particular tradition, but adequate to *both*. Therefore, it is only *through* the interreligious dialogue, and as it were, at its end, that we come back to a faithful and critical understanding of our own religion. Orthodoxy and critique do not exclude each other, rather, they complement each other, but only from the point of view of a truly *global* theology.

The method of the interreligious dialogue, and therefore also of the theology of religions, turns out to be a circular movement. The end leads back to the beginning. This circular structure of thought is typical of all genuinely *hermeneutical* methods. It is hermeneutical in that it begins from an implicit "fore-conception" or anticipation of meaning, not in order to progress to new and unheard of results, but in order to come back to itself through the explication of what was already there. Methodical inquiry here, however, is not, as in the empirical, phenomenological and dialectical methods which Panikkar terms "morphological" and "diachronical," fundamentally limited in scope. Since it is only in the encounter with other forms of thought that our own becomes at all questionable to us, no hermeneutics which remains within one tradition can claim critical competence for itself without reservations.[58] Only diatopical hermeneutics, which operates in the realm *between* religions and cultures and aims at a universal horizon of encounter — only such a method of understanding fulfills the requirement of radical critique demanded of all thinking today, while at the same time remaining faithful to (i.e., bound-back, *re-ligare*) revelation and thus not giving up the claim to orthodoxy.

In conclusion, we should note that Panikkar always emphasizes that it is not the goal of the interreligious dialogue "to obtain agreement at the cost of fundamental . . . principles."[59] By means of an incessant mutual criticism and correction the dialogue brings about an ever-deeper understanding of what is revealed in the various religions. Panikkar closes his defense for a non-exclusive religiosity with the remark:

> I can only be free from a certain type of Christianity or Hinduism (and for that matter from a certain type of Buddhism and Secularism) if I become a better Christian and a better Hindu.[60]

In summary, on the basis of Panikkar's many important theoretical contributions to interreligious understanding we have reconstructed the following steps of a *method* for the theology of religions:

---

58. It is for this reason that neither the "regressive hermeneutics" of a psychoanalytic model nor the "progressive hermeneutics" (Paul Ricoeur) of a model based upon Hegelian dialectics can really claim universality and thus the right to criticize ideology as Jürgen Habermas, for example, asserts. Furthermore, no hermeneutics which limits itself to the historical retrieval of founding texts, as does Gadamer's philosophical hermeneutics, can fulfill this requirement.

59. Panikkar, *The Unknown Christ of Hinduism,* p. 7.

60. Ibid., p. x.

1. One begins with a faithful and critical understanding of one's own tradition — an understanding won with all reliable methods which we have at our disposal: empirical, historical-critical, philological, phenomenological, etc.

2. In the same way, an understanding of another tradition is acquired.

3. This understanding becomes conviction. One experiences a genuine *conversion.*

4. An internal *intra* religious dialogue begins between the two convictions. One searches for a *common language* capable of expressing the truth of both religions.

5. The internal intrareligious dialogue becomes an external *inter* religious dialogue when one lays one's new interpretation before representatives of the other tradition.

6. Steps 1 through 5 are presupposed for all partners in dialogue.

7. New interpretations are tested for their "orthodoxy" in both traditions. If they are found inadequate, one returns to the level of the intrareligious dialogue and begins again.

PART IV

Response

14

A Self-Critical Dialogue
RAIMON PANIKKAR

ἐδιξησάμην ἐηεωυτόν
I practice self-critique

Herakleitos (Fr. 101)

METHODOLOGICAL REFLECTIONS

Self-Critique

A festschrift, as this literary genre is usually called, purports to be a *fest,* i.e., a "feast" to celebrate "someone" for "some reason."[1] For celebration I am always ready. Life itself is a celebration, and I understand wisdom (*sophia*) as the art and science of Life (1993a). Philosophy (*philo-sophia*) would then be the love of the art and science of Life, viz., of the praxis and theory of living — and not of human life alone: the wisdom of love.

The "someone" I do not take to be my ego, but certainly it has something to do with me, that unique mirror of the real that responds by my name: the mystery of the name! We concelebrate then a common intellectual feast in the person of this someone, who in no way is the owner of the intellect celebrated in the "feast." Ideas cannot have copyright. We are all to be congratulated. The "some reason" belongs to the fact that some ideas which have been written down are alive and have become incarnated in action. Contemplation is both theory and praxis.

---

1. For the sake of brevity, I shall not cite my own writings mentioned in the various essays in this book. I shall, however, give references in parentheses to places in my writings where I develop matters discussed in this response. They are keyed to the Bibliography at the end of this book, which is divided into one section for books and another for shorter works. References to books will have a year or a year and a letter to indicate the work referred to; for example, "1993a" refers to *A Dwelling Place for Wisdom* in the books section. Shorter works will be referred to by a year and a number to indicate exactly the article being cited; for example, "1990/2" refers to "The Ongoing Dialogue."

As the incumbent of such a *festschrift* I should perform the duty, first of all, of thanking each and every one of the contributors to this volume, and not only the actual authors, but also all those who did express willingness or even sent papers which the editor did not include in this volume. There could be no higher honor for a philosopher than the "feast" in which the thoughts that have nurtured his life are studied, criticized, put into practice. If the crystallization of one's life in some intellectual writings finds echo, sympathy, critique and, specially, is found to have transforming power, this is a reason for joy and gratitude.

My gratitude is both for praise and criticism. The former stimulates me to be worthy of it. The latter offers me the opportunity to pursue the dialogue entering into that difficult but fruitful activity of self-criticism. By self-critical dialogue I mean the activity of the whole person rethinking and re-examining one's own spiritual and intellectual life after having listened carefully to the reception of one's thoughts in the minds of others. The sceptic philosophers were often called seekers, enquirers, investigators. Let us recall that *skepsis* means also perception, observation, search. This much to situate Herakleitos's motto: I *scrutinize myself* — my Self: the Self (re)searching into itself, a self-examination.

I am not going to give a perfunctory response, nor will I try to put my record "straight" clarifying some allegedly misinterpreted facts or ideas. I shall simply try to spell out and deepen what I have been asked to do. I feel that we are all engaged in the same venture of probing together some of the major issues of our times. I build on and rely upon the wisdom of the contributors in order to attempt a further step — leaving, of course, most of the things still unsaid. I am just reacting to some of the issues of the volume.

Listening to, i.e., obeying (*ob-audire*), the Herakleitean motto, I have to add that this constant scrutiny belongs to the human vocation as such. It is then not pride to say that I have taken upon myself the task of striving to find out the sense of my life, and of life in the entire universe. This is the task of authentic philosophy.

Most human traditions, including the western until the "Enlightenment," have believed that to every human being is given the opportunity of making sense of one's own life. Whether because there is a God, *karma,* providence, an innate power of the mind, a revelation, or because the universe is an ordered *kosmos* (*ṛta, ordo*), or whatever, the fact is that the awareness that Man is an intelligent being amounted to the conviction that everybody could find himself or herself in the universe. There were, of course, *terrae incognitae,* partial enigmas and opaque spheres of the real, but they were nevertheless mapped, although closed territories. In this sense the animistic universe of Ptolomeus (which included the Divine) was far more complete than the mechanistic world of Copernicus — notwithstanding the higher mathematical precision of the latter. From the greeks until the birth of modern science western Man lived in a finite world and fini-tude meant perfection, as the very etymology of the word suggests, so that infinite perfection would amount to a contradiction in terms. Around the time of Descartes this confidence breaks down. The case of his contemporary, Come-nius, offers us a contrast. We can know everything, he says (obviously not in the restricted sense of modern science), because we can find the very limits of our knowledge knowing that above which we cannot go (*Janua rerum,* IV). The gnostic optimism of *homo sapiens* was shattered once human wisdom became the competence of a specialized and highly sophisticated rational faculty (1993a). Once knowledge ceases to be saving knowledge the door is open for competitive specializations.

Pre-modern western Man still had the confidence that, because there was a living God and human destiny was headed toward a glorious divinization, Man had a given power to steer through life in order to reach his or her destiny.

Modern science has shattered the gnostic optimism, i.e., the conscious confidence that Man *is* an intellectual being, and thus can know all that is needed for life, happiness and salvation. Human health, for instance, was not in the hands of esoteric specialists who have studied over long years and then have, of course, to earn more and more money. Human existence was not dependent on the efficient functioning of the megamachine of a modern State, so that services may run smoothly. There were a cosmic order and a social fabric, maintained by a hierarchical structure of reality itself — all abuses of the elites notwithstanding. Traditional knowledge purported to lead to understanding and transformation, not to certainty. This was the obsession of Descartes: *scire* should lead to *certitudo* — (*Wissen* to *Gewissheit*). Most agnosticisms have emerged because of the wrong equation between *gnōsis* and *certainty* (up to political *security*). The ancients knew that *dubitatio est scientiae initium* (doubt is the beginning of knowledge); its goal is not security, but joy and freedom, as so many texts from East and West affirm.

Let no one imagine that I have a rosy picture of the past and want to turn back the clock of human history. But not all was dark in the past, just as all is not negative in the present. Yet, it is our duty to learn from the wisdom of our ancestors and to criticize the present, precisely to improve it.

I would say that it is the urgent task of philosophy to recover in a critical (and thus doubting, provisional and not apodictical) way the sense of the whole, a holistic wisdom. I do not consider myself a special creature because I claim to have something more than a fragmented vision of reality.

I would like to use the privilege provided by this occasion by informally conversing with the authors in a friendly and constructive way. This will have but a sad result: the chapters I most agree with and the ideas I most cherish will receive least attention. I apologize. Be it only said that silence is the best tribute. But the chapters stand.

I shall present my reflections touching upon some of the main problems referred to in the chapters.

Mediation and Communication

Joseph Prabhu presented to me one of the most formidable philosophical questions, the problem of mediation, which he afterward decided to drop in favor of his more general contribution as editor. This question lurks underneath more than one contribution, and it seems fair to offer some comments on the problem. It is indeed one of the pivots upon which the entire Enlightenment hinges (although we may recall Arnold Gehlen's sarcastic remark that while the premises of the Enlightenment are dead, their consequences are still very much alive).

The problem of mediation, in fact, stems from the strenuous effort of the Enlightenment to solve by means of an autonomous epistemology the older ontological question of relationships. How could we, epistemologically, i.e., critically, relate different things? I have been asked how can I relate them to eternity? How do I relate to *kosmos,* the *theos* and the *anthropos* in the cosmotheandric intuition? How can I find criteria to mediate between some principles and the norms for ethical decisions?

To be sure, how we can justify epistemological mediations was the crux of post-cartesian philosophy. To ignore this would amount to the "slumber" of precritical thinking, Kant would say. I should certainly not skip this central question.

We should distinguish first of all, mediation from instrumentalization. An *instrument* is a device we use. It is something our body or our mind uses in order to enhance our power. To some extent we are the makers of the instrument, and we use it as such. *Mediation* is not an instrument; it is not a machine we build or a concept we utilize. Mediation is seen as a required bridge which in some sense is already there, like a platonic idea which we need only to discover. It is the link which relates, unites, directs, "mediates." To manipulate mediation is political demagogy or another sort of abuse of power.

Here Modernity overpowers Aristotle, in spite of its indebtedness to him in other fields, and falls back on Plato in trying to avoid metaphysical platonism. If all knowledge has to become critical knowledge and critical knowledge is conceptual knowledge, the problem of mediation is both necessary and unsolvable. Either the concept is the idea and the idea is the real thing (reality) or the concept is just a *medium quo,* a simple instrument. It has to relate the inner world of our mind with the external world of our senses. Here lies the difficulty and perhaps the philosophical crux of modern western philosophy. Here I insert my radical challenge.

I am not allying myself with Kierkegaard (*Begrebet Angest* I, 3; etc.) in order to criticize Hegel, or with buddhist philosophers (Mādhyamika) in order to debunk the vedāntins. The issue, as Descartes would say (*Regula* 3), is not one of history but of science in the traditional sense of knowledge.

Mediation was already a problem for Plato and specially for Plotinus and the neoplatonics. The One needs mediations in order to unfold itself in the respective emanations. It seems that if we want to avoid an undifferentiated monism without falling into an unrelated atomism we need to make room for the question of mediation. And in fact mediation has become an almost indispensable hypothesis. Knowledge is mostly seen as mediation, Christ is called a mediator, hermeneutics is sheer mediation. Hermes, the mediator of intelligibility, is the messenger of the Gods. But who is the Absolute, the Christ, the Gods, the Knower? Ultimately, what is Reality?

My commentary is

a) very simple in its *formulation,*

b) relatively easy in its *critique* of mediation, and

c) exceedingly difficult in *substituting* it by another intelligible hypothesis.

The Locus of Mediation

We should distinguish mediation in its restricted sense as an epistemological problem (*Vermittlung* in Hegel) from the more general ontological question of the middle (*mesiteia, meson, mesotēs, medium* and the in-between, *Dazwischen*). Epistemological mediation has become the necessary method of our reflexive knowledge in modern western philosophy.

The starting point is simply this: all our knowledge must be ultimately based on immediacy, experience, *anubhāva,* intuition (clear and distinct ideas), symbolic awareness, *apauruṣeyatva,* and the like, i.e., on something which does not need, *for us,* a further foundation or justification. There must be something immediate, i.e., something which does not need mediation — unless, as we shall see, mediation is seen as just another word for communion (*com-munus*). Otherwise we would fall into a barren *regressus in infinitum.* If all knowledge were mediated without something immediately known, and as such accepted, we would be entangled in that regression — unless knower, knowledge and known coalesce, as Plotinus says (*Ennead* VI, 7, 41). Searching ever backward for the foundation of any answer and not finding it we could never return to affirm anything and would have to renounce any judgment. We could only accept a certain provisionality in all our dealings with reality, the intellectual act included, so that we simply stop for heuristic or pragmatic reasons in order to establish a relative and provisional body of doctrines. This explains why modern science starts with axioms (or postulated premises — hypotheses) which preserve the rationality of what is based upon them, but which sever us from a direct contact with the real. Modern science is pure mathematical formalism. The crisis of contemporary science is, in a way, due to the fact that Descartes's and Galilei's firm belief that the true world consists of mathematical forms may not correspond any longer to the very discoveries of science.

Whatever the validity and foundations of our knowledge, we believe we know something, and in fact we make judgments on things and events — albeit to affirm that we know that our formulations are non-absolute precisely because they are mediated.

Any mediated knowledge reaches the status of knowledge because some mediator has brought the raw fact, the premises, the surmise, the sentiment, the impressions, or whatever, to the feet of our knowing power, and this has adopted the stranger, assimilated the object, made it its own, after having checked the credentials of the mediator. The diatribes of Descartes and Francis Bacon against imagination as a wrong mediator are well known. Pascal calls it "maîtresse d'erreur et de fausseté."

Among the many names I have used as synonymous for the immediacy of the starting point, one word has been avoided: *evidence*. If taken in its ciceronian sense (translating *enargeia,* i.e., *perspicuitas*) or in its medieval sense (distinguishing between objective evidence and propositional evidence) I could have used it. But today (with apologies to Brentano, Husserl and others) the cartesian notion (*simplex mentis inspectio*) is prevalent — in spite of the fact that Descartes uses the name only sparingly. Here, *evidence* has lost its metaphorical reference to light and stands practically for certainty (*certitudo*). There is no doubt that evidence leads to certainty, but the *mentis certitudo* is not equivalent to human foundation, unless Man is reduced to cogitation (*res cogitans*) and the *cogito* to mental operations. The cosmic confidence (I am going to suggest later) does not need to be based on mental certainty.

My commentary is that the problem of mediation arises out of the split between ontology and epistemology which was perhaps necessary to reach critical consciousness, but which, once established, cannot be healed if the split is not overcome by a more mature philosophy, which being aware of the distinction (epistemology/ontology, subject/object) does not break it in two pieces. The question is not what kind of mediation, but what is it that makes mediation necessary. Kierkegaard saw it rightly when, criticizing Hegel, he affirmed that the need of mediation comes from the assumption that reality is rational. We may go further, now including Kierkegaard in the critique, and assert that mediation becomes an indispensable concept only when we start from a dualistic conception of reality.

We have already said that our problem is how to overcome the necessity of mediation without "going back" to an undifferentiated whole, that is, without falling into monism. Which is the status of knowledge? of science? of the *logos?* "The logos is one," says Bacon's favorite quotation from Heraclitus (fr.2), "but the majority lives as if they had a private understanding *phronēsis.*"

Indeed, the post-cartesian as well as the non-hegelian way of approaching the problem often goes under the name of parallelism, be it epistemological (subject/object) or psychological (mind/body). Modalism (Spinoza), occasionalism (Malebranche), pre-established harmony (Leibniz), and later on vitalism (Bergson), and the many names around the "*Identitätstheorien*" and the "isomorphisms" of the last and present centuries are but different forms of parallelism. "Ordo, et connexio idearum idem est, ac ordo, et connexio rerum" is the lapidary sentence of Spinoza (Eth. II, 7). Mediation is then substituted by a bracketing of causality which has reached up to modern natural sciences like the "implicate order" of D. Bohm or the "morphogenetic fields" of R. Sheldrake.

Mediation becomes necessary once we have reduced thinking to "scientific" know-how, and intelligibility to rational, almost spatial "encapsulation." By this last word I mean the alleged rational intelligibility when something is perceived as contained in a larger concept. We could speak of the geometric predominance of science. In fact, until the last years of the last century (Hilbert's *Grundlagen der Geometrie,* 1899) Euclid's axioms (perhaps with exception of the famous last one of the "parallels") were practically considered as evident (because of spatial evidence). But even later, when in mathematics (including geometry) the "evidences" were substituted by postulates, the main and almost unique rule governing them was that of induction and deduction. Or, in a more general way, inference has been considered the practically unique scientific method. With the exception of so-called immediate inference (which is rather explicitation) all other (discursive) inferences are mediations. Thinking has become calculus: induction and deduction.

Mediation is then the bringing of the particular concept into a larger concept which embraces the former, or the linking of the two concepts through a previously accepted rule which is based on the same principle of geometrical evidence. By means of the syllogism we bring in contact, we mediate, two prima facie unrelated concepts by a middle term which "contains" the premises. By means of postulates or axioms we mediate the gap between two or more independent items. In short, mediation is the mailman of intelligibility.

My hypothesis submits that mediation has no *ultimate* relevance, because reality is neither one nor many, and the nature of the entire reality is constitutively relational. Here the śaiva notion that "all is related to all" (*sarvam sarvātmakam*) comes to mind. Or the christian notion of "God being all in all" (*ta panta en pasin*) also could be recalled. We may also mention the buddhist insight of the *pratītiya-samutpāda,* which I have translated as radical relativity. Interestingly enough Nishitani Keiji speaks also of "circuminsessional relationships." All this tends to make us aware that all that exists is a net of relationships, without taking sides now in the dispute between the *ātmavādin* and the *anātmavādin.* Certainly, any net has its knots, but these are precisely the agglomeration of the threads of the net, *pudgala.* The relations here, as in the Trinity, are not quantitative; they are constitutive of the real. It is not as if there were things, of whatever type, which afterwards, "we" relate. It is rather that the warp and woof of reality is constituted by such relations. Things do not need to be extrinsically mediated, they *are* inasmuch as they commune with each other.

Intelligibility does not entail the famous objective "reductio ad unum" because the knowing subject can never be fully abstracted from the known object. Polarity (advaita, trinity) is an ultimate character of reality — and shortcircuiting the poles brings only darkness (monarchic despotism).

And with this I have already mentioned the world view which makes mediation unnecessary, but first I should spell out my critique.

Critique

If the nature of the real is rational, and the rational is the real, if the ultimate structure of reality is dialectical, if absolute monotheism is the case, if the knower is a conqueror of an alien known,... under these and similar assumptions we certainly need mediation (Vermittlung), for we are neither absolute reality nor pure rationality. In sum, Hegel offers one of the most profound constructions of a rational world view: "Vermittlung durch Aufhebung der Vermittlung" ("mediation by means of overcoming mediation").

But that great *If* is a gratuitous assumption, when not begging the question — as I have tried to show elsewhere concerning monotheism: the existence of an "omniscient" Supreme Being does not amount to affirming that this Being knows everything that *is,* unless we previously identify Being with Intelligibility — the *is* with the *is-knowable* (1988/2).

In a word, mediation installs reason at the top of everything — also because to doubt it we need the very reason we want to contest. But doubt is only unbearable to rationalism.

An upaniṣadic reflection on the *mahāvākyāni* as suggested in my *Mantra-mañjarī* (1977) or the aristotelian principle about the soul being in some way everything (*De anima* III, 8), or the pauline view that in God we live, and move, and are (*Acts,* 17, 28), or the averroistic interpretation of the active intellect (*al-'aql al-fa' 'āl*) would be pertinent here. All these views seem to point to an underlying unity, a common structure, being, spirit, . . . which makes "mediation" unnecessary at the ultimate level, and meaningful at the level of the hierarchical structure of reality (cf. Thomas Aquinas *Contra Gentes* III, 83, as I commented long ago) (1951, 2nd ed. 1972, pp. 238–48).

There is mediation needed for the "secondary causes," but the Prime Cause does not require it. The Prime Cause is immanent, i.e., immediate cause of any effect. God does not need any mediator. "He" is immediately present in every being (and this is fundamental for the Christology I am going to defend).

My critique is that on the ultimate level mediation is neither required nor rationally convincing, because it only postpones the problem. In order that the mediator mediates it will need another mediator and *sic ad infinitum.*

We have here a similar example to the famous discussions around the "Third Man" *tritos anthropos,* which was the strong argument of Aristotle (*Met.* I, 990 b, 18; etc.) for the immanence (non-separability) of the Platonic ideas. But if the mediation (in our case) is immanent how does it mediate the two parties in itself? How does it reach immediacy, unity in itself? Hegel is right: *Vermittlung* is *Unmittelbarkeit,* the mediated knowledge, the reflexive knowledge is immediate with an immediacy superior to the first immediacy (*unvermittelte Unmittelbarkeit*).

Én kaì Pollá (Plat. *Phileb.* 15 D and Arist. *Met.* IV, 2; 1003 a 33) has been since Plato the way of presenting the question of the ultimate structure of reality. It should be noted that once we put the question this way we cannot escape Platonism; and this is the quintessence of all Western philosophy, *pace* Whitehead. If we begin by asking whether Being is one or multiple we are already assuming an intellect, a mind, a *nous* for which reality appears either as one or as many. Reality has already split itself into an asking knower and a "thing" known, into a subject and an object.

We may say that it is reality itself which obliges us to put the question. We have then the Platonic-Hegelian-Marxist line. We may also say that our *Dasein* is the very question. We have then the Aristotelian-scholastic-Heideggerian line — in spite of the many differences among those "six" philosophies, and without going further back to Parmenides and Heraclitus. Our point here is only this: The alleged dilemma of the "One or the Many," which translates into the option monism/dualism (plurality) is methodologically an uncritical dilemma because it erects discursive reason (*ratiocinatio*) as the ultimate judge of reality. The *advaita* position I am going to defend is critically aware that the very question which creates the mentioned dilemma begs what it questions.

In fact, to ask whether reality is an ultimate unity or an irreducible diversity, besides the dialectical implication of "identity and difference" (there is not the one without the other), assumes already not only the "ontological difference" but the *ontological* split which automatically degrades *symbolical awareness* to a knowledge of second rank. It upgrades, on the contrary, the question of mediation to the central issue of reality — and thus of dialectical philosophy.

Put in simple words: any mediation has to mediate between two different entities. We have A, Z and the mediator M. Besides the aporia that M has to partake of A and Z, and be at the same time different from A and Z, my hypothesis says that A partakes of Z in an analogous way as that in which M partakes of A and Z, like the "medium" in a syllogism, although we do not "see" it immediately. If A and Z were not ontologically related, the function of M would be illusory; it could not truly mediate between A and Z. Mediation is only an epistemological device made necessary once the divorce between ontology and epistemology is perpetrated.

Reality is not A, Z and M as three independent entities. Reality is the interdependence, or rather the innerdependence, i.e., the constitutive relationship between the three. There is no A without Z and M, nor Z without the other two, nor M without both. A is A only in relation to Z. An isolated A does not exist; it is an abstraction. Ultimately, A is not an independent and self-subsisting A with only external (accidental) links with Z, by means of M. The very reality of A relates existentially and essentially to the reality of Z and M.

There is no need of epistemological mediation because ontologically everything is ultimate mediation, or rather communion. Everything is, because it mediates. Everything is in relation because everything is relation, or, if we take the person to be essentially relationship, enlarging the notion of person, everything is personal. The philosophical way of expressing this intuition was to affirm that everything is alive, and the "theological" formulation was that of the ancient greeks and many other religions, that everything is "full of Gods" (Arist., *Met.* I, 3; 989 b 20 sq.). The universe is a uni-verse — not a unity, but a concurrence, *concursus, perichorēsis,* a universal rhythm. We may here simply recall the "Buddhist" comment of Plotinus: "How, then, does Unity give rise to Multiplicity? By its omnipresence...and...in virtue of its being nowhere" (*Ennead* III, 9, 4).

I have already mentioned that the notion of *symbolic awareness* would be my epistemological answer to the question of mediation (1979a, pp. 301–302). Symbolic awareness is immediate awareness. Symbolic awareness does not need mediation. The symbol is always immediate, non-mediated. The symbol is symbol precisely because it does not require mediation. There is no possible hermeneutics of a symbol. The symbol is symbol because it symbolizes — not because it "hermeneuticizes" (i.e., because it gives an interpretation of itself).

If we need an interpretation, a mediation, in order that the symbol symbolizes, this other element by which we interpret the symbol would be the real symbol (1981/4).

I may express all this by recalling the intuition of the Vedic Wisdom, as understood by its traditional exegetes, the *mīmāmsāka-s*. They developed the idea, so often misunderstood and ridiculed, of *apauruṣeyatva:* the Vedas having no author, not being mediated knowledge. The Vedas are Vedas because they do not need mediation. They are immediate; there is no author lurking behind to explain the meaning of the symbols. Śabara Svāmin says explicitly that nobody has linked the Vedic words with meaning. They are *apauruṣeya,* without a human mediator. If an author were needed we would again need a third agency to explain what the author means. If the symbol is not *svayamprakāśa* self-illuminating, self-refulgent, as a later tradition will say, it is not a symbol. That which a thing reveals immediately to us of itself, that is the real symbol — which, of course, includes the consciousness (the knower) for "whom" the symbol is symbol. In this sense the Vedas are symbols; in Western parlance, primordial revelation. This latter word is a loaded notion, and it may lead to a misunderstanding if we assume a revealer behind the revelation, who would then have to clarify to us the meaning of revelation and who would then be more fundamental than revelation itself. Mīmāmsā is atheistic. There is no God behind. And in this sense Madhva says that *apauruṣeya* means the very speech of the Creator. It is improper to say that the philosophies of India have not known the critical paradigm of the european Enlightenment (cf. *pramā, pramāṇa, prameya, pramātā pramiti* . . . [valid knowledge, means of valid knowledge, object of knowledge, knowing subject, act of knowledge . . . from the root *mā* (*mens,* mind) to measure]), but the primordial problem is seen from a different perspective. The epistemological question is not ultimate. There is no split between epistemology and ontology. The *logos* of the *on* itself. Ontology becomes epistemology only when the *verbum entis* becomes the *verbum mentis,* i.e., when our *logos* divorces the *on.*

Am I not falling into a precritical situation? Not at all, for three main reasons.

a) From a "sociology of knowledge" point of view there is simply no possible way of going back. Once the critical question arises we cannot legitimately silence it.

b) We are in a postcritical period which submits to critique also "*pure* reason" and discovers, first of all, that it is not so pure. Hegel's pathos is not self-critical. He writes in his *Philosophy of Religion:* "Das Denken ist der absolute Richter, vor dem der Inhalt sich bewähren soll" ("Thinking is the absolute judge before whom the very contents [of thought] must stand the test [prove themselves]"). Furthermore, if "pure" reason is the foundation of itself, either we beg the question or we simply trust in reason beyond its own rational domain; i.e., we trust that reason mirrors reality.

c) The very awareness of the act of knowing does not vouch for its independence from the ontological question — to put it briefly. Elsewhere I have criticized the "hunter's epistemology" and defended the intrinsic ontological character of epistemology. A political translation of all this today is the *ecological* crisis. In the hunter's epistemology a subject searches for a target, the object, and "shoots" at it once it has been properly focused, having found the "clear and distinct" idea. Ontological knowledge, on the other hand, requires the knower so to grow as to be able to embrace the known — to reach a certain identification between the two.

So far the critique of mediation on the ultimate level. We should not confuse our critique of mediation with the practical and pragmatic need for intermediaries.

The Alternative

As a plausible substitute for mediation I would like to use here an ancient and polysemic word: *communicatio.* It obviously suggests *communio* and implies *communis,* communality. It is formed of *com* (*cum*) and *munis* (*munia, munus*), the latter word meaning task, office, duty, function. *Com-munis* amounts to being coresponsible, *mit-verpflichtet,* to share in the same task. We are sharing in the word, says the Ṛg Veda (I, 164, 37). *Communis* corresponds to the Greek *Koinos* and is opposed to *proprius,* one's own, peculiar, particular. *Communicatio idiomatum* is a *terminus technicus* in christian theology. The greeks already used the word *anakoinosis* in our sense of communication of ideas to somebody with the intention of inviting the hearer to partake in the counsel, as Cicero still reports (*De oratione,* III, 204).[2]

In the contemporary world many thinkers have made ample use of the word before it was seized by the so-called information sciences. I have in mind F. Ebner, K. Jaspers, N. Berdiaev, Gabriel Marcel, J. Habermas, and many others. I would like to use it in a manner closer to Jaspers and Berdiaev, sympathetic, perhaps to Habermas, but in an almost opposite, although not contradictory way to modern usage. Communication is not just passing information among individuals, but (re)establishing communion. What makes communication possible is not mediation but the more original communion which communication (re)constructs. I am not necessarily assuming the platonic or the christian myth, but have in mind most of the world myths, although not particularly relying on any of them.

I am saying only this. Communication takes place because it is possible, and it is possible because of a more original communality among all beings. In short, we can understand each other because we have something in common. We may call it Being, Nature or Human Nature, Matter, the Mystical Body of Christ, of Buddha, or whatever. There is an original situation which is common; this commonality is the matrix out of which communication takes place, which creates something new, previously nonexistent.

---

2. Our root *mei* means to change (cf. *mutation* and in sanskrit *ni-māyā*). *Communio* is exchange and *communicatio* implies a *Schicksalgemeinschaft,* a common destiny. If we relate it to *moenia* (wall) *communis* is the *Hausgenosse,* the person who lives within the same walls — although modern philology criticizes this etymology.

Communication is a most natural act. Stars communicate, the solar system is a set of communications. We may call them gravitation, cosmic energy, light and what not. Minerals, plants, animals, humans and angels communicate. The Divine is pure communication (or it would stifle in its incommunicability). Reality is pure communicability. And communication perdures because it is not a one-directional flow ending in a monistic omega point (of any type) but a rhythmic exchange which is precisely the very nature of reality.

To be sure, we are mainly concerned with human communication, i.e., with the conscious act of reaching the other by means of knowledge. This is certainly the case, but we should not excommunicate ourselves so much from the earth and matter as to believe we are the absolute kings of creation. Human knowledge is a special kind of communication, and the *animal loquens* speaks of all those other forms of communication.

In order for communication to take place we do not need to do anything artificial. Communication is primordial, original. Human communication may be indeed a complicated affair but its basis is the cosmotheandric communality. The ecological consequences should be patent: any excommunication of Man from the "rest" of reality is anti-natural, inhuman and, ultimately, destructive. If we need mediation to communicate with the earth all ecological disasters are at the door (1993d). The need for mediation assumes that the other is not I, and thus we need an intermediary to bridge the gulf. The centrality given to mediation betrays the ignorance of the thou-dimension of reality: the "Dulosigkeit" of Ferdinand Ebner. This very customary way of presenting the question in the third person (for instance: "The other *is* not me," "What *is* reality?") makes mediation indispensable in order that the object that (it) *is* may reach the subject that (I) *am*. We need then mediation from the "A is B" to the "I know that A is B." Once we put the question in terms of an objective *is*, we need mediations to reach the subject. Since the cartesian *cogito,* stressing the first person (the subject), up to modern science, stressing the *it*, still called third person, there has been a forgetting of the *thou,* and we have created an unbridgeable gulf between spirit and matter, subject and object. But the I, Thou and It belong together (1986/2). The *proton pseudos* of idealism was to reduce reality to the dialectical paradigm I/Not-I, forgetting the Thou, which alone prevents the I from swallowing the Not-I: idealism or materialism; in a word, monism. The Thou is neither I nor Not-I. The I does not need mediation in order to reach the Thou; nor the Thou to reach the I. They belong together. There is no I without a Thou, no Thou without an I. The solipsism of the I is self-contradictory the moment it speaks or becomes conscious of itself. A Thou is necessary for any I-awareness.

I am tempted to link this forgetting of the *thou,* which has reduced all that is not an *I* to an *it,* an object, with the dominant patriarchalism of the last millennia during which, by and large and with important exceptions, women have been objects of males, whether by admiration, dominion or exploitation. I signal also the intriguing disappearance of the dual in modern languages. "I and Thou" form not a plural, but a dual. Grammar is not as irrelevant as modern nominalism tends to imagine.

Personalism may not be the best word if we reduce it to human relations. But it may help if taken in the traditional sense of the Christian *una persona,* the buddhist buddha-nature or the karmic universal solidarity.

An important contribution to this problem is the upaniṣadic idea of universal correlations. As a matter of fact, this is another recurrent idea from China to medieval Europe ("as in heaven so on earth"). The task of the person is to become actively aware of those correlations. Persons can do it, because they constitute the very warp and woof of the real. I shall still return to this problem in the section dealing with what I have called *Christophany* (see also 1993d).

Mythos and Logos

Bettina Bäumer and Harold Coward deal from different angles with one of the most important aspects of today's human problematic: that of language, and that of the language of the myth, respectively. They have presented the problem in a creative way, and I would like to continue that line of thought. In fact, 1980/1 was only half of my essay. The other half is still unpublished, although some ideas are elaborated in 1986/6.

I include my comments in the methodological part because this is not the place to develop an entire philosophy of language. I shall limit myself to a couple of considerations.

From this methodological aspect my overall comment says that any approach to human problems by the sole means of the *logos* is one-sided, even without reducing *logos* to *ratio.*

Here I would like to underscore the importance of not taking language as a mere instrument by which we "humans" conduct our business; the inextricable and constitutive relationship between *mythos* and *logos;* and the need of becoming aware of the silence preceding both.

Language as the First Revelation of Being

Language creates reality. This goes against the modern grain. It goes against the nominalistic and "computerizing" trends of our times. I submit that the *animal loquens* is not just using a code for passing information. Human speech is creating reality when uttering authentic words. Words have power not only over other mortals; the elements also obey the word (cf. *Mt* 8: 26–27). By the word Man shares actively in the shaping of history and in the making of the world (cf. *AV* IV, 1). As I have repeated time and again, that which Ramon Llull called the *affatus* (or *effatus*), the speech (as the sixth human sense), is a sharing in the Word, which, according to many traditions, is the Power by which all things have been and are being made.

I have written about the need to complete the paradigm Being-Thinking by the triad Being-Speaking-Thinking. Speaking is the freedom of Being which speaks without having itself to conform to the structures of Thinking (1990/8). Here I would situate the fundamental locus of language.

I submit that language, besides being simply an instrument of thinking, is, in a more momentous way, the first manifestation of Being. To put it somewhat paradoxically: language is prior to thought — although, of course, we cannot thoughtfully, i.e., reflexively, sever thought from language. On the ontic level this break would be insanity; on the ontological just a lie (1986/6). In short Being speaks, or, as Śabara already said: Language speaks. The ultimate structure of anything consists in *res, notio, verbum,* the thing, the notion (of which the concept is only a class), and the word — and not only *res* and *notio.*

We may ask whether the old parmenidean paradigm of Thinking and Being does not suffice, following which, all that "is" is either a thing or a thought. Through thinking we reach Being. Man is *res cogitans.* We can think thoughts and beings. Thought transcends itself and has its proper intentionality. It intends either things in *natura rerum* or ideas in the intelligible world.

Why then, on this ultimate level, also words? If thoughts are reflections on things, are not words expressions of thought? My answer here is an emphatic no. Words are more — not less — than translations of thoughts. It is almost the opposite: thoughts are interpretations of language. Language is more than an instrument of communication between thinking beings. The word, or linguisticality, if one so prefers, is the very womb in which communication and meaning can take place. But language is more than this. Language is the first "revelation" of Being.

Communication, we said, implies an original communion which makes communication possible. But how does communication come about? What does communication add to the more basic and often implicit communion? Is it only "unconcealment"? But who or what produces it? How do we communicate?

Here is where I introduce the traditional tripartite scheme, reflected in the cosmotheandric intuition (1977/7 and 1990/8). The triadic structure of reality is an ancient and almost universal tradition, as the two bulky volumes of E. Schadel *Bibliotheca Trinitariorum* (München, 1984, 1988) show. Prior to or rather between the relationship Thinking/Being there is Language, the Word. How do we overcome solipsism? How do we relate to each other? The bond is language in its widest sense. Interestingly enough, for some indic schools of philosophy, *cestā,* gesture (effort, and accidentally also *mudra*), besides *śabda,* word, is a *pramāṇa,* a means of valid knowledge.

To say that language is what makes communication possible sounds almost trite. But this affirmation does not mean language is a mere psychological divide or just an instrument we use. We should ask: How is it that the instrument works? It can only work because the word itself belongs to this primordial reality in which we all share (*RV* I, 164, 37). We would remain unconnected monads, incommunicable atoms, if there were not language, if the word did not dwell within us. Were it not for language we would stifle in our thoughts. The human world is a linguistic universe. The word is the agora of reality, and Man is the custodian.

Myth as Part of Language

Regarding the second point, I am glad neither Coward nor Bäumer has aligned me with Nietzsche's and post-nietzschean attacks against western logocentrism. Agreeing with J. Habermas that we need to overcome the "Paradigma der Bewusstseinsphilosophie" and with K. O. Apel regarding the "Logosauszeichnung der menschlichen Sprache," learning also from F. Ebner and E. Rosenstock-Huessy besides many others, I feel that the western tradition has suffered from a lopsided development of the *logos*. Perhaps this is a side effect of the preponderance given to scripture and later to the printing press? But my point is neither to criticize the West nor to defend irrationality, but to integrate or rather to bring to light the intrinsic relationship between *mythos* and *logos*.

The word is not only *logos,* reason and reasonable word, but also *mythos*. With the *logos* alone we cannot do justice to the human experience and thus to the respective self-understandings of religions and traditions. *Mythos* is also language and therefore carries with it a certain intelligibility, although not of rational evidence. Man is not only endowed with rational consciousness, but also possesses mythical awareness, which is different from the former. The symbolic world belongs to this mythical awareness. Symbols are the bricks out of which the *mythos* is constructed, although we should not imagine symbols to be objects as bricks are things. The subject for whom the symbol is symbol belongs to it. The symbol is not objectifiable (1970a, pp. 7ff).

It is not enough to grant condescendingly to the *mythos* a status in the lower range of the emotions and instincts. *Mythos* is not irrationality. Precisely because there is no subordinationism of the *mythos* to the *logos,* the categories of rationality and/or irrationality are not applicable to the world of the *mythos* (1989/5). We would impoverish our world, our human life and the universe immensely if we were to reduce reality to what the *logos* tells us about it. There is also another telling. Or, rather, both *mythos* and *logos* constitute our telling, our human language.

On the other hand, we should not subordinate the *logos* to the *mythos* either. This would be irrationality, besides being inexpressible — for it would amount to the *logos* committing suicide. It is the mutual relationship which opens up a view to the cosmotheandric intuition, as we shall see.

I have never played with the *logos* alone or with the *mythos* alone. What I contest in many academic discussions is precisely the underlying myth of the discussions. The present scene pays heed again to what artists, poets and many thinkers have been saying since Esau spurned his primogeniture, the Vedas affirmed that the highest heaven, perhaps, did not know the mystery of reality, the Tao declared itself silence, and the peoples of the world danced and put ornaments in their buildings and on their bodies without for that matter renouncing or neglecting rationality. Since my first essays I have been striving for the internal harmony between *mythos* and *logos* (1944/1). Not by bread alone, not by *mythos* or by *logos* alone, does Man live.

Our first task is to understand ourselves, to strive to become intelligible synthesis — not necessarily a system. Experience is paramount, life has the priority, praxis always leads. Our life is at the foundation of all our thoughts.

But a logically subsequent, although ontologically simultaneous task is to make ourselves intelligible to others. If we live within a homogeneous myth this is relatively easy. The context is taken for granted. The context is the undiscussed canvas on which we put our ideas and judge our actions. But north american academia is not the european intellectual scene, nor can the indic world be equated to either of them. And besides the professional intellectuals there are many other forces in this world of ours. Surely we need communication, dialogue.

Dialogue is truly *dia-logos;* it pierces the *logos* and touches the *mythos.* If we do not share the same myth, the dialogue will have to create it. But this is a task prior to dialectics. Both *mythos* and *logos* pervade everything, but they cannot live in isolation. I do not propose a dialectical alternative, a substitution of one paradigm for another, as if it all were a question of accepting one or another model. I question the very need of models in order to think and specially to live humanly. Here lies the momentum of challenging Parmenides's paradigm.

Bettina Bäumer asks whether a mantra is mythical language and tends to say that it is not. Without wanting to be unnecessarily paradoxical, but just for the sake of clarifying my notion of myth, I may say that when we ask whether anything is a pure myth, it has ceased, by this very fact, to be a myth and has become mythology or a mythologumenon. The mantra, I would say, is a symbol which sheds off its mythical character the moment we cease to believe in it as mantra and take it as a simple nominal sound or phrase, even if powerful, because of the effects ("vibrations") it triggers. You chant the mantra or recite it or simply meditate on it because you believe in it, although you may formulate your belief in very different more or less rational explanations. Ultimately you recite the mantra for some inexplicable "reason." It is for you something very real, and you will be somewhat uncomfortable attempting to explain it to somebody who does not have at least a certain sympathy, propensity or empathy with it.

"Whoever shall invoke (*epikalesētai/invocaverit*) the name of the Lord shall be saved" said the foundational discourse of Peter (*Acts* 2: 21), echoed by Paul (*Rom* 10: 13), following the Jewish and other traditions. If you don't believe you will not understand, said *Isaiah* (7:9) nor even exist (according to another possible rendering). The ancient *disciplina arcani* was not magic esotericism. It was demanded by the situation itself. If one does not believe in the act (word, action...) one is performing, that "act" is not the same as the act that the believer is performing (meaning, reenacting...). Here would apply my distinction between *noēma* and *pisteuma* (1978, p. 89).

So much has been written recently on mantra that I should not enlarge the list. We have now the rich bibliography by the late H. P. Alper in *Understanding Mantras.* But a philosophical reflection on mantra may be an appendix to what I have been saying. Mantra, *vāc, śabda-brahman,* Bṛhaspati, *logos,* all point to the primordiality of the word, and thus of language.

The Silence of the Word

Rounding out my commentary on *mythos* and *logos* I mention the place of silence in any meditation on the word. Any word erupts out of the silence. It is silence which makes it possible. Silence is its matrix. The "silence of the word" would be a contradiction in terms if taken in the sense of the objective genitive: the word has no silence. The word is such because it shatters away silence. The phrase should be taken as a subjective genitive. The word comes from and in this sense belongs to silence. The relation is non-dualistic — which did lead me to speak of an advaitic genitive ("God's world" being a momentous example). Silence and word are worlds apart, and yet they belong to each other in intrinsic relationship. Silence is "silence of the word," and word is the "word of (out of) silence." Word would not be word if it would not "word" silence, if it would not emerge of silence. Silence would not be silence if it would not be "silenced" by the word, if it would not be that which makes silence to be what it is, absence of word.

Silence stands here for no-*logos,* no-word, no-intelligibility and even no-rationality, without equating it with irrationality.

Perhaps in this context we should introduce the name of "spirit" (*rūaḥ, ātman, pneuma, Geist...*). The spirit is utterly different, though not separable from the *logos.* Western civilization has subordinated the spirit to rationality with momentous consequences, which I will not spell out now. The formidable question of the void, emptiness, *śūnyatā,* even nothingness, *asat* and the like lurks here. I mention it solely in order to disclose the overall myth from which I write (cf. 1979a, pp. 257–75; 1989).

THE CROSSCULTURAL DIALOGUE

Diatopical Hermeneutics

The pair praxis-theory, like *mythos-logos,* forms a constitutive polarity of reality. The one is not without the other. Christian thinkers had meditated upon the jewish wisdom of *Sirach* 42: 25: "All things go in pairs, one the opposite of the other; He has made nothing incomplete. One thing supplements the virtues of another" (see also 33: 15). Praxis and theory belong together. We see it in the actual political situation. History conditions our thinking. In our time, we have both reactionary movements (like those of 1815 and 1990 speaking of a "New World Order") and the collapse of the monocultural world view (which is the essence of colonialism). We cannot properly know, let alone judge the world from a single standpoint. In sum, a crosscultural approach is called for. There is no doubt that the present-day interest in and need of crosscultural studies stems from a praxis situation and not from a pure theory critical of itself. Christian missions and western colonialism would continue convinced of their superiority were it not for the actual existential changes in the political situation of the world — and also, of course, the other way round. "All things go in pairs."

David Krieger's chapter highlights in an excellent way the method I consider proper for the interreligious dialogue, and which, as he himself points out, is valid also for any crosscultural dialogue. Indeed, religion and culture cannot be separated. Religion gives culture its ultimate content, and culture gives religion its proper language (1989/6).

For this very reason I distinguish between *common language,* indispensable for any encounter, and *universal language,* about which I am critical and rather sceptical. There cannot be a truly supracultural language. Any language is good product and a symbol of a culture; when we reach some crosscultural communication we enrich precisely the respective cultures by introducing some new elements.

A common language does not mean a universal language. Language is always dialogical. It is in dialogue that we perform any linguistic activity. We search for common languages between a hindu and a christian, an atheist and a monotheist, a thai and a portuguese, a leftist and a conservative. But we cannot actually speak all those languages at the same time. We ourselves are bound to speak different languages in different situations lest we be misunderstood. While expressing my own opinions I have found myself using almost contrary statements and giving different emphases to words when speaking with a jew or with a buddhist. Instead of reducing languages to uniformity we are creating new languages. Krieger rightly describes such encounters as founding events.

Krieger speaks of "functional equivalence," which was how I introduced what I later came to call, refining the notion, *homeomorphic equivalents.* I mention it because of the political relevance of this notion. We are all too prone to monocultural approaches to our political situation. The outcome is war. Let me give a concrete case. I believe that the idea of homeomorphic equivalents helps in finding the middle path between those who, under the guise of defending "The Universal Declaration of Human Rights," would propagate one single ideology, and those who reacting against that imposition, would not abide by "The Universal Declaration of Human Rights," branding it as imperialist or what not, and feel free to transgress those rights. The "Declaration" is certainly not universal, but it is up to other cultures and religions to discover within their own traditions the homeomorphic equivalent(s) so as to be able to defend what we would call the dignity of the person — which would be the factual common language for those engaged in our present-day discussions.

I signal here what I have called *diatopical hermeneutics* in order to do justice to the crosscultural dialogue. The apt method for understanding two different contexts springing from two separate myths is different from the method suitable for relating two different texts.

I am thankful to Krieger for signaling a certain ambiguity in my use of dialectics. I wish I had published my seminar given at the Banaras Hindu University in the fifties on "Dialogue and Dialectics." Krieger is right in pointing out, in a footnote, that my scheme of the "three kairological moments in human consciousness" should not be used as a transcultural paradigm as if we could fix the totality of the human experience in one single scheme. I may say on my behalf that accepting heuristically the myth of history I felt somewhat justified in using such a temporal pattern. But I should have been perhaps more clear in specifying that it was one particular language. That temporal pattern did help me to situate the human condition seen from one particular perspective through which we may envisage the whole. It is an example of the *pars pro toto* effect.

This leads me to clarify a point which has been raised again and again. Am I not contradicting myself criticizing universalism, i.e., acknowledging the factual incommensurability of ultimate rational systems, and at the same time offering a pattern which seems to claim universal validity? Am I not defeating my purpose criticizing the global syndrome (one universal language, one government, market economy, global ethics...) and advancing a universal argument against such totalitarian attempts?

I may be right or wrong regarding universalism or pluralism (about this, later), but my position is still coherent. We should distinguish between the coherence and absolute universal validity of any statement. *Coherence* means that we "stick together" "adhering" to the recognized "inherent" rules of a particular field, not "hesitating" to denounce as false what is "incoherent" within that particular framework. *Universal validity* entails that what we affirm or deny is the case under any circumstance. I, for instance, condemn human torture under any, for me, foreseeable circumstance. But I have to acknowledge that one of my "stances" is the infinite or divine dignity of the human person, which I also have to recognize is not a universal "stance" — as much as I believe in it. In other words, the *ought to be* cannot be based "outside" or "beyond" the *Being that is*. Prescriptive rules are more than merely descriptive statements. But the rule presumes a ruler, a *rex* which regulates and is acknowledged as such. We need a myth.

Indeed we all have a *pro toto* pretension, but it is only one particular way of approaching the whole as we see it in our particular horizon (myth). This is what I have called the *pars pro toto* effect. It is a non-universal way of approaching from our particular perspective the universality we all intend. It is a particular language speaking about the general realm of Being.

Our universalistic instinct is so embedded in our psyche that it may be necessary to spell out that Being itself is only a formal concept and that the *totum* of the *pars pro toto* effect is not Being in itself but an intended *totum in parte,* an undefined *totum* in the horizon under which we situate our consciousness. We may claim "objective" validity, but this amounts to claiming objective validity from the subjective point from which a particular subject, belonging to a limited time and space, culture and psychology, envisages the "objective." Furthermore, universal objectivity (assuming it were possible) does not cover universal subjectivity. We may claim to speak for all objects of a previously defined class, but we cannot pretend to include in that class all subjects without depriving them of their subjectivity, i.e., of what makes them subjects: sources of consciousness endowed with the power of making another classification or none at all.

Only a universal Subject, an absolute I, could reasonably make a statement with universal validity. And even then the universal validity of the absolute Subject could only claim absolute objectivity and subjectivity under the gratuitous assumption that on that absolute level object and subject, i.e., Being and Consciousness, coalesce. A fortiori any proposition made by a finite subject cannot make such a claim a priori. *If* the knowing subjects are real, no single subject can claim to speak for all other subjects, and thus reasonably raise the claim to universality. With such an apparently universal affirmation it should become apparent that this attitude does not spurn rationality. To claim that one single subject speaks for all subjects is a mere contradiction: a subject is one who speaks for itself. Democracy, for instance, functions on the basis of that stupendous — and often naive — confidence that others, to whom we have given our "vote," can speak for us in the affairs of the *res publica,* but no human subject can abdicate what makes it a subject: autochthonous consciousness (with all that it entails). Human dignity and thinking are inalienable aspects of Man — but again this is valid insofar as it expresses and qualifies a tautology for those who see it as such. A tautology is merely formal: "A=A." This is David Hilbert's formalism in mathematics. A qualified tautology converts it into a "material" statement referring to things. This would be the position of Gottlob Frege in mathematics. When universal statements claim a universal applicability their universality is reduced, by the translation, to the accepted congruence with the "facts." For many of us Man's dignity is an ontic absolute. But this is not accepted by most of the political and economic powers in our world today. I endorse here fully the position of Paul Knitter, about which more later. We operate always within an accepted myth.

In other words, the subjective aspect of any affirmation with the claim to universal validity does not encompass the totality of human beings. It will remain always *our* affirmation. If at all, only an a posteriori statement could claim universal validity within a particular horizon offered by a given myth in a limited field in time and space. Nobody can encompass the universal range of the human experience. This is what I express with my reflections on language. Each universal statement is couched in a language, and no language is universal and presuppositionless (1990/8).

I should specify once again here that the so-called formal and meta-languages are not universal. They may claim a certain universal validity only when their very particular formalisms and premises have been adopted.

To affirm that 0.5+0.5=1 here and everywhere, today and forever, is not a valid objection on two accounts. First, we are not dealing here with mere "formal" exactness, but with affirmations about reality. We have to do with statements like "there is God," "reason is the essence of Man," "the second principle of thermodynamics is universally valid," which do not bracket the subjective and "material," aspect of reality. Our query is not merely "logical."

Second, even that arithmetical example is not really universally objective. It is an abstraction which has only an intentional (and generally uncritical) reference to real objects. This abstraction is meaningful only under a complex set of assumptions, like equivalence between Being and Thinking, thinking and numbering, and so on, which are not universal. The equation 0.5+0.5 blue=1 object has little meaning; 0.5+0.5=1 is here meaningless. But even ½ cow+½ cow is certainly not always equal to 1 cow. In fact, 0.5+0.5=1 only where 0.5 and 0.5 mean nothing outside their own self-referential formal system. It is a mere abstraction, which can be extrapolated only under very limited conditions and accepted postulates — valid as it is in the field of numbers, which is a very useful but limited form of thought.

In short, my criticism of universalism is not a universal affirmation (which is impossible — as I argue). It tallies with my defense of pluralism, which is not a pluralistic statement (which has no meaning). It is simply my opinion, which I am striving to defend in a convincing manner. And this is already our next point.

Pluralism

The question of pluralism has emerged as one of the stumbling blocks of all that I am trying to defend. Carney, Cobb and Larson all touch upon this problem. As the first only touches it obliquely, I shall come to his contribution in the next section.

I am struck by my convergence with John Cobb. I agree with him. Relativity is not relativism. The *pars pro toto* effect is at work everywhere. My metaphysics is as particular as any other one. It is my metaphysical window. I see the *totum in parte*.

There is but one element I introduce into the picture which situates my metaphysical stance. It may be close to the "total matrix" of process philosophy — although without claiming to be total. It is *myth*, a myth which, as I have said, has an inner relationship with the *logos*. Such a relationship, of course, can be articulated only by means of the *logos*, and therefore can be spelled out only one-sidedly.

We may pursue a little more the metaphor of the window. We all see through our respective windows. The more perfect the window the less conspicuous it is; we may easily forget that we are looking through a window, so transparent has it become for us. We do not see our windows, our myths. But there is still more. We realize that there are other people looking through different windows. We may even contest the alleged correctness of the visions through other windows, but we hear others describing to us their respective sceneries. Let me insist. Pluralism does not claim to see through all the windows or to control all (or some) of them. Pluralism simply acknowledges the existence of other windows. It simply hears and respects the speech of others, enters into dialogue with them. The indispensable function of language appears here. This is the locus for dialogue both dialectical (over against an acknowledged logical background) and dialogical (allowing the other to pierce through our own *logos*). We see through our windows, but listening to others speak we hear other languages. And the others tell us that we also are looking through a window. Through language we communicate with the wider human world. Language, we have already said, is the bond of humanness. For this reason the closing of the dialogue may lead to war — and war is the degradation of the human. Now, in order to understand the language of the other we need to "stand-under" the same myth. We need to peep into some opening of the other's window. And my conviction, against intellectual and political technocrats, is that there is no universal television screen from which we *all* may see "one world."

I may insert here an important remark which belongs to a historically enlarged sociology of knowledge. We all see through our respective windows. In order to become aware of the relevance of other windows, without dismissing or ignoring them, we need to *hear* the witnessing of our neighbors — no longer ignored as barbarians from whom we have nothing to learn. In short, the *logos* has a constitutive dimension: the *hearing* of it. The *logos* is not only the spoken word, it is equally the heard word. We speak in order to be heard — and not just by ourselves. Dialogue is duologue and not a crossing of monologues. Language is not just speaking. It is also hearing. The lack of attention to hearing the other stands at the root of the lack of pluralism of most colonial civilizations — not just the western. "Faith comes from hearing!" said Paul (*Rom.* 10: 17). (Tellingly enough, the New English Bible, as well as the Jerusalem Bible and other modern translations distort the text.) I am tempted to sum it all up by saying that pluralism is the art of listening.

Be that as it may, we all operate within a given myth, in which we believe, and which is the matrix of our respective processes of intelligibility. Myths are not only geographically and historically distributed; they are also kairologically active. There is emerging, for instance, a sort of common myth among the people presently engaged and interested in such theoretical issues. This is related to the common language that the dialogue is creating — as we already said.

There is today the western myth and even the myth of humanity as we, the "literate," understand the world. The rejection of cannibalism is, for instance, a shared myth (with apologies to the old Caribs of the West Indies from whom the word stems). This is not the case with the condemnation of capitalism, although one may think that unless we eliminate it from the scene humanity is going to fall into social cannibalism. The ideas of the unity of the human race, of the earth, and of the universe, are contemporary myths. They are taken for granted (by those who believe in them).

The self-relativization John Cobb so convincingly speaks of is an example of what I am saying. We are able to relativize and even to relativize ourselves precisely because the ground is an unspoken myth, a "matrix" we take for granted. I am thankful for his contribution, which shows how one can arrive at similar positions from different perspectives.

Before responding to Gerald Larson's well-organized critique of pluralism, I will try to make myself understood without insisting on what I have written in essays cited and uncited by him (1991/7). The difficulty may lie in the fact that my hypothesis dares to touch the most treasured principle of the dominant philosophy of our times: "reason, inductive and deductive" as our basic instrument for making sense of reality and configuring human life. Or, to put it another way, my hypothesis goes against the modern scientific paradigm as being the sole serious intellectual exercise; it goes against the dominance of the modern pan-mathematical method. Understanding does not come by calculating. The latin culture distinguishes between *ratio* (reason) and *ratiocinatio* (discursive reasoning, induction and deduction).

The modern West, or the Enlightenment, may be proud of its discoveries. I do not dispute this. I only point out that the price for the so-called critical discovery is the blindness about other realms of reality, including the human reality. One cannot have one's cake and eat it, as I am reminded.

Besides the rather insulting manner in which the Enlightenment has treated its predecessors (obscurantist slumber, superstitious naiveté, pre-copernican galimatias . . .), its blind trust in "pure" reason appears rather pedantic today. Other periods were, after all, not so naive.

We may recall the classical *pramāṇavāda* of indic philosophies or the *triplex oculus* of christian scholasticism to convince us that uncritical ingenuity has not always been the case. The *mīmāmsā,* for instance, recognizes *pratyaksa* (perception), *anumāna* (inference), *upamāna* (comparison), *arthāpati* (postulation, presumption), *anupaladhi* (non-cognition), *śabda-pramāṇa* (verbal authority, word). Hugh of Saint Victor, as another example, speaks of the *oculus carnis, oculus rationis* and *oculus contemplationis.* In a word, not everything is reducible to reason, although reason may be a necessary fellow-traveler in all human transactions. But so are the other two eyes, for that matter. Or, as I would say, not all is *logos* in Man, although this is a statement of the *logos.* The *logos,* in stating this, does not deny itself; it transcends and relativizes itself, i.e., it does not proclaim itself an absolute.

I formulate pluralism by saying that truth belongs not only to the realm of the *logos,* but that it pertains also to the order of the *mythos.* "The Myth of Pluralism" was explicitly the title of a study of mine. (See 1979/2).

I shall reduce my comments to three: Clarification of the notion, methodological remarks, and a dialogical response.

Clarification of the Notion

It should be clear that I do not understand by pluralism what is currently meant nowadays when people speak of "pluralistic society," "theological pluralism," or pluralisms of many sorts. This usage means a tolerant, open, and a more or less sophisticated stand which accepts or finds a place for a diversity of life styles, doctrines or religions. This is certainly a positive value and an indispensable attitude, but I understand by pluralism something more basic (1961/1).

Pluralism, as a word touching upon the nature of reality, is a polysemic name. It has a long history. Some pre-socratics were supposed to be pluralists, and today there is the talk about pluralisms of all sorts: political, civil, demographic, practical, psychological, ethical, historical, religious, mythical, functional, logical, intellectual, theoretical, epistemological, metaphysical, philosophical, monadological, cultural, harmonic, implicit, mere, relative, utter, absolute, and so on and so forth. C. Wolff, I. Kant, F. C. S. Schiller, W. James, H. Laski, M. Scheler, H. Albert, and many of our contemporaries have dealt thematically with the problem of pluralism.

Larson calls my "pluralism" "theoretical pluralism" in order to stress that it is not a merely pragmatic or practical pluralism. I reject that adjective and feel that emphasizing this epithet is what leads Larson to find fault with it. It all depends, of course, on what we understand by *theory.* Pluralism, as I understand it, puts today the strictest challenge to the monarchy of reason — ultimately to monotheism.

I take pluralism to be not a metaphysical view of the universe (although it may entail one — or many), but a fundamental *human attitude: aptitudo,* that for which I am *aptus,* fit.[3]

The "one and the many" has been, not only since Plato but since the ancient egyptians (see Erik Hornung) the main concern of the Western philosophical mind. Histories of philosophy use to treat pluralism as the third grand system after monism and dualism. We may recall Bertrand Russell's "absolute pluralism." By using the word *Pluralism,* on the other hand, I intend something more than making an objective statement about the world or against the "Identitätsphilosophie" (idealism), the "block universe" (D. Davidson), the monistic world view, or in favor of the "pluralistic universe" (W. James) — without mentioning all the names that history of philosophy tells us. All our talk of crosscultural studies and mutual fecundation would remain barren if we had not the daring to break the cultural frontiers which, like "iron curtains" and "Berlin walls," isolate peoples, cultures and religions.

A crosscultural incursion into this problematic could use the word *pluralism* to mean *advaita,* although in an original way. Pluralism is not plurality: pluralism suggests that reality is neither a unity nor a plurality. The indic mind introducing the word *advaita* stresses the negation of duality (and the temptation is *ekatva,* monism). The homeomorphic western equivalent could use the world *pluralism* to stress the irreducibility of ultimate world views — whereby what is ultimate is again subject to (pluralistic) discussion. If *advaita* is qualified monism, pluralism is qualified plurality. But *advaita* could as well be designated as qualified dualism and pluralism as qualified unity. It is to this ultimate depth that the problem of pluralism leads us.

The problem of pluralism is primarily not a question of ethical convenience or political prudence, or even an epistemological answer to the subject-object split, but a philosophical question regarding reality.

I shall limit myself here to describing the pluralistic attitude in face of conflicting truth-claims — to follow the consecrated, although for me unconvincing, language (as if we could make any claim about truth outside its *a-letheia*).

Pluralism takes a critical attitude which does not see the absolute necessity — and eventually the convenience — of reducing everything to one single truth, without for that matter allowing for a proliferation of truths — since every truth has its own field and boundaries. The pluralistic attitude does not suffer from any compelling obsession to reduce everything to absolute unity, without for that matter subscribing to any ultimate duality, since this is not the only alternative to monism. The pluralistic attitude accepts the stance that reality may be of such

---

3. Sanskrit: *āpta, āpnoti:* he reaches, obtains, attains (because it suits my character); the indoeuropean root being *āp (ep)*: to hold, take, reach.

a nature that nobody, no single human group to be sure can coherently claim to exhaust the universal range of the human experience. The "reason" is that reality may not be totally objectifiable, because we, the subjects, are also part of it.

I am saying that knowledge, by its nature, demands a knower (not necessarily an individualistic one). Any integral knowledge, therefore, cannot prescind the "objective" knowledge from the knowing subject. All knowledge is "personal knowledge," and this is, to quote M. Polanyi, not an imperfection but a "vital component" of knowledge itself. Pluralism does not make an objective statement about the world. It simply implies the awareness that knowledge is always the knowledge of a subject and that an absolute subject (assuming it existed) would have only an absolute objective knowledge of all that is knowable. For an absolute knower, object and subject coalesce. But the absolute object of the absolute subject covers the entire reality only under the assumption that reality is totally intelligible, which is what pluralism does not need to assume (1988/2). The total intelligibility of reality is a gratuitous assumption which is not necessary for functioning of our mind — unlike, for instance, the principle of non-contradiction on the mental plane. The principle of non-contradiction puts an extrinsic barrier to our calculating mind: If we think A to be the case, we cannot think the identical A to be Non-A. The Non-A puts a boundary to our intelligibility of A — which amounts to saying that to know A entails not knowing Non-A. To assume, on the other hand, that reality is absolutely intelligible leaves no room for any unintelligible reality. Non-being would be an illusion (which would give to the *vyavahārika* an illusory status in relation to the *paramārthika,* to speak in vedāntic categories). Pluralism is incompatible with any absolutism. I am not saying absolute idealism is false; I am stating that it is not warranted. It may be presupposed or posed, but it is not necessary — besides being against immediate human experience. And this is congruent with the idea of the Divine as absolute Freedom.

It may help to describe our understanding of pluralism from a history of ideas point of view.

In this context I would define culture, over against nature, as the substitution of things by objects. I take things to be ontic presence in human awareness, and objects to be ontological constructs of reflexive thinking. Nature is a world of things. Things are more or less animate. They have an *animus.* This amounts to saying that things are not only objects but also subjects. Culture, on the other hand, is a world of states of consciousness or fields of awareness. There are objects, *objecta:* "things thrown," that is put before awareness so that we are capable of thinking about them. Since Socrates in the western world and Sāmkhya in the indic scene, the *concept* has taken an upper hand over all other states of consciousness. Now, concepts are a special kind of objects. They are the rational distillate, as it were, of those states of consciousness which allow themselves to be classified as intelligible units. They do not have a life of their own, they are (valid) where they have been conceived. Concepts qua concepts need to be immutable — otherwise conceptual knowledge would be impossible. If a concept changes its meaning, by this fact it turns into a different concept — sometimes under the same name.

Culture is the cultivation of nature in order to produce an artificial universe, the world of culture. Nature and culture are intertwined. Man is a cultural animal. Its *animus* begets a universe of objects. Man needs to cultivate not only the Earth, but also itself. The human nature is a cultural one. *Cultura animi*, incidentally, is how Cicero defines philosophy. Cultivation of the *ātman* is how we could translate it for the indic spirit, and *cultura idearum* would be the socratic-platonic heritage of western philosophy. The cultivation of ideas meant cultivation of real world (and of Man in it), as long as ideas were believed to be real entities, but became the cultivation of abstract concepts once the platonic aura faded away.

Here is where pluralism fits in: in the awareness that the world of objects has no existence of its own. Objects are intellectual entities; they depend on the subject which has "put them before" our awareness. This subject is generally not an individual but a collective society in a given time and place. These intellectual constructs form a more or less complete universe, which is what we generally call the world of culture. Now, the salient feature of our present-day situation is the overwhelming predominance of a single culture. The predominant culture today is a conceptual culture of a western brand, although extended all over among the "elites" of the world. It is the particular culture which has created the world of concepts where "civilized" Man lives. In this cultural world there is place for tolerance, dialogue and condemnation, but there is no room for pluralism. Our modern world is a cultural world of concepts, but concepts, we already said, are not flexible. The intrinsic intentionality of a concept is to be univocal. We may substitute a better one, or make a conceptual distinction splitting a single concept into two, if need be. It is plain that in a conceptual culture, there is hardly place for pluralism as coexistence of cultures.

Pluralism is precisely the recognition that there may be several centers of intelligibility, that the world in which we live is not only a world of concepts but of subjects as well — and subjects cannot be co-opted into objects, much less into concepts, without ceasing to be subjects.

There is another important chapter related to pluralism which should be at least mentioned. This chapter is, of course, the founded mistrust of reason and the ambivalence of the human imagination. I have in mind, first of all, the symbolic awareness developed in the twentieth-century philosophers for instance, the *idola* of Francis Bacon, Luther's notion of reason, the critique of all systems by Condillac and the overall attacks of Nietzsche, among many others. Perhaps, after all, our reason is neither so "pure" nor so powerful. But we do not open this chapter of western thought, which would make our criticism much easier, because we defend pluralism even within the strictest assumptions of reason.

In sum, I understand by pluralism that *fundamental human attitude* which is critically aware both of the factual irreducibility (thus incompatibility) of different human systems purporting to render reality intelligible, and of the radical non-necessity of reducing reality to one single center of intelligibility, making thus unnecessary an *absolute* decision in favor of a particular human system with universal validity — or even one Supreme Being.

Saying that it is a *fundamental* attitude, I am suggesting that it does not belong to any particular conceptual construction. Saying that it is a *human* attitude implies that it is existentially human, i.e., a human praxis, and that we are conscious of it. Now, this awareness is critical and twofold. *Critical* here means reflexive and aware of its needs for foundation. *Twofold* means that this awareness is both conscious of its own perspective and of its relativity.

The critical foundation of pluralism consists in applying to itself what it criticizes in all systems: that any foundation is simply a place where we halt because we think that it does not need any further foundation. This can be only a belief which may act as a pragmatic postulate based on what I have called cosmic confidence — about which later.

Concerning the twofold awareness we may say this much. The first awareness (perspectivism) offers no major difficulty. We, from the vantage point of our particular system, detect the incompatibility between our belief-system and another one. We may hold, for instance, to the metaphysical correspondence between Thinking and Being or the cosmological belief in a Supreme Being. From these perspectives a non-univocal view of the relation between the Consciousness and Reality, or a non-monotheistic belief is incompatible with the first stance. The respective systems — each from the other viewpoint — cannot both be true. We shall stick to one and judge the other ultimately false — although we are aware that our two different metaphysical options are due to a diverse perspective on those very issues. We would look then into the ground on which one perspective appears to be more plausible than the other and either shift the discussion to that ground or recognize the relative validity of the other perspective. We touch here our second point.

The second awareness (relativity) is more complex. Let us imagine three mutually irreducible views of reality: A, B, and C. From the perspective of system B, we may see not only the falsity of systems A and C, but also their evil consequences. We shall refute those systems and, if we can, we shall also combat them with the means, which, according to our system, are truthful, ethical, and effective. Up to here there is not yet pluralism. Pluralism appears when we critically realize that our standpoint and our system cannot claim to be so absolute as to judge the others as *absolutely* untrue or evil. Pluralism struggles against absolutism not by an (equally absolute) anti-absolutism, but by relativizing all absolutisms by means of searching for their contextuality.

Roman christianity during the european Middle Ages held that islam was a false religion, and heretics more harmful to the people than "terrorists" today. The church safeguarded the intimacy of human conscience so that a bona fide muslim or a condemned heretic could still go straight to heaven (*de internis non judicat ecclesia*), but the *bonum commune* demanded they should be persecuted or punished — like the modern prison system. The Roman Church, because of its belief in the unfathomable divine transcendence, does not pronounce an absolute judgment. In this sense it has held a certain transcendent pluralism, but politically and doctrinally it was not pluralistic.

The pluralistic attitude, as I have elaborated elsewhere (1979/2; 1990a, pp. 75ff.), has its origin in human praxis, and it entails two insights: first, that our own knowledge is not absolute, and second, that the knowledge represented by systems A and C has other subjects of understanding and self-understanding so that we, from our vantage point, cannot claim to represent the totality of the situation — although, from our part, we shall oppose those systems.

Another example may clarify this point. Let us assume that I believe the capitalist system to be theoretically wrong and ethically evil. I hold a belief-system which justifies the anti-capitalist stance. I shall direct all my endeavors to dismantling the capitalist ideology, and I shall use those means which are congruent with my world view. I may believe in the power of ideas, or in the effectiveness of political pressure, or in the force of disruption, or what not.

A non-pluralistic attitude will try to uncover the anthropological and metaphysical roots of capitalism and eventually come to the conclusion, if successful, that the notion of Man and reality implied in capitalism is absolutely wrong, even if disguised by the many layers of mediations. The fight will be to the bitter end — only deterred by strategies of how to attain the best results in eliminating capitalism.

A pluralistic attitude will also fight capitalism, but it will ponder the fact that an important group of people do not share such a negative opinion — although our "hero" will denounce the obnoxious motives hidden behind the capitalist ideology. Nevertheless, our staunch anti-capitalist will recognize the fact that some people, not only in good conscience, but with for them good reason, continue to defend capitalism. The outcome will be to relativize one's own stance and yet to continue fighting capitalism. The dialogical and also dialectical dialogue are here called for, as well as a praxis changing the entrenched structures of capitalism. But the pluralist is equally aware that utterly destroying capitalism may also harm his or her own anti-capitalist stance. The struggle will go on; it could perhaps lead up to a *certain* guerrilla action or *maquis* although not to a full-fledged *guerra* (war), certainly not to an absolute crusade to crush the "evil." The pluralist will be forced to recognize (I spoke of the role of the praxis) that the capitalist system is also a "legitimate" option *in the eyes of its defenders*. This will lead to a relativization of both one's own and the other's position, making room thus for a common agonistic arena. It may lead to a shifting of one or either position, or perhaps not practically, though theoretically, the possibility remains open. Eventually, the destructive tensions may turn into creative polarities. One may not see how this is feasible, but the possibility is not excluded a priori. Pluralism does not solve the dilemma, but it prevents the reduction of reality to lemmas.

It is clear that, in this sense, pluralism cannot be a supersystem. It has nothing to do with "an underlying identity to religious diversity." There is no "fundamental pluralist insight." We cannot manipulate pluralism as a dialectical factor. We cannot rally the pluralistic folks against the non-pluralists. Larson is right. There cannot be a "theoretical pluralism," understanding theory in a restricted way different from the classical *theoria*. Pluralism is a human attitude, not a "theoretical system." As I have said time and again, it entails the acceptance of the "irreducibility of praxis to theory." The praxis presents us with unforeseen and insoluble problems, and we cannot postpone *ad kalendas graecas* the concrete decisions of our lives. Pluralism, in a way, shatters the eschatological expectations which lurk behind so many desacralized and religious behaviors: "We do not know today, but Science will solve 'it' . . . in the future"; "meanwhile I obey the Church, the scientific establishment, or follow the *status quo*."

Pluralism makes us aware of our contingency, i.e., of our limitations, and shows us how to cope with a lack of *total* security and certainty and how to live with our vulnerability. Experience begins to convince us that an escalation of defenses of all types and a proliferation of suspicion have a contrary effect. In pluralism we take our stance and risk our life.

This sociological comment leads me to a more metaphysical consideration. Thomas Dean, in his most acute critique on my notion of pluralism, asks whether by "admitting opacity into Being and Truth but not into Reason or Logos" I am not "unwittingly *perpetuating,* rather than truly *rethinking* the very concept of *logos* or reason" that I criticize.[4] I fully agree with Dean and with Heidegger whom he cites, and with so many others since Herakleitos (frgs. 12, 49, 91, etc., the famous *panta rei* in Greece, and the *Nāsadīya Sūkta* (RV X, 129) in India, that the *logos* is a dynamic force that never ceases to "unconceal" (*alēthēs*) itself in a never-ending dialectic. I take for granted that we cannot freeze the *logos,* that truth, even the "smallest" truth is always infinite and ultimately mysterious, that there is a *fluxus quo* which will never permit us to freeze anything real, that reality and the *logos* itself are open-ended as it were. But pluralism affirms more — not less — than this. It affirms more than an eschatological stance, even if the *eschaton* is "never" to come. For intrinsic coherence I do not speak of an opacity of the *logos*. *Logos* for me entails intelligibility, and the *logos* would cease to be *logos* if it were not intelligible. An unintelligible *logos, quoad se,* of course (and not *quoad nos*), would represent a contradiction in terms. But I do not subscribe to a panlogism; I am aware of the limits of the *logos*. Being, on the other hand, may have an opaque facet precisely because it remains outside the light of the *logos* — or, in christian vocabulary, because the Father, while equal to the Son (*Logos*), *is not* the Son. I do not speak of opacity of the *logos,* but I believe I have insisted enough in saying that the *logos* is not the whole Man.

We can, of course, maintain that pluralism is wrong and give reasons for it. The reasons will amount to saying that "our" system, or basic-mini-system, is true and thus any other different explanation must be short of the truth.

---

4. *Toward a Universal Theology of Religion,* ed. L. Swidler (Maryknoll, N.Y.: Orbis Books, 1987), p. 171.

I have said "basic-mini-system" in order to make room for the most common objection against pluralism, namely that there are some underlying principles which are common to all because they belong to human nature. They form the basic-mini-system, the human core which defies pluralism: "Don't kill your father," "Two and two are four," "We all want to eat...."

This brings me again to the point regarding myth: any basic-system is valid only within a particular myth. It is the prevalent myth at a certain period or place, but the myth is not universal. We all know that there have been civilizations which considered it necessary and merciful to kill the father-figure of the king, and there have been other peoples which have not accepted the translatability into numerical figures of any real thing, so that two houses are not only unequal to two pigs but also to two other houses. The basic-system is accepted only within a certain myth, even if we call it the degree of evolution of human consciousness or simply progress. We know well that progress is a myth not shared by all. We all want to eat, up to the point that this wish does not interfere with our religious (jaina) *samlekhana* (ritual progressive fasting unto death), our political agitation, our recovery of health or what not.

Human invariants should not be confounded with "cultural universals." The former exist (everybody speaks, eats, sleeps, rejoices...). The latter do not (every culture speaks *a* language and has a specific understanding of the meaning of eating, sleeping, rejoicing...).

To be sure, there is a "transcendental relationship" between the human invariants and the cultural universals. This means that we cannot speak of the former without the language of the latter, i.e., outside a particular language. In other words, the (universal) human invariant is a formal concept — meaningful only in a particular material concept belonging already to one culture (or group of them).

In *The Journal of Religious Pluralism,* Richard P. Hayes takes pluralism "to signify not the mere acknowledgement that there is a variety but the celebration of this variety... the attitude that variety is health and therefore something to be desired" (1991/I, 1, p. 65). And he convincingly argues that neither Buddha nor buddhism is pluralist. I agree with this latter affirmation.

But his prior sentence does not fully represent my notion of pluralism. I do not consider pluralism an ideology, as Hayes does (pp. 93–95), and Larson affirms.

Let us take a cue from this formulation and repeat that, for me, pluralism is neither *necessarily* the celebration of variety nor *always* to be desired. It may be so sometimes, specially when confronted with exclusivist and fanatical or narrow-minded approaches, but in general it is a scandal to human thought, a challenge to human intelligence and a thorn to any culture. Pluralism is rather the acknowledgement of our contingency, of our limitation, of our inability to handle problems as we would like. It is the often painful but possibly cathartic revelation (if the word is permitted without fundamentalist underpinnings) of the other, who is unassimilable to us. And yet the other may be wrong, evil, an obstacle for consensus or for any sensible progress. But who is going to deny that this is precisely the actual human condition?

Let me be precise: First, no single religion as such can be pluralistic. Religions can (and I add, should) be open, tolerant, not absolutistic, but each religion has a set of beliefs, practices, rules which may be different and even contradictory to the corresponding features of another religion. Pluralism has nothing to do with a superficially conciliatory eclecticism.

Second, no single philosophy as such can be pluralistic either. The moment we formulate whatsoever, we do it claiming truth, in a language and within a framework which is our context. And even if we claim universality this is *our claim,* which is not identical with an actual universality.

Third, pluralism is not a supersystem, a meta-language, a referee in the human disputes, an intellectual panacea. Pluralism is an open, human attitude, which therefore entails an intellectual dimension that overcomes any kind of solipsism, as if we — any we — were alone in the universe, the masters of it, the holders of the Absolute.

As I wrote more than twenty years ago, while we can understand plurality (it is simply a fact), we cannot coherently understand pluralism (as a system). A pluralistic system would be an ideology in the pejorative sense of the word, a procrustean bed into which we fit contradictory diversities just to serve our purposes, a supersystem artificially concocted to dominate a given situation. In this sense, I am "contra pluralism." For decades I have lived with universalistic roman catholics and inclusivistic vedāntins. As I have argued — sometimes exciting the *furor theologicus* of "orthodox" hindus and catholics — the famous simile of the elephant in a dark room (identified diversely as a pillar, an ivory piece, etc.) is the most blatant example of an anti-pluralistic attitude; all the others are partial, all say some truth, but only I (we) know the whole elephant. Authentic pluralists know that they do not know the elephant either, and, based on the testimony of the others, doubt that anybody knows the elephant. They assume further that the "elephant" which vedāntins, catholics, skeptics, philosophers, and so forth claim to know may well be either an empty concept or another part of a still more complete living Being.

Finally, in this objective sense I am not pluralist; nobody is a pluralist. My opinions, beliefs, philosophy, or religion are as limited, vulnerable, debatable and subjected to critique as any other. I am not saying that there are not people claiming to know the whole elephant, or that they are wrong. I am saying that they are not pluralists.

Methodological Remarks

My point here is that pluralism is an attitude the study of which obviously elicits a peculiar method; this method is the dialogical dialogue, as I have described several times. It does not preclude criticism and refutation. It only precludes blank condemnation, absolute verdicts, total break of communication, demand of unconditional surrender. It does not exclude the dialectical approach, but it is not reducible to it.

In the preceding section we have been unearthing the metaphysical implication of pluralism. We can always look for a metaphysical "foundation" of any human act. But pluralism, as an attitude, has a kind of free-wheeling value which makes it useful as a method, even while subscribing to other metaphysical assumptions. It is the method of peaceful approach, dialogical dialogue, two-way learning, mutual respect, and the like. It prevents us from fanaticisms of all sorts.

Pluralism entails a method, but it does not offer an alternative to the existing systems. To the hypothesis of the "universal theology of religion" the pluralistic critique does not consist in offering a "pluralistic theology of religion" but criticizing the absolute claims of any given "universal theology of religion." There is no "pluralistic theology of religion." This is a statement of fact. There are diverse theologies of religion and also other homeomorphic equivalents. This does not mean that any theology of religion should not attempt to cover the widest possible range of data and interpretations, not claim validity and not present itself as having a relative universality. It means that any such "theology of religion" is conscious of the radical relativity of its assumptions and starting points, beginning with the limitations of the words *theology* and *religion.*

I pay attention to methodology, because we need a multiperspectival and crosscultural approach to world problems. This is, for me, urgent, important — and obvious. What the pluralistic attitude does is to prevent, with intrinsic reasons, any method or set of methods from declaring itself sufficient to approach a problem. Here we touch questions of praxis of immense relevance. Peace and conflict-resolution demand such a pluralistic attitude — and I refrain now from elaborating further (see 1989/2; 1993e).

Dialogical Response

The preceding pages might have clarified my position and perhaps dispelled some misunderstandings. I have the task now to address myself to the thoughtful chapter of Gerald Larson. I begin with a sense of gratitude and, startlingly enough, of fellowship in the same struggle for what the greeks called *akribia,* which Hegel might have translated as "Anstrengung des Begriffs" (as he called philosophy). I have, in fact, the feeling that Larson is fighting a different pluralism, so that we might have a purely semantic discrepancy. Nevertheless, for the sake of further clarification, I may try to respond.

I am happy to have elicited Larson's brilliant critique. I shall attempt here what I have called the dialogical dialogue. It may very well be that Larson sees more than I am capable of seeing in my defense of pluralism. I sense he fears I may end by condoning evil, tampering with truth, and falling into relativism; that I may be incapable of taking a stance, and amorphous enough as to put up with everything, contributing thus in a nefarious way to present-day disorientation in theory and praxis, in religion and politics, in life in general.

To reassert that this is not my intention is obvious for me. I have, nevertheless, to re-examine whether or not my position leads to what Larson and I abhor. We have then already a point of convergence. A second point of agreement is that neither of us would like to abandon rationality and fall into irrationalism.

To begin with, being coherent with a pluralistic attitude, I have to say that I agree with him that "there is no such thing as a theoretical pluralist position." It would be a contradiction in terms. I did write something similar when criticizing Nāgārjuna's Mādhyamika as interpreted by T. R. V. Murti (1996/2).

However, the negation of theoretical pluralism is not synonymous with the statement that pluralism, as I have described it, has no philosophical basis or that it cannot be defended philosophically — where, of course, the notion of philosophy is not restricted to rationalism.

Larson links pluralism with "a literally mindless ideology" of a decadent moment in world history "at which it is increasingly obvious that theoretical and practical Marxism is bankrupt" and no other moment is in view. Pluralism makes "a virtue out of a necessity." Two comments are in place here, one positive and one negative.

To make a virtue out of a necessity is the most realistic attitude, probably the most humane and certainly one of the pivots of a critical sociology of knowledge. We do not live in utopia, we do not philosophize *in vacuo,* we do not think outside of and independent from our factual situation. It is certainly true that pluralism, right or wrong, is the cry of the hour, the need of the day. It is praxis that triggers theory, which subsequently conditions praxis. Our discourse would have been impossible at the high pitch of the european Enlightenment a couple of centuries ago. Colonialism, which I have defined as the belief in the monophormism of culture, would not allow any talk about pluralism. But it is interesting and revealing that Larson quotes disapprovingly this ancient proverb, as if virtue would fall directly from heaven. To make a virtue out of necessity is not necessarily a vice.

The negative comment is the following. I have a different reading of the world situation and would be not overly obsessed with the allegedly last gasps of marxism and thus interpret the mainly political phenomena of our times as the failure of the pluralisms of the left and of the right. At any rate, my notion of pluralism does not marginalize "intellectual life." On the contrary, it may offer something, and something very critical at that, regarding the Gulf War and the "New World Order," for instance. It may give the nerve to resist the bulldozing of the mind and triumphalistic attitudes of supposedly well-intentioned attempts at establishing an earthly paradise on a global basis. Unless we take a pluralistic attitude as we intellectually analyze the political problems of the world, we face the danger of becoming either mere lackeys of the present system or angry contestants of the status quo without any possible dialogue except radical contestation tamed only by sheer impotency of effecting any change.

The shortest philosophical formulation of the pluralistic attitude would probably be the statement that the very nature of truth is pluralistic (1990/7). But pluralism would never affirm that truth is plural. The interplay between *mythos* and *logos* is present in all our intellectual enterprise. Some forty years ago I wrote an essay which was the fruit of my personal religious experience: truth cannot be a merely "essential" aspect of reality. It has an existential character also (1956/1). Simplifying and cutting through the jungle of present and past discussions on the nature of truth, I would come to the following summary: *truth is self-identity.* This purports to be, of course, a phenomenological statement. The ontological statement would be: *truth is the manifestation of that self-identity.* And the epistemological statement would affirm that *truth is the intellectual formulation of that same self-identity.* This was an ancient tradition still clearly echoed by Comenius when saying that "truth is the link (*vinculum*) of beings" (*Janua rerum* XIV, 9). It can only be the bond of a thing with itself, its self-identity. The sanskrit expression for truth (if we translate it this way, says clearly that truth is the very "beingness" of the thing: *satyam,* real, actual, true. Untruth, on the other hand, is not "unbeing" or "unbeingness," but disorder: *anṛtam* (falsehood), which is *anṛtu* (out of season). Untruth is something contrary to the cosmic order (*ṛta*), disturbing the harmony of reality.

We should avoid the confusion between reality and conceptual scaffolding. The statement that truth itself is pluralistic does not mean at all that truth is plural. There are not many truths. This would be a contradiction *in adjecto.* Similarly, truth is not one either. Either this is a barren tautology (truth is truth), or a dogmatic position (truth is one) postulating that a being can only manifest itself in one and the same way. We may notice again the captivity of Being under the power of Thinking. The statement that truth is pluralistic means that the self-identity of each and every being is precisely self-identity because it is irreducible to any alterity. Truth is not an *aliud* of the thing but its own *idipsum.* The truth of every being makes its uniqueness, and thus its dignity. It cannot be replaced by anything else, it cannot be treated as a means for something alien — or alienating.

Saying this, am I not trying to avoid a freezing objectification and conceptualization of truth by falling into the opposite extreme of making truth a sheer subjective notion? It would seem so if the preceding paragraph were understood as coming from individualistic premises. Truth is never *my* truth. Truth is always a relation in which the subject is involved, but of which the subject is not the boss. Truth is neither merely objective nor purely subjective. Truth takes us from the domination of the one or the other, the object or the subject. Truth is an objective and subjective *agreement* (where the sanskrit *gūrtas* [*gūrtiḥ*] and the latin *gratus* open up a world of *grace* and *celebration*).

Truth is not objectifiable either. We cannot speak of truth drawing its meaning on a blackboard. When the scholastics, for instance, defended the proposition that truth lies in the statement, they were defending it in a non-nominalistic world. Statements were more than simple algebraic equations. The direct link to things was not broken. Statements were ontologically laden and not merely nominal sentences. "Each thing refers to each being in the same way that it refers to its truth" we could thus render those intriguing words of Aristotle: *ekastou hōs eusei tou einai houtō kai tēs alētheias* (*Met.* II, 1, 993 b 30).

Larson is right in detecting the importance of the question of pluralism. Pluralism is an ultimate attitude and thus, it is not self-defeating as any formulation of relativism (which is not to be equated with relativity), but certainly self-referential, relativistically self-referential, like all ultimate issues are: being is being, A is A, reason is reasonable, evidence is self-proving, etc. Here lies its importance, that it enlarges and deepens the principles on which human coexistence may thrive (1962/1).

I have now to react to a double question. Is there place for error? What is the criterion for falsehood?

The first question is common to pluralistic and non-pluralistic attitudes. There is certainly a place for error. When the self-identity is denied, stifled, deformed, broken, be it existentially, be it thwarted in its manifestation or formulation, there is error. Many religious and philosophical traditions have related error and sin, *avidyā* and bondage, ignorance and damnation, etc. We have already mentioned that *anṛta,* the absence of *ṛta* (order, cosmic harmony), is one of the sanskrit words for error. Human freedom would have but little meaning without this capacity of forging one's own way and the possibility of failing to do it. I agree that there can be no privileged [pluralist] position. Any position is a concrete stance standing somewhere and saying some particular thing which in no way has an exceptional status. Within our system of thought, culture, religion, philosophy we have definite convictions which allow us to brand something as error and/or evil. Pluralism is not blind to error or evil, but it does not absolutize any position.

The second question, regarding the criteria for discriminating truth from falsehood, is where the pluralistic attitude takes a relativistic stance against other positions which accept some kind of absolute norms or criteria.

In order to be brief I give two examples, one logical and the other ethical.

Is the principle of non-contradiction not an absolute criterion for truth? Without indulging now in logical subtleties I shall say only this much. To begin with, non-contradiction is only a negative and not a positive criterion. Anything which goes against the principle of non-contradiction cannot be correct; but truth is not measured by this principle. "Christopher Columbus did not sail to what we now call America" is not true and not contradictory. The particle and wave theories of matter are contradictory (*qua hypotheses*) and yet fulfill on an equal (though imperfect) basis the condition of physico-mathematical adequacy. But we cannot limit the case to such "truisms." As the very name of the principle indicates, it is a principle of non-contradiction, i.e., of diction, of saying, of language. We mean language as meaningful language, as utterances which say something about reality. Some saying and its contra-*dictory* cannot be said in truth. We grant the validity of this principle where it belongs: language. But from language to reality there is a jump. Relativity still holds. Here it is the relativity of language. In sum, we have negative truth-criteria for language (the non-contra-dictory), but not for Being.

We also have ethical criteria, but they are not absolute. Each culture segregates its own criteria — and discusses them, often hotly. Let us recall the present issues of divorce, abortion, death penalty, war, capitalism and the like.

I, for one, unambiguously condemn the dropping of the atomic bombs, the nazi holocaust and the hunting of africans to bring them as slaves to America, but I meet many people whom I respect who defend similar practices as a lesser evil (Kurdistan, Rwanda, the Persian Gulf, etc.). I cannot condone slavery as an institution, and yet we have to acknowledge that for centuries "good people," including politicians, thinkers, and saints, practically approved of slavery and defended the existence of outcasts. Cannibalism and human sacrifice may be other extreme cases. The condemnation of these examples belongs today to the common myth of our humanness. But not too long ago people whom we would call humans and even humane practiced those horrendous acts. In our times, I would include war as an example of an institution which has not (yet?) found a common mythical rejection.

At a certain moment in space and time we may share some common myth which allows for some common criteria. We all condemn nazism and stalin-ism — I suppose. But we live in diachronic moments also. I have already given the controversial issues of war and capitalism. We have to take cognizance of the fact that our human criteria do not coalesce. I shall not abandon my criteria, and according to them I shall struggle against what I consider harmful, inhuman, wrong, evil. But I shall not extrapolate and absolutize my criteria. The theory of *svadharma,* besides possible and actual abuses, could be a hint of pluralism.

The difficulty arises when we have to cross cultural boundaries, and have first to work out the criteria which will allow us to make judgments without imposing our ethical notions on others.

Christophany

The chapters by Carney, Sheridan, D'Sa and Lanzetta directly touch upon the christological problem, although Podgorski, Knitter and Cousins relate also to it (1972/2). I feel that I am questioned about my identity and my convictions, and for this reason I shall adopt an almost autobiographical stance. It is more a confession than an elaborate response. It is a conversation with friends.

The Question of Identity

I have stressed time and again that identity has been taken to mean what differentiates a thing from another, *singularity,* or what identifies a thing with itself, disregarding differences, *individuality* (1964, pp. 39–41; 1975/7).

When I am asked about my religious identity I am asked about my beliefs. Belief is neither an artificial superstructure nor magic. A believer is not a blind follower of somebody or some idea, but a person who has become aware of the transcendental relation between one's own being and the conscious life one lives. I say, on purpose, "life" and not "ideas," because for me belief involves praxis as much as theory. And when I speak of orthopraxis and orthodoxy I in-clude in this "ortho" the critical awareness that both theory and praxis flow from the very core of our being. I do not share the conviction that theory is the cause of praxis or praxis the cause of theory. Both belong together in a non-dualistic manner. There is not the one without the other. The ancients knew it when they called prudence the highest virtue, because it unites, in an unbroken harmony, theory and praxis. Prudence is insightful action and practical knowledge.

Belief is not a superimposition, an *adhyāsa,* but the human translation of faith, and, thus, translation in both theory and praxis. Belief has an intellectual dimension and a practical side. Faith, on the other hand, is that constitutive human dimension which is expressed in belief and reenacted in the act of faith.

The relation between faith and belief is a transcendental relation. Naked faith, as it were, unexpressed faith, unconscious faith may have potential existence, but it does not actually exist. Faith is active, it is a power, it is probably the most genuinely human dimension. This faith exists and acts; it manifests itself and is effective when it becomes actualized in one particular form or another, when it is expressed, translated, made effective in a concrete way. It is the so-called act of faith which, according to most religious traditions, has saving power. One aspect of this act is its intellectual manifestation. Man is an intellectual being and in a special way a rational creature. Belief entails this human way of expressing one's faith. The relation is transcendental in this sense. There is no faith without belief and no belief without faith lurking behind, as it were. We cannot separate the two. But we must distinguish them. Faith is not a "thing in itself" which appears in belief. Faith is not a transcendent substance or a separate entity above and beyond. Faith is transcendental to belief.

Man "has" faith in a similar way as Man is endowed with reason and feelings. Any human act entails normally a more or less implicit actualization of faith, reason and feelings. We act because we believe something, have a certain reason for it and feel something in doing it. Religious beliefs are ultimate beliefs concerning ourselves and/or life, reality — in whatever name we may couch this sense of ultimacy.

Christian identity: christianness. As intellectual beings born in a particular culture in time and space we are given the language in which to articulate those beliefs which we may purify, criticize and change all our lives. One of these matrices is the broadly called christian tradition.

In this sense I confess and recognize myself a christian. I understand this affirmation neither as a mere label that I can put on and off nor as an uncritical and irrevocable identification between my being and my christian confession. There is a *via media* between being a dilettante and a fanatic.

I confess myself a christian because I recognize my personal identity as belonging to a human historical tradition which calls itself christian (1991/8). I am not an isolated gnostic. My *ecclesia* is the christian one. It is an existential belonging which does not exclude, but precisely demands, a personal intellectual assimilation, an interpretation and critique, of this appurtenance. I should say that I follow the traditional understanding of church as *Mysterion Kosmikon ecclesia ab Abel, corpus Christi mysticum,* and not mainly, and, much less, exclusively, as an organization. This allows me to accept the traditional christian belief that "outside the church there is no salvation," because this is the meaning of church, and the visible christian *ecclesia* only a concrete form of this cosmic communion of the entire universe (1963b, pp. 63–77) outside which there is no salvation. This is a qualified tautology indeed. I would carefully distinguish between religion and sect.

I am a christian, i.e., I confess myself a christian as I recognize myself a man of the twentieth century belonging to the indo-european cultural stem. I do not identify myself exhaustively with my chronological and ethnic background. I, for one, strive to overcome many limitations endowed with this historical phylum, but I cannot deny those facts. I have seen and "suffered" too many westerners wanting to "become" hindus and ending by being either artificially uprooted or still christians in spite of themselves. We cannot deny upbringing, history, archetypes, *karma* — and yet we may want to, or even should, transcend all those factors. But overcoming is not synonymous with repression or denial.

Some may think that this is a very "hindu" idea of what it is to be a christian. It may or it may not be, but I do not feel the need to apologize, nor does this fact prove that it is a wrong notion or even an unchristian one.

Indeed, if I declare myself a christian it is because my belief tallies with what I believe to be the core of the christian belief and I recognize myself in communion with the christian church. Communion does not mean for me party discipline, blind fellowship, or uncritical agreement with the general policies of a particular official church in a given period of time or chunk of space. Religious affiliation, I submit, is neither accidental membership in a club nor biological belonging to a particular clan. It is the recognition of a *sui-generis* existing bond whose specificity does not need now to be spelled out. And having said affiliation I may recall that there are many mansions in the Father's house. My distinction of christianness from christendom and christianity goes in the same direction (1992/3).

How far my theological writings fall into the christian present-day orthodoxy is not for me to judge. My concern is with truth and truthfulness. I am always open to correction. I would like to say only this much: First, that unless one excommunicates oneself willingly no power on earth can sever us from the divine love which is in Christ, to quote St. Paul (*Rom.* 8:38–39). Second, that we should not fall into the modern rationalistic trap of cartesian origin, of identifying religion with mere doctrine, although the relationship is an intimate one. Doctrine is a form of intellectual communication, and doctrines are important, but they are not the only thing, either in religion or in Man. I do not identify myself with a *res cogitans. Cogitatio quasi coagitatio* knew the scholastics, which Monsieur Descartes probably forgot. This leads me to my second confession.

Hindu identity. I would probably not assert so unambiguously my christian identity if I would not as well confess myself a hindu. I accept what I believe to be my hindu *karma,* and I acknowledge my hindu *dharma.* Both are existential facts that I neither rebuke nor repress. They form part of my being as much as one's parents are "parts" of oneself. We are what we are, although in this *are* our will and our intellect play an important, but not exclusive, role. We are not just what we want to be, or what we think we are. Our reality is more powerful than both our will and our intellect, although we are also the fruit of our own construction. We are cocreators of our being, but our demiurgical activity is that of shaping ourselves out of given materials and also with lent instruments.

I am saying, of course, that I am a person (a knot in a net of relationships) and not a mere individual internally severed from the rest of the universe. My personhood is not an isolated "me." Many of the theological and philosophical difficulties of the modern mind would fade away if we would overcome the modern western myth of individualism. Our roots also belong to us, and *karma* (history) is also part of our being.

If I am a hindu it is not, of course, a matter of sheer choice, or mere will, sympathy and/or intellectual agreement — as if it all were an individualistic affair. It is simply an existential reality which I freely accept, having broken christian prejudices of exclusivisms and inclusivisms. This implies, of course, a personal experience and a constant preoccupation with acquiring the wisdom of the tradition one comes from. Many hindu intellectuals have said that only a "reincarnated" *rishi* could have written the *Mantramañjarī*.

Indeed it is less problematic to confess myself a hindu than a christian, because the hindu tradition emphasizes the existential aspect of belonging, whereas the christian tradition emphasizes the essential aspect of orthodoxy (1969/3, pp. 436–41). There are no specifically declared hindu doctrines. Yet belonging is not a matter of choice or sympathy either. One needs a *sampradāya,* so to say. Belonging is an existential fact. The *sanātana dharma* and the *ecclesia ab Abel* are homeomorphic equivalents. Both notions acknowledge the belonging to a cosmic order.

Two sub-identities. I do not need to go on with personal confessions. I am also a buddhist and a secularist at heart, as I have often said.

I call these two belongings sub-identities for personal and philosophical reasons. Personally I have discovered secularity after having experienced to the full, I would dare say, the most severe roman catholic tradition. And I have discovered buddhism also after having plunged into the most strict vedāntic orthodoxy.

The philosophical reason also should be patent. We have here, curiously enough, a case for the correspondence between phylogenesis and ontogenesis. In fact, modern secularity, although very different from the ideology of secularism and the historical events of the western secularization, is related to those other movements. This very fact could partly explain why in modern India secularity is often called secularism — although the Constitution of the country only uses the word "secular." Praxis and theory also are intermingled here. Contemporary secularity, standing for the definitive character of the spatio-temporal, i.e., material structures of reality, can be fully grasped — and in fact this awareness has clearly emerged — after the two mentioned phenomena. In the dialectic between the sacred and the profane, and mediating between the two extremes of an all-swallowing sacredness and an equally all-bulldozing secularism, stands as a middle way the insight of secularity. I call it *Sacred Secularity,* which is also the title of one of my forthcoming books.

Similarly, buddhism did not come out of the blue in a no-man's land. It was the understandable reaction to a brahmanic and world-denying spirituality which the Buddha overcame with his Middle Way. Not without reason buddhism began as a monastic movement, a *sangha* which acted as a leaven outside India and was reabsorbed in its land of origin — historical factors and needed qualifications notwithstanding.

In a word, my christian identity has led me to understand and accept what I call secularity. And my hindu identity has equally conduced me to the *anātman* insight, or rather to the "non-experience" of the *anātmavāda* — without specifying it further now.

The Harmonic Quaternitas

Lived life has led me to this *quaternitas* without a split in my being, i.e., without destroying a dimensionless center. We should not experiment with religions (1975/6). We should experience rather their power and accept their gift — which like our destiny may not always be a pleasant one. One may burn one's own passport (a novel invention) because of the crimes of the country, but one still remains a german, a north american, a japanese or a spaniard. Religious affiliation, I repeat, is neither a matter of *mere* choice nor of brute fact. No jewish mother, hindu father, christian baptism, muslim birth or any merely objective fact makes me a real jew, hindu, christian, muslim or whatever. These facts may be necessary conditions, but they are not sufficient ones if religion is to be less than a genetic fact and more than a social feature. But neither mere will, mere sympathy nor intellectual empathy makes me a member of those religious traditions. I am enamored of islamic sufism. This does not make me a muslim. There is a *via media* which constitutes the deepest aspect of human identity, which is religious identity. This required an entire theological reflection on the nature of sacraments or samskāras, which are neither magical imprints incorporated into one's being nor merely accidental qualities depending one one's whims. The traditional beliefs of *karma* (*karmasaṁgraha*), *buddhakāya,* "mystical body of Christ," and the like are all notions which indicate a blending between a subjective and an objective participation in a religious body.

On the other hand, in order to avoid a split personality, a certain symbiosis is indispensable. The synthesis or rather harmony, is:

 i) risky but simple on the existential level,

 ii) complicated on the speculative level, and

 iii) difficult but possible on the intercultural level.

Existential level. On the existential level it is risky, because it demands a spiritual temperature (*tapas*) to harmonize divergent attitudes so as not to turn schizophrenic; it requires a fidelity to one's own authenticity, which is not exempt from dangers. I am reminded of the spirituality of swimming against the current (*ūrdhvaṁsrotas*) as the Dhammapāda puts it (*uddhaṁsoto:* XVI, 10). Whoever will reach the Source has to swim against the current, echoes chinese wisdom. Only living fish swim upstream. If you seem to owe allegiances to more than one country, academia, church, institution or "trade union" (of any sort), you may lose your job or be considered an unreliable person; you are not tenured anywhere, if you display too many flags. Even nonmilitary establishments often demand exclusive loyalty.

On the other hand, it is simpler than it may appear from the outside, since the only thing one needs is a kind of critical but passive fidelity to one's deeper self, to the *ātman* or to the Holy Spirit. Religious identity, I repeat, is not party membership (a part of a whole), but fidelity to the wholeness of one's being, which is at the same time related to the Whole. I may add here that it all is of a feminine simplicity of accepting life as a gift, facts as revelation and events as challenges. You do not need to choose, but you have to purify your heart (1993e).

Speculative level. On the speculative level the task is complicated. Cultures and religions, let alone countries and institutions, usually have grown and developed caring jealously for their own identity by differentiation.

Either/or is a common frame of mind. But the complexity is intrinsic because no amount of good will or existential sympathy may eliminate the strictures of thinking and the rights of the principle of non-contradiction on which is based the choice of "either/or" between two contradictory statements.

But the task is imperative. If religious traditions continue ignoring and often misrepresenting each other, when not playing dirty games, there will be no peace on earth. Religious harmony does not mean monolithic unity.

A christian interpretation of hinduism and a hindu interpretation of christianity may be preliminary steps toward a mutual fecundation which may yield a hindu-christian theology — to utilize an expression which I now find inadequate. I have tried to do both, fully aware that those were only preliminary steps (1963d; 1967a; 1970/2). I have even made an effort at a manifesto for a hindu-christian theology (1979/1).

Intercultural level. On the intercultural level the difficulties compound. I may repeat here the powerful metaphor of language. We may speak several languages. We learn a second language more or less translating mentally from the first. The first remains the obliged point of reference. But we can also acquire connaturality with more than one language so that we no longer translate from the mother tongue. We think and experience the world in that other language also. Translation is no longer needed. On the contrary, we begin to be critical of translations, precisely because we live naturally in two universes of discourse.

Saying that each religion, or rather each religious tradition, is a language, is more than a metaphor. We affirm that each religion is a new language. But this affirmation should be understood without subscribing to three main "myths" of modernity: a diffused platonism, a crypto-kantianism and a nominalistic idea of language. We do not need to assume that the ideal world has an independent and stronger existence than our sublunar beings. We do not need to subscribe to the opinion that there is a "thing in itself" of which language or religion are but manifestations or appearances. Nor do we need to understand the languages as just different linguistic codes saying the same thing. Languages are not diverse *phenomena* of the same *noumenon;* they are not *mere* instruments for passing information.

This is the crux of interculturality. To cross cultural and religious boundaries in our age of passports and competition is indeed dangerous and imperative, difficult but not impossible. The problems are not only of a purely intellectual character. They are also of a political nature and depend upon economic factors and psychological reactions. We cannot abolish history overnight with its aftereffects of colonialism, exploitation, mistrust, deceit and fights from all sides. Religions are more than intellectual constructs.

A look at the last fifty years may astonish us with the results achieved. In spite of understandable counterreactions, "ecumenical ecumenism" is in the air and a sizeable part of the religious traditions have abandoned exclusivisms and intolerances and are open to dialogue. I may give an example.

A Kenotic Christology

I have been asked time and again to clarify my position regarding the very title of one of my books: *The Unknown Christ of Hinduism.* I shall comment upon it as an example of the need and difficulty of crosscultural dialogue. My study did not refer to the known Christ of christians or to any "Christ in itself" of which christians know one aspect and hindus another aspect under another name — paraphrasing the already mentioned simile of the elephant. Nor is there an "ideal Christ" in any gnostic fashion. As Sheridan rightly points out, the language and discourse of that book was a christian one, and attempted to explain to christians some hindu intuitions.

What does it mean? It means this. Each religious tradition has a claim to a potential fullness. Now, this claim should not be confused with a claim to universality. "Completeness," incidentally, is the first meaning of the word *catholic* which has been interpreted as geographical universality only by the expansive european spirit. Religions are projects of *salvation* — using this word as standing for the goal of Man's life in whatever sense. Each religion is a project to help, enlighten, transform... the concrete person for the fulfillment of human life. Each religion aspires to the whole as a whole and not to one of its parts. The whole of man means human salvation, as the very etymologies of the two words already indicate (whole, health, *salus, salvus, sarvam*). This whole is nevertheless "contained" in a reflection, image, mirror of reality. It is again the *pars pro toto effect.* The *totum* is *in parte,* but the *totum* as an image, is whole in the small and in the greater mirror.

Let us reenact the christian plea as I would make it: If I am a christian and have found in Christ the central symbol of my existence (giving to the word symbol its full meaning) I am not satisfied with being partial, having just my part of the cake and simply acknowledging that others are happy with other parts, as a stray is happy with a second bone I throw to it so that it may not quarrel with my own dog. A christian (*pace* John's Gospel, Corinthians, Ephesians, Colossians, and even Romans) believes he or she has access to the *Logos,* the Firstborn, the Alpha and Omega, the light of the entire universe created and uncreated. And christian tradition calls this symbol with a name which seems to be the bone of discordance: a common name, the *anointed,* which is a powerful jewish symbol, the *Māshīaḥ (Māshūaḥ),* and became a proper name in the hellenized form: *Christos.* This *Christ* was identified with important (trinitarian) qualifications with God on the one hand (Son of God), and with no less important (incarnational) qualifications with Jesus (Son of Man) on the other hand. This is the central symbol of the christian tradition — a myriad of interpretations notwithstanding. In this Christ lie all the treasures of the fathomable Godhead, to quote St. Paul again. Seeing him one sees the Father, "fons et origo totius divinitatis," as the Councils of Toledo in the spirit of Nicea and Chalcedon described the silent Mystery of the Father (to use Irenaeus's phrase).

At the same time, I am fully convinced that neither my ego, nor all christians nor even all my fellow human beings are ever going to exhaust the knowledge of such a Mystery. I discover at the same time that there are other people, other world views, other religions (other windows). I may not even be able to formulate how they experience reality, ignoring the parameters into which they fit their respective experiences. I cannot say that they affirm, in different words, the "same thing" I do. I often do not even comprehend their talk. Sometimes I cannot say even that they are at logger-heads with my ideas. I am not saying anything about their beliefs, much less about what they should believe. I do not have the knowledge, and certainly not the authority. Although Jahweh tells me to slaughter the moabites or the amalekites I shall react as Śaṅkara, who, believing in the absoluteness of the Vedas, wrote he would not believe that the fire does not burn even if a thousand Vedas would say it.

In that book I only said that "the Unknown Christ" is the way the christian will react when hearing about other religions, hinduism in this case. The christian cannot but believe (as the buddhists have also said with the same words and practically all religions in similar ways) that all that has been said about truth, goodness and beauty are aspects of the Mystery which each tradition calls by its own name and the christian calls Christ.

There is a perverted reading of this sentence, and history shows the havoc produced by it: the inversion of subject and predicate and the freezing substantialization of the subject. The sentence does not say that christianity is the whole truth, goodness and beauty. This would be the perversion of the order of the things and of christianity. The sentence says that the word *christian* stands for goodness, truth and beauty whatever they may be. The sentence should not be interpreted as saying that Christ, my Christ — much less Jesus of Nazareth — has the monopoly of truth. It says, on the contrary, that truth, whatever (ultimate) truth, whatever (ultimate) value, is Christ — certainly an Unknown Christ: the Mystery (which the christians may say is the mystery of Christ). The christians will use this word *Christ,* because it is a christian word, but cannot say that this is the word the hindu should use, nor even that both are speaking about the same "thing." The "Mystery" is not a "thing." The discussion about "things" belongs to a different level.

I insist, "the Unknown Christ" is not an "idea" or a "thing in itself," which christians call Christ. There is no co-opting others into the christian language. To say "Unknown Christ" may be the best form the christian is able to interpret, inasmuch as this is possible, the nature of other religions. It is a specifically christian language, which stands precisely for the validity and truth of other religions — leaving aside the possible perversions of religion. And if a translation is needed then it would be erroneous to assume that Christ here means Krishna, *sakti* or Īśvara, as if these names were the names hindus give to the *christian* Christ. These names which refer to the Ultimate (Mystery) — and no name is neutral — may or may not tally with the contents the christian ascribes to the name of Christ.

The common difficulty in understanding the title of that book, I assume, is both practical and theoretical. *Practical,* because so many crimes have been committed in the name of Christ — and God even more — that many people are allergic to this name. One should respect feelings, but at the same time use discernment. Not every german is a nazi, every jew a fanatic, every muslim intolerant, every north american an imperialist. . . . *Theoretical,* because of both the unqualified identification of Christ with Jesus of Nazareth and the substantialization of Christ as a "thing in itself." The christian recognizes Christ (the Mystery) *in* and *through* Jesus, but Christ (the risen Jesus for the christian) is not identical with Jesus. We have here once again the confusion between mathematics and reality, the "formal" with the "material" concept. If A=B, B=A, but this formalism is not to be confused with the actual nature of reality. The substantialization of Christ is the other theoretical difficulty. The symbol *Christ* does not denote an anthropomorphic individual. In the Eucharist, the christian believes, there is the real presence of Christ, which obviously does not mean that Holy Communion amounts to chewing the proteins of Jesus, the son of Mary, nor to eating another individual called Christ. And this may be more than enough to clarify my position.

My mirror reflects the whole, and from my mirror I call Christ the whole, since I cannot renounce the wholeness of my being and my vision of reality. But it is not by looking through my window that I am going to know what the whole looks like seen through another window. From my window I will have to speak of an Unknown — and because my name for this mystery is Christ, I will call it Unknown Christ. In a word, Christ is the christian name for the Unknown — to whom, incidentally, the book was dedicated.

But one should immediately add that this is a christian, and a particular christian, way of expressing a vision which may have other homomorphic equivalents in other traditions.

What else could I attempt here than a timid approach to a non-compelling "theology"? Should I recall Diderot's phrase in his *Oeuvres esthétiques* that any creative person "seduces rather than guides"? How could I not defend nonviolence and not chastise the use of reason as a weapon? (1996/4). How could I not dedicate myself more to the complex problems of the *jñānavādins* and take perhaps too much for granted the *bhaktimārga?* I felt I should take the bull by the horns and not skip the symbol Christ, taking refuge in God, the Divine, the Spirit, or simply Love. I am too much of a buddhist not to know that God is as controversial and non-universal as any other symbol, besides the inconvenience of being neither concrete nor historical.

I have tried to speak the christian language, and perhaps I have neglected to give "equal time" to the hindu language, or the buddhist one for that matter, except in my more philosophical studies (1989; 1977; 1993/1). My point has always been that we do not need to water down the insights of one tradition in order to put forward the intuitions of another. We do not meet each other by chopping off all our differences but by climbing to the peaks of the diverse traditions.

Another comment may clarify my approach. It could also serve as another example of how I do not separate *logos* and *mythos.*

I have found myself taking part in christological discussions about the uniqueness of Christ; in fact, I have somewhat reluctantly taken sides and only obliquely stated my overall critique. I could hardly reveal that for me it is a pseudo-problem, which started since the loss of corporate identity (ecclesial in this case) and crystallized as a problem since modern science became the paradigm of intelligibility.

Single events are not the object of "scientific" knowledge. Scientific knowledge of the so-called hard sciences has to integrate the event into a pattern, and has to be able to find a "law" of behavior. It needs to predict. Love, on the other hand, entails the discovery of the uniqueness of a thing. A "scientific" jar is a single specimen among many jars. If it breaks I can replace it by another one, probably an almost identical one. If I love a particular jar, that jar is for me unique. I am sad if it breaks. I cannot and will not replace it with another one. It has something irreplaceable. It makes a difference if someone dies or if the dead one happens to be my father. The loving approach to things is of another kind than the scientific one. Modern science has to exclude love from its approach to things. The scientific world is a loveless universe. It needs to abstract individuality. Love has no place in it. It approaches things in an impersonal and quantifiable manner. Nothing is said here against modern science. But something is said against taking modern science as the only paradigm of knowledge.

The question of the uniqueness of Christ appears as a problem once we approach Christ without love, i.e., "scientifically." We try to find his identification and not to discover his identity when love is absent (1972/2). Now, the question is not that theologians (or scientists for that matter) are loveless people or that they do not love Christ. The problem is that love is not an acknowledged epistemological tool — and even more, that epistemology is served from ontology.

The "contamination" of scientific thinking has brought about another more delicate and moral issue which appears almost scandalous seen from the outside. It is the result of the split between the intellect and the spirit, between intellectual life and spiritual life, and the subsequent specialization within theology itself (speculative, positive, historical, spiritual, moral, and so on). If the uniqueness of Christ should mean that he is the only exclusive Savior, only for those who recognize him, if heaven is only for christians, a noble soul, a bodhisattva, an egoless saint may well be inclined to renounce that privilege and feel that he or she cannot be happy, fulfilled and really saved (whole, liberated) if fellow beings are denied, without any fault of theirs, the same benefit. I am expressing in a crude way the feeling of more than one outsider. In gentle terms I wrote about the need to overcome a tribal Christology as the prophets of Israel overcame the notion of a tribal God and transformed it into a more universal and loving symbol.

The problem is, further, that while the Christology of the last two millennia has operated mainly within the myth of history and with the greek *logos,* the *christophany* of the third millennium (as I would call it) has to consider the possibility of a radical mutation, a true *meta-noia.* I mean not changing the direction of the *nous* itself, but overcoming the merely mental (1990/10). Clearly enough, with such "thoughts" one cannot expect a warm reception among many professional colleagues. If every real thing or event for me is unique, where is the problem?

POLITICS

I use this word *politics* in its anthropological and even metaphysical sense (1978/1). Here belong the three parts of this section. All our speculations would be an ivory-tower exercise if they did not reach the political level. Man is a political animal, as Aristotle said and practically all human traditions believe: Man is community.

The Radical Trinity

It may sound paradoxical, and to some perhaps preposterous, that a section on the Trinity is included under the general heading of politics.

It is on purpose that I mention here the chapters by Cousins and Podgorski. This is consonant with what I call *Sacred Secularity.* Religion is not separable from politics, although it must be carefully distinguished from it. Like the temporal and the external, the sacred needs to be seen in a non-dualistic way if we are to overcome the present-day fragmentations and dichotomies which lead the world toward premature catastrophe. A divine Trinity severed from human history and the cosmos would remain a museum piece in a theological cabinet.

We limit our comments to three.

God beyond God

To Cousin's chapter I would say that it is not necessary for me to postulate a Godhead beyond God, be it like Eckhart or Tillich, because this divine *Abgrund* is precisely the Father. I should not expand further now on these problems which, as I said, have a direct relevance for the world. What we need today is not a cosmetic alteration of the present order but a radically new understanding of Man's role in the universe. For this, both a christian experience of the Trinity and the wisdom of other traditions become indispensable (1984/5; *The Conflict of Kosmologies* [forthcoming]).

If God is identified as the Supreme Being there is a certain justification to assume that there is a pure Being or a Godhead beyond God. The "God beyond God" is needed once we interpret God to be a being, albeit supreme. God as the Supreme Being is still a being, even if we call it supreme and use the name analogically. God as the Supreme Being is still a refined anthropomorphism: the Highest Entity. Man remains the model, and not only the obliged relational point of reference. Anthropomorphism is the lurking danger of monotheism. And this is why, in order to avoid it, monotheism has to stress transcendence so much and be suspicious of immanence. Now, monotheism or antimonotheism (called atheism) is a feature of western culture. Even apparently so "clear-cut" a question as asking "Why is there Being rather than Nothing?" unconsciously still asks "Why is there a Supreme Being rather than Nothing?" Otherwise the question could not arise. One (my) being asks for (other) beings and for (a supreme) Being. "Why after all is there existence [not *being*] rather than nothing?" was the classical metaphysical question. Only we, the little beings, can ask such a why — and rightly so. "Why this world?," "Why are we?," "Why is there a Supreme Entity?" are legitimate questions. "Why Being?" has no meaning. Who asks? And what does it ask? An ultimate why is a self-contradiction. It amounts to asking what is beyond the Beyondless (what is beyond the "last" star? — either it is not the "last" or there is no beyond). "There is no-Beyond" amounts to "Beyond is-not." To ask is already an intentional act outside oneself; it is an epistemological act toward transcendence. An absolute Being (not a Supreme Entity) does not ask whether "there is" a why for its Being — it does not ask anything.

Here is the locus of the cosmotheandric intuition. The radical Trinity is neither monotheism, nor tritheism. The hypothesis of a God beyond God becomes unnecessary and the question of the Why does not arise. The "Beyond" (the son) is the father, the Presence is the Son, and the Absence is the Spirit. But I should not repeat myself (1973).

I am not identifying in an unqualified way Father, Non-being, Baselessness (and Abyss), *śūnyatā, wu-wei* and similar notions. Nor is God a cultural universal. None of these notions is the "same." They are *homeomorphic equivalents.* I can never insist sufficiently that the cross-cultural or interreligious approach requires a proper methodology.

Advaita

We have already stated that *advaita* is not monism. *Advaita* represents the overcoming of rationalism without abandoning the intellect. We have also stated that *advaita* and Trinity are two homeomorphic equivalents for the ultimate structure of reality (1991/5). And the cosmotheandric or theanthropocosmic intuition would like to be a qualified version of those ultimate insights. *Advaita* amounts to an ultimate challenge to intelligibility presented by the human intellect itself: we discover the impossibility of a total intellectual transparency (intelligibility).

A simile may spare us longer elaborations. One only needs to read Proclus's comment on Book X of Euclid's *Elementa* to realize what a shock the discovery of irrational numbers represented for the human mind. The simplest discovery was linked with Pythagoras's theorem about the right-angles triangle (when we divide a square by a diagonal) whose diagonal (hypotenuse) is incommensurable with the two other sides. That the square of the hypotenuse equals the sum of the two other squares was already known to egyptians, babylonians, indians and chinese, although in Pythagoras the proof is given on a general theoretical basis for any such triangle. But the quandary arises when we scrutinize the meaning of the equation and try to relate the members, i.e., to measure the one with the other.

It is easily proved that a finite coefficient k linking the hypotenuse with the two equal sides of the right-angled triangle cannot exist. If at all k should be an irrational number — and so it is called. The actual relationship is expressed by the irrational number $\sqrt{2}$. This means that a simple geometrical figure like the right-angled triangle with equal sides cannot consist of a finite number of points. If we use n and m points for the sides there are no kn or km points to build the hypotenuse. It means, in a word, that the triangle cannot be exactly measured in units, however small we may conceive them. This is extraordinary. It should have remained truly an esoteric doctrine, and this is why it is said that the Gods punished the first Man who revealed what is ineffable and unimaginable. He died in a shipwreck, Proclus tells us. One cannot violate the mystery, Proclus explains further. The sides and the hypotenuse (like the radius and the circumference) are incommensurable. With one single measure we cannot encompass reality.

There is no end to an irrational number. If we use it, it is an illegitimate substitute for the real triangle. And if we begin speculating about the infinite then Zeno of Elea also dispels our rational calculus and disturbs our thinking: Achilles will never be able to reach the tortoise if there are infinite intermediary points to cross. We may, of course, introduce all kinds of irrational and imaginary numbers. Our mind will handle them only when we abstract them from the real. To abstract means to subtract something. Doing this we should remain aware of two features of this operation: we have left something out (a chunk of the real thing has been neglected, set aside), and the very operation may have wounded (modified) the thing. Once again we unconsciously translate the equation Thinking-Being into Calculating-Being. The ancients said that matter was not thinkable in rational terms.

This mathematical example may help to introduce the notion of *advaita* if we do not forget that it is only a simile. Using the word *advaita* or non-duality we do not refer to indian philosophical systems; we refer to a negation of monism without "falling" into dualism. *Advaita* is not a weakened monism or relative dualism, but an independent and third possible experience of reality.

An intelligible description of it needs this apophatic expression of *a-dvaita* (non-duality), because authentic *advaita* in no way spurns reason and rationality, and we, as rational beings, need to express ourselves "componendo et dividendo," as the Divus Thomas would say, stitching things together and tearing them apart, or, more academically stated, by synthesis and analysis, induction and deduction. It is only in denying the apparent duality of reality, without falling into the temptation of putting everything into one bag, that we may approach the advaitic intuition in an intelligible way. It says *neti, neti.* But this is possible only if the *iti,* the "this" of the *na-iti,* appears forcefully and really to our field of vision. Reality is neither one nor two. It is not one, for we cannot deny evidence: we experience multiplicity. It is not two, for we cannot deny that any duality, epistemologically, logically and metaphysically presupposes an underlying unity which allows that it be doubted, as it were. As it should be stressed time and again, the advaitic intuition is not the denial of reason but the transcending of it. Overcoming the intellect does not mean to deny it. This would still be an intellectual act. *Advaita* has its reasons that reason does not know, we could say, paraphrasing the well-known pascalian phrase: "Le coeur a ses raisons que la raison ne connaît point."

The negation of both a dualistic and a monistic structure of reality, because of the fact that we cannot bring reality into an intelligible oneness, is the very core of *advaita. Advaita* does not say that Being *is* non-dual. If Being were non-dual (and not-plural), we think logically it would have to be one. This is monism. *Advaita* says that Being *is-not* dual, that duality *is-not* the case. And it adds further that Being *is-not* one. *Advaita* does not make an objective statement about reality: "Being is not-two." If not-two includes also not-three, etc., the rational deduction would be that "Being is one." To deny it would amount to plain contradiction. *Advaita* refuses the *is* (one or two) and says instead Being is-not — one or two. Being has no predicate. The *is* of our rational thinking does not need to be identical with the Being of our awareness. It challenges, precisely, objectivity on the ultimate level, because it discovers that our own thinking is equally non-dual; it can not be reduced to an absolute unity; it is constitutively polar. It challenges subjectivity equally, precisely because it refuses to postulate the necessary transparency of reality to our thinking, to any thinking. Thinking and Being are two irreducible "dimensions" of reality, dimensions which are neither identical (monism) nor different (dualism).

We *speak* about Being (reality), but we are aware that our speech is not exhaustively covered by our *thinking.* The parmenidian scheme of Thinking and Being needs the complement (or rather supplement) of Being-Speaking-Thinking (1990/8).

This touches upon the basic question about the nature of reality and its triadic structure: Father, Son and Spirit; Heaven, Earth and Man; Things, Concepts and Words; and so forth. Here I find a *formal* human invariant. This is what I call the cosmotheandric or theanthropocosmic intuition: the *theos,* the *anthropos* and the *kosmos* as the three constitutive dimensions of reality — different but inseparable (1985/1; 1986/2; 1988/2; 1989/5; 1993c).

Perichorēsis

This suggestive word, which in classical greek simply means "rotation" (from a verb meaning "to go around and dance") has been utilized by christian theology to express the trinitarian *circumincessio* (*circuminsessio*), that is, the movement in the divine Trinity by which immanence and transcendence are overcome (cf. Jn. 10: 38 and also BG IX, 405). It is the trinitarian dance by which the Father empties himself from all that "he" is, and so does the Son, and so does the Spirit, in order that Life goes on giving and receiving. In other words, each "person" is fully in the other one; they are circumincessional as it were. *Rota in medio rotae* ("like a wheel within a wheel") was a favorite passage (Ez. 10:10) commented on by christian mystics.

It is interesting to know that this word, which in neoplatonism was used to express the relation between body and soul (in dynamic interchange), was applied by Gregory of Nazianzen to the union of the human and the divine natures in Christ. Later (and John Damascene consecrates it), the word is applied to the Trinity.

I am within tradition, although transcending it (as any *traditio* demands), when I apply this notion to the radical Trinity, i.e., to reality. "The Trinity is the measure of all things" wrote Marsilio Ficino (*De amore, II, 1*) quoting the pythagoreans. This is the *circumincessio* between the Divine, the Human and the Cosmic.

I have been asked how do I relate the Three. In other words, who is in control? My answer is clear: nobody is the boss. Ultimately the question is a pseudo-problem, because the "persons," or the Divine, the Human and the Cosmic, are not three entities, three beings — who would need a higher being (God beyond God) to keep the order and give them unity (or even harmony). The "dimensions" are irreducible and yet inseparable. For this reason identity and difference do not apply, as there is not a "fourth" (common) background over against which any comparison of identity or difference could be made. The dynamism between the "three" is free, not preconceived, or pre-directed (by whom?). Reality is not a pre-planned comedy. Here lies our dignity and responsibility, to be associated with the very destiny of the universe. The ultimate is irreducible to anything else. Unity and plurality (and the so-called Trinity or *Advaita* is neither of them) are intellectual reductionisms.

My last comment here underscores what has been said. To be Man is not just to be a small piece of intelligent matter crawling in the universe or a great individual walking on earth. Man is a conscious agent in the very destiny of the universe. This may explain why I speak of the radical trinity.

I will not elaborate further, but I felt I had to make this comment, which introduces our next problem.

Cosmic Confidence

Knitter's chapter touches upon another personal concern of mine. The character of this festschrift may perhaps condone the style of my response. He touches profound fibers in me, and I feel I should be forgiven if I react with my heart as much as with my mind. This should be taken as an expression of my gratitude.

The Critique

Knitter's critique is rich in lessons for me. It shows how easily misunderstandings can arise. I fully share his concern. How could I not? I would not like to be second to anybody in the thirst for justice. I find the justification of my life in my total dedication to Justice, or in the Gospel words: for "the Kingdom and its Justice."

Knitter makes a convincing plea, and I join my forces and my voice with his, to direct the activity of religious institutions in the direction of socio-economic and political justice. I have, in season and sometimes out of season, remarked that there is no justification without justice. Knitter would like to rally all the potential forces of institutionalized religions to struggle for a common cause: the elimination of the unjust situation of the world, including man-manipulated hunger, human exploitation, wars, crushing of minorities, abuse (when not even worse) of the poor, neglect of the feminine aspect of Man and of reality. I would also make, besides the ecological warning, the plea for animals, plants and minerals as subjects in their own right and not only objects for human use or knowledge. I speak of *ecosophy,* animism and the cosmotheandric intra-connection (*perichorēsis*). He wants to let us forget "byzantine" questions and discover the essential task of religion: "human welfare." His project is noble and utterly convincing. I am with him, and, qualifying his phrase, I would include the Divine plus the cosmic in his "human," and salvation (liberation) plus ful-fillment (joy) in his "welfare." But this should not distract us from the priority to be given to the "human," because it is closer to our possibilities of acting. Yet, all this is interconnected. All too often religions as institutions have been excessively concerned with "celestial" matters. Knitter's political effort to spur "religions" to enhance the *humanum* can be sure of my collaboration (1993e).

Knitter has still another very important point to stress: the importance and priority of praxis. If we begin to be engaged in this praxis, our ideas will flow from it and will likely be the right ones. His project is also political, and I would like to join efforts.

I stress my agreement because I feel that, if he has misunderstood some of my thoughts, I am to blame for not stating clearly enough that the context in which he situates my dialogue with others is hardly my personal milieu.

I would like to remark that I do not speak of "a pluralist model" or of "the validity of many religions." Nor do I feel touched by the charge of defend-ing in a colonialistic spirit the uniqueness of the christian event. I have stated time and again that any event is unique and that within the myth of history the christic event has its "unique" relevance. For me, pluralism does not mean that "there are many absolutes." On the contrary, the pluralistic attitude recognizes the contradiction of such an affirmation. The "something in common" I am al-leged to defend would be, if at all, empty nothingness, *śūnyatā.* I may be right or wrong, but I have made clear since the very outset what I mean by pluralism. But the fact is that I do not find a better word than *pluralism* and so I stick to it, maverick or not.

It is refreshing to hear that I stress the "utter differences between religions" when generally I am accused of trespassing religious constituencies and even blurring religious boundaries.

But I have to take Knitter's criticism very seriously if he sees in me the danger of complacency in one's own positions and "delight in diversity," as if we should not struggle with all our forces to eliminate injustice and error. I might have given the impression of condoning evil because I do not preach a new crusade and total war against it. I agree with Knitter's criteria, but I do not absolutize them.

Let me give a concrete example, which sums up hundreds of similar situations in which I have found myself.

Calcutta is an effervescent city in all senses of the word. I have walked, talked and engaged in social action with some monks of the Sri Ramakrishna Mission. My first reactions, in the early fifties, were Knitter's. The monks chided what seemed to them my "over-sentimentalism" and "christian prejudices." They intended to "sober my indignation" in face of the sufferings and injustices by their hammering home to me that the meaning of life is not to live on earth more or less comfortably; that without *karma* I was bound to be without any answer; that an "all-loving Father" would not convince anyone; that without the realization that this world is *māyā* I would not be able, first, to evaluate the situation, certainly not as the people themselves do, and second, that this "over-excitement" of mine would only work countereffectively; and so on. And, in fact, all the charitable agencies in the last fifty years have not improved the situation substantially.

We should not ignore the different underlying presuppositions, perceptions, sense of urgency and even of priorities. My friends were even suspicious that the "theologies of liberation" might be tricks of the CIA and other agencies, or as the most sophisticated would tell me, fruit of the "Zeitgeist" of the West in order to sell the products of western-born (although Japan-made) technology and solve its internal problems. I spare you my answer of how one could so perniciously twist so noble a concern.

Or, to give another example. What would be Knitter's reaction when speaking with one of the most famous philosophers of India, not a hindu fanatic, who confidentially confessed to me that, for him, one of the models of the christian spirit was Adolf Hitler, who at least had the advantage of expressing crudely and without hypocrisy his feelings of superiority and scorn for non-aryans (call them pagans)? Was he not a baptized member of the church and with religious leanings during his first youth? Had he not simply drawn the lessons of christian intolerance and cruelty? One cannot brush these frontal attacks aside eschewing the suspicion that slogans like "preferential option," "freedom of the press," "equality for all" serve the powers that be to neutralize the cry of the radicals and go on with business as usual. The political arena is more complex than many religions imagine. And yet I agree with Knitter that we cannot separate the two realms (1974/3; 1993e).

For half a century I have been saying that the "Sitz im Leben" of the inter-religious dialogue is not the comfortable chair of the academic, the position of power of the churchman or the luxury of the westerner — notwithstanding the oversimplification. "We" should listen to the accusation of paternalism when we speculate on the preferential option.

I have been with the mother of the starving child. She has given up the hope that the child will live. Death is too far advanced. She wants only that the older brother may survive and the starving one may quickly pass away without much suffering. She does not want my remedies and words, which she knows do not work and change nothing. There are millions of those "poor," sufficiently "conscientized" to know that all our "options" are just this, options, decisions, intentions, words, programs, and at best (and yet tragically countereffective) money. I have lived also with old folks and experienced that they realistically did not expect a miracle from me. They expected love, sympathy, a fraternal cry, my time and company — and eventually a consoling word that, in spite of the fact that there is no personal solution nor will there be any change in the village, that, transcending all these "tragedies," there is Life, Sun, Air, Bhagavan, Ram, a little meal, a liberating belief that we are just a passing wave, and that like the snatched flower we had our time and it was wonderful to have had what we had. Opiate? Resignation? One thousand five hundred children under the age of five starve every day due mainly to the third world debt, debt whose warranted repayment some still debate. But the poor countries have no other option lest they get worse off. And for thirty years now the situation has been deteriorating. What are we going to say to them *today?* They cannot wait for tomorrow. They expect a word for them, not for their children.

My personal religion is shaped by these and many other experiences. But I am not imposing this as the only model. I feel and believe this is what we should do: join hands to dismantle what I call the technocratic complex. But soon I find other people who neither share my opinions nor agree with my options. Of course, I strive to convince them of how "wrong" they are and how "right" I am. But my pluralistic attitude, not my pluralistic opinions (nobody can have a pluralistic opinion), leads me to take them seriously, to play the dialogue fairly, to relativize my arguments without giving them up. I shun all messianisms — or, as some jews would put it: the Messiah will come at the end of times, that is, he will never come — in time.

May I give vent to a suspicion with fear and trembling? I can't help suspecting that the "option for the poor" is becoming so obvious that it is evolving as a placebo for Church and State so as to appease the scruples of the best, give them the impression that something is being done, give Nobel Prizes to Mother Teresas and proceed with business as usual. The world today has 100 million street-children crawling in the great cities of our "civilized" world, and 320 million women under the broken ceilings of the slums. So little is done that from various sources politicians reckon that in two centuries the street-children and female slumdwellers will number in the hundreds of millions. One fifth of the population of the world consumes 70 percent of all metals and 85 percent of all forests (official figures of the UN for 1994 according to *Le Monde diplomatique,* July 1995, p. 22). And still we hear voices complaining that the poor peoples consume too much firewood. Meanwhile, all agree that we have to opt for the poor.... The problems are overwhelming and cry for a radical transformation.

I beg not to be misunderstood. I take the theology of liberation to be one of the most important spiritual and intellectual achievements of our times. It liberates, first of all, theology from the many bondages of the last centuries. It recovers the genuine scope of traditional wisdom which is, as practically all religious traditions claim, to liberate Man and clarify the way to Freedom, Salvation, Joy, *mokṣa, nirvāṇa*. . . . On the other hand, I underscore the real danger of being manipulated or simply absorbed, and thus neutralized, by the powerful status quo of today's technocratic complex. Furthermore, I signal also its predominantly monocultural character in spite of the now timidly emerging "asian and african theologies of liberation."

Some Clarifications

I feel I have shown that I share Knitter's *pathos,* that I am within the same *ethos*. Only our *logos* is somewhat different. And here is a concrete case of pluralism due to the ultimate ineffability of the real. He sees that the "preferential option may help my position and purify it from its dangers."

I accept the offer. A christian Christology today — it is not a redundance — should see in Christ not so much the triumphant symbol of past cosmologies as the liberating symbol for the oppressed and as another word for Justice. I cannot agree more.

But I am tempted to do likewise, that is, to reinforce his position of a preferential option for the oppressed (for the *dalit* movements in India, for instance) by stressing "cosmic confidence" as the basis. The concern for the poor presupposes precisely a cosmic confidence. In fact, why do we get so indignant at injustice, premature deaths, and sufferings if not because we assume a cosmic confidence in reality, in which somehow we trust and believe that life cannot be so senseless, unjust and cruel as to justify such manmade oppressions? It is that cosmic confidence which triggers the healthy decision of the "option." It is the awareness of injustice which leads to the "option." But this injustice is only detected because of our presupposition that there is a *cosmic order* which the injustice has precisely violated.

Here are still some further reflections of a fellow-traveler.

The cosmic confidence is the conviction, belief, myth, acceptance, experience or even postulate that reality is the ultimate ground we have in order to make some sense of anything, find that life has a certain value, the world a certain consistency, our thinking a certain truth and words a certain meaning. We say "certain" or "some sense" because we cannot exclude the most disparate interpretations of this sense. The very idea that the world may be in chaos or sheer illusion has meaning only over the background of a cosmic order which we assume in order to negate it. Cosmic confidence arises from the awareness that the universe is a *kosmos,* that we are conscious participants in the universe, whatever degree of reality, sense or purpose we may attribute to it. Cosmic confidence constitutes an ultimate background for all our actions and activities.

Cosmic confidence exists ontically in any living being if the awareness is latent, ontologically if it is conscious. The very act of committing suicide is a vindication of cosmic confidence. The suicide commits the suicidal act precisely because of the felt unbearable gap between the expected cosmic confidence and its collapse in personal life. Cosmic confidence is needed even in order to proclaim life as absurd or to espouse nihilism. It is only over against the background of a cosmic confidence that despair, absurdity and nihilism say what they want to say. We have to trust reality, even to mistrust everything else. The word *confidence* should not misguide us to imagine that cosmic confidence dreams of a paradise. It is the confidence that is cosmic; it is not our trust that the world is a harmonious universe, according to some subjective and a priori patterns. The harmony of reality is not a preconceived harmony, as if we knew beforehand how the universe has to be. I imagine that Herakleitos, the genial aristocrat from Ephesos, had experienced something similar which led him to utter the words: "Invisible harmony is stronger than the visible" (fr. 54). The invisible, ultimate order of the universe is the source of our ideas about truth, beauty — and their contraries. The order of the cosmos is the ultimate order of things and our last criterion to say what is order and what is disorder. Ultimately the cosmic confidence is a qualified tautology — as all ultimate issues are. A qualified tautology, as we already mentioned, amounts to the jump from a formal analytical proposition to an ontological sentence, tautology which appears to us as a priori because of the myth within which we think and act.

I may be allowed to insist because I have been sometimes misunderstood. Cosmic confidence is not trust in the world, confidence in the cosmos. It is the confidence *of* the cosmos itself, of which we form a part inasmuch as we simply are. It is a subjective genitive: the confidence itself is a cosmic fact of which we are more or less aware, and which we presuppose all the time. If the cosmos, understood here as a name for the entire reality, had not an intrinsic "consistency" and were not the very source of all our scale of values, we could not develop that basic attitude which is at the root of all our thoughts and feelings. Reality is our last instance. Cosmic confidence is not our interpretation of the world. It is that awareness which makes any interpretation possible. What the principle of non-contradiction does in the logical field the cosmic confidence performs in the ultimate order of reality. We cannot deny the principle of non-contradiction without presupposing it already. We cannot disclaim a cosmic order without assuming it already. Cosmic confidence is the awareness of this state of affairs. The vedic notion of *ṛta* or cosmic order may be a homeomorphic equivalent of what we are saying.

It should be clear by now that cosmic confidence is not the epistemological certainty of Descartes. Cosmic confidence is not trust in our ideas. It is also not the heideggerian "Grundbefindlichkeit der Angst." Dread may be a basic character of human existence, and it may give us even a warning against a naive belief in our reason, but it is not the very presupposition of our being in the cosmos. A monk once asked the famous chinese master Chao-Chou (Joshu): "What is the unique and ultimate word of truth?" The monk replied "Yes!" The commentaries I know take the answer as a prima facie unintelligible koan, as other similar reactions to related questions: "Clean the dishes!," "Go fishing!" and the like. I take it to be a literal, straight and precise answer: Yes, Amen,

Aum, affirmation of what is, acceptance of reality, enlightened vision without intermediaries, realization of that very trust. This cosmic confidence is rather like that first act of the intellect in which there is neither trust nor falsehood, as Aristotle reported and Thomas Aquinas commented (*III De Anima* 6; *Perih.* I, 1 b a 9; etc.). It is the awareness of our being in and of the universe.

Confidence has something to do with trust, faith, as the word suggests, and with hope as well. And we have it because we love.

There is another reason I call it *confidence*. It is indeed an act of trust, but trust after all. It is not logical evidence. If Thinking and Being, as I maintain, do not need to coalesce perfectly, our reliance on Being cannot be proved or shown by mere reason. We trust reality as it *is* and not because we are able to comprehend it or capable of understanding it — although this transcending of reason lies within the power of the intellect.

It should be clear that this confidence and the option for the poor do not belong to the same universe of discourse. The former is ultimate, the latter a moral option — and both required.

The Option for the Poor

The option for the poor is first of all an option. I underscore that, for me, it is an imperative option, a decision a responsible person has to take today, specially the intellectual. But it is an option — an option which liberates us indeed.

As option I have a threefold comment to offer, first, cultural, second, anthropological, and third, crosscultural.

The *counter-cultural comment* is this. It corresponds to the genius of the last centuries of the western world to rely on the primacy of the will, at least since the *devotio moderna*. "Our basic being is in the will," said Schelling, epitomizing the modern western genius. It is a question of an option, of an act of the will, of a moral decision because it is an ethical imperative. An imperative is something which is commanded, and which we willingly obey — or disobey. It is an order which we give to ourselves or which we detect as imposed by the situation or some authority. We make a decision (de-cision, *Ent-scheidung*), i.e., a free "cutting" of all our other possibilities. We could do otherwise but being sensitive to the demands of justice, we curtail our privileges in order to offer our talents to the "poor" and put our lives at the service of the destitute. I believe it is the proper and most moral decision to take.

The *anthropological comment,* related to the crosscultural one, is this. Any option reposes in the will, the will is supposed to be free — and even rational. Our will decides to make that option because we are convinced that it is the proper thing to do, see reasons for it, and an elementary sense of humanness justifies our option. It all reposes on a reflexive choice. I wonder if Christ made an option to die on the Cross, if Francis of Assisi made an option to embrace poverty, if Luther made an option ("Here I stand and I can't do otherwise!"), or even if a loving mother makes an option to kiss her child or to spend a sleepless night beside her ailing baby, or an artist paints a canvas, an author writes a poem or a composer creates music out of clear options of love, service, beauty or whatever. It is something stronger than options, more powerful than decisions. Before the left hand may know what the right hand has to do, the right has already done it. Any person in love, any passionate intellectual, any artist, any saint will understand this. Thus the paramount importance of the purity of heart from which spontaneously the most authentic acts flow. The crime of Ananias was not to have indulged in "legal business" after all, but the fact that such a thought had simply entered in his heart. This was what Peter chastised and what cost Ananias his life.

I feel I have no option but to strive for justice. I have no option but to stand at the side of the oppressed. I have no option but to speak the truth. I have no alternative other than to set my life at stake for the sake of peace. My conscience has no other option. The traditional christian language spoke of vocation. God calls. Man hears, and obeys (*ob-audire*). We may certainly say no, but the yes is not the result of an option. It is the only possible way to live in freedom and joy, to be oneself. The authentic call, in this traditional language, may come from God, but through the heart, from the innermost core of our being. When it is a question of giving witness to truth (Jesus said) do not think beforehand (1993b).

The *crosscultural comment* relativizes the role of will and reminds us that other cultures often do not start from those premises. They may not build on the will or use the language of decisions. The ethic of the Upaniṣads, for instance, could offer us another language. This was my previous caveat concerning the critique of monoculturalism of the "option."

This is a very delicate problem because it touches our sensibilities, our myth. Each culture is an encompassing myth within which we have our specific world view.

The option for the poor, in an exclusive historical myth, leads to a tragic sense of life which may trigger a reaction of callousness for the poor or a sense of impotent rebellion. Within the framework of dialectical materialism the so-called conscientization leads to despair. With merely historical conscientization the oppressed become conscious that for many of them there will be no liberation at all. In spite of all our most strenuous efforts to opt for the liberation of the oppressed, thousands of children are going to starve *today,* and millions of refugees and victims of wars are not going to be liberated in their lifetime. We may console *ourselves* with the view of a brighter future, but what is our answer for those people? Either there is a transhistorical reality (now or later) or there is no hope for them.

The target of this criticism is not the theology of liberation — and certainly not the case of Paul Knitter. The theology of liberation is first of all "theology," and this *theos* vouches for the transcendent dimension I am defending. Indeed, this in no way condones our apathy, indifference or resignation. Without the preferential option for the poor, the situation would be worse, and much has been achieved by our conscious engagement for justice. But this does not deny the fact that for many the option remains ineffective.

Here is where traditional cultures speaking of heaven, *karma*, nirvāṇa, God and brahman have something essential to contribute. To realize that my life has a meaning (sense) which is *life*, even if I have been invited to the banquet of Life just for a few moments, is the only saving hope for many and another exemplification of what I mean by cosmic confidence.

Surreptitious Technocentrism

Last and certainly not least comes my comment on Dussel's qualified defense of technology. It is fitting that it is my last comment, precisely because it all should end in a transformative praxis of the human condition.

I shall make three sorts of comments: (a) crosscultural, (b) philosophical, and (c) ethical. But I preface all of them expressing a deep communication with Dussel. We share similar concerns. I sympathize deeply with his intentions and also with his spirited defense of a neglected side of Marx, all the more important today since we very much need again to hear his stand for the "oppressed." I also, like him, do not share the triumphalistic attitude of liberal capitalism, although I offer different alternatives than Dussel. This is a friendly critique with the aim of clarifying the issue. We are in the same boat.

Crosscultural

My main comment to Dussel's chapter refers to its monoculturalism. This may be, incidentally, the common denominator of all my previous reactions as well. The solution, for me, is not more roads, hospitals and computers, although, within certain limits, to some elites of the First World (even if living in eastern or southern enclaves) these may be helpful. An example of this attitude is Dussel's question: "What is the solution?" He searches for solutions before critically considering the possibility that the very problem may look different from another perspective, not to say culture. It may even be a different problem altogether. To be sure, Dussel analyzes the "essence of technology" (about which later), but he does it with the same technological parameters I would question, precisely because they are foreign to the cultures to which we want to offer a more humane "solution." The West, even if secularized, has been deeply influenced by its missionary and messianic spirit — important distinctions notwithstanding.

From the predominant perspective of the modern West I think Dussel is right. There is no other alternative to the impasse, as he calls it. Any other alternative would be affected by the same universal syndrome I am criticizing all the time. If I am against technocentrism as the universal panacea, I would also be against any other universal ideology. There is no single all-embracing alternative. But there are alternatives — many, and valid. If we look for a single alternative to modern technocratic culture, we are once again bowing down to the monophormism of a colonialistic attitude — and still worse, to a monodimensional notion of *logos*.

I can well imagine that the only existing alternative in Latinamerica may appear to be the so-called appropriate technology. In fact, official Latinamerica operates within the orbit of the western world. White Latinamerica belongs, in fact, to the western world. This is why it feels, and rightly so, marginalized, peripheral. Apparently the center is New York, Paris, London (Moscow once upon a time) and money at all times. If I were to tell citizens of Varanasi that they do not dwell in the center of the world, their poverty would change into misery and their joy and hope into despair. After the cultural genocide of the indigenous peoples in the Americas, which began five hundred years ago, I understand that the immense majority of the present-day population has even lost the memory of the archetypes of their cultures — although precisely on the occasion of the fifth centenary the world learns not only about the facts of the past, but also of the will of the american First Nations to build a culture of their own. Are we, in the name of science and technology, going to commit the same acts which the conquistadors did in the name of God and Empire? Are we going to consider only one single Way as the immigrants did? Are we going to reduce cultures to mere folklore, tolerated as long as the "natives" join the world-market, understand english, or spanish, buy the products of "our" industries, and adopt the technological way of life? Let us recall that there are fifty million indigenous people on the american continent (there were probably almost 100 million half a millennium ago).

Needless to say, these words are not directed to the friend who has done stupendous work in understanding Ibero-America. I am referring here to the question of the universality of technology. This is not the moment to recall, for instance, the names of Tupac Amaru, Martí, or more recently the events in Chiapas (about which Dussel has written a memorable commentary). I mention them here just as indicators of another sensibility.

This is the problem, and if it is risky and difficult to change the course of history, it is going to be more risky and catastrophic if we want to preserve the status quo, allowing only for accidental reforms to the predominant techno-scientific system. This is the real test for crosscultural studies. They are not there to offer mere solutions or to entertain people. They are there to change the very vision of the problems, thus, the problems themselves. "Those are the poor," said the "third-world helper" to his overseer — from overseas, of course. "We are not the poor," retorted the people, "we are mazatecos!" — and proud of it.

I know well that the evolutionary work of thinking, describing the history of humanity as if following the arrow of time, has led us to believe that modern science is universal and our astronomic and physico-chemical cosmology the definitive acquisition for the peoples of the Earth. Have we not gone to the moon? We are prone to relativize the kosmologies of other civilizations. But we become upset at the thought that "our" astronomy may be not so true as the caste of the scientists tells us today.

I have written extensively on this (among others, 1963/4; 1971/4; 1984/8; 1988/1). I mention it in order to underline the importance of the question and the need for a crosscultural methodology if we are to consider other cultures as equal partners in dialogue. There is no real dialogue if I have my pockets full of dollars and you in your hands a few devaluated pesos. But equally there is no dialogue if I have my brain full of powerful technologies and you your heart filled with deep but fragile hopes.

Dussel's espoused socialism is still a variant of the technocratic system. I would not call the mayan culture, which he knows so well, another form of socialism. Socialism has to do with "socializing" the means of industrial production. The mayan culture was not individualistic so as to need "socialization," nor the mayan agriculture like the modern industrial techniculture. But, of course, all is a question of explaining our words. I submit that the adequate level of the discussion is not here but on the crosscultural plane. This is what allows me to speak of technocentrism as the most pernicious ideology, because it is subtler than all the ethnocentrisms so widely criticized today.

I do not need to convince my friend, who knows my position, but I should stress for the reader that I am not advocating a going back to idealized old times or to bucolic village life, that I am not defending a negative and otherworldly ascetism. On the contrary, like Thomas Aquinas (advocating human happiness for this earthly life without having to expect an eschatological fulfillment) I am defending an enhancement of our quality of life and human joy through our "emancipation from technology" (1984/6).

Dussel finds a dilemma between the need of the peripheral peoples for an accelerated development, on the one side, and the ecological question on the other side. If India were to have the number of cars the United States of America has (or consume the same amount of paper), the human race would soon disappear. But who on earth is going to convince the people with an inferior GNP that they should now renounce the "comforts" the "developed nations" have enjoyed? No wonder that dictatorships are needed to keep "law and order." Within the western scheme the impasse is serious. To solve the problem we need the collaboration of other cultures. Many of these cultures, for instance, will help us realize that neither "development" nor "ecology" is capable of handling the human condition. The "solution," I submit, is not to solve the dilemma by an "adequate (western) technology," but to break this ultimately false dilemma by a radical transformation of our world — including our world view. Crosscultural studies are demanding!

Acceleration is not the solution. Modern acceleration is a rupture of the human and cosmic rhythms (made possible by the domination of machines of the second degree), and thus offers no worldwide constructive solution. In the long run, or rather in the span of a few generations, the remedies are going to be worse than the malady. The facts today are already proving it. Acceleration should be substituted by harmony with the human and cosmic rhythms. The drama is that these very words sound romantic or hollow to technocratic ears.

Ecology is often seen as "business as usual," as continuing the exploitation of nature, only with more care, scientific know-how, and some recycling. Other cultures have a radically different view of nature. Nature is alive and thus not an object for Man. Males learn slowly today that women are not objects of their sex-drives, power-thirst or even objects of care and love. Modern Man has still to learn that nature is not an object for human greed — or condescending protection. To this end I have tried to introduce the notion of *ecosophy,* which stands for the wisdom of the Earth in the sense of the subjective genitive, i.e., as the very wisdom of the Earth in which Man shares and which Man represents. I began to use *ecosophy* in my classes at the University of California without knowing that practically at the same time Arne Naess had also coined this word, although filling it with another meaning altogether. A crosscultural perspective offers more than just cosmetics.

I submit that modern science is as provincial and limited as any other science in human history, although it has advantages for us and corresponds to our degree of civilization. We should not overlook the fact that modern science has very particular assumptions about the nature of matter, energy, time and space which are far from being universal and compatible with the world views of other cultures (1987/8).

Philosophical

But even from a western perspective I do not share Dussel's technological optimism. He honors me by aligning my ideas with those of Heidegger on these matters. I shall not comment on this, because I am not offering a response but only attempting to clarify my position.

I would begin by recalling my more basic critique of modern science much before my criticism of present-day technology. I enunciate, without elaborating, my main thesis: *Modern science is perverse.* It has perverted the meaning of words by converting them into terms. For modern science, time is no longer the life-span of things but the derivate of space and velocity. Space is no longer the habitat and larger body of things, but just a measure; matter is just another parameter related to force and acceleration; and similar reductionisms with fire, light, energy and the like. Words (fire, light, space, time, and so forth) are historico-cultural crystallizations of human experiences; terms (modern scientific names) are pragmatic labels to indicate measurable magnitudes (1980/1).

Modern technoscience has two essential features. First, it has to operate with abstractions, which we may call numeric measurements. There is something fascinating and grand with mathematical algorithms. The confusion begins when scientific terms are interpreted as real words. Due to the spectacular success of modern science, people take scientific abstractions for the reality from which they have been abstracted.

And this remnant from the scientific abstraction is the most important aspect of human experience. I mention here just one element of what remains outside the scientific abstraction. This is the character of uniqueness. Single events are not, and cannot be the subject matter of modern science. Modern science needs some regularity, some repetition, some implicit laws at least. Anything unique escapes the very field of modern science. Now, any human experience is unique, any conscious act of Man acquires its humanness precisely because of its irrepeatability, its uniqueness: today and not tomorrow, me and not the other, you and not another person, my hand, my friend, spouse, child, country, planet....

To put it in a nutshell, in the dialogue between Bellarmino and Galilei regarding the ultimate question of science (not of course concerning Vatican politics), Bellarmino was right and Galilei wrong. There cannot be real science (knowledge, *scientia, gnōsis, jñāna*) disconnected from a (theo-) cosmological context, and vice versa, there can be no theology without science. The fragmentation of knowledge, which began at that time, brought about the fragmentation of the knower, as I have repeatedly said. The perversion is, of course, not a moral perversion; much less does it relate to the scientific community. It concerns the very method of knowing and its substitution by calculating (playing with pebbles: *calculi*). We can calculate without love, but we cannot truly know without love. The meaning of the word *scientia* has been overturned (perverted).

The second point to underscore is the difference between *technē* and technology. The former is a human invariant; the latter is the fruit of one particular culture. The universalization of technology brings about the much discussed westernization of the world. My submission is that there has been a mutation in the change from *technē* or techniques to modern technology.

There is nothing new, certainly not for a scholar of Marx like Dussel, in stating that a quantitative change brings about a qualitative one. The passing from the machine of first degree to the machine of the second degree is connected with the difference between *technē* and technology. The former is art, work, symbiosis with nature, and benefits the planet — beginning with the individual artisan. The sources of energy of the first-degree machine respect the energy-rhythms of nature. The second-degree machine breaks, through artificial acceleration, the cosmic rhythms of the natural order and utilizes artificial (unnatural) sources of energy which are not renewable. I would follow here the beautiful study by Dussel: ours is a sacramental world. The plant "enjoys" being eaten by the animal. This belongs to the cosmic circle (play). The plant "becomes" thus an animal; so does the small animal when eaten by the big one and both by Man. It is a eucharistic "commerce." Man in its turn is called upon to be transformed (eaten up) and become risen, divinized, enlightened, realized, liberated. But this cosmotheandric circle is broken if we convert agriculture, which is a sort of love-making with the Earth, into agribusiness, which amounts to the violation of Nature, significantly called world "resources," for the profit of the exploiter.

Not only economy, but the very nature of industrial and scientific labor has undergone a qualitative change since the time of Marx; his analyses assume an idea of labor and industry which is no longer real today. Labor as the lending of the laborers' own efforts in order to produce, even if not interpreted in a crude corporal way, is no longer the issue. The very idea of salary begins to prove alienating. Human activity is not just production of goods. The reign of freedom is not the span of free time we have after labor. We should overcome that type of anthropology. I subscribe to most of Dussel's analyses. My point is that technology is not what he describes. Technology is the trojan horse for the westernization of the world. It may be that this is the way to go, but we should not dream then of allowing other cultures to survive.

Perhaps another example will help to explain the very transformation in the ways of thinking I am advocating. A majority of experts seems to agree that we need to put "limits to growth," although they disagree on the means to adopt. The very idea that we have to put limits to the growth of an organism (say, an endless growth of an individual) shows that it has lost the homeostasis of a healthy organism. I have argued elsewhere (1986/4) that the present-day technocratic organization has lost its own ontonomic regulation (and even that this cancer of our social system has its correlation with the cancer of individual organisms). I am not saying here anything against medicines for curing the cancer of society or of individual bodies. I am simply stating that this loss of homeostasis in our social organism is the symptom of a congenital ailment, and that to restore health we cannot be satisfied with an accurate diagnosis but have to find an etiological remedy. The causes are, I have said, the loss of the cosmic rhythms. The limits to growth cannot be attained by any sort of pills. No technological devices will cure the technological diseases, no dictatorial growth-control of children, cars or business will be a stable and natural solution. We need cosmic confidence much more than technological superstitions.

Ethical

One conviction I share in an unambiguous way with Dussel: our present system is unjust. We have to change it. He proposes a liberating production. And here my doubts begin. I propose a liberation from production and substitution by reproduction. In nature things reproduce themselves — and we may obviously assist and even direct (*ducere*) this process. I certainly advocate a transformation, a metamorphosis. Here again it is a question of respecting the cosmic rhythms — without violating them through acceleration. It takes nine months for a child to be born (by human reproduction and not production of humans) — and twenty-four for an elephant (without jurassic parks). If it is a question of production, the poor population are bound to be the losers. The participation of the southern countries in the general export power of the world was 31 percent in 1950 and decreased to 17 percent in 1970. At present it is still worse. The transfer of capital from the South to the North, which soars to billions of dollars, has increased since the very beginning of the world-market economy. This is built into the system, and it does not matter if the technocratic complex is managed by a socialist or a liberal ideology. If one-fourth of the human population has no drinking water, and the lowest one-fifth gets 1.4 percent of the world's GNP while the upper one-fifth gets 84.7 percent (as of 1994); or if the world already consumes at least three times more energy than the earth can sustainably support (of which 80 percent is plundered by 20 percent of the world population), the changes cannot be mere redistribution of goods.

This is why I plead for a transformation of the system. By transformation I understand something more than reformation, which is how I read Dussel. He thinks, it seems to me, that if we succeed in passing from the capitalist system to the socialist one we have solved the problem. No doubt socialism allows for a more just repartition of goods, but capitalism is "better" for sheer production, disregarding, of course, the human factor. I argue that reform is not enough, and that destruction by violent means is unethical and countereffective. In sum, neither reformation nor deformation is what I advocate; I advocate transformation. This implies an ethical stance. This is why the problem of technology is not a technological problem. It is a human problem. What is at stake is not better distribution of goods, but the very notion of the good.

Another point I should clarify regards the ethics of means and ends. I do not think that the problem of technology is solved simply by an ethic drawn from the individualistic moral of the good or bad use of allegedly neutral instruments. A sword can be good, in traditional parlance, if used to defend the widow, or bad if used to wound my brother. With an atomic bomb it is more difficult to follow this line of argument. But when dealing with complex systems and sociological situations we cannot be satisfied with tranquilizing our individual consciences because we do not harm anybody by drawing a salary from a complex "defense" industry or earning money by speculating in the market. I fear this traditional way of tranquilizing our consciences, so as to harness the simple people into collaborating with the powers that be, is not convincing anymore and it is one of the causes of the political violence everywhere. Gandhi's noncooperation movement and passive nonviolence should tell us much. John's Gospel of saying *no* to the System is equally telling. Naught for our comfort! The responsibility of the intellectual is greater than that of the simple citizen. We touch problems of extraordinary importance.

Another point of total agreement is that we must get out of the present situation. And I have the same sense of urgency that my friend has.

I understand all the reasons of prudence, which I may be tempted to call short-sighted or provisional, but which are certainly "realistic." It is enormously difficult, and sociologically speaking impossible, to emancipate the present-day generations from this technocratic addiction. But more risky still is to satisfy oneself with accidental reforms tinkering with the System. One simple argument will suffice: the present state of affairs has no future.

There is a startling consensus in the world today, that if we continue in the present state of affairs, by the next decade over three-quarters of the human population will live in subhuman conditions. We advocate birth control, although we do not think it possible to stop producing cars, and yet one car in ten years pollutes the world fifteen times more than a child in the same time — without including the infrastructure of roads, steel, etc. We do not consider real alternatives even thinkable, and we go on consoling ourselves that "we" shall make it by a sort of a technological *deus ex machina*. The majority of our species will not make "it." This is no time for quibbling with petty moral justifications. We hear the slogan "act locally, think globally." The intellectual formulation is weak: no global thinking is possible. We can think only from a given horizon. But the intention of the saying is quite correct. We have to act locally following the kantian moral imperative: to act imagining that our rule of conduct could become a universal rule, an injunction, at least, for all those who are in a similar situation. By this simple rule we cannot morally perform most of the actions we do. If everybody globally would have a car, or every country would export more than import. . . .

The present technocratic system forces all of us who are inside it to consume far beyond what a normal human being should. We have broken the cosmic rhythms. This is why I wonder at Dussel's optimism, although I am so (tem-piternally) optimistic as to allow myself to be (temporarily) pessimistic. The experience of the last thirty years during which the situation has deteriorated, does not allow us to go on dreaming of a "better world" without radical changes which demand from us a personal transformation. We have to act. But I resist acting in the direction of prolonging the agony of a system which will lead us to catastrophe. And I am not so fatalistic as to think that there is no way of a total transformation in comparison with which the changes of Europe in these last years will look like ripples. If all our discussions help us and the world to this transformation, the festschrift will not have been in vain. I am full of gratitude to my friends.

Bibliography
Selected Writings of Raimon Panikkar

BOOKS

1948 *F. H. Jacobi y la filosofía del sentimiento.* Buenos Aires (Sapientia).

1951 *El concepto de naturaleza: Análisis histórico y metafísico de un concepto.* Madrid (Consejo Superior de Investigaciones Científicas); 2nd, rev. ed., Madrid (CSIC) 1972.

1960 *La India: Gente, cultura y creencias.* Madrid (Rialp).

1961 *Patriotismo y cristiandad.* Madrid (Rialp).

1963a *Ontonomía de la ciencia: Sobre el sentido de la ciencia y sus relaciones con la filosofía.* Madrid (Gredos).

1963b *Humanismo y Cruz.* Madrid (Rialp).

1963c *L'incontro delle religioni nel mondo contemporaneo: Morfosociologia dell' ecumenismo.* Rome (Edizione Internazionali Sociali).

1963d *Die vielen Götter und der eine Herr: Beiträge zum ökumenischen Gespräch der Weltreligionen.* Weilheim/Obb. (O. W. Barth).

1964 "Religion and Religions" (manuscript); *Religione e Religioni: Concordanza funzionale, essenziale ed esistenziale delle religioni; studio filosofico sulla natura storica e dinamica della religione.* Brescia (Morcelliana).

1966 *Maya e Apocalisse: l'incontro dell'induismo e del cristianesimo.* Rome (Abete).

1967a *Kerygma und Indien: Zur heilsgeschichtlichen Problematik der christlichen Begegnung mit Indien.* Hamburg (Reich).

1967b "Indian Letters" (manuscript); *Offenbarung und Verkündigung: Indische Briefe.* Freiburg (Herder).

1967c *Técnica y tiempo.* Buenos Aires (Columba).

1968 *La gioia pasquale.* Vicenza (La Locusta).

1970a *L'homme qui devient Dieu: la foi dimension constitutive de l'homme.* Paris (Aubier).

1970b *La presenza de Dio.* Vicenza (La Locusta).

1970c *Le mystère du culte dans l'hindouisme et le christianisme.* Paris (Cerf).

1972a *Dimensioni mariane della vita.* Vicenza (La Locusta).

1972b *Cometas: Fragmentos de un diario espiritual de la postguerra.* Madrid (Euramérica).

1973 *The Trinity and the Religious Experience of Man: Icon, Person, Mystery,* 2nd enlarged edition. London (DLT); Maryknoll, N.Y. (Orbis Books) 1975.

1975 *Spiritualità indù: Lineamenti.* Brescia (Morcelliana).

1977 *The Vedic Experience: Mantramañjarī, An Anthology of the Vedas for Modern Man and Contemporary Celebration.* Berkeley (University of California Press); London (DLT) 1977; 2nd ed., Pondicherry (All India Books) 1983; New Delhi (Motilal Banarsidass) 1989.

1978 *The Intrareligious Dialogue.* New York (Paulist) 1978; 2nd ed., Bangalore (ATC) 1984.

1979a *Myth, Faith and Hermeneutics.* New York (Paulist) 1979; 2nd ed., Bangalore (ATC) 1983.

1979b *Culto y secularización: apuntes para una antropología litúrgica,* rev. ed. Madrid (Marova).

1981 *The Unknown Christ of Hinduism: Towards an Ecumenical Christophany.* Rev. and enlarged edition. London (DLT) 1981; Maryknoll, N.Y. (Orbis Books) 1981; Bangalore (ATC) 1982.

1982 *Blessed Simplicity: The Monk as Universal Archetype,* with contributions by E. Cousins, C. Tholens, M. Dardenne, A. Veilleux, M. B. Pennington, and P. Soleri. New York (Seabury).

1989 *The Silence of God: The Answer of the Buddha.* Maryknoll, N.Y. (Orbis Books).

1990a *La torre di Babele: Pace e pluralismo.* San Domenico di Fiesole (Edizioni Cultura della Pace).

1990b *Sobre el diálogo intercultural,* trans. and intro. de J. R. López de la Osa. Salamanca (San Esteban).

1993a *A Dwelling Place for Wisdom.* Louisville, Ky. (Westminster/John Knox Press).

1993b *La nueva inocencia.* Estella (Verbo Divino).

1993c *The Cosmotheandric Experience: Emerging Religious Consciousness,* ed. with intro. Scott Eastham. Maryknoll, N.Y. (Orbis Books).

1993d *Ecosofia: la nuova saggezza — per una spiritualità della terra.* Assisi (Cittadella Editrice).

1993e   *Paz y desarme cultural.* Santander (Sal Terrae); *Peace and Cultural Disarmament.* Louisville, Ky. (Westminster/John Knox Press) 1995.

SHORTER WORKS

1944

1. "Síntesis: Visión de síntesis del universo," *Arbor* (Madrid) 1, pp. 5–40.
2. "La ciencia biomatemática," *Arbor* (Madrid) 3, pp. 349ff.

1945

1. "La entropía y el fin del mundo: Un problema de cosmología," *Revista de Filosofía* (Madrid) IV, 13, pp. 287–318.
2. "El indeterminismo científico," *Anales de Física y Química* (Madrid) XLI, 396, pp. 573–605.

1947

1. "Max Planck (1858–1947)," *Arbor* (Madrid) 24, pp. 387–406.

1950

1. "El átomo de tiempo," *Arbor* (Madrid) 49, pp. 1–32.

1951

1. "La novedad que en el concepto de naturaleza introduce el cristianismo," *Tijdschrift voor Philosophie* (Leuven) XIII, 2, pp. 236–262.
2. "La naturaleza de la ciencia físico-matemática," *Sapientia* (Buenos Aires) 19, pp. 36–46.
3. "El cristianismo no es un humanismo," *Arbor* (Madrid) 62, pp. 165–168.
4. "Patria y cristiandad," *Documentos* (San Sebastián) 8, pp. 107–122.

1952

1. "El objeto del patriotismo: la patria," *Politeia* (Fribourg) IV, 2–3, pp. 172–178.
2. "Cristiandad y Cruz: Una investigación teológico-histórica," *Arbor* (Madrid) 84, pp. 337–352.
3. "La Virgen María," Prefacio a J. Guitton, *La Virgen María,* Madrid (Rialp), pp. 7–48.

1953

1. "Le concept d'ontonomie," *Actes de XIé Congrés International de Philosophie.* Bruxélles 20–26 Aug. 1953. Vol. 3. Louvain (Nauwelaerts), pp. 182–188.

1956

1. "Die existentielle Phänomenologie der Wahrheit," *Philosophisches Jahrbuch der Görresgesellschaft* (München) 64, pp. 27–54.

2. "Sur l'anthropologie du prochain," *Actes du VIIIé Congrés des Sociétés de Philosophie de langue française. L'homme et son prochain.* Paris (PUF), pp. 228–231.

1957

1. "The Sanctity of St. John of the Cross and of St. Teresa," *Prabuddha Bharata* (Mayavati, Almora) 3, pp. 273–278.

1961

1. "Pluralismus, Toleranz und Christenheit," *Pluralismus, Toleranz und Christenheit.* Nürnberg (Abendländische Akademie), pp. 117–142.

2. "La Misa como 'consecratio temporis.' La tempiternidad," *Sanctum Sacrificium* (Zaragoza) [V Congreso Eucarístico Nacional], pp. 75–93.

3. "Una meditación teológica sobre el Africa," *Nuestro Tiempo* (Pamplona) 83, pp. 533–542.

4. "El sentido cósmico de la ciencia," *Sapientia* (Buenos Aires) XVI, 60, pp. 90–111.

5. "Algunos aspectos fenomenológicos de la espiritualidad hindú de hoy," *Nuestro Tiempo* (Pamplona) 88, pp. 1181–1207.

6. "La demitizzazione nell'incontro tra cristianesimo e induismo," *Il problema della demitizzazione* (Archivio di Filosofia). Ed. E. Castelli, Padova (CEDAM) 1–2, pp. 243–266.

1962

1. "Le fondement du pluralisme herméneutique dans l'hindouisme," *Demitizzazione e immagine.* Ed. E. Castelli, Padova (CEDAM), pp. 243–269.

2. "Forme e crisi della spiritualità contemporanea," *Studi Cattolici* (Roma) VI, 33, pp. 5–19.

3. "Meditación sobre Melquisedec," *Nuestro Tiempo* (Pamplona) IX, 102, pp. 675–695.

1963

1. Espíritu religioso del pueblo castellano," *Nuestro Tiempo* (Pamplona) 111, pp. 3–16.

2. "La confidencia: Análisis de un sentimiento," *Revista de Filosofía* (Madrid) XXII, 84–85, pp. 43–62.

3. "Una consideración teológica sobre los medios de comunicación social," *Atlántida* (Madrid) I, 4, pp. 435–441.

4. "Europa und die Frage nach der kulturellen Einheit der Menschheit," *Das europäische Erbe in der heutigen Welt.* Nürnberg (Abendländische Akademie), pp. 9–36.

5. "Der zerbrochene Krug: Zur indischen Symbolhaftigkeit," *Antaios* (Stuttgart) IV, 6, pp. 556–571.

6. "Sur l'herméneutique de la tradition dans l'hindouisme: Pour un dialogue avec le christianisme," *Ermeneutica e Tradizione*. Ed. E. Castelli. Padova (CEDAM), pp. 343–370.

1964

1. "Technique et temps: la technochronie," *Tecnica e casistica*. Ed. E. Castelli. Padova (CEDAM), pp. 195–229.

2. "Das erste Bild des Buddha: Zur Einführung in den buddhistischen Apophatismus," *Antaios* (Stuttgart) VI, 4, pp. 373–385.

1965

1. "Advaita e Bhakti: Lettera da Vrindaban," *Humanitas* (Brescia) 10, pp. 991–1001.

2. "Morale du mythe et mythe de la morale," *Démythisation et morale*. Ed. E. Castelli. Paris (Aubier), pp. 393–413.

3. "Relations of Christian to their Non-Christian Surroundings," *Indian Ecclesiastical Studies* (Belgium) IV, 3/4, pp. 303–348.

1966

1. "La foi dimension constitutive de l'homme," *Mythe et foi*. Ed. E. Castelli. Paris (Aubier), pp. 17–63.

2. "The 'Crisis' of Mādhyamika and Indian Philosophy Today," *Philosophy East & West* (Honolulu) XVI, 3/4, pp. 117–131.

3. "La problemática dell' 'aggiornamento' monástico," *Visioni attuali sulla vita monastica*. Ed. G. M. Brasó Montserrat (Abadia de Montserrat), pp. 221–230.

1967

1. "Aktion und Kontemplation in indischen Kultmysterium," *Kult und Kontemplation in Ost und West*. Hrsg. Abtei Niederaltaich. Regensburg (Pustet), pp. 46–59.

2. "La faute originante ou l'immolation créatrice: Le Mythe de Prajāpati," *Le mythe de la peine*. Ed. E. Castelli. Paris (Aubier), pp. 65–100.

3. "Dialogue between Ian and Ray: Is Jesus Christ Unique?," *Theoria to Theory* (Cambridge, U.K.) 1, pp. 127–137.

1968

1. "Herméneutique de la liberté de la religion: La religion comme liberté," *L'herméneutique de la liberté religieuse*. Ed. E. Castelli. Paris (Aubier), pp. 57–86.

2. "The European University Tradition and the Renascent World Cultures," *A Challenge to the European University*. Ed. S. K. Oliver. Geneva (World Council of Churches), pp. 72–86.

3. "Ogni autentica religione è via di salvezza," *Incontro tra le religioni*. Roma (Mondadori), pp. 107–124.

4. "The Internal Dialogue. The Insufficiency of the So-Called Phenomenological 'Epoché' in the Religious Encounter," *Religion and Society* (Bangalore) XV, 3, pp. 55–66.

5. "Toward an Ecumenical Theandric Spirituality," *Journal of Ecumenical Studies* (Philadelphia) V, 3, pp. 507–534.

6. "Philosophy and Theology, Reason and Faith: An Essay in Terminological Clarification," *The Concept of Philosophy.* Varanasi (Centre of Advanced Study in Philosophy), Banaras Hindu University, pp. 507–534.

1969

1. "Le silence et la parole. Le sourire du Bouddha," *L'analyse du langage théologique. Le nom de Dieu.* Ed. E. Castelli. Paris (Aubier), pp. 121–134.

2. "Christianity and World Religions," *Christianity.* Patiala (Punjabi University), pp. 78–127.

3. "Algunos aspectos de la espiritualidad hindú," *Historia de la espiritualidad.* Ed. L. Sala Balust y B. Jiménez Duque. Barcelona (Flors), pp. 433–542.

4. "Metatheology or Diacritical Theology as Fundamental Theology," *Concilium* (Nijmegen) VI, 5, pp. 21–27.

5. "La présence de Dieu," *La Vie Spirituelle.* Paris (Cerf), pp. 527–533.

6. "The People of God and the Cities of Man," *People and Cities.* Ed. Stephen Verney. London (Collins, Fontana Books), pp. 190–221.

1970

1. "Le sujet de l'infaillibilité: Solipsisme et Vérification," *L'infaillibilité, son aspect philosophique et théologique.* Ed. E. Castelli. Paris (Aubier), pp. 423–445.

2. "Buddhismo e Ateismo," *L'ateismo contemporaneo.* Ed. Facultà filosofica della Pontificia Università Salesiana di Roma. Vol. 4, Torino (Società Editrice Internazionale), pp. 449–476.

3. "Menneskehedens enhed, menneskehedens splittelse," *Nordisk Missions-Tidsskrift* (Copenhagen) II, 81, pp. 92–98.

4. "The Supreme Experience: The Ways of West and East," *New Dimensions in Religious Experience.* Ed. George Devine. Staten Island, N.Y. (Alba House), pp. 69–93.

5. "Die Zukunft kommt nicht später," *Vom Sinn der Tradition.* Hrsg. L. Reinisch. München (Beck), pp. 53–64.

6. "Fe y creencia. Sobre la experiencia multireligiosa. Un fragmento autobiográfico objetivado," *Homenaje a Xavier Zubiri.* Vol. 2, Madrid (Editorial Moneda y Crédito), pp. 435–459.

7. "The Myth of Incest as Symbol for Redemption in Vedic India," *Types of Redemption.* Eds. R. J. Zwi Werblowsky and C. J. Bleeker. Leiden (E. J. Brill), pp. 130–144.

1971

1. "Die Philosophie in der geistigen Situation der Zeit," *Akten des XIV. Internationalen Kongresses für Philosophie.* Wien, 2–9 Sept., 1968. Bd. VI. Wien (Herder), pp. 75–87.

2. "La loi du karma et la dimension historique de l'homme," *La théologie de l'histoire. Herméneutique et eschatologie.* Ed. E. Castelli. Paris (Aubier), pp. 205–230.

3. "The Relation of the Gospels to Hindu Culture and Religion," *Jesus and Man's Hope* (Pittsburgh) 2, Pittsburgh Theological Seminary, pp. 247–261.

4. Il messaggio dell'India di ieri al mondo di oggi," *Filosofia* (Torino) XXIX, 1, pp. 3–28.

5. "Faith, a Constitutive Dimension of Man," *Journal of Ecumenical Studies* (Philadelphia) VIII, 2, pp. 223–254.

6. "Philosophy of Religion in the Contemporary Encounter of Cultures," *Contemporary Philosophy: A Survey.* Ed. R. Klibansky. Firenze (La Nuova Italia Editrice), pp. 221–242.

7. "Nirvána and the Awareness of the Absolute," *The God Experience.* Essays in Hope (The Cardinal Bea Lectures). Vol. 2. Ed. J. P. Whelan. New York & Toronto (Newman), pp. 81–99.

8. "Christ, Abel and Melchizedek," *Jeevadhara* (Kottayam) I, 5, pp. 391–403.

9. "Der Mythos der Zukunft," *Zukunft der Theologie, Theologie der Zukunft.* Wien, Freiburg, Basel (Herder), pp. 17–26.

10. "Gottesdienst in einem säkularisierten Zeitalter," *Gottesdienst in einem säkularisierten Zeitalter.* Kassel (Stauda), pp. 49–110.

11. "Indology as a Cross-Cultural Catalyst," *Numen* (Amsterdam) XVIII, 3, pp. 173–179.

1972

1. "Témoignage et dialogue," *Le Témoignage.* Ed. E. Castelli. Paris (Aubier), pp. 367–388.

2. "Salvation in Christ: Concreteness and Universality, the Supername," Inaugural Lecture at the Ecumenical Institute of Advanced Theological Study. Tantur, Jerusalem, pp. 1–81.

3. " 'Super hanc petram' Due principi ecclesiologici: la roccia e le chiavi," *Legge e Vangelo. Discussione su una legge fondamentale per la Chiesa.* Brescia (Paideia), pp. 135–145.

4. "śūnyatā and Pleroma: The Buddhist and Christian Response to the Human Predicament," *Religion and the Humanizing of Man.* Ed. J. M. Robinson. Waterloo, Ont. (Council on the Study of Religion), pp. 67–86.

1973

1. "Tolérance, Idéologie et Mythe," *Démythisation et Idéologie.* Ed. E. Castelli. Paris (Aubier), pp. 191–206.

2. "Monólogo con Vicente Fatone," *Obras Completas de Vicente Fatone.* Buenos Aires (Sudamericana) II, pp. 7–16.

3. "Philosophy and Revolution: The Text, the Context and the Texture," *Philosophy East and West* (Honolulu) XXIII, 3, pp. 315–322.

4. "The Category of Growth in Comparative Religion: A Critical Self-Examination," *Harvard Theological Review* (Cambridge, Mass.) LXVI, 1, pp. 113–140.

5. "Common Patterns of Eastern and Western Scholasticism," *Diogenes* (Firenze) 83, pp. 103–113.

1974

1. "Toward a Typology of Time and Temporality in the Ancient Indian Tradition," *Philosophy East & West* (Honolulu) XXIV, 2, pp. 161–164.

2. "The Hindu Ecclesial Consciousness: Some Ecclesiological Reflections," *Jeevadhara* (Kottayam) 21, pp. 199–205.

3. "Have 'Religions' the Monopoly on Religion?," *Journal of Ecumenical Studies* (Philadelphia) XI, 3, pp. 515–517.

4. "The Silence of the Word: Non-Dualistic Polarities," *Cross Currents* (New York) XXIV, 2–3, pp. 154–171.

5. "Le mythe comme histoire sacrée: Shunahshepa, un mythe de la condition humaine," *Le Sacré.* Ed. E. Castelli. Paris (Aubier), pp. 243–315.

1975

1. "El presente tempiterno: Una apostilla a la historia de la salvación y a la teología de la liberación," *Teología y mundo contemporáneo.* Homenaje a Karl Rahner. Ed. A. Vargas-Machuca. Madrid (Ediciones Cristiandad), pp. 133–175.

2. "Temps et histoire dans la tradition de l'Inde," *Les Cultures et le Temps,* Paris (UNESCO and Payot), pp. 73–101.

3. "Verstehen als Überzeugtsein," *Neue Anthropologie* VII, *Philosophische Antropologie.* Hrsg. von H. G. Gadamer and P. Vogler. Stuttgart (Thieme), pp. 132–167.

4. "Seed-Thoughts in Cross-Cultural Studies," *Monchanin* (Montreal) VIII, 50, pp. 1–73.

5. "Le temps circulaire: Temporisation et temporalité," *Temporalité et Aliénation.* Ed. E. Castelli. Paris (Aubier), pp. 207–246.

6. "Some Notes on Syncretism and Eclecticism Related to the Growth of Human Consciousness," *Religious Syncretism in Antiquity: Essays in Conversation with Geo Widengren.* Ed. B. Pearson. Missoula, Mont. (Scholars Press), pp. 47–62.

7. "Singularity and Individuality: The Double Principle of Individuation," *Revue Internationale de Philosophie* (Bruxélles) 11/112, 1–2, pp. 141–166.

1976

1. "La sécularisation de l'herméneutique: Le cas du Christ: fils de l'homme et fils de Dieu," *Herméneutique de la sécularisation.* Ed. E. Castelli. Paris (Aubier), pp. 213–248.

2. "La visione cosmoteandrica: il senso religioso emergente de terzo millennio," *Vecchi e nuovi Dei.* Torino (Editoriale Valentino), pp. 521–544.

1977

1. "La philosophie de la religion devant le pluralisme philosophique et la pluralité des religions," *La philosophie de la religion.* Ed. E. Castelli. Paris (Aubier), pp. 193–201.

2. "The New Innocence," *Cross Currents* (New York) XXVII, 1, pp. 7–15.

3. "Social Ministry and Ministry of Word and Worship (Some Considerations from the Asian Background)," *Ministries in the Church* (Hong Kong) Feb.–March, pp. 1–20.

4. "The Time of Death: The Death of Time. An Indian Reflection," *La réflexion sur la mort* — 2e Symposium International de Philosophie. Athénes (Ecole Libre de Philosophie 'Pléton'), pp. 102–120.

5. "Eine unvollendete Symphonie," *Erinnerung an Martin Heidegger.* Hrsg. G. Neske. Pfullingen (Neske), pp. 173–178.

6. "Creation and Nothingness. Creation: ex nihilo sed non in nihilum. Nothingness: ad quem sed non a quo," *Theologische Zeitschrift.* Volume in honor of Professor Fritz Buri (Basel) 33, pp. 344–352.

7. "Colligite Fragmenta: For an Integration of Reality," *From Alienation to At-Oneness.* Proceedings of the Theology Institute of Villanova University. Ed. F. A. Eigo. Villanova, Pa. (The Villanova University Press), pp. 19–91.

8. "Man as a Ritual Being," *Chicago Studies* (Chicago) XVI, 1, pp. 5–28.

1978

1. "Religion ou Politique? Y a-t-il une solution au dilemme de l'Occident?," *Religione e Politica.* (Archivio di Filosofia). Ed. M. M. Olivetti. Padova (CEDAM), pp. 73–82.

2. "Time and Sacrifice. The Sacrifice of Time and the Ritual of Modernity," *The Study of Time III.* Ed. J. T. Fraser. New York (Springer), pp. 683–727.

3. "The Texture of a Text: In Response to Paul Ricoeur," *Point of Contact* (New York) II, 1, pp. 51–64.

4. "The Vitality and Role of Indian Philosophy Today," *Indian Philosophical Quarterly* (Poona) V, 4, pp. 673–692.

5. " 'Gedankenfreie' Meditation oder seinserfüllte Gelassenheit?," *Munen Musô. Ungegenständliche Meditation.* Festschrift für Hugo M. Enomiya-Lassalle. Hrsg. G. Stachel. Mainz (Grünewald), pp. 309–316.

6. "The Bostonian Verities: A Comment on the Boston Affirmations," *Andover Newton Quarterly* (Andover) XVIII, 3, pp. 145–153.

7. "Action and Contemplation as Categories of Religious Understanding," *Contemplation and Action in World Religions.* Eds. Y. Ibish and I. Marculescu. A Rothko Chapel Book. Seattle and London (University of Washington Press), pp. 85–104.

8. "Philosophy as Life-Style," *Philosophers on Their Own Work.* Bern, etc. (Lang) Vol. 4, pp. 193–207.

1979

1. "Rtatattva: A Preface to a Hindu-Christian Theology," *Jeevadhara* (Kottayam) IX, 49, pp. 6–63.

2. "The Myth of Pluralism: The Tower of Babel — A Meditation on Non-Violence," *Cross Currents:* "Panikkar in Santa Barbara," (New York) XXIX, 2, pp. 197–230.

3. "La religión del futuro o la crisis del concepto de religión — la religiosidad humana," *Civiltà delle Macchine* (Roma) XXVII, 4–6, pp. 82–91.

1980

1. "Words and Terms," *Esistenza, Mito, Ermeneutica* (Scritti per Enrico Castelli). Ed. M. M. Olivetti (Archivio di Filosofia) Padova (CEDAM) II, pp. 117–133.

2. "Hermeneutics of Comparative Religion: Paradigms and Models," *Journal of Dharma* (Bangalore) V, 1, pp. 38–51.

3. "Aporias in the Comparative Philosophy of Religion," *Man and World* (The Hague, Boston, London) XIII, 3–4, pp. 357–383.

1981

1. "Indian Theology: A Theological Mutation," *Theologizing in India.* Ed. M. Amaladoss, T. K. John, G. Gispert-Sauch. Bangalore (TPI), pp. 23–42.

2. "L'eau et la mort: Réflexion interculturelle sur une métaphore," *Filosofia e religione di fronte alla morte.* Ed. M. M. Olivetti (Archivio di Filosofia) Padova (CEDAM), pp. 481–502.

3. "Athens or Jerusalem? Philosophy or Religion?," *Logos* (Santa Clara) 2, pp. 21–39.

4. "Per una lettura transculturale del simbolo," *Quaderni di psicoterapia infantile.* Roma (Borla), pp. 53–91; Dibattio, pp. 113–123.

5. "The Contemplative Mood: A Challenge to Modernity," *Cross Currents* (New York) XXXI, 3, pp. 261–272.

1982

1. "El círculo: sólo si el tiempo es circular vale la pena romperlo," *Octavio Paz.* Ed. Pere Gimferrer. Madrid (Taurus), pp. 215–222.

2. "Auf dem Wege zu einem ökumenischen Ökumemismus," *Ökumene. Möglichkeiten und Grenzen heute.* Hrsg. K. Froehlich. Gewidmet Oscar Cullmann. Tübingen (Mohr), pp. 140–150.

3. "Sobre l'hinduismo i el cristianismo: Una qüestión de vida cristiana," *Qüestions de vida cristiana* (Montserrat) 114, pp. 54–72.

4. "La notion des droits de l'homme est-elle un concept occidental?," *Diogène* (Paris) 120, pp. 87–115.

5. "Alternative à la culture moderne," *Interculture* (Montréal) 77, pp. 5–25.

6. "Letter to Abhishiktananda — On Eastern-Western Monasticism," *Studies in Formative Spirituality* (Pittsburgh) III, 3, pp. 427–451.

1983

1. "The End of History: The Threefold Structure of Human Time-Consciousness," *Teilhard and the Unity of Knowledge.* Ed. T. M. King and J. F. Salmon. New York (Paulist), pp. 83–141.

1984

1. "The Dialogical Dialogue," *The World's Religious Traditions.* "Current Perspectives in Religious Studies." Essays in honor of Wilfred Cantwell Smith. Ed. F. Whaling. Edinburgh (T. & T. Clark), pp. 201–221.

2. "La pau politica com objectiu religiós," *Qüestions de vida cristiana* (Montserrat) 121, pp. 86–95.

3. "La interpellación de l'Asia al cristianismo," *Teología i Vida.* Barcelona (Claret), pp. 81–93.

4. "Religious Pluralism: The Metaphysical Challenge," *Religious Pluralism* (Boston) V, pp. 97–115.

5. "Sein und Nichts: Fragender Durchblick auf die entfaltete Problematik," *Sein und Nichts in der abendländischen Mystik.* Hrsg. W. Strolz. Freiburg, Basel, Wien (Herder), pp. 107–123.

6. "L'émancipation de la technologie," *Interculture* (Montréal) 85, pp. 22–37.

7. "The Dream of an Indian Ecclesiology," *Searching for an Indian Ecclesiology,* Bangalore (ATC), pp. 24–54. Ed. G. van Leuwen (The Statement, Papers and the Proceedings of the Seventh Annual Meeting of the Indian Theological Association, Nagpur, Oct. 21–23, 1983).

8. "The Destiny of Technological Civilization: An Ancient Buddhist Legend: Romavisaya," *Alternatives* (New York and Delhi) X, 2, pp. 237–253.

9. "The Catholic Experience Towards a Theanthropocosmic Vision," *Was ist die Natur.* Kyoto, Japan (Hazokan), pp. 83–107. (Ed. The Institut für interkulturelle Forschung in Japan) (Japanese).

10. "Yama: A Myth of the Primordial Man," *Journal of Indo-European Studies.* Essays in memory of Karl Kerényi. Ed. E. C. Polomé. Monograph Series (Washington) 4, p. 28–38.

1985

1. "Der Mensch, ein trinitarisches Mysterium," *Die Verantwortung des Menschen für eine bewohnbare Welt im Christentum, Hinduismus und Buddhismus.* Hrsg. R. Panikkar und W. Strolz. Freiburg (Herder), pp. 147–190.

2. "Dios en las religiones," *Mission Abierta* (Madrid) 5–6, pp. 85–102.

3. "Présentation: Un traité de spiritualité," Préface to N. Shânta: *La voie Jaina: histoire, spiritualité, vie des ascètes pèlerlines de l'Inde.* Paris (OEIL), pp. 17–32.

4. Què vol dir avui confessar-se cristiâ?," *Qüestions de vida cristiana* (Montserrat) 128–129, pp. 86–111.

5. "The Harmony of the Vedic World," Foreword to J. Miller, *The Vision of the Cosmic Order in the Vedas.* London (Routledge, Kegan Paul), pp. xi–xix.

6. "La Vocación humana es fundamentalmente religiosa," *Anthropos* (Barcelona) 53/54, pp. 16–22.

1986

1. "La montée vers le fond," Preface â H. Le Saux (Abhishitananda) *La montée au fond du coeur, Le journal intime du moine chrétien-sannyāsī hindou.* Paris (OEIL), pp. i-xxvii.

2. "The Threefold Linguistic Intrasubjectivity," *Interrsoggettività Socialità Religione.* Ed. M. M. Olivetti. *Archivio di Filosofia* (Roma) LIV, 1/3, pp. 593–606.

3. "La dialéctica de la razón armada," *Concordia* (Frankfurt) 9, pp. 68–89. [Entrevista realizada por R. Fornet-Betancourt y A. Gómez-Müller.]

4. "Medicina y Religión," *Jano* (Madrid) XXI, 737, pp. 12–48.

5. "Religiöse Eintracht als Ziel," Einführung zum *Ramon Llull, Buch vom Heiden und drei Weisen.* Freiburg (Herder), pp. 10–18.

6. "Verità — Errore — Bugia — Esperienza Psicoanalitíca," *Quaderni di psicoterapia infantile* (Roma) 13, pp. 14–110.

1987

1. "Theology as Theopraxis," *Socio-Cultural Analysis in Theologizing.* Ed. K. Pathil C.M.I. (Tenth Annual Meeting of the ITA, Mangalore, 28–31 Dec. 1986). Bangalore (ITC), pp. 162–169.

2. "Theomythia and Theology: Mythos and Logos," *Festschrift für Walter Strolz.* Nov., pp. 251–257.

3. "The Challenge of Religious Studies to the Issues of Our Times," Foreword to S. Eastham, *Nucleus.* "Reconnecting Science and Religion in the Nuclear Age." Santa Fe, N.M. (Bear & Co.), pp. xiii–xxxviii.

4. "L'humor i el llenguatge," *Qüestions de vida cristiana* (Montserrat) 137, pp. 25–34.

5. "The Jordan, The Tiber and the Ganges: Three Kairological Moments of Christic Self-Consciousness," *The Myth of Christian Uniqueness: Toward a Pluralistic Theology of Religions.* Eds. J. Hick and P. F. Knitter. Maryknoll, N.Y. (Orbis Books), pp. 89–116.

6. "The Invisible Harmony: A Universal Theory of Religion or a Cosmic Confidence in Reality?," *Toward a Universal Theology of Religion.* Ed. L. Swidler. Maryknoll, N.Y. (Orbis Books), pp. 118–153.

7. "Deity," *The Encyclopedia of Religion.* Ed. M. Eliade. New York (Macmillan). Vol. 4, pp. 264–276.

8. "El 'tecnocentrisme' algunes tesis sobre tecnolgia," *Qüestions de vida cristiana* (Montserrat) 139, pp. 84–99.

1988

1. "Antinomias entre la cosmología moderna y las cosmologías tradicionales," *Entwicklung zur Menschlichkeit durch Begegnung westlicher und östlicher Kultur.* Akten des IV. Interkontinentalen Kolloquiums zur philosophischen Insistenzanthropologie 1–6 September 1986 an der Universität Bamberg. Hrsg. von H. Beck und I. Quiles. Frankfurt am Main (Lang), pp. 213–219.

2. "The Unknown Knower," *Réflexions sur la liberté humaine. Gedanken zur menschlichen Freiheit. Concepts of Human Freedom.* Festschrift in Honor of André Mercier on the Occasion of his 75th Birthday. Ed. M. Svilar. Berne (Lang), pp. 133–159.

3. "Chosenness and Universality: Can Both Claims Be Simultaneously Maintained?," *Sharing Worship. Communicatio in Sacris*. Ed. P. Puthanangady. Bangalore (National Biblical Catechetical & Liturgical Centre), pp. 229–250.

4. "Instead of a Foreword: An Open Letter," D. Veliath, *Theological Approach and Understanding of Religions*. "Jean Daniélou and Raimundo Panikkar, A Study in Contrast," Bangalore (Kristy Jyoti College), pp. v-xiv.

5. "What Is Comparative Philosophy Comparing?," *Interpreting Across Boundaries*. "New Essays in Comparative Philosophy." Eds. G. J. Larson and E. Deutsch. Princeton, N.J. (Princeton University Press), pp. 116–136.

1989

1. "Anima Mundi — vita hominis — spiritus Dei. Some Aspects of a Cosmotheandric Spirituality," *Actualitas omnium actuum*. Festschrift für Heinrich Beck. Hrsg. E. Schadel. Frankfurt am Main (Lang), pp. 341–356.

2. "Epistula de pace," Response to *Philosophia pacis: Homenaje a Raimon Panikkar*. Madrid (Símbolo Editorial), 15pp. [pro manuscripto].

3. "In Christ There Is Neither Hindu nor Christian: Perspectives on Hindu-Christian Dialogue," *Religious Issues and Interreligious Dialogues*. Eds. C. Wei-hsun Fu and G. E. Spiegler. New York (Greenwood), pp, 475–490.

4. "Autoconciencia cristiana y religiones," *Fe cristiana y sociedad moderna*. Vol. 26, Madrid (S.M.), pp. 199–267.

5. "Mythos und Logos: Mythologische und rationale Weltsichten," *Geist und Natur*. Hrsg. H. P. Dürr and W. Ch. Zimmerli. Bern, München, Wien (Scherz), pp. 206–220.

6. "L' home i la seva por," Varis autors, *L'Home i les seves pors*. Barcelona (Llar del llibre), pp. 23–36.

1990

1. "La sfida dell'incontro planetario tra i popoli," *Rivolgimenti*. "Dialoghi di fine millennio." Ed. M. Guzzi. Genova (Marietti), pp. 16–36.

2. "The Ongoing Dialogue," Foreword to *Hindu-Christian Dialogue*. "Perspectives and Encounters." Ed. H. Coward. Maryknoll, N.Y. (Orbis Books), pp. ix-xviii.

3. "Cosmic Evolution, Human History and Trinitarian Life," *The Teilhard Review* (London) XXV, 3, pp. 62–71.

4. "Ekklesia and Mandiram, Two Symbols of Human Spirituality," (Foreword) *Studies in Formative Spirituality* (Pennsylvania) XI, 3, pp. 277–284.

5. "Gott näher treten," *Gott näher treten*. "Begegnung mit dem Ganz Anderen." Hrsg. von U. Baatz. Wien (Herder) pp. 135–144.

6. "Vorwort: Eine alte sicht der Wirklichkeit," Bede Griffiths. *Die Neue Wirklichkeit*. München (Aquamarin), pp. 7–19.

7. "The Pluralism of Truth," *World Faiths Insight* (New York and London) XXVI (October), pp. 7–16.

8. "Thinking and Being," *Du Vrai, Du Beau, Du Bien*. Études Philosophiques présentées au Professeur Evanghélos A. Moutsopoulos. Paris (Vrin), pp. 39–42.

9. "The Experiential 'Argument' of Abhinavagupta. A Cross-cultural Consideration," *L'argomento ontologico*. Ed. M. M. Olivetti. Biblioteca dell' *'Archivio di Filosofia'* (Padova) LVIII, 1/3, pp. 489–520.

10. "The Christian Challenge for the Third Millennium," *Christian Mission and Interreligious Dialogue*. Eds. P. Mojzes and L. Swidler. Lewiston, N.Y. (Mellen), pp. 113–125.

11. "Gespräch mit R. Panikkar," C. von Barloewen. *Vom Primat der Kultur*. "Essays zur vergleichenden Kulturbetrachtung." München (Eberhard), pp. 375–411.

12. "The New Role of Christian Universities in Asia," *The Role of Persons of Other Faiths and Traditions as Teachers in Christian Universities and Colleges*. Ed. P. B. Mansap Sihm, Workshop of the Association of Christian Universities & Colleges in Asia [ACUCA] (Oct. 24–26, 1989), Bangkok (Assumption University), pp. 15–34.

13. "Raimon Panikkar," by Ron Miltenburg in *Art Meets Science and Spirituality in a Changing Economy*, s-Gravenhage (SDU), pp. 330–345.

1991

1. "L'hinduisme," *Les intuïcions fonamentals de les grans religions*. Barcelona (Cruïlla), pp. 73–83.

2. "El buddhisme," *Les intuïcions fonamentals de les grns religions*. Barcelona (Cruïlla), pp. 87–97.

3. "There Is No Outer without Inner Space," *Concepts of Space, Ancient and Modern*. Ed. K. Vatsyayan. New Delhi (Abhinav), pp. 7–38.

4. "Begegnung der Religionen: Das univermeidliche Gespräch," *Dialog der Religionen* (München) I, 1, pp. 9–39.

5. "Advaita und Trinität," *Wissenschaftler und Weise. Die Konferenz*. Hrsg. P. Michael, Grafing (Aquamarin), pp. 77–99.

6. "Can Theology Be Transcultural?," *Pluralism and Oppression*. "Theology in World Perspective." Ed. P. F. Knitter [Annual Publication of the College Theology Society, 1988, vol. 34], Lanham, Md. (University Press of America), pp. 3–22.

7. "Novenario," [Sobre Dios] *El Ciervo* (Barcelona) XXXIX (489) (Diciembre), pp. 9–10.

8. "On Catholic Identity," *Warren Lecture Series in Catholic Studies*, No. 17 Public Lecture. The University of Tulsa (October 4, 1991).

1992

1. "A Nonary of Priorities," *Revisioning Philosophy*. Ed. J. Ogilvy, Albany, N.Y. (State University of New York Press), pp. 235–246.

2. "Filosofia e teologia: una distinzione superata: Note per una discussione," *Filosofia e Teologia nel futuro dell 'Europa* a cura di Giovanni Ferretti (Atti del V Colloquio su Filosofia e Religione/Macerata 24–27 Ottobre 1990) Genova (Marietti), pp. 185–196.

3. "L'albada de la cristiania," *Qüestions de vida Cristiana* (Montserrat) 161 (Abril), pp. 34–44.

4. "Méditation européenne aprés un démi-millenaire," *1492–1992 Conquête et Évangile en Amérique Latine*. Questions pour Europe aujourd'hui. Actes du Colloque réalisé à Lyon du 28 au 30 Janvier 1992 à l'université catholique de Lyon, Lyon (Profac) 1992, pp. 29–52.

5. "A Christophany for Our Times," *Theology Digest* (Saint Louis) Spring, pp. 3–21.

6. "Are the Words of Scripture Universal Religious Categories? The Case of Christian Language for the Third Millennium." *Religione, Parola, Scrittura*. Ed. M. M. Olivetti. Biblioteca dell'Archivio di Filosofia (CEDAM), pp. 377–387.

1993

1. "Satapathaprajña: Should We Speak of Philosophy in Classical India? A Case of Homeomorphic Equivalents," *Contemporary Philosophy. A New Survey*. Ed. G. Floistad Dordrecht/Boston/London (Kluwer Academic Publishers). Vol, 7, pp. 11–67.

2. "La diversidad como presupuesto para la armonía entre los pueblos," *Wiñay Marka* (Barcelona) Nr. 20 (Mayo), pp. 15–20.

3. "Reflexions sobre religió i Europa," *Qüestions de Vida Cristiana* (Montserrat) 168, pp. 70–84.

4. "Les religions i la cultura de la pau," *Qüestions de Vida Cristiana* (Montserrat) 169, pp. 13–38.

Other Titles in the Faith Meets Faith Series